Human Rights and Development in International Law

This book addresses the legal issues raised by the interaction between human rights and development in contemporary international law. In particular, it charts the parameters of international law that states have to take into account in order to protect human rights in the process of development. In doing so, it departs from traditional analyses, where human rights are mainly considered as a political dimension of development. Rather, the book suggests focusing on human rights as a system of international norms establishing minimum standards of protection of individuals and minimum standards applicable in all circumstances on what is essential for a dignified existence.

The various dimensions covered in the book include: the discourse on human rights and development interrelationship, particularly *opinio juris* and the practice of states on the question; the notion of international assistance and cooperation in human rights law, under legal regimes such as international humanitarian law, and emerging rules in the area of protection of persons in the event of disasters; the extraterritorial scope of economic, social and cultural rights treaties; and legal principles on the respect for human rights in externally designed and planned development activities. Analysis of these topics sheds light on the question of whether international law as it stands today addresses most of the issues concerning the protection of human rights in the development process.

Tahmina Karimova is a public international law lawyer. She has advised states, UN specialised agencies and programmes (ILO, UNDP, UNWomen), international organizations and NGOs on matters of international law, development and human rights. She holds a diploma of jurist from the Tajik State National University, an LLM from the University of Essex and a PhD in International Law from the University of Geneva and IHEID.

Human Rights and International Law
Series Editor: Professor Surya P. Subedi, O.B.E.

This series will explore human rights law's place within the international legal order, offering much-needed interdisciplinary and global perspectives on human rights' increasingly central role in the development and implementation of international law and policy.

Human Rights and International Law is committed to providing critical and contextual accounts of human rights' relationship with international law theory and practice. To achieve this, volumes in the series will take a thematic approach that focuses on major debates in the field, looking at how human rights impacts on areas as diverse and divisive as security, terrorism, climate change, refugee law, migration, bioethics, natural resources and international trade.

Exploring the interaction, interrelationship and potential conflicts between human rights and other branches of international law, books in the series will address both historical development and contemporary contexts, before outlining the most urgent questions facing scholars and policy makers today.

Available titles:

Human Rights and Charity Law
International Perspectives
Kerry O'Halloran

Forthcoming titles:

Adoption Law and Human Rights
International Perspectives
Kerry O'Halloran

The Right to Truth in International Law
Victims' Rights in Human Rights and International Criminal Law
Melanie Klinkner and Howard Davis

Business and Human Rights
History, Law and Policy – Bridging the Accountability Gap
Nadia Bernaz

Extracting Accountability from Non-State Actors in International Law
Assessing the Scope for Direct Regulation
Lee James McConnell

About the series editor

Professor Surya P. Subedi, O.B.E. is Professor of International Law, University of Leeds, member of the Institut de Droit International and former UN Special Rapporteur for human rights in Cambodia.

Human Rights and Development in International Law

Tahmina Karimova

LONDON AND NEW YORK

First published 2016 by Routledge

2 Park Square, Milton Park, Abingdon, Oxfordshire OX14 4RN

52 Vanderbilt Avenue, New York, NY 10017

Routledge is an imprint of the Taylor & Francis Group, an informa business

First issued in paperback 2020

British Library Cataloguing in Publication Data
A catalogue record for this book is available from the British Library

Library of Congress Cataloging-in-Publication Data
Names: Karimova, Tahmina, author.
Title: Human rights and development in international law / Tahmina
    Karimova.
Description: New York, NY : Routledge, 2016. | Series: Human rights
    and international law | Includes bibliographical references and
    index. | Description based on print version record and CIP data
    provided by publisher; resource not viewed.
Identifiers: LCCN 2015041293 (print) | LCCN 2015041193
    (ebook) | ISBN 9781315665283 (ebk) | ISBN 9781138957138 (hbk)
Subjects: LCSH: Human rights. | Right to development. |
    International law. | International cooperation.
Classification: LCC K3240 (print) | LCC K3240 .K372 2016 (ebook) |
    DDC 341.4/8—dc23
LC record available at http://lccn.loc.gov/2015041293

ISBN: 978-1-138-95713-8 (hbk)
ISBN: 978-0-367-59667-5 (pbk)

Typeset in Galliard
by Apex CoVantage, LLC

To my grandfather Karim

Contents

Table of abbreviations

AAA	Accra Agenda for Action
AAAA	Addis Ababa Action Agenda
ACHPR	African Charter on Human and Peoples' Rights
ACHR	American Convention on Human Rights
AComHPR	African Commission on Human and Peoples' Rights
ACP	States African, Caribbean and Pacific States Parties to the Lomé Convention
AOPP	Action-Oriented Policy Paper on Human Rights
API	Protocol Additional to the Geneva Conventions of 12 August 1949, and relating to the Protection of Victims of International Armed Conflicts, 8 June 1977
CEDAW	Convention on the Elimination of All Forms of Discrimination against Women
CERD	International Convention on the Elimination of all Forms of Racial Discrimination
CERDS	1974 Charter of Economic Rights and Duties of States
CESCR	Committee on Economic, Social and Cultural Rights
CRC	Convention on the Rights of the Child
CRPD	Convention on the Rights of Persons with Disabilities
CUP	Cambridge University Press
DAC (OECD)	Development Assistance Committee
DD II/III/IV	Development Decades II-IV (of the UN)
DRD	Declaration on the Right to Development
EBRD	European Bank for Reconstruction and Development
EC	European Community
ECHR	European Convention on Human Rights
EComHR	European Commission of Human Rights
ECOSOC	Economic and Social Council (of the UN)
ECtHR	European Court of Human Rights
EEC	European Economic Community
ESC rights	Economic, social and cultural rights
ETOs	Extraterritorial Obligations
EU	European Union

FAO	Food and Agriculture Organization
GA	General Assembly (of the UN)
GNI	Gross National Income
GNP	Gross National Product
HIPC	Highly Indebted Poor Countries
HLTF	High-Level Task Force on the Implementation of the Right to Development
HRBA	Human Rights Based Approaches
HRC	United Nations Human Rights Council
IAComHR	Inter-American Commission on Human Rights
IACtHR	Inter-American Court of Human Rights
IBRD (World Bank)	International Bank for Reconstruction and Development
ICC	International Criminal Court
ICCPR	International Covenant on Civil and Political Rights
ICERD	Convention on the Elimination of All Forms of Racial Discrimination
ICESCR	International Covenant on Economic, Social and Cultural Rights
ICJ	International Court of Justice
ICRC	International Committee of the Red Cross
ICRC Study	Henckaerts and Doswald-Beck (eds), *Customary International Humanitarian Law*, Cambridge: CUP, 2005
ICTY	International Criminal Tribunal for the Former Yugoslavia
IDA	International Development Association
IDI	Institut de Droit International
IDL	International Development Law
IFIs	International Financial Institutions
IHL	International Humanitarian Law
ILA	International Law Association
ILC	International Law Commission
ILO	International Labour Organization
IMF	International Monetary Fund
MDG	Millennium Development Goals
MDRI	Multilateral Debt Relief Initiative
NAM	Non-Aligned Movement
NEPAD	New Partnership for Africa's Development
NGO	Non-governmental organization
NIEO	New International Economic Order
ODA	Official Development Assistance
OECD	Organization for Economic Cooperation and Development
OHCHR	Office of High Commissioner for Human Rights
OP-ICESCR	Optional Protocol to International Covenant on Economic, Social and Cultural Rights
OUP	Oxford University Press

OWG	Open Working Group
PCD	Policy Coherence for Development
PCIJ	Permanent Court of International Justice
PRSs	Poverty Reduction Strategies
Recueil des Cours	Recueil des Cours de l'Académie de Droit International de la Haye
RtD	Right to Development
SAP	Structural Adjustment Program
SDGs	Sustainable Development Goals
SSC	South–South Cooperation
SUNFED	Special United Nations Fund for Economic Development
UDHR	Universal Declaration of Human Rights
UN	United Nations
UNCTAD	United Nations Conference on Trade and Development
UNDP	United Nations Development Programme
UNESCO	UN Educational, Scientific and Cultural Organization
UNICEF	United Nations Children's Fund
USA	United States of America (also given as US)
VCLT	Vienna Convention on the Law of Treaties
WB	World Bank
WHO	World Health Organization
WW II	World War II

Foreword

At the end of the month of September 2015, the General Assembly of the United Nations adopted the 2030 Agenda for Sustainable Development.[1] There are several ways to look at the significance of this document which finds no precedent back to the year 2000 with the adoption of the Millennium Declaration.

One may consider the document adopted in 2015 as illustrating in a most dramatic way the tremendous number of economic, social and ecological challenges to which all the peoples of the Earth as parts of humanity are faced for the decades to come. But one should not limit oneself to this dramatic dimension. While some of the eight goals of the Millennium Goals have virtually been already achieved, one should take this document as a serious demonstration of the determination of the UN Member States to enhance their cooperation in favour of an economic development that at the same time is respectful of the global environment and of human dignity.

Eradication of poverty is presented in the Agenda as 'the greatest global challenge and indispensable requirement for sustainable development', and the major contribution of this document is probably to provide a renewed roadmap to the international community for the next 15 years, pointing at the same time to the interlinkages and to the integrated nature of the different components of a development which cannot be sustainable if it is not also based on the respect for the fundamental civil, political and socio-economic rights.

The 2030 Agenda manifests the ambition of the international community to provide itself with a legal framework integrating what appears in the history of the United Nations as having remained for too long as distinct preoccupations and initially perceived as belonging to different fields of international law: human rights law, the international law of economic development and the protection of the global environment. Still, this integrative process is to be considered as a much demanding task which cannot be achieved otherwise than by increasing in a critical way the level of cooperation between several components of the international community, starting with States and their governments.

---

1 Transforming Our World: the 2030 Agenda for Sustainable Development, UN doc. A/70/L.1.

But the question remains as to how to integrate human rights and particularly in their legal dimension in this development framework? This is precisely the purpose of the book written by Tahmina Karimova. As the result of long years of systematic research, this impressive work discusses the human rights and development interface; it comes to the conclusion that so far human rights have had a limited impact on the development praxis as international legal norms even if development overlaps with many provisions of the treaties protecting, in particular, the economic, social and cultural rights.

How to change this situation? In order to try and answer this question, Ms Karimova reconsiders legal issues raised by the interaction between human rights and development in contemporary international law focusing on the nature and scope of states' obligations regarding international assistance and cooperation as provided by human rights treaties. Her approach consists in juxtaposing the legally binding human rights obligations with the instrumentalist approach, whereby respect for human rights are represented as merely options rather than strictly binding legal obligations. The author demonstrates, however, how international law progressively evolved in this respect from demands for structural changes at the international level that emphasized the role of affirmative action towards a focus placed, more recently, on how to realize development policies and practices without interfering with the enjoyment of human rights.

No doubt, the UN Charter creates legally binding obligations on states to cooperate for human rights. But at the same time, the present normative evolution points to the necessity of enlarging the concept of development which should be interpreted as including the requirement that development policies and practices respect human rights; an approach of which we have earlier noticed that it is, and rightly so, the one retained by the 2030 Agenda. Overall, Ms Karimova is able to put together closely interlinked development and human rights elements into a new image, structured by international assistance and cooperation. This special focus is a new one; it leads to a much better understanding of the interrelationship of the legal and political bases of development processes.

The reading of this book is probably the best way to address the question of whether and in which respect the 2030 Agenda for Sustainable Development points to the correct direction for transforming the world, which, indeed, needs it.

Pierre-Marie Dupuy
Emeritus Professor
University of Paris (Panthéon-Assas)
Graduate Institute of International and
Development Studies – Geneva
International Arbitrator
2015 ASIL Manley
Hudson Medal

Acknowledgements

First and foremost, I would like to gratefully acknowledge the academic guidance of Professor Pierre-Marie Dupuy, who supervised the doctoral thesis on which this book is based. I was in a privileged position to receive his invaluable advice on international law, its directions and his precious insights on the grand project called '*le droit international au développement*'. I am grateful for his encouragement to pursue my research. I have also had the honour to have prominent international law professors, namely Professor Andrew Clapham and Professor Eibe Riedel, as members of the PhD jury to examine the present work. I would like to take this opportunity to express my gratitude for their guidance, invaluable comments and suggestions.

I am greatly indebted to Stuart-Casey Maslen for editing the whole manuscript and providing me with substantive and editorial comments. I was fortunate and very honoured to have had the opportunity of meeting several academics and international lawyers, before, during and after my research on the topic, who have, knowingly or otherwise, helped me to form my ideas and my arguments about human rights law. I would like to specifically mention Professor Vera Gowlland-Debbas, Mona Rishmawi and Sandra Ratjen. I should also like to thank friends and colleagues who have provided comments and helped to improve the drafts: particularly, Dr Christophe Golay, Heather Northcott, Dr Ivona Truscan, Dr Ioana Cismas and Dr Krisztina Huzsti-Orban for their comments and views on various chapters of this manuscript. Thank you for your kindness.

Equally, my warm thoughts and gratitude go to those whom I have met during my doctoral studies and who with their presence, friendship and affection contributed to the accomplishment of the final outcome. A few persons need to be mentioned specifically: my dear friends Alessia Rosetti, Ilaria Vena, Jean Abboud, Adineh Abghari – thank you for standing by me in many various ways, and to Farrah Hawana and Janis Grzybowski for blending into the legal picture some realist takes on life and politics. I should also like to thank Milena Costas Trascasas, Mara Lisa Arizaga, Sebastiaan Verelst, Martha Cuadros-Buechner, Cristina Bondioni and Natalija Erjavec for their company in the most challenging times. I would be greatly remiss were I not to mention dear Vincenza and Carmelo Giacca for their hospitality and generosity.

I owe debts of gratitude to Routledge and especially Professor Surya Subedi for expressing their interest in my research. Special acknowledgements are

xx   *Acknowledgements*

due to the Routledge publishing team, including Katherine Carpenter and Olivia Manley, for their support throughout the process as well as colleagues from the Routledge team, including Hayley Kennard and Marie Roberts for their work on the final manuscript. For great assistance in the editorial process, I am greatly indebted to Jeni Lloyd, who has patiently edited this work under tight deadlines.

This book has benefited immeasurably from my frequent journeys to Italy, Tajikistan and Turkey and my stay in Switzerland. More fundamentally, I could not have completed my research without the warmth and calmness of the 'Villa Moynier'. In some respect, this book is based on thoughts moulded and developed in the seat of the Geneva Academy of International Humanitarian Law and Human Rights.

I also wish to thank Gilles Giacca for his love and partnership throughout these years – and support in that cold period in the now distant January of 2014. Finally, the idea of developing this book would have never materialized without the absolute and unwavering support of my parents and my brother Akmal. Their strength, grace, wit and faith in 'continuing' has guided me like a compass in this life. This book is dedicated to them with much love. *Modar va Padari aziz. In kitob ba shumo bakhshida meshavad. Be muhabbatu dastgirii behamtoi shumo, in kitob nuri ruzro namedid.*

T.K.

I   Introduction

Introduction

The relationship between human rights and development is one of the oldest debates between two issues of concern to international society, with no clear answers yet provided by the course of evolution. There is general agreement that human rights and development are interrelated. However, it is at this point that consensus ends and divergences begin, particularly when one tries to articulate on which level they converge. The main criticism, and a problem for human rights, is the failure of the development praxis to see human rights in their totality and, rather, see only their partial aspects.

This predicament can be explained in the following terms. The development framework does not see its relationship with human rights in terms of the potential overlap between the material scope of human rights treaties and development activities. Consequently, it does not automatically align its practice with the human rights treaties. Rather, the engagement of development practice with human rights has been largely selective. For development, human rights are more about democracy, rule of law, good governance, and transparency. Increasingly we hear words and phrases such as equity, empowerment, listening to the voices of the poor and their participation in decisions affecting their lives, all of which have roots in the human rights discipline.

What development seems to carefully avoid is incorporating the defining feature of human rights, namely, their legal parameters. We still can observe that the value of human rights is seen to the extent that it is conducive to the attainment of development objectives; development may take human rights into account when it is necessary or conducive to this end. Taken together, they result in a situation where human rights standards are perceived as inapplicable to the development actors' own conduct.

While these parameters disturb the balance between rationales underlying human rights, they crucially inform us that it is the recognition of a link between human rights and development which defines the scope of human rights in development debates. The question is whether recognition is a defining moment. Is it a prerequisite? What if there are certain cases where the link between human rights and development is automatic, rather than a matter of choice, irrespective of the existence of their mutual compatibility? At the same time, this outcome is also symptomatic of a need to critically reflect whether, in reality, human rights law and international law in general can provide a basic framework within which most of the concerns related to the human rights and development interface can be addressed. The main question is whether non-arbitrary ways exist to determine the place of human rights in development.

1 Reframing human rights in the development debate

Several important stages of the 'human rights and development' debate can be distinguished. An early and explicit recognition of the links between human rights and development culminated in the formulation of the concept of a right to development. This concept not only contributed to the transformation of the way in which human rights are conceived and implemented, but also shifted the focus on the international dimension of human rights from the outer margins to the very centre of development debates.[1] The right to development has been, and possibly still is, ahead of the curve on many important issues in the field, except that its nature and ambit remain ambiguous at best and at worst unrecognized outside the United Nations.

The most recent phase of the human rights and development debate re-emerged in the post-Cold War climate, as a number of events provided a fertile ground to discuss their convergence.[2] Human rights marched into the development discourse in tandem with democracy and a 'good governance' agenda, resulting in a new and influential sensibility regarding their mutual reinforcement. But has this led to substantive progress in increasing the integration of human rights into development? Where do we stand in the current state of debate, and what can we make out of it?

The past decades has seen a rise in prominence of human rights in development practice. Since the 1993 World Conference on Human Rights in Vienna, the idea that development and human rights are mutually reinforcing has been consistently repeated in a number of diverse contexts.[3] In 2005, the UN Secretary-General's report, *In Larger Freedom*, underlined intimate links between security, development and human rights.[4] Similarly, the 2005 World Summit outcome

1 P. Alston, 'Introduction', in P. Alston (ed.), *Peoples' Rights*, OUP: 2005, p. 1.
2 This change was not only due to the collapse of 'socialism' in the East, but also corresponded to the period of harsh criticism of social and economic failures produced by development in the 1980s. R. Jolly, 'Adjustment with a Human Face: A UNICEF Record and Perspective on 1980s', 19(12) *World Development* (1991), pp. 1807–1821.
3 UN GA, Vienna Declaration and Programme of Action, UN doc. A/CONF.157/23, 12 July 1993, para. 74.
4 Report of the Secretary-General, In Larger Freedom: Towards Development, Security and Human Rights for All, UN doc. A/59/2005, 21 March 2005. For an analysis, see M. Nowak, 'The Three Pillars of the United Nations: Security, Development and Human Rights', in E. Salomon, A. Tostensen and W. Vandenhole (eds), *Casting the Net Wider: Human Rights, Development and New Duty-Bearers*, Intersentia: 2007, pp. 25–43.

document reaffirmed that 'development, peace and security and human rights are interlinked and mutually reinforcing' and that 'the promotion and protection of the full enjoyment of all human rights and fundamental freedoms for all are essential to advance development'.[5] A wide variety of initiatives on rights-based development have been undertaken by the UN, bilateral aid agencies, and non-governmental organizations.[6] The Development Assistance Committee (DAC) of the Organization for Economic Cooperation and Development (OECD) approved an Action-Oriented Policy Paper on Human Rights and Development.[7] The World Bank too has made public statements which acknowledge 'connections' and positive linkages between human rights and development.[8] Its approach has been to accept human rights in a general fashion.[9] There seems to be a consensus among virtually all development cooperation actors that development and human rights are interrelated. The essential task for the human rights discipline is to go beyond this discourse and try to understand what it actually means.

Despite strong policy statements on the importance attached to human rights in development discourse, academia and civil society reveal, as a reality, the fact that the change of discourse amounts to no more than rhetoric incorporation.[10] The most visible indications in support of this conclusion are the Millennium Development Goals (MDG), the 'single' most important development agenda, and the prolific commentary of UN human rights bodies and the human rights community more generally, all of which urge an integration of a human rights normative

---

5 UN GA Resolution 60/1, 2005 World Summit Outcome, 16 October 2005, paras. 9 and 12.
6 See e.g. United Nations, The Human Rights Based Approach to Development Cooperation – Towards a Common Understanding Among UN Agencies (the 'Stamford Statement'), adopted at a meeting which was held at Stamford, Connecticut, 3–5 May 2003, www.undg.org/index.cfm?P=221.
7 In particular, the AOPP stated: 'The importance of human rights for development is widely recognised. Human rights and equitable, sustainable development are mutually reinforcing. Human rights have intrinsic value, and achieving them is seen as an objective in its own right. But human rights are also a critical factor for the long-term sustainability of development.' OECD, *DAC Action-Oriented Policy Paper on Human Rights and Development*, OECD: 2007, p. 3.
8 For example, a publication of the World Bank on the occasion of the 50th anniversary of the UDHR stated: 'The Bank contributes directly to the fulfilment of many human rights articulated in the Universal Declaration. Through its support of primary education, health care and nutrition, sanitation, housing and the environment, the Bank has helped hundreds of millions of people attain crucial economic and social rights. In other areas, the Bank's contributions are necessarily less direct, but perhaps equally significant. By helping to fight corruption, improve transparency and accountability in governance, strengthening judicial systems and modernizing financial sectors, the Bank contributes to building environments in which people are better able to pursue a broader range of human rights.' WB, *Development and Human Rights: the Role of the World Bank*, 1998, p. 3.
9 A. Palacio, 'The Way Forward: Human Rights and the World Bank', in S. Puri (ed.), *Development Outreach*, World Bank Institute: 2006, pp. 35–36.
10 P. Uvin, 'From the Right to Development to the Rights-based Approach: How "Human Rights" Entered Development', 17 (4–5) *Development in Practice* (2007), pp. 597–606.

framework into development.[11] One could hardly disagree with Alston, who analogized the current state of debate between human rights and development to the metaphor of 'ships passing one another in the night, each with little awareness that the other is there, and with little if any sustained engagement with one another'.[12]

In order to better capture the criticism of the human rights community, it is suggested to have a closer look at how human rights *are* characterized in development policy debates, thus allowing an assessment of the extent to which convergence between human rights and development has taken place.[13] Three interrelated and broad aspects of the current state of affairs can be mapped out at this juncture.

First, the prevailing development approach to human rights integrates only a selected number of elements from human rights discourse, largely focusing on certain civil and political rights.[14] Mainstream thinking *uses* human rights almost interchangeably with democracy or good governance, but seldom, if ever, links the main area of intervention for development policies and programmes (i.e. education, health, living standards, income generation, women, etc.) to the realization of social and economic human rights.[15] The DAC, for example, highlights

---

11 See e.g. Joint statement of the Chairpersons of the United Nations Human Rights Treaty Bodies, presented at the High-level Plenary Meeting of the General Assembly on the Millennium Development Goals, New York, 20–22 September 2010, www.ohchr.org/en/News Events/Pages/DisplayNews.aspx?NewsID=10329&LangID=E.

12 P. Alston, 'Ships Passing in the Night: The Current State of the Human Rights and Development Debate Seen Through the Lens of the Millennium Development Goals', 27 (3) *Human Rights Quarterly* (2005), pp. 755–829, p. 825.

13 E. Jouannet, 'How to Depart from the Existing Dire Condition of Development', in A. Cassese (ed.), *Realizing Utopia: The Future of International Law*, OUP: 2012, pp. 392–417.

14 A detailed case-by-case analysis of the practice of individual states donors is likely to reveal a more nuanced picture of the state of affairs. See Chapter 11 for the various strands of approaches on the topic. Some donors appear to make human rights as an overarching objective of their activities. However, it should be mentioned that mere references to human rights do not necessarily show how policies are translated into practice. See e.g. G. Dijkstra, *The New Aid Paradigm – A Case for Policy Incoherence*, Background Paper for World Economic and Social Survey, 2010, available at http://www.un.org/en/development/desa/policy/wess/wess_bg_papers/bp_wess2010_dijkstra.pdf.

15 In a study, it was argued that most human rights interventions have focused on civil and political rights. Examples included 'freedom of expression (e.g. media projects) or due process (e.g. rule of law programmes) . . . investing in organisations (e.g. national human rights institutions), processes and procedures (e.g. democratisation, including elections, parties, civic education) and structures (e.g. capacity building of state or civil society)'. However, human rights are only 'mainstreamed' in education, health, housing, etc. programming. OECD, *Integrating Human Rights into Development Donor Approaches, Experiences And Challenges*, OECD: 2006, pp. 41, 44. A second edition of the study, published in 2013, does not seem to be able to trace any progress in this regard. It concludes: 'While at a policy level governments are committed to the indivisibility of all human rights, within development cooperation human rights work has tended to be narrowly construed around civil and political rights. This narrow focus in part explains why there is limited evidence and advice to date on how governance interventions can strengthen the realization of all rights, including economic and social rights.' World Bank and Organisation for Economic Co-operation and Development, *Integrating Human Rights into Development: Donor Approaches, Experiences, and Challenges*, 2nd edition, The World Bank and the OECD: 2013, p. 59.

the role of human rights as related to effective states, democratic governance, and the empowerment of citizens.[16] Socio-economic rights, which seem to be directly implicated in the poverty agenda of development actors, are rarely invoked, and cumulative evidence from diverse policy instruments show little regard for and understanding of these rights.

The practice of coupling 'human rights' with the 'democracy' and 'good governance' agenda has been highly controversial.[17] Some authors criticized conflating all of these themes as counterproductive for human rights;[18] linking governance and human rights tends to dilute socio-economic human rights.[19] While democracy and good governance may play an important role in the protection of human rights, the exclusive focus on these themes has strengthened the notion of human rights as a *political* dimension of development. This approach, in part, plays into the hands of those who view human rights in development as an additional layer of donor conditionality. Separation, therefore, may be necessary for the very preservation of the 'legitimacy' of human rights.[20]

Confining human rights only to their political dimension can effectively divert attention from the human rights obligations of donors, since it is the internal structure of the recipient state that is targeted. It also deflects attention from the fact that the development process implicates vital social and economic arrangements

16 It stipulates: 'Human rights are at the heart of effective states, democratic governance and empowered citizens. Effective states are those that control their territories, have open, transparent, accountable and inclusive political institutions, thriving economies, low levels of corruption, and are built on the principles of the rule of law.' OECD, *DAC Action-Oriented Policy Paper on Human Rights and Development*, OECD: 2007, p. 3.
17 From a strictly legal perspective, or, rather, a traditional international law point of view, a potential tension of promoting democracy may arise with the idea that internal state structures are matters of domestic jurisdiction. The ICJ in the *Nicaragua* case, in response to the argument of the US that Nicaragua breached international commitments to hold free elections and enact democratic reforms, pronounced that these matters were of 'exclusive jurisdiction provided of course that it does not violate any obligation of international law. Every State possesses a fundamental right to choose and implement its own political, economic and social systems.' ICJ, *Military and Paramilitary Activities in and against Nicaragua Case (Nicaragua v. United States of America)* (Merits) 1986, ICJ Rep 14, para. 258. At the same time, the practice seems to be in the direction of change, see e.g. Commission on Human Rights, Resolution 1999/57 on Promotion of the right to democracy, 27 April 1999, p. 4.
18 Concerns include the tendency to reducing democracy to electoralism, while human rights are largely seen to be 'politically neutral' and hence universally sustainable. L. Chun, 'Human Rights and Democracy: The Case for Decoupling', in 5(3) *International Journal of Human Rights* (2001), pp. 19–44, p. 35; K. Tomasevski, *Development Aid and Human Rights Revisited*, 2nd edition, Pinter Publishers: 1993, p. 13.
19 The language and definitions used in policy debates are very important. 'Naming or labelling the social context', Barnett and Finnemore write, 'establishes the parameters, the very boundaries, of acceptable action.' M.N. Barnett and M. Finnemore, 'The Politics, Power, and Pathologies of International Organizations', 53(4) *International Organization* (1999), pp. 699–732, p. 711.
20 M. Monshipouri, and C.E. Welch, 'The Search for International Human Rights and Justice: Coming to Terms with the New Global Realities', 23(2) *Human Rights Quarterly* (2001), pp. 370–401, p. 385.

and is capable itself of having a negative impact on the rights of individuals. Controversies over human rights in the development debate, and particularly 'the politicization debate',[21] can be avoided if human rights are defined strictly by the development actors' own mandate.[22]

Second, it appears that the consensus that development and human rights are complementary has *not* been articulated (as of yet) in legal terms.[23] It may, perhaps, have taken place in the form of recognition of their factual or substantive overlap and at the level of human rights principles.[24] Human rights concepts and principles may therefore be incorporated. Their expression as legal 'obligations', however, is avoided.[25]

The literature on the issue has frequently taken the position of the international financial institutions (the World Bank and International Monetary Fund, referred to as the IFIs) as a point of departure. This is not surprising given the prominent role these institutions have played in shaping the debate. Significant energy has been expended on the subject of political prohibition provisions in the institutional mandates of the IFIs, so as to 'prohibit' engagement with human rights in light of their political nature.[26]

---

21 E. Jouannet, 'How to Depart from the Existing Dire Condition of Development', in A. Cassese (ed.), *Realizing Utopia: The Future of International Law*, OUP: 2012, pp. 392–417, p. 400–401. Rajagopal notes, 'The idea that human rights can be hegemonic can strike its core believers as nothing less than sacrilege.' Discussing the various uses of human rights, he states that the end of Cold War marked the new birth of hegemonic role of human rights. 'In the economic sphere the World Bank and IMF, as well as several bilateral agencies, embraced a market-friendly conception of human rights.' B. Rajagopal, 'Counter-hegemonic International Law: rethinking human rights and development as a Third World strategy', 27(5) *Third World Quarterly* (2006), pp. 767–783.

22 K. Tomasevski, 'The Influence of the World Bank and IMF on Economic and Social Rights,' 64 *Nordic Journal of International Law* (1995), pp. 385–395, p. 395.

23 S. McInerney-Lankford, 'Human Rights and Development: Some Institutional Perspectives', 25(3) *Netherlands Quarterly of Human Rights* (2007), p. 490.

24 For example, the former President of the World Bank, James Wolfensohn, asserted: 'we tend to approach such matters [rights] from an economic and from a social point of view, taking out objectives which are articulated in the Universal Declaration and in the Covenants. But *rather than referring back to those documents*, we reflect their contents within the context of seeking to address the question of poverty.' J.D. Wolfensohn, 'Some Reflections on Human Rights and Development', in P. Alston and M. Robinson (eds), *Human Rights and Development: Towards Mutual Reinforcement*, OUP: 2005, p. 22. Similarly, convergence is visible at the level of human rights principles. The OECD policy paper notes that '[t]here is growing consensus on the value of human rights principles – such as participation, non-discrimination and accountability – for good and sustainable development practice' as their application builds on and strengthens good and sustainable development practice. See OECD, *DAC Action-Oriented Policy Paper on Human Rights and Development*, OECD: 2007, p. 3.

25 A. Clapham, *Human Rights Obligations of Non-State Actors*, OUP: 2006, p. 138.

26 From the perspective of the World Bank, see I.F.I. Shihata, 'Exclusion of Political Considerations in the Bank's Articles – Its Meaning and Scope in the Context of the Institution's Evolution', in I.F.I. Shihata, F. Tschofen and A.R. Parra (eds), *The World Bank in a Changing World: Selected Essays*, Martinus Nijhoff Publishers: 1991; I.F.I. Shihata, 'Political Activity Prohibited', in I.F.I. Shihata, *The World Bank Legal Paper*, Martinus Nijhoff Publishers: 2000, p. 219. For

To explain the disconnect between human rights and development, theory has thus been preoccupied with discussion of the mandate and legal constraints, as well as limitations to the disciplinal and institutional arrangements. By so doing, it is submitted here that the doctrine might have lost sight of the fact that such debates primarily deal with the question of the *extent* to which development institutions *should promote* human rights. To illustrate this point, it is useful to recall that in development circles, the value of human rights continues to be seen in instrumentalist terms.[27] The following mode of thought underlies this approach: development may take human rights into account when it is necessary or conducive to the attainment of development goals. Applying the logic of empirical evidence (e.g. where there is no causal link between human rights and development), however, renders the relevance of human rights remote.

The human rights community has followed suit by providing 'instrumental', 'operational effectiveness' and 'added value' arguments in support of this consequentialist paradigm.[28] 'Ever since human rights entered the development lexicon in the 1990s', Mac Darrow writes, 'their proponents have been pressed to demonstrate the "value added", in instrumental and presumptively quantifiable terms, of human rights in development. Rightly or wrongly, this remains the dominant framing of human rights in development debates.'[29]

The merit of using practical value arguments, or terms conformable to the field of development, need not be downplayed. Such a treatment of the issue, in one stroke of a brush, does not simply write off the many different legal parameters involved in the human rights and development continuum but crucially formulates the question in a way that effectively distorts the problem. The instrumentalist view of human rights defines the question of respect for human rights as an option – a matter of choice – rather than as a matter of legally binding obligations. Within this line of thinking, there is an automatic presupposition that compliance with human rights norms is dependent on recognition of the links between development and human rights. It is instead proposed that the

---

the arguments from human rights perspective see S. Skogly, *The Human Rights Obligations of the World Bank and the International Monetary Fund*, Cavendish Press: 2001; M. Darrow, *Between Light and Shadow: the World Bank, the IMF and International Human Rights Law*, Oxford, Hart Publishing: 2003.

27 S. McInerney-Lankford and H.O. Sano, *Human Rights Indicators in Development: An Introduction*, A World Bank Study, WB: 2010; OECD (DAC), *Integrating Human Rights into Development: Donor Approaches, Experiences and Challenges*, OECD: 2006.

28 For example, Mary Robinson has stated: 'There is so much practical benefit to be gained by expressly embracing the right to development, by integrating rights-based approaches to development, and by harnessing the instruments, mechanisms, and norms of the United Nations human rights programme to serve the cause of development.' M. Robinson, *Development and Rights: The Undeniable Nexus*, OHCHR: 2000, www.unhchr.ch/huricane/huricane.nsf/0/F31C625AA489D31BC125690A0053C8DE?opendocument.

29 M. Darrow, 'The Millennium Development Goals: Milestones or Millstones? Human Rights Priorities for the Post-2015 Development Agenda', 15(1) *Yale Human Rights and Development Journal* (2012), pp. 55–127, p. 83.

engagement of development actors with human rights issues should be defined within their own areas of operations. Put in these terms, the development praxis must ensure that its activities *respect* human rights.[30] The Committee on Social, Economic and Cultural Rights has stressed that:

> the core obligations of economic, social and cultural rights have a crucial role to play in national and international developmental policies, including anti-poverty strategies. When grouped together, the core obligations establish an international minimum threshold that all developmental policies should be designed to respect . . . [i]f a national or international anti-poverty strategy does not reflect this minimum threshold, it is inconsistent with the legally binding obligations of the State party.[31]

In other words, when states conduct their development cooperation activities, they are bound to, at a minimum, respect human rights. How development policies can *promote* or *protect* human rights, in addition to the minimum requirement of 'do no harm', appears to be little more than a choice for development institutions. To further highlight the lack of due attention to human rights as a matter of legal obligation, it is useful to compare how obligations in the area of environment have been integrated into development policies.[32] The World Bank Operational Policy on Environmental Assessment is a good example of how obligations in the area of environment can be accommodated in development operations.[33]

Third, as a consequence of the first two factors, human rights rarely, if ever, apply to the development actors' own conduct. The debate is pervaded by the view that human rights treaties address the obligations of a state towards its citizens and do not engage the responsibility of the donors. In the context of the

---

30 For the IMF legal counsel, 'the applicability of human rights to development to ensure that its actions do not produce negative effects on the former . . . would depend on a finding that the human rights in question are part of general international law. It is further argued that since the human rights often most directly implicated in the development process such as socio-economic rights have not reached such a status, their applicability therefore is problematic.' F. Gianviti, *Substantive Issues Arising in the Implementation of ICESCR: Working Paper*, UN doc. E/C.12/2001/WP.5, 7 May 2001, paras. 17–20.

31 CESCR, Statement on Poverty and the International Covenant on Economic, Social and Cultural Rights, UN doc. E/2002/22-E/C.12/2001/17, annex VII, para. 17, 10 May 2001.

32 In a similar vein, increased attention is being paid to issues of policy coherence between actors of economic policy-making. See for example paragraph 5 of the Uruguay Round Declaration on the Contribution of the World Trade Organization to Achieving Greater Coherence in Global Economic Policymaking.

33 Viz. 'EA [environmental assessment] . . . takes into account . . . obligations of the country, pertaining to project activities, under relevant *international environmental treaties and agreements*. The Bank does not finance project activities that would contravene such country obligations, as identified during the EA.' World Bank, O.P. 4.01- Environmental Assessment, January 1999, para. 3 (emphasis added).

activities of development institutions, such as the IFIs, arguments of institutional limitation are often invoked. Even if, as in recent years, the World Bank and the International Monetary Fund have somewhat moderated their approaches, they are far from accepting that any 'responsibility exists to ensure compatibility' with human rights.[34] While emphasis has been placed on 'good governance' as well as on the 'social' and 'political' aspects of development policy, 'no systematic process has been put in place for considering the impact of lending practices on the enjoyment of human rights'.[35]

Furthermore, the much-celebrated World Bank's Safeguard Policies, including environmental assessments, involuntary resettlement, and indigenous peoples, pertain only to the investment-lending policies and practices of the Bank, or, to put it simply, to the world of *projects*.[36] It is often overlooked that the World Bank also provides *development policy lending* that finances poverty reduction schemes throughout the world, as well as debt relief, such as the Highly Indebted Poor Countries (HIPC) initiatives, that are exempt from comparable safeguard policies.[37] Consequently, the Inspection Panel (the accountability mechanism established to address cases of adverse impact of WB-financed operations) has no mandate to receive requests concerning development policy lending of the World Bank.[38] One can even argue that keeping the focus on the political dimension of human rights effectively ensured that human rights concepts applied mainly to the recipient state's relationship with its citizens rather than to the 'development' activities of donors.

Based on these examples, it appears that human rights have not been internalized by development processes in a meaningful way. Human rights have not been conceived of as a system of international norms establishing minimum standards of protection of individuals applicable in all circumstances. To give effect to these norms, states, depending on the circumstances, are under a negative obligation

34 S. Marks and A. Clapham, *International Human Rights Lexicon*, OUP: 2005, p. 190.
35 *Ibid*.
36 See the World Bank Group, www.worldbank.org. It is important to note that currently the World Bank is in the process of revising and adapting its Safeguard Policies. See WB, 'Review and Update of the World Bank Safeguard Policies', https://consultations.worldbank.org/consultation/review-and-update-world-bank-safeguard-policies. For comments on the initial draft, see the letter of Special Procedures mandate holders to the World Bank concerning the review of its Safeguards policies, 12 December 2014, www.ohchr.org/Documents/Issues/EPoverty/WorldBank.pdf.
37 See generally, Investment and Development Policy Operations at www.worldbank.org.; WB, OP 8.60 – Development Policy Lending, March 2012; BP 8.60 – Development Policy Lending, February 2012; World Bank, *Development Policy Lending Retrospective: Flexibility, Customization and Results, World Bank, Operations Policy And Country Services*, 27 October 2009, p. 1.
38 Paragraph 12 of the Resolution establishing the Inspection Panel stipulates: 'The affected party must demonstrate that its rights or interests have been or are likely to be directly affected by an action or omission of the Bank as a result of a failure of the Bank to follow its operational policies and procedures with respect to the design, appraisal and/or implementation of a *project* financed by the Bank.' Resolution No. IBRD 93–10 and Resolution No. IDA 93–6, '*The World Bank Inspection Panel*', 22 September 1993 (emphasis added).

not to interfere with human rights and, in certain situations, are even under a positive obligation to facilitate their achievement. Put in these terms, it seems that basic human rights law premises bear little impact on the policy and practice of development. Such an outcome is inevitable, as human rights norms *do not guide* the discussion on human rights in development.

In this context, the key question that emerges is, how are we to read the integration of human rights into development? Can human rights, as currently employed, have only certain entrenched usages in the context of development? Can they be taken seriously as a matter of legal obligations? Can human rights references be properly construed with legal implications for development as a matter of international law? What are the potential implications of human rights for development?

As a preliminary remark, it is possible to identify two primary barriers to the integration of human rights in the context of development. First, in normative terms, it is suggested that the legal relationship between human rights and development has yet to be established. If we take into consideration the above example of integrating obligations under environmental law into the operational frameworks of the development institutions, there is no logical reason why development policies and practices should not, and, indeed, every reason why they should, integrate the legal dimension of human rights. Examples of such practice may be found in The European Bank for Reconstruction and Development (EBRD) and the New Partnership for Africa's Development (NEPAD),[39] both of which have accommodated human rights obligations in their development policies and activities.[40]

The second barrier exists at a conceptual level. While the repercussions of economic, social and cultural rights are fundamental to development cooperation (and vice versa), they are rarely incorporated in development analyses. This raises a question about the definition of 'human rights' referred to when states take actions to promote human rights in the international scene. This may be explained by the prevailing divide between two sets of rights: (i) civil and political, and (ii) economic, social and cultural. Such a proposition may seem trite and contrary to the accepted minimum consensus on indivisibility of rights, but it has not been taken as a relevant factor to explain the neglect of these rights in the development process.[41]

---

39 African Union, NEPAD Framework Document, October 2001, www.nepad.org/system/files/NEPAD%20Framework%20%28English%29.pdf.

40 EBRD makes direct reference to international conventions, including those related to human rights in its Environmental and Social Policy, which states: 'The EBRD will not knowingly finance projects that would contravene obligations under international treaties and agreements related to environmental protection, human rights and sustainable development as identified through project appraisal.' See EBRD, Environmental and Social Policy, May 2008, para. 9.

41 In particular, from the donors' perspective, 'development policies should be kept separate from the issues of human rights (which at best should be used to assess the compatibility of those policies and practices with human rights norms, but could not be the basis of development models. That would be too close to accepting the legitimacy of economic, social and cultural rights, which most of the major donors were not fully prepared to do).' A. Sengupta, 'Implementing the Right to Development', in N. Schrijver and Friedle Weiss (eds), *International Law and Sustainable Development*, Martinus Nijhoff Publishers: 2004, p. 365.

2 Introducing the perspective of international human rights obligations

It is proposed that the specific criteria for *linking* human rights and development need to be sought within a human rights legal framework.[42] The scope of engagement of donors and multilateral development agencies with human rights can be identified with reference to human rights treaties. This will ensure 'the application of *uniform* and *universal* legal obligations' to the conduct of all parties to the development process.[43]

Article 2(1) of the International Covenant on Economic, Social and Cultural Rights (ICESCR) would seem to be a starting point towards providing an answer to most of the questions on the human rights and development discourse. The Covenant, in line with the direction of the UN Charter, has absorbed 'development', qualifying it as an important means for the achievement of human rights.[44] Economic development and the enabling international economic order can be said to constitute a *conditio sine qua non* for the full realization of the socio-economic rights of individuals.[45] Development measures can thus serve as a framework within which economic and social rights can be defined and realized.[46] Furthermore, development cooperation is of relevance from a human rights perspective, as aid can make additional resources available for the realization of rights.[47]

The problem, of course, is that the legal nature from which the foregoing parameters are inferred has been controversial. The provision on assistance and cooperation has given way to multiple interpretations. It does not provide

---

42 K. Tomasevski, *Development Aid and Human Rights*, St Martin's Press: 1989, p. 125.
43 *Ibid.* (emphasis added).
44 See UN GA, International Covenant on Economic, Social and Cultural Rights, 16 December 1966, United Nations, Treaty Series, Vol. 993, p. 3; UN GA, Convention on the Rights of the Child, 20 November 1989, United Nations, Treaty Series, Vol. 1577, p. 3; UN GA, Convention on the Rights of Persons with Disabilities: resolution adopted by the General Assembly, UN doc. A/RES/61/106, 24 January 2007.
45 Report of the Secretary General, Progressive Development of the Principles and Norms of International Law Relating to the New International Economic Order, UN doc. A/39/504/Add.1, 23 October 1984, para. 212.
46 This of course can only be the case if development cooperation is designed within the framework of international human rights law. K. Tomasevski, 'Human Rights Obligations: Making Education Available, Accessible, Acceptable and Adaptable', *Right to Education Primer No. 3*, SIDA: 2001, p. 8.
47 In certain contexts, aid is a major source of financing. In 2010, the Palestinian Authority (PA) received net ODA of US$2.5 billion accounting for some 31% of its GDP. In 2008, the volume of aid it received amounted to a 49% share of its GNI. The United States, European Union, UN and Arab countries are the top donors. Aid Effectiveness: Palestinian Territory, 4th High Level Forum on Aid Effectiveness, Busan, Korea, www.aideffectiveness.org/busanhlf4/en/countries/middle-east/735.html. Afghanistan and Iraq are two examples of least developed countries that receive a high concentration of official development assistance. OECD, *Resource Flows to Fragile and Conflict-Affected States 2010*, OECD: 2010, www.oecd.org/dataoecd/51/52/46043367.pdf.

a ready understanding of the term, as its definition can be attributable to its composite origins, viz. the UN Charter, international development law, right to development discourse, development theory, or, as Jouannet would put it, to the '*welfare-inducing international law*' in general.[48]

The controversies surrounding the international assistance and cooperation as found in Article 2(1) of ICESCR did not prevent it from being used as a guiding principle to structure the international dimension of human rights obligations. This is particularly so, as the provision does not exhaust its normative force among developing countries. A core question underlying the concept is whether 'there are any standards which define a level of indigence, of lack of ability to fulfil basic needs which is unacceptable for the world order. And what are the legal consequences, if any, which are triggered by such a situation'?'[49] It therefore remains to be seen whether, on the basis of Article 2(1), it is possible to construct a framework that will address most of the concerns relevant to the development framework from a legal point of view.

The normative concerns of human rights treaties with development are not only confined to the questions of resources; compliance with human rights is equally paramount. This is because development policies and practices substantially overlap with the rights of individuals in the areas of health, education, standards of living, and sanitation, and are capable of impacting on human rights positively and negatively, directly and indirectly. Legal discourse as a consequence has been preoccupied with a question of how to ensure that economic and/or development policies do not conflict with individuals' human rights.[50] In simple terms: if the purpose of development is an individual, as officially proclaimed by the global policies, is it not the purpose that directs the rules?[51]

If, traditionally, human rights scholarship took the international assistance and cooperation as a basic framework of law to guide human rights in development debate, a new direction in legal argumentation had given away to a more nuanced understanding of the issue. One way for the human rights community to argue for adherence to human rights norms was to advocate for extraterritorial obligations. Yet another way to achieve adherence to human rights law is through analogous application of the principles and rules developed in international environmental law. These legal ideas may help us to construe a more complex analysis of the main questions.

There are several new elements that provide a context for revisiting development and human rights interrelationship. First, as the year 2015 marks the end of the MDG cycle and the turning point for shaping the international community's

---

48 E. Jouannet, 'What is the Use of International Law? International Law as a 21st Century Guardian of Welfare', in 28 *Michigan Journal of International Law* (2006–2007), pp. 815–862.

49 M. Bothe, Environment, Development, Resources, 318 *Recueil des Cours* (2005), p. 380.

50 P. Alston, *Development and the Rule of Law: Prevention Versus Cure as a Human Rights Strategy*, International Commission of Jurists: 1981, p. 71.

51 The formulation is taken from E. Jouannet, *The Liberal-Welfarist Law of Nations: A History of International Law*, CUP: 2012.

development project for the next 15 years, a time for evaluation and critical reflection prompts consideration as to whether human rights provide a legitimate framework for action. Second, the current global crises may fundamentally challenge and change perspectives on issues that were traditionally of concern to developing states, such as equity, rule of law in international economic relations, and the impact of financial institutions on the socio-economic rights of individuals, to name a few. There are visible signs that the international community seems to be gradually moving towards embracing concepts applicable to all states regardless of the level of development.[52] Concepts such as a global social protection floor may gradually and eventually replace the poverty discourse.[53]

It is interesting also to observe that transgovernmental regulatory frameworks of global economic affairs, such as the G20 (Group of Twenty), which have rarely put 'poverty' at the fore of their agenda in the past, are beginning to speak of human rights (i.e. full respect of 'fundamental principles and rights at work').[54] While practical effects of the inclusion of human rights in this sort of forum are yet to be seen, its insertion should be interpreted in a symbolic way; questions of responding to a minimum set of needs essential for the survival of the human person come to the fore, i.e. well-being is becoming a common interest of all.

In the doctrine, the theoretical analysis of the relationship between human rights and development has reached its peak. New writings seem to offer little innovative thinking on the legal dimensions of the subject matter, with much of the debate characterized by circularity. If, relatively recently, academic debates have concentrated on the controversial practices of conditionality and accountability challenges posed by IFIs, currently there is a sense of crisis in the development and human rights debate. On the one hand, the debate is becoming somewhat of an isolated genre, limited either to the right to development or

---

52 See the discussion in Chapter II on post-2015 development agenda.
53 'The notion of the social protection floor is anchored in the fundamental principle of social justice, and in the specific universal right of everyone to social security and to a standard of living adequate for the health and well-being of themselves and their families. Provisions made within the framework of the floor relate to a range of rights listed in the Universal Declaration of Human Rights. The core idea is that no one should live below a certain income level and everyone should at least have access to basic social services.' ILO, *Social Protection Floor for a Fair and Inclusive Globalization Report of the Advisory Group chaired by Michelle Bachelet*, ILO: 2011, p. 25. See also, ILO, Resolution concerning the recurrent discussion on social protection (social security), adopted by the ILC at its 100th session, June 2011; ILO, Social Protection Floors for Social Justice and a Fair Globalization, Report IV, document for the ILC 2012, 101st session, 28 February 2012; European Commission, Social Protection for Inclusive Development, European Development Report 2010, Brussels 2011; CEPAL, Protección social inclusiva in América latina, Santiago, 2011. For an excellent review of the relevant global policy frameworks see F. Mestrum, *Social Protection Floor: Beyond Poverty Reduction?*, Global Social Justice, 15 March 2012.
54 G20 Leaders' Communiqué Brisbane Summit, 15–16 November 2014; G20 Leaders' Declaration, Saint Petersburg Declaration, September 2013; G20 Leaders Declaration, Los Cabos on 18–19 June 2012 and Cannes Final Declaration '*Building Our Common Future: Renewed Collective Action For The Benefit Of All*', G20-G8 Cannes, France 2011.

to the critical comments on the integration of human rights into development goals which are frequently of minimal importance to the core issues. On the other hand, emerging areas, such as extraterritorial human rights obligations, are receiving greater attention, while the development and human rights intersection remains either at the margins of writings, or, is not fully understood in light of the context from which the development and human rights debate emerges.

In reality, the human rights and development relationship sits at the intersection of many delicate and controversial issues of concern to the current international legal order. The relationship between human rights and development provokes the following questions: allocation and distribution of resources: the protection and promotion of social and economic rights, particularly from the negative effects of globalization and the market; the international dimension of human rights obligations; the use of human rights in foreign policy; and the collective dimension of human rights. At the UN only, the development and human rights interface surfaces in the debates on right to development,[55] international cooperation for the promotion and protection of human rights,[56] human rights and international solidarity,[57] extreme poverty and human rights,[58] the effects of foreign debt and other related international financial obligations of states on the full enjoyment of human rights,[59] the question of a democratic and equitable international order,[60] and, as of recently, the unilateral coercive measures.[61]

55 See the Intergovernmental Working Group on the Right to Development, www.ohchr.org.
56 See Human Rights Council Advisory Committee, 'Study on the Enhancement of International Cooperation in the field of human rights, pursuant to Human Rights Council Resolution 13/23', UN doc. A/HRC/19/74, 29 February 2012: see also the latest Human Rights Council Resolution 28/2, Enhancement of international cooperation in the field of human rights, UN doc. A/HRC/28/L.1, 26 March 2015.
57 In Resolution 2005/55, the Commission on Human Rights decided to appoint the Independent Expert on Human Rights and International Solidarity. Ultimately, the work of the Independent Expert is to lead to the drafting of a Declaration on the right of peoples and individuals to international solidarity in UN Commission on Human Rights, Human Rights Resolution 2005/55: Human Rights and International Solidarity, UN doc. E/CN.4/RES/2005/55, 20 April 2005.
58 See the mandate of the Special Rapporteur on Extreme Poverty and Human Rights, since 1998.
59 See the work of the Independent Expert on the effects of foreign debt and other related international financial obligations of states on the full enjoyment of all human rights, particularly economic, social and cultural rights. In the beginning, two different mandates were established by the Commission on Human Rights: the mandate of the Independent Expert on structural adjustment policies in 1997 and the mandate of the Special Rapporteur on the effects of foreign debt on the full enjoyment of economic, social and cultural rights in 1998. These two mandates were discontinued in 2000 when the mandate of the Independent Expert on the effects of structural adjustment policies and foreign debt was set up.
60 In its recent Resolution 18/16 of 13 October 2011, the Human Rights Council decided to establish a special procedures mandate. Independent expert on the promotion of a democratic and equitable international order, Human Rights Council Resolution 18/16, Promotion of a democratic and equitable international order, UN doc. A/HRC/RES/18/6, 13 October 2011.
61 Human Rights Council Resolution 27 / 21, Human rights and unilateral coercive measures, UN doc. A/HRC/ RES/ 27/ 21, 3 October 2014.

All of these debates occur in a fragmented manner within subdisciplinary fields, with little effort being made to bridge issues that can be common to most of them. It is suggested that at least two questions identified in this section underlie all of these debates. First, whether there is a legal requirement under international law upon states to cooperate and assist? Second, whether there are possible limits imposed on the external activities of states by human rights? In other words, the second question is concerned with identifying the legal framework applicable to states when they engage in activities which potentially affects the socio-economic rights of individuals residing abroad. Assessment of these questions may ultimately shed light on whether international law, as it stands today, requires more than is actually seen in terms of practice.

3 Connections between development and human rights: Basic questions further delimited

The interface between human rights and development incorporates a multitude of diverse and complex aspects, including a wide variety of human rights norms and a potentially vast number of situations that may arise in a development context. To define the limits of the scope of this book, it is necessary to distinguish it from other related themes by way of charting various aspects of the topic. This book will be concerned with a narrow issue identified in the previous section: the question of assistance and cooperation, which is identified as a source of law providing legal criteria for the development and human rights interface, and the question of the compliance, i.e. *respect*, for human rights in the context of development. There are a few other issues that are relevant to the present subject but are beyond its scope.

One of the dimensions of the human rights and development topic is the issue of *enforcement* of human rights in development, often discussed in the relevant literature under the rubric of human rights conditionality in development. This subject is often presented as controversial. However, contrary to what may appear at first glance, international law provides a framework for analysis of the relevant legal issues. The legal questions in play will vary according to the specifics of each case, and may depend on the legal relations between the parties (donor and recipient), as well as the nature of violations. It is nonetheless possible to frame the issue in very general terms.

The basic question is whether development aid can be used to enforce compliance with or respond to violations of international human rights norms in a concerned state (e.g. recipients of development aid), including through the suspension or cancellation of agreements and, if so, what are the legal limits? Here a distinction can be drawn between obligations deriving from treaty regimes and those derived from customary international law. International human rights agreements envisage a system of accountability, and the answers to most of the questions can be found in the relevant human rights treaty (or its interpretation). Some human rights treaties prescribe a specific means of enforcement,[62] while others remain silent on the issue.[63] States, of course, enjoy the discretion of employing methods to comply with their obligations by other means not foreseen in the treaty itself.[64]

The accountability mechanisms prescribed by international human rights treaties do not preclude recourse to mechanisms of international law, provided that certain conditions are met. The Draft Articles on the Responsibility of States for Internationally Wrongful Acts make clear that the specific framework embodied by special rules take precedence.[65] The International Court of Justice adopted the same position in the *Nicaragua* case;[66] however, it further specified that the rule is only valid as long as the prescribed mechanism is functioning.[67] In addition, not all international human rights treaties provide for an inter-state procedure. For those that do, the choice to be bound by the relevant provision(s) is optional. In light of the fact that none of these universal level procedures have ever been used, Bruno Simma has suggested that they 'should not be regarded as exhausting the matter of enforcement . . . When human rights treaties provide no meaningful enforcement in case of States alleging violations by other States, recourse to the general law of responsibility, such as rules on counter-measures . . . should be available.'[68]

The important point to make here is that termination of aid is not necessarily problematic and is not as unregulated as might be suggested, when situated

62 International Covenant on Civil and Political Rights: Article 41; Convention against Torture: Article 21; International Convention on the Elimination of All Forms of Racial Discrimination: Article 11; International Convention on the Protection of the Right of All Migrant Workers and Members of Their Families: Article 76. In contrast, regional mechanisms are considered more sophisticated on the issue: ECHR: Article 33 (as amended by Protocol 11); ACHR: Article 45; ACHPR (Banjul Charter): Article 49.
63 International Covenant on Economic, Social and Cultural Rights and Convention on the Rights of the Child. However, with the adoption of the Optional Protocol to the ICESCR, adopted by GA Res A/RES/63/117, on 10 December 2008, and the Optional Protocol to the Convention on the Rights of the Child (OPCRC) on a communications procedure adopted by the UN General Assembly on 19 December 2011, the situation has changed.
64 U. Khaliq, *Ethical Dimensions of the Foreign Policy of the European Union: A Legal Appraisal*, CUP: 2008, p. 40.
65 Article 55 of the Draft Articles on the Responsibility of States stipulate 'These articles do not apply where and to the extent that the conditions for the existence of an internationally wrongful act or the content or implementation of the international responsibility of a State are governed by special rules of international law.' See also Commentary to Article 55, in International Law Commission, Report of the International Law Commission 53rd session (23 April – 1 June and 2 July – 10 August 2001), GAOR, 56th session, Suppl. No. 10, UN doc. A/56/10, p. 358.
66 ICJ, *Military and Paramilitary Activities in und against Nicaragua (Nicaragua v. United States of America)*, Judgment, ICJ Reports 1986, paras. 267 and 268, where the Court stipulated: 'In any event, while the United States might form its own appraisal of the situation as to respect for human rights in Nicaragua, the use of force could not be the appropriate method to monitor or ensure such respect.'
67 B. Simma, 'Human Rights and State Responsibility', in A. Reinisch and U. Kriebaum (eds), *The Law of International Relations – Liber Amicorum Hanspeter Neuhold*, Eleven International Publishing: 2007, pp. 362–363.
68 *Ibid.*, p. 365.

within the scope of the lawful measures to which a state, other than an injured state, may resort. In addition, as noted above, states may have a legitimate interest in ensuring other States Parties comply with their human rights treaty obligations.[69] Equally, the legality of the enforcement of human rights obligations, including through development-related measures, can derive from customary international law. In this instance, the content of the norms will be, strictly speaking, confined to a limited set of norms, particularly those recognized as *erga omnes*. The countermeasures are not without limits[70] and are subject to compliance with a set of rules.[71] For example, suspension of a development cooperation treaty is subject to the provisions of the Vienna Convention on the Law of the Treaties.[72] Particularly in relation to development agreements of a humanitarian nature, due regard should be taken of Article 60(5), which concerns the protection of the human person contained in treaties of a humanitarian character.[73]

Similarly, the Articles on State Responsibility identify a set of obligations not affected by countermeasures, which include the protection of fundamental human rights and obligations of a humanitarian character. In its General Comment on the effect of economic sanctions on civilian populations, the Committee on Economic, Social and Cultural Rights addressed countermeasures undertaken by states individually and as a group of states.[74] It asserted that sanctions should

---

69 ILC Commentaries to the Articles on State Responsibility cite the case of Netherlands-Suriname in 1982, when the Dutch Government suspended a bilateral treaty on development assistance as an example of countermeasures although justified differently (fundamental change of circumstances). Christian Tams's study of countermeasures also cites the example of EC Member States denunciation of the 1983 Cooperation Agreement with Yugoslavia also qualified as *clausula rebus sic stantibus*. Tams gives examples of other cases involving suspension of development assistance as countermeasures. See C. Tams, *Enforcing Obligations Erga Omnes in International Law*, CUP: 2005, p. 207ff. See also Section 703 of the Third Restatement which states: 'a State does not violate international law when it shapes its trade, aid or other national policies to influence a State to abide by recognized human rights standards'. *Restatement of the Law (Third) of Foreign Relations of the United States* (American Law Institutive Publishers, 1987).
70 *Military and Paramilitary Activities in und against Nicaragua (Nicaragua v. United States of America)*, *supra* note 60, para. 205, in which the Court specified that the 'choice of political, economic, social and cultural system and the formulation of foreign policy' are matters of domestic prerogative.
71 Article 50 of the Draft Articles on the Responsibility of States for Internationally Wrongful Acts; see also Chapter VI, section on International law and cross-border aspects of socio-economic rights.
72 Articles 54 to 64 of the Vienna Convention on the Law of the Treaties (VCLT) governing situations of termination or suspension of the treaties.
73 Article 60 of the VCLT identifies the situations of termination or suspension of a treaty as a consequence of its breach, and paragraph 5 stipulates: 'Paragraphs 1 to 3 do not apply to provisions relating to the protection of the human person contained in treaties of a humanitarian character, in particular to provisions prohibiting any form of reprisals against persons protected by such treaties.'
74 Other potential legal issues may arise with regards to prohibition of coercion. See the relevant section of Chapter VI.

18   *Introduction*

'always take full account of the provisions of the International Covenant on Economic, Social and Cultural Rights'.[75] From the above overview, it becomes apparent that most of the controversies surrounding human rights conditionality in development are more sufficiently regulated by international law than may appear at first glance. Rather, the controversies surrounding the topic relate to the inconsistent and selective practices, which are influenced by foreign policy considerations rather than the needs of individuals.[76]

Furthermore, it is not possible to discuss the nexus between human rights and development without dealing in some detail with the notion of sustainable development. Sustainable development clearly is conceptually based on human rights, among other things, but evolution of the doctrine on the subject has so far concerned itself with the environmental aspect. The International Law Association (ILA) rightly puts emphasis on the challenge of 'integration' and how not to lose sight of human rights and development issues in the pursuit of intergenerational equity.[77] In one of its reports the ILA reiterated the obscurity in the relationship between different elements of the sustainable development concept, namely environmental protection, social improvement, economic development, gender empowerment, and promotion of respect for human rights.[78]

The question of integration is perhaps one of the biggest challenges: how could various and quite different lines of legal rules, standards and policies in all of these

75 CESCR, General Comment No. 8, The relationship between economic sanctions and respect for economic, social and cultural rights, UN doc. E/C.12/1997/8, 12 December 1997, para. 1.
76 K. Tomasevski, Monitoring Human Rights Aspects of Sustainable Development, 8 *American University Journal of Law and Policy* (1992), p. 81; See also K. Tomasevski, *Development Aid and Human Rights, Contextualising the International Covenant on Economic, Social and Cultural Rights: Assessing the Economic Deficit, op. cit.*, (Describing the practice of sanctions, uses of human rights in aid, pp. 61–95); K. Tomasevski, *Responding to Human Rights Violations: 1946–1999*, Martinus Nijhoff Publishers: 2000; and C. Pinelli, 'Conditionality', *Max Planck Encyclopaedia of International Law*, www.mpepil.com.
77 The concomitant aspect of it is that sustainable development speaks of 'basic human needs', which raises important issues as to whether it satisfies the absolute non-derogable minimum requirement developed in human rights law practice. And if the doctrine of sustainable development maintains as one of its principles poverty eradication, the question is, how does this principle legally relate to human rights law? For the discussion see ILA, Report of the Seventy-First Conference, 71 *International Law Association Conference Report* (2004), pp. 574–575.
78 The report further highlighted the relationship of human rights and sustainable development as follows: 'A further challenge is the role of human rights law within the sustainable development process. These are two topics that are clearly complementary – both reflect a wider and more inclusive understanding of the international community. However, beyond the level of political language . . . – there may be less commonality between them than is first imagined. For instance, emphasis upon a human right to a healthy environment risks the marginalisation of developmental considerations, if not appropriately implemented.' ILA, Report of the Seventy-First Conference, 71 *International Law Association Conference Report* (2004), pp. 574–575.

areas – development, human rights, environment and economic relations – be linked to each other and be mutually accommodated so as to produce a coherent system of concepts? Obviously the two concepts pull together different metrics; what is clear is that the concepts of human rights and sustainable development are not the same, and the formulation of the next sustainable development agenda, through 2030, may well serve as a test case for their interoperability.[79]

4 Possible limitations of the 'human rights and development' intersection

4.1 *Human rights law*

At the outset, it is important to mention some critical comments made about the 'limits' of human rights in the development discourse. First, there is some scepticism as to the capacity of human rights to grapple effectively with issues of the material well-being of individuals through development. On one account, human rights *law* (as opposed to human *rights*)[80] is saddled with serious constraints that limit its contribution to human development.[81] According to this perspective, human rights law traditionally visualizes consequences for the state only in regard to its individuals *within* its national frontiers. Given that development is a multi-actor process, any attempt to apply human rights law in development will require 'broadening the circle of duty-bearers' for human development.

Legal strategies developed to date, such as the right to development and the more innovative but rapidly evolving approach based on responsibility through extraterritorial application of human rights, are insufficient, as they remain controversial.

Second, it is questioned whether the individualist approach of human rights is a suitable device to respond to issues of a systemic nature.[82] Developmental

---

79 For commentaries on the Conference on Sustainable Development, Rio +20, see J. Vinuales, Concept obèse, le développement durable se meurt, *Le Temps*, 24 August 2012.
80 For international human rights law theory as distinct from the theory of human rights and the theory of international human rights see F. Mégret, 'International Human Rights Law Theory', in A. Orakhelashvili (ed.), *Research Handbook on the Theory and History of International Law*, Research Handbooks in International Law Series, Edward Elgar: 2011, pp. 199–231, p. 200.
81 W. Vandenhole, 'The Limits of Human Rights Law in Human Development' in E. Claes, W. Devroe and B. Keirsbilck (eds), *Facing the Limits of the Law*, Springer: 2009, 355–374, p. 355.
82 For earlier criticism on the conceptual suitability including western and non-western notions of individualism see K. Tomasevski, 'The Influence of the World Bank and IMF on Economic and Social Rights', 64 *Nordic Journal of International Law* (1995), pp. 385–395, and J. Donnelly, *Universal Human Rights in Theory and Practice*, Cornell University Press: pp. 57–60. See also S.P. Marks, B. Rudolf, K. De Feyter and N. Schrijver, 'The Role of International Law' in OHCHR, *Realizing the Right to Development Essays in Commemoration of 25 Years of the United Nations Declaration on the Right to Development*, UN: 2013, pp. 445–468.

human rights are particularly susceptible to the difficulties of definitions and collective challenges, which do not easily fit with the individualistic approach of
human rights.[83] One of the concerns underlying such an argument seems to be
the issue related to the individual nature of remedies provided under human
rights law, and to the question of duty-bearers.[84]

While each of the concerns outlined above require perusal of great magni-
tude, at this point, a general and brief comment is in order. With regard to the
first criticism, it suffices to point out that sometimes, the positioning of human
rights law as governing the relationship between the individual and the state con-
ceals the important characteristic of human rights treaties. Human rights treaties,
although *sui generis*, operate in the realm of international law. It is often forgot-
ten that remedies for violation of human rights treaties remain within the boundaries of international law.[85] Although, 'in human rights agreements the promissee
[a state to which the obligation runs] is a state, while the true beneficiary is an
individual[,] . . . that does not detract from the right of any state party to an
agreement to seek its observance by others'.[86] Simma's conclusive analysis on
the theory of the objective obligations under human rights treaties may provide
some key ingredients to understanding the capacity of human rights law to instigate changes at the international and national levels concerning socio-economic
development.[87]

Human rights, as is well known, do not embody the traditional type of treaties
between states based on reciprocity and mutual benefit.[88] This has given rise to
the theory of 'absolute' or 'objective' obligations, to which human rights treaties
purportedly belong. This theory was further developed in the jurisprudence of

---

83 It is said that the concept of collective rights has been fitted so far only in the area of indigenous rights.

84 W. Vandenhole, 'The Limits of Human Rights Law in Human Development', *op. cit.*, pp.
356, 364ff.

85 For the contrary view, see J.S. Watson, 'The Limited Utility of International Law in the
Protection of Human Rights', 74 *Proceedings of the ASIL* (1980), pp. 1–6.

86 Louis Henkin notes: 'I state this with confidence.' He rejects the view of others who have
argued that 'human rights agreements that establish special remedies or "machinery" intend
these to be exclusive and replace the ordinary remedies between parties for violations of
international agreements generally.' Recalling the famous *obiter dictum* of the ICJ in the
Barcelona Traction case on the obligations towards international community as a whole
which concern all states, he points out that Articles 55 and 56 of the UN Charter, 'can also
be considered *erga omnes*'. L. Henkin, 'International Human Rights as "Rights"', 1 *Cardozo
Law Review* (1979), pp. 425–447, p. 431, footnote 24.

87 B. Simma, 'From Bilateralism to Community Interest in International Law', 250 *Recueil
de Cours* (1994), p. 372. See also, L. Henkin, 'International Human Rights as "Rights"',
op. cit., pp. 425–447; in M. Kamminga, *Inter-state Accountability for Violations of Human
Rights*, University of Pennsylvania Press: 1992, p. 149ff.

88 See ICJ, *Reservations to the Convention on the Prevention and Punishment of the Crime of
Genocide*, ICJ Pleadings, p. 64.

regional human rights mechanisms.[89] In 1978, the European Court of Human Rights in the case of *Ireland v. United Kingdom* developed this theory by pronouncing that:

> Unlike international treaties of the classic kind, the Convention comprises more than reciprocal engagements between contracting States. It creates, over and above a network of mutual, bilateral undertakings, objective obligations which . . . benefit from 'collective enforcement'.[90]

When reading these passages, Simma warns against hasty conclusions. More specifically, qualification of human rights treaties as treaties not producing an 'exchange of tangible benefits' should not lead to an assertion 'that such absence of factual, or "sociological" reciprocity, as it were, leads to the absence of reciprocal legal rights and duties proper'.[91] As the International Court of Justice confirmed in the *South West Africa* case, states can have rights which do not 'necessarily relate to anything material or "tangible", and can be infringed even though no prejudice of a material kind has been suffered'.[92]

In the *Ireland v. United Kingdom* case, quoted above, the European Court of Human Rights does not isolate human rights treaties from its *milieu*, but manages instead to 'free' the category of human rights from the 'adverse effects of reciprocity'. The important point to be made here is that human rights treaties may establish an objective order 'in so far as its legal architecture goes beyond the creation of correlative inter-State rights and duties along the contractual model'.[93] It is this 'inter-state' compliance (or even enforceability) envisaged in human rights treaties, or, put differently, the assumption of duties and obligations between states as set in human rights treaties, that is the main remedy to address systemic and structural issues.[94] This not only concerns situations of breaches,

---

89 The European Commission of Human Rights dealt with the issue for the first time in the *Pfunders* case (ECHR, 4 *Yearbook of the European Convention on Human rights* (1961), p. 116 et seq) and subsequently in a number of cases. European Commission of Human Rights, *Cyprus v. Turkey*, 21 *Yearbook of the European Convention on Human Rights* (1978), p. 101ff., p. 226ff.; *Chrysostomos et al.*, 34 *Yearbook of the European Convention on Human Rights* (1991), p. 35ff., p. 52. Inter-American Court of Human Rights issued an Advisory Opinion on the subject matter. IACtHR, *The Effect of Reservations on the Entry Into Force of the American Convention on Human Rights (Arts. 74 and 75)*, Advisory Opinion OC-2/82, September 24, 1982, Inter-Am. Ct. H.R. (Ser. A) No. 2 (1982).

90 ECtHR, *Ireland v United Kingdom*, Series A, No. 25 (1978), p. 90.

91 B. Simma, From Bilateralism to Community Interest in International Law, *Recueil des Cours*, Vol. 250 (1994), p. 369.

92 ICJ, *South West Africa Cases (Ethiopia v. South Africa)*, Second Phase, ICJ Reports 1966, p. 32.

93 B. Simma, From Bilateralism to Community Interest in International Law, *op. cit.*, p. 372.

94 Menno Kamminga recalls the regime of reservations as an evidence of reciprocity in human rights treaties. With reference to individual reservations of certain states in regard to various

but it also emphasizes that states are mutually bound and have a responsibility 'to keep the treaties alive'.[95]

The Covenant on Economic, Social and Cultural Rights has also been established in the framework of the inter-state rights and obligations. Article 23 requires that:

> The States Parties to the present Covenant agree *that international action for the achievement of the rights recognized* in the present Covenant includes such methods as the conclusion of conventions, the adoption of recommendations, the furnishing of technical assistance and the holding of regional meetings and technical meetings for the purpose of consultation and study organized in conjunction with the Governments concerned. [emphasis added]

This provision clearly recognizes the role of all contracting states to contribute to the realization of economic, social and cultural rights in any given State Party.[96] It also assumes that every state has an interest in the performance by every other State Party, of its obligations. This analysis is also directly applicable to the debate on whether the right to development can be formulated as a human right when in fact it concerns the states *inter se.*

The main 'limitation' of human rights treaties is that their 'reciprocal' feature does not contribute to the performance of the states.[97] Perhaps the most crucial aspects of human rights in development is the issue of accountability and the continuing uncertainty regarding the precise scope of obligations.[98] The human

---

human rights treaties such as ICCPR, CEDAW, ICERD, etc., he convincingly interprets these reservations as a manifestation of the 'individual interest' of states in observance of human rights treaties by the other parties rather than being merely an expression of a collective interest, in M. Kamminga, *Inter-state Accountability for Violations of Human Rights, op. cit.*, p. 136ff.

95 B. Simma, 'Mainstreaming Human Rights: The Contribution of the International Court of Justice', 3(1) *Journal of International Dispute Settlement* (2012), pp. 7–29, p. 23.

96 This issue was discussed in debates concerning International Cooperation in the negotiation of the Convention on the Rights of Persons with Disabilities. While the EU held that 'IC [international cooperation] is about implementation, not a specific right of individuals . . . These are general references stating that implementation horizontally will not be possible without IC', Chile made clear that 'The Article [international cooperation] clarifies States' commitments under this Convention. Responding to the EU's concerns that IC was not about individual rights, it stated that international public law has always served to regulate the obligations of States and just a few decades ago, individuals were introduced as subjects of international law. This does not exclude a provision referring to relations among States and regulating the horizontal nature of IC.' Sixth Session of the Ad Hoc Committee, Summaries of the Sixth Session, Vol. 7, Issue no. 1, 1 August 2005, www.un.org/esa/socdev/enable/rights/ahc6sum1Aug.htm.

97 One exception at the universal level could be the case brought before the ICJ in ICJ, *Questions relating to the Obligation to Prosecute or Extradite (Belgium v. Senegal)*, Judgment of 20 July 2012.

98 K. Tomasevski, 'Monitoring Human Rights Aspects of Sustainable Development', *op. cit.*, p. 96.

rights that are most often directly implicated by the development intervention, viz. socio-economic rights, have only begun their path towards justiciability at the international level. The deficit of accountability, both at international and national levels, has rendered questions of ensuring the compliance of development with human rights indeterminate.

Potential constraints can be seen, not so much with the conceptual underpinnings of human rights law (being individual-oriented), but with a structural approach to human rights in general.[99] Any structural approach to human rights realization, or any long-term solution for development, is hinged upon economic issues.[100] Legal theory, as known, will always face constraints when embroiled in 'the shifting and unruly facts of international politics, economics and social justice'.[101] Consequently, there may be a number of factors preventing developing states from achieving socio-economic progress; problems of an internal character, such as a lack of will or capacity, or even care, can inhibit progress.[102] Yet, locating the responsibility for failure to deliver development within a nation state is only part of the picture.

99 Alston has pertinently described the limitations here: '[the] potential danger is that the structural approach will become identified with a sweepingly broad, non-legal, economically or sociologically oriented approach. Its impact then would be to downplay the importance of other, specifically legal, approaches to human rights issues, to move the focus of UN human rights activities away from specifics towards global economic problems and generally "to disappear into the clouds of a universality that leaves the larger world stranded far below". There is a touch of irony in the fact that, on the one hand an unduly legalistic approach gave rise to the need for a radical departure from existing approaches to the promotion of human rights, while on the other hand the adoption of a preventive approach to human rights serves to emphasize the need not to lose sight of the firm legal foundations of the modern concept of human rights. For without constant reference to the various legal standards that have been painstakingly negotiated, adopted and ratified, we are no further along the road to human dignity.' P. Alston, *Development and the Rule of Law: Prevention Versus Cure as a Human Rights Strategy*, International Commission of Jurists (1981), p. 20.
100 The capacity of a state to meet its commitments to the realization of basic needs of the population within its jurisdiction is dependent on the economic issues, as resources are crucial for the realisation of all human rights.
101 O. Schachter, 'The Evolving International Law of Development', 15 *Columbia Journal of Transnational Law* 1 (1976), pp. 1–16, p. 1. In the words of the High-Level Task Force on the Implementation of the Right to Development, 'the greatest challenge for the implementation of the right to development, in theory and practice, is to reconcile the conceptual approaches of human rights and economics; in other words, how to maintain a holistic vision of human rights, implying indivisible and interdependent norms aimed at maximizing the well-being of all individuals and peoples, while introducing the concerns of development based on sound economic policies that foster growth with equity' in High-Level Task Force on the Implementation of the Right to Development, The Right to Development in Practice: Provisional Lessons Learnt, OHCHR, *Realizing the Right to Development Essays in Commemoration of 25 Years of the United Nations Declaration on the Right to Development*, UN: 2013, pp. 469–484.
102 As de Feyter notes, 'Developing States have been only partially successful in bringing about development. Lack of success may have resulted from lack of care. Government policies may have focused on elite interest. They may have been more concerned with national than

At a deeper level, however, human rights and development are not antitheti-
cal, as is sometimes projected. Human rights have been shaped by the dominant
development paradigms of 'modernity' – a move from backwardness to progress. According to Rajagopal, the legal classification of socio-economic human
rights and the corollary obligations of states have been based on an economic
rationale, and more specifically on a specific model of economy where the role
of the state was predominant (the so-called first 'all-state' stage of the development covering the 1950s to 1970s). This not only contrasts but also contradicts
the current market-based model of development.[103] The notion of human rights
thus 'remains too deeply mired within the progressivist and teleological impera-
tives set by the development discourse, and therefore cannot be counted upon
in an unproblematic way as an emancipatory narrative of resistance to violence
unleashed by development encounter'.[104] By this logic, one must ask whether
human rights could actually be able to question the 'development' process?

4.2 *The role of law in development (cooperation)*

The second major limitation concerning the present subject relates to the relationship between development and law, which has always been uncertain. This
is partly due to the susceptibility of development to conflict, being by definition
'an intervention to affect change'.[105] The existence of legal rules in the area of
development aid has been raised in the past. Back in 1968, the International Law
Commission was suggested to study a 'particularly urgent' subject matter related
to the legal principles of reciprocal assistance between states in economic matters.[106] It was stated that:

> The time had now come to consider the question whether there was a
> legal obligation on the richly endowed countries to render assistance to

---

with social security. In such cases, the remedy is fairly straightforward. What is required is
a change in government policy. Or, if necessary, a change in government or in the organisation of political life.' K. de Feyter, *World Development Law: Sharing Responsibility for
Development*, Intersentia: 2001, p. 67.
103 Louis Henkin similarly explains: '[b]orn after various socialisms were established and
spreading, and commitment to welfare economics and the welfare states was nearly universal, international human rights implied rather a conception of government as designed for
all purposes and seasons. The rights . . . [implied] a government that is activist, intervening,
planning and committed to economic-social programs for the society that would redound
as economic – social rights for the individual.' L. Henkin, 'International Human Rights as
"Rights"', *op. cit.*, p. 434.
104 B. Rajagopal, *International Law from Below: Development, Social Movements and Third
World Resistance, op. cit.*, p. 33.
105 K. Tomasevski, 'Monitoring Human Rights Aspects of Sustainable Development', *op. cit.*,
p. 88.
106 International Law Commission, Summary record of the 977th meeting, Extract from the
Yearbook of the International Law Commission, 1968, Vol. I, UN doc. A/CN.4/SR.977,
para. 27.

those countries which needed it and if so, what was the scope of that obligation.[107]

The subsequent Secretary-General's *Survey of International Law* took note of a proliferate body of multilateral and bilateral agreements, as well as instruments not governed by international law but which gave rise to a certain practice with common trends. A question addressed by the report was concerned with whether, in view of all accumulated practice, it can be said that a body of customary law was emerging, including the obligation to render assistance. The reflection on this issue did not produce much comment in the report apart from a submission that 'no such obligation as that suggested has been accepted in positive law'. At most, 'there is an imperfect obligation to take certain actions towards certain objectives within particular institutional and procedural arrangements', which in any case were 'at an early stage of their development, and that the time is not yet ripe for any attempt to spell out an obligation in concrete legal terms'.[108]

The principles embodying this area of law, as broadly articulated by the New International Economic Order, did not reach the level of a 'legal concept'. Almost five decades later, there is little to suggest that any progress has been made.[109] To address the title of this section, the expression used by Michael Bothe comes to mind: 'Market mechanisms are trusted, not legal regulation.'[110] Economic growth is a predominant concern of development. It is therefore hardly surprising that no general legal framework for development exists today.[111] Those

107 *Ibid.* The work of the Economic and Social Council of the United Nations, the Marshall Plan, the organization in Europe of three economic communities, the progress made towards economic integration in Central America, the establishment of a Latin American free trade area, and the President Kennedy's Alliance for Progress were all deemed to be expressions of the duty of states to render assistance to one another in economic matters.

108 The Secretary General's Survey of International Law identified three areas: (i) international legal rules and measures concerning the regulation and co-ordination of the economic activities of States; (ii) international trade; (iii) economic and technical assistance. 'Although not exclusively so, the achievements of the Commission have been in areas of traditional international law.' Survey of international law – Working Paper prepared by the Secretary-General in the light of the decision of the Commission to review its programme of work, Extract from the Yearbook of the International Law Commission 1971, vol. II(2), UN doc. A/CN.4/245 (1971), http://untreaty.un.org/ilc/documentation/english/a_cn4_245.pdf. M. Flory, 'Adapting International Law to the Development of the Third World', 26 *Journal of African Law* 1982, p. 12.

109 On the whole, the regulatory framework of the development assistance is composed of instruments, standards, procedures that guide the transfer of aid and its use, and reporting. This all is encompassed by the category of the Official Development Assistance (ODA). ODA is defined in following terms: (i) provided by official agencies, including state and local governments, or by their executive agencies; and (ii) each transaction of which: a) is administered with the promotion of the economic development and welfare of developing countries as its main objective; and b) is concessional in character and conveys a grant element of at least 25% (calculated at a rate of discount of 10%). OECD, *Factsheet 'Is It ODA?'*, OECD: November 2008.

110 M. Bothe, Environment, Development, Resources, 318 *Recueil des Cours* (2005), p. 505.

111 *Ibid.*

few normative solutions offered to address development problems did not prove efficient, and according to some assessments, simply 'failed'.[112] An additional impediment for legal regulation is the changing definition of development. Consequently, the legal landscape of development cannot be canvassed by definition, because there is no consensus as to whether this law should capture the reality of development as it *is*, or instead be oriented towards what it should be.[113]

A number of commentators pointed to the EU and the ACP partnership as something closest to a legal regime.[114] Other regimes do not, as yet, enjoy such an appraisal. The balance sheet for the role (as well as the rule) of law in international development has engendered harsh criticism. One commentator has pointed out that '[i]nsufficiently legalised and never fully accepted, IDL [international development law] has never succeeded in establishing itself completely, and in so doing, it has unfortunately created a lot more misunderstanding than it has led to advances'.[115] What is more, the turning of development towards poverty is thought to be a fundamental reorientation and even abandonment of the more structural problems.[116]

In addition, the last decade has seen a substantial diversification of actors, as well as a proliferation of sources and channels of aid. The current development landscape has evolved and grown in complexity, as new and non-traditional, southern donors, or the South–South Cooperation (SSC), as they are referred to, are increasingly playing a significant role.[117] These changes have significant

---

112 E. Jouannet, 'How to Depart from the Existing Dire Condition of Development', *op. cit.*, p. 404. UNCTAD, *The Least Developed Countries Report 2010: Towards a New International Development Architecture for LDCs*, UN: 2010.

113 K. Tomasevski, 'Monitoring Human Rights Aspects of Sustainable Development', in 8 *American University Journal of Law and Policy* (1992), p. 89.

114 E.g. Partnership Agreement between the members of the African, Caribbean and Pacific Group of States and the European Community and its Member States.

115 E. Jouannet, 'How to Depart from the Existing Dire Condition of Development', *op. cit.*, p. 404.

116 Speaking of the MDGs, Emmanuelle Jouannet states: 'the current fight against poverty and extreme poverty contributes in any event to endorsing the idea that it is impossible to find political and legal solutions for the all-round development of developing countries . . . [T]hus we no longer speak of socio-economic inequalities in the texts relating to poverty, as the problem has gone. LDCs and developing countries are regarded as now having only one central problem, that of poverty, so that the fight against poverty will be the key to everything, along with the market. But the fight against poverty is not economic and social development, and ways to address social and economic inequalities are far more difficult and challenging for states than the means needed to eradicate poverty.' *Ibid.*, p. 403–404.

117 While these so-called 'new donors' have been in operation for quite some time, their visibility has increased in the last decade due to their contribution to the development assistance. The South-South Cooperation as a notion takes its roots in the Asian-African Conference, known as the Bandung Conference, in 1955, and the creation of the G-77 Group in the 1960s. For the role of the emerging economies in development cooperation see A. Sumner and R. Mallett, *The Future of Foreign Aid Development Cooperation and the New Geography of Global Poverty*, Palgrave Macmillan: 2012; C. Gore, 'The New Development

ramifications for international development and, ultimately, for the concept of development itself.

The policies and practices of new donors do not easily yield to generalizations, as no systematization of their activities has taken place yet. On the other hand, their integration into the existing, traditional development cooperation schemes is problematic, as these new actors reject the basic premises of the OECD–DAC and do not regard themselves as donors or providers of assistance.[118] In fact, the SSC do not consider their cooperation as a replacement of the traditional North–South cooperation and thus liable to the same standards.[119] The G-77 and China guiding principles for South–South cooperation state that '[f]inancial contributions from other developing countries should not be seen as official development assistance (ODA) from these countries to other countries of the South. These are merely expressions of solidarity and cooperation borne out of shared experiences and sympathies.'[120]

Consequently, a consensus opinion has emerged that there is no uniform global North or South any more in the dynamics of development; this signals the transition from the concept of aid to that of cooperation and possibly may guide development. The present, 'more complex architecture' of development cooperation contributes to a fragmentation of the global development structure and raises questions as to the coherence and effectiveness of the system.[121] It

---

Cooperation Landscape: Actors, Approaches, Architecture', in 25 *Journal of International Development* (2013), pp. 769–786; T. Abdel-Malek, *The Global Partnership for Effective Development Cooperation: Origins, Actions and Future Prospects*, Deutsches Institut für Entwicklungspolitik, Bonn: 2015; and N.A. Besharati, *Common Goals and Differential Commitments: The Role of Emerging Economies in Global Development*, German Development Institute, Discussion Paper No. 26, 2013.

118 For instance, China's Policy on Foreign Aid states: 'When providing foreign assistance, China adheres to the principles of not imposing any political conditions, not interfering in the internal affairs of the recipient countries and fully respecting their right to independently choosing their own paths and models of development. The basic principles China upholds in providing foreign assistance are mutual respect, equality, keeping promise, mutual benefits and win-win.' White Paper on China's Foreign Aid (2014), www.china. org.cn/government/whitepaper/node_7209074.htm.

119 Guiding principles 3 and 4 read respectively as follows: 'South–South cooperation must not be seen as a replacement for North–South cooperation. Strengthening South–South cooperation must not be a measure of coping with the receding interest of the developed world in assisting developing countries' and 'Cooperation between countries of the South must not be analysed and evaluated using the same standards as those used for North–South relations.' in G-77 and China guiding principles for South–South cooperation, found in UNCTAD, *Economic Development in Africa Report 2010, South-South Cooperation: Africa and the New Forms of Development Partnership*, UN 2010, p. 17.

120 *op. cit.*

121 Recent attempts, particularly in the Fourth High Level Forum on Aid Effectiveness in Busan (2011), to integrate these new donors into the operational framework in accordance with the same development policy principles and procedures as DAC donors did not yield much results. The outcome document of Busan included a paragraph that demonstrates

may, however, also bring new opportunities; the entry of new actors onto the scene introduces an element of competition with traditional donors, including 'a competition on the norms ruling the transfer of aid'.[122]

The question is, why is the role of law in development important for human rights purposes? The multiplicity of actors, processes and non-law instruments characterizing development today has one important disadvantage: the absence of an arbiter. While a case can be made to invoke human rights aspects in the legal regimes of investment, trade, intellectual property, etc., this is not quite possible in the framework of development, characterized by discretion and a lack of fixed rules.

5 Remarks on approach

This book approaches the interface of human rights and development cooperation from an international law perspective. It does so through a survey of the legal aspects of the human rights and development intersection, namely by reviewing the sources relevant to the debate with a view to contributing to the understanding of the concepts of international cooperation and assistance that have increasingly become a main point of reference. Legal and extra-legal aspects are probably more strongly interrelated in the concept of the human rights and development intersection than in any other area of the human rights discipline. This poses limitations and difficulties in the study of the practice, since instead of reliance on the jurisprudence of international human rights' judicial and quasi-judicial bodies, references are more often being made to treaties, interpretations and statements of the UN human rights bodies, and to policy frameworks of the major development actors.

To expand the analysis and increase its relevance, this book takes into account a number of other elements. First, this includes an assessment of state practice as reflected in the domestic legislation, donor state policies and guidelines on human rights, and State Parties' periodic reports to the treaty monitoring bodies as well as the dialogue with them. Second, the study analyses states' international legal commitments under other regimes, such as international humanitarian law and emerging rules in the area of protection of persons in the event of disasters,

---

the point well: 'The nature, modalities and responsibilities that apply to South–South co-operation differ from those that apply to North–South co-operation. At the same time, we recognise that we are all part of a development agenda in which we participate on the basis of common goals and shared principles. In this context, we encourage increased efforts to support effective co-operation based on our specific country situations. The principles, commitments and actions agreed in the outcome document in Busan shall be the reference for South-South partners on a voluntary basis.' Busan Partnership for Effective Development Co-operation, November 2011, para. 2.

122 Philipp Dann usefully instructs us that these actors may 'provide new insights and instruments, set other priorities and thus strengthen the system'. P. Dann, *The Law of Development Cooperation: A Comparative Analysis of the World Bank, the EU and Germany*, CUP: 2013, p. 153.

as are currently elaborated by the International Law Commission. These two areas may not only provide inspiration for a dynamic interpretation of the scope and extent of states' various obligations of both a procedural and substantive kind, but may also lead to a better understanding of the implications and challenges in operationalizing obligations of states *inter se*, concerning protection of individuals. It is often pre-supposed that there is no legal obligation as such to provide assistance to meet human rights obligations (including through assistance to development). However, adopting such an approach from the very start is reductivist and disregards important directions and debates in which different areas of international law, as well as the practice of individual states, are heading. What seems less clear, however, is on which basis this should be: moral, political or legal?

It is important to be clear with one's key terms from the very beginning. The focus is on conceptual legal development, not on pragmatic efforts to make human rights practically relevant to the development cooperation. Although frequent references are made to the IFIs throughout this book, the study will focus on the analysis of legal obligations of states in the area of realization of human rights in the development context. There are a number of reasons for this, not least the availability of extensive assessment of the responsibility of non-state actors. The most important reason, however, is that states are a logical starting point for identifying the legal aspects of the topic in question.[123]

6 Outline of the book

This work structures the legal ideas and arguments concerning the relationship between human rights and development, according to the evolution of discourse.

It starts with characterizing and contextualizing the two parallel discourses: development on the one hand and human rights on the other. This historical assessment forms an important background for the emergence of different legal ideas about the relationship between development and human rights (Chapter II). It further sets the broader context, which situates human rights within the wider processes of the development discourse, and identifies also the current status of human rights integration in the main development policy and operational instruments at multilateral and bilateral settings.

Chapter III proceeds from the first doctrinal encounter between human rights and development, which gave rise to the concept of the right to development. It provides an overview of the content of the right to development and how it visualizes the relationship between human rights and development. What

---

123 As well noted, '[r]etaining a focus on States' obligations under human rights treaties would underscore their extension to State actions in all international fora, from the UN Human Rights Council or UN human rights treaty bodies, to UN General Assembly, and its second Committee on Economic and Financial Matters, the European Union, the OECD or in IFIs.' S. McInerney-Lankford, 'Human Rights and Development: Some Institutional Perspectives', *op. cit.*, p. 490.

becomes apparent from the discussion is that it is the international dimension of the right to development, giving rise to inter-state obligations, which makes the right contentious and politically unacceptable. This takes us to the examination of the concept of the obligation to cooperate, as reflected in the UN Charter and in the International Covenant on Economic, Social and Cultural Rights (ICE-SCR), which traditionally has served as a legal basis for the right to development discourse.

The obligation to cooperate for human rights is envisaged in the Charter of the United Nations, the ICESCR, and other treaties incorporating economic, social and cultural rights. Chapter IV introduces the subject by providing basic elements of the context – the law of cooperation – the logic of which underpins the UN Charter and the ICESCR. This chapter proposes a rather long 'journey' to assess the nature and meaning of cooperation and assistance, and suggests searching for answers outside the strict confines of debates on human rights and development. For example, international humanitarian law and the current draft rules on the protection of persons in the event of disaster are areas of law equally rooted in the same principles of cooperation, solidarity and human dignity.

Finally, Chapters V and VI develop an idea that flows from the previous discussions; the main concern for the relationship between development and human rights is not only a question of resources, but, effectively, one of compliance, to ensure that development does not harm individuals. How to ensure that economic and/or development policies do not conflict with human rights obligations is a crucial challenge. This chapter traces the legal sources of the requirement that states are to respect the human rights of individuals residing abroad and suggests that general principles of international law may be an appropriate avenue to address these issues.

II Development from a human rights perspective

Introduction

Development thinking is an area dominated by economic and policy consider-ations based more on *realpolitik* than law.[1] At the same time, perceptions of, and approaches to, development, as reflected in the development institutions, have influenced the legal responses and scope and content of norms.[2]

This chapter will proceed from an overview of the development landscape and the history of its moorings in human rights, moving with greater refinement to actual practice, that is, existing policies and practices. It does so, in the first place, by sketching the evolution and changing trends of development policy think-ing and the legal discourse, including its human rights dimension. This will, in part, involve examining the actors/institutions, the objective of their relationship and the means and instruments of their interaction, including legal and policy frameworks.

The purpose is not only to canvas the institutional and policy environment of development but also to discuss what can be made of the many different uses of human rights in development discourse and practice. Such analysis signals the extent to which human rights discourse 'infiltrates' development frameworks and whether these frameworks support the confluence of human rights and develop-ment or, on the contrary, confirm their separate evolution.

1 The changing notion of 'development'

When addressing the reach of international law to the questions of development, and in particular, development as a problem of international legal order, ques-tions arise as to what development is and how to determine its 'insufficiency'

1 M. Virally, 'La 2ᵉ décennie des Nations Unies pour le développement – Essai d'interprétation para-juridique', 16 *Annuaire français de droit international* (1970), pp. 9–33, p. 9.
2 M. Hirsch, 'Developing Countries', *Max Planck Encyclopaedia of Public International law*, www.mpepil.com, para. 9.

(or 'sufficiency'). Historically, and to date, the prevalent criteria are expressed in terms of Gross National Product (GNP) in calculating the level of development. But beyond this core economic element, other criteria have been introduced, such as the 'human dimension' as articulated by the UN Development Programme's Human Development Index and the relatively recent concept of 'intergenerational equity' reflected in the notion of 'sustainability'.

Crudely put, there is no accepted definition of development. Some consensus exists on what development *should not be*, and over time new dimensions have been added by development theory, practice and policy to the aforesaid basic econometric definition. Consequently, as Tomasevski has justly observed, '[t]he legal framework for development remains controversial because of disagreements as to whether the law should be oriented towards an ideal or whether it should follow prevalent practice'.[3]

There is general agreement that responses to the challenge of development require efforts at two levels.[4] Intra-state solutions to development challenges require adequate policies within developing countries. The second level is inter-state, i.e. international measures that articulate possible rights and duties of states *inter se* regarding development. The two levels are closely interlinked. As Virally explains, '[i]l s'agit toutefois . . . d'un ensemble cohérent, donc de mesures qui se complètes les unes les autres et, souvent, se conditionnent mutuellement, de sorte que les défaillances enregistrées dans un secteur déterminé risquent d'avoir un effet cumulatif et de compromettre toute la stratégie'.[5] All international debate and economic, political and, at times, legal measures concentrate around these two dimensions.

1.1 The development paradigm

The traditional narrative is that the concept of development is largely a product of economic and political events following World War II.[6] Yet its initial manifestations date back to an even earlier period.[7] In effect, the internationalization of

---

3 K. Tomasevski, 'Monitoring Human Rights Aspects of Sustainable Development', 8 *American University Journal of Law and Policy* (1992), p. 89.

4 The UN SG's Agenda for Development states: 'For sustained growth to take place, two conditions are necessary; a supportive national environment, and a favourable international climate. Without appropriate national policies, no amount of assistance, bilateral or multilateral, will lead to sustained growth. On the contrary, assistance given in this way can reinforce dependence on the outside world. Without a favourable international climate, domestic policy reform will be difficult to achieve, threatening the success of reforms and increasing the hardships suffered by the population.' Report of the Secretary-General, Agenda for Development, UN doc. A/48/935, para. 46.

5 M. Virally, 'La 2e décennie des Nations Unies pour le développement – Essai d'interprétation para-juridique', *op. cit.*, pp. 9–33, p. 17.

6 F. Snyder, 'Law and Development in the Light of Dependency Theory', 14 *Law and Society Review* (1980), p. 724; See also G. Rist, *The History of the Development: from Western Origins to Global Faith*, Zedbooks: 2002, p. 69.

7 For an in-depth analysis of the Mandate System of the League of Nations as the precursor to current development practice (ranging from classic developmental planning to specialized

the 'social domain', and the attendant poverty and welfare discourse, has its roots in the League of Nations.[8] Article 22 of the Covenant of the League of Nations addressed development within its mandate system and is said to have invented the first principle of development, i.e. 'well-being and development' of peoples.[9] According to the Covenant this was 'a sacred trust of civilisation'.[10] This concept of development was further developed in Article 55 of the UN Charter, together with the references to human rights.

The notion of development in its modern understanding emerged during post-WWII reconstruction in Europe. It was coined by US President Truman in his Four Point Speech,[11] in which every nation was called upon to work jointly through the UN and its specialized agencies 'whenever practicable' for the achievement of 'peace, plenty, and freedom'. The concluding part of the Fourth Point included a solidarity and human rights tone stating that '[o]nly by helping the least fortunate of its members to help themselves can the human family achieve the decent, satisfying life that is the right of all people'.[12] Some authors ascribe a symbolic significance to the Fourth Point, as it had set in motion the basic premises of development thinking and reconfigured global power structures.[13] The discovery of 'underdevelopment' as area of intervention in the 1950s thus put poverty 'squarely on the international agenda'.[14]

---

agencies, standard setting in socio-economic spheres to petition processes) or even as a foundation of the apparatus of development ('the institutional link in transition between colonialism and development'), see B. Rajagopal, *International Law from Below: Development, Social Movements and Third World Resistance*, CUP: 2003, in particular, p. 50ff.

8 *Ibid.*, p. 108.

9 Precedents to the Mandate system included Article VI of the General Act of the Berlin Conference in 1885 and Article 11 of Convention Revising the General Act of Berlin, 26 February 1885, and the General Act and Declaration of Brussels, 2 July 1890, according to which the European Powers 'exercising sovereign rights or authority in African territories will continue to watch over the preservation of the native populations and *to supervise the improvement of the conditions of their moral and material well-being*' (emphasis added).

10 Article 22 of the League of Nations already contains some parameters of the development known and existent to the current discourse on development. Article 22 states that the best way to implement this principle (e.g. well-being and development of respective people) is 'that the tutelage of such peoples should be entrusted to advanced nations who by reason of their resources, their experience or their geographical position can best undertake this responsibility, and who are willing to accept it, and that this tutelage should be exercised by them as Mandatories on behalf of the League.' Furthermore, '[t]he character of the mandate must differ according to the stage of the development of the people, the geographical situation of the territory, its economic conditions and other similar circumstance.' See also an example of domestic development legislation of the time, the British Colonial Development Act of 1929.

11 The US President Truman's Point Four at the Inaugural Address of 1949 is believed to have launched the 'development age'. For a full reproduction of the speech see G. Rist, *The History of the Development: from Western Origins to Global Faith, op. cit.*, pp. 71–72.

12 Reproduced in G. Rist, *ibid.*

13 A. Escobar, 'Power and Visibility: Development and the Invention and Management of the Third World', 3(4) Cultural Anthropology (1988), pp. 428–443, p. 429.

14 B. Rajagopal, *International Law from Below: Development, Social Movements and Third World Resistance, op. cit.*, p. 106.

As to the responses to development (or lack of it), they remain as controversial as the concept itself. Social sciences have constructed different theories and models to explain the causes of underdevelopment. Different approaches to underdevelopment have been predominant at different times. In the 1950s and early 1960s, the 'modernization theory' prevailed.[15] At national level, the theory encouraged industrialization, while internationally this approach found its expression in the invention of development aid, the rise of technical assistance with its different modalities, and the transfer of resources and technologies from rich countries to poor ones.[16]

While the UN Charter recognized the importance of promoting 'conditions of economic progress and development' and 'the solutions of international economic, social, health, and related problems', it did not vest adequate powers in the UN to implement this mandate, much less to secure it a mandate to manage global economic development. The UN Charter instead trusted that states would make good on their pledges 'to take joint or separate actions in cooperation with the UN'.[17] Relevant institutional arrangements were designed outside the UN, at the Bretton Woods Conference, where decision-making did not rely on the principle of equal representation. At this time, human rights were not yet situated within development discourse. At this stage, only at the UN, the focus of development in terms of human well-being was limited to 'basic needs'.[18]

Quick results did not emerge from capital transfers, and growth did not benefit the poor. Underlying assumptions of the modernization approach were widely criticized, particularly by dependency theorists in the late 1960s and 1970s,[19] and the idea of 'basic needs' started to gain support among development institutions.[20] At the international level, the problem of development was seen as part of

15 It assumed 'development' as a historical and evolutionary process, where society undergoes the stages of growth taking off from the state of a traditional society with the final form of growth being the age of 'high-mass consumption'. W.W. Rostow, *The Stages of Economic Growth: A Non-Communist Manifesto*, CUP: 1960, pp. 4–16. See also for detailed explanation of the modernization T. Dos Santos, 'The Crisis of Development Theory and the Problem of Dependence in Latin America', in Henry Bernstein (ed.), *Underdevelopment and Development: The Third World Today*, Penguin Books: 1973, pp. 58–59.
16 J. Macrae, *Aiding Recovery? The Crisis of Aid in Chronic Political Emergencies*, Zed Books: 2001, p. 13.
17 Articles 55 and 56, UN Charter.
18 Stokke notes that the UN agencies were active in forming the strategy of basic needs, with their emphasis on public services. O. Stokke, *UN and Development: From Aid to Cooperation*, IUP Press: 2009, pp. 10–11.
19 For a thorough discussion of the theory see T. Dos Santos, 'The Structure of Dependence', 60 *The American Economic Review* 2, Papers and Proceedings of the Eighty-second Annual Meeting of the American Economic Association (May, 1970), pp. 231–236, p. 231. A. Escobar, *Encountering Development: The Making and Unmaking of the Third World*, Princeton University Press: 1995, p. 82. See also for differences between *dependencia* theories from previous ones in F. Snyder, 'Law and Development in the Light of Dependency Theory', 14 *Law and Society Review* (1980), p. 724.
20 E.H. Jacoby, 'Dilemma of the World Bank: Comment to the Annual Report 1972', 4(3) *Development and Change*, p. 95.

the structural disequilibrium of the world economy. Such an approach paralleled the political climate of the time between North and South after decolonization, and the East–West dynamics created a fertile environment for enhancing the position of the developing countries.[21] Essentially, decolonized states quickly realized that the existing structures of the economic order were not particularly beneficial to them.[22]

1.2 The New International Economic Order

Dependencia (dependency) theories nourished developing countries' vision of the causes of existing inequalities.[23] One of the first moves of '[the] large majority of the new world . . . poor, weak, underdeveloped',[24] in addition to their legal independence, was to acquire political and economic independence, as expressed in 1962 UN General Assembly Declaration on Permanent Sovereignty over Natural Resources.[25] Paragraph 1 of the Declaration required sovereignty to be exercised in the interest of a state's 'national development and of the well-being of the people of the State'. This principle was regarded as the economic extension of the right of peoples to self-determination. René-Jean Dupuy described the birth of the new dimension of self-determination in following terms:

> Si les thèmes qui informent le droit des peuples à disposer d'eux-mêmes sont identiques à ceux que proféraient les révolutionnaires de 1789 et de 1793, ils n'étaient pas dans la situation où se trouvent les peuples livrés à la faim, à la maladie, à l'analphabétisme. C'est ce qui donne à la formulation du droit des peuples, de nos jours, son nouveau timbre : il n'est plus une protestation libérale mais est devenu une revendication sociale en même temps qu'une affirmation d'indépendance . . . C'est pourquoi le droit des peuples, d'essence politique dans son principe originel, se dédouble en droit des peuples à disposer de leurs ressources . . . L'indépendance politique qu'il suppose n'a pas de sens autrement qu'assortie de l'indépendance économique.[26]

---

21 Bedjaoui describes the context of the time as follows: 'un contexte connu pour avoir été triplement "euphorique": l'euphorie des indépendances en chaîne des anciennes colonies, celle du "pouvoir du nombre" au sein de l'Assemblée générale de l'ONU et, enfin, celle du socialisme et de l'interventionnisme étatique, l'un et l'autre devenus une mode'. Bedjaoui, M., 'L'humanité en quête de paix et de développement', Cours général de droit international public (2004), Vol. II, 325 *Recueil des Cours* (2006), p. 148.

22 Imbalances were identified in terms of trade, foreign investment, and the conduct of transnational corporations among others.

23 UN GA Resolution 3201 (S-VI), Declaration on the Establishment of a New International Economic Order, 1 May 1974, para. 2.

24 R. Anand, *Confrontation or Cooperation? International Law and Developing Countries*, Martinus Nijhoff Publishers: 1987, p. 44.

25 UN GA Resolution 1803 (XVII), Permanent Sovereignty over Natural Resources, 14 December 1962.

26 R.-J. Dupuy, Communauté internationale et disparités de développement : cours général de droit international public, 165 *Recueil des Cours* (1979), pp. 139–140.

In a favourable political condition, developing countries formulated more 'demands' through appeal to the international community[27] to address problems of unfavourable terms of international trade, and operation of financial and monetary systems, in particular participation in international economic institutions. An attempt was made to shift financial and monetary decision-making to the United Nations. A set of principles was elaborated through the Declaration on the Establishment of a New International Economic Order (NIEO)[28] and the 1974 Charter of Economic Rights and Duties of States (CERDS),[29] mainly addressing North–South relations. Resolutions 3201 on NIEO comprised a list of 20 principles, and Resolution 3202 setting out the NIEO Programme of Action outlined areas that were to be put in place by 'all efforts'.[30] This programme emphasized two aspects. First, that assistance had to be given on terms 'as determined' by developing states themselves and, second, there was a preference for collective action through the UN in the implementation of the NIEO. This had to take place in an environment where developing countries were to be protected from external interference, and would not be required to honour their reciprocal obligations.

As defined in the Programme, one of the urgent actions to follow these resolutions was 'to establish generally accepted norms to govern international economic relations systematically' with an aim 'to establish a just order' by means of 'a charter to protect the rights of all countries, and in particular the developing States'.[31] Thus, a set of rules was formulated in the CERDS. The Charter included principles partially based on accepted rules of international law[32] and those that included elements causing division between developing and developed

27 With reference to the international community, R.-J. Dupuy remarked: 'La communauté internationale fournit des interlocuteurs aux pauvres : sans eux leur interpellation se perdrait dans le désert d'un monde irresponsable. Voilà pourquoi le tiers monde utilise le concept communautaire comme un mythe politique, comme une idée force qui, et à travers la mauvaise conscience des puissants, ouvre son chemin à la nuit du 4 août.' *Ibid.*, p. 122.

28 UN GA Resolution 3201(S-VI), Declaration on the Establishment of a New International Economic Order, UN doc. A/RES/S-6/3201, 1 May 1974, para. 6; UN GA Resolution 3202 (S-VI), Programme of Action on the Establishment of a New International Economic Order, Doc. A/RES/3202 (S-VI), 1 May 1974.

29 UN GA Resolution 3281 (XXIX), Charter of Economic Rights and Duties of States, 12 December 1974.

30 It included problems of raw materials and primary commodities as related to trade and development; the reform of the international monetary system; industrialization; transfer of technology; regulation of transnational corporations; prompt adoption of the Charter of Economic Rights and Duties of States; promotion of cooperation among developing countries; assistance in the exercise of permanent sovereignty over natural resources; the strengthening of the role of the United Nations system in the field of international economic cooperation; and the launching of 'special programs' by the United Nations to mitigate the difficulties encountered by specific developing countries.

31 United Nations Conference on Trade and Development Resolution 45 (III) of 18 May 1972.

32 E.g. respect to sovereignty, territorial integrity and political independence of states, acceptance of the sovereign equality of all states, principles of non-intervention and *pacta sunt servanda.*

states concerning the level of compensation for expropriation of foreign property and regulation of the activities of the transnational corporations.[33] These attempts to change the structure and content of international law[34] were not supported by the main addressees, i.e. industrialized states. According to one commentator:

> The resolutions of the NIEO were forced through the General Assembly in a lamentable atmosphere. They were not negotiated solutions but a partisan set of demands . . . As for the Charter of Economic Rights and Duties of States, it is not international law, and happily so, for in some respects it is sound, but in other respects, quite nationalistic and unsound.[35]

At the UN, steps were taken to follow up the Declaration and Charter by elaborating the legal principles and norms of international economic law pertaining to legal aspects of the NIEO. Despite a series of resolutions by the UN General Assembly on the matter, this ambitious project of consolidating and progressively developing principles and rules did not materialize, because they apparently went outside the remit of existing principles and 'had not yet crossed the threshold of *lex lata*'.[36] States with advanced economies, therefore, 'were able to control the nature and extent of the reform of the economic system'.[37]

Indeed, one significant aspect of the entire endeavour was the role it assigned to legal rules (and international law more generally) in relation to the problem of development. The NIEO was the most important legal *desideratum* to transform the economic relations between states to make it fairer and to accommodate the needs of the poor majority. In general, the normative structure, as developed in the UN through successive declarations and international development strategies, provided the basis for systematization of the normative framework of a branch called international development law.[38] However, as Georges Abi-Saab has rightly noted, 'this impressive normative structure has remained very fragile because the basis of obligation of the industrialized countries to act according to these principles was very controversial'.[39]

---

33 NIEO included measures of economic content such as the integrated commodity programme, the generalized preference scheme in trade, financial flows in form of aid, the codes of conduct for multinationals and the transfer of technology and of legal political nature aiming at strengthening the position of developing countries in the international economic system, such as extension of the principle of permanent sovereignty over natural wealth and resources and the demand for full and effective participation in international economic decision-making, etc.

34 M. Bothe, 'Environment, Development, Resources', 318 *Recueil des Cours* (2005), p. 385.

35 S. Schwebel, 'A Commentary', in T.M.C. Asser Institute (ed.), *International Law and Grotian Heritages*, The Hague, T.M.C. Asser Institute: 1985, p. 142.

36 G. Abi-Saab, 'Wither the International Community', 9 (2) *European Journal of International Law* (1998), pp. 248–265.

37 D. French, ' "From Seoul With Love" – The Continuing Relevance Of The 1986 Seoul ILA Declaration on Progressive Development of Principles of Public International Law Relating to a New International Economic Order', 55 *Netherlands International Law Review* (2008), p. 9.

38 G. Abi-Saab, 'Wither the International Community', *op. cit.*, p. 263.

39 *Ibid.*

At the same time a more careful analysis of NIEO suggests that it was 'neither new nor fundamentally radical'. It was not radical, as it did not question the fundamental development paradigm – e.g. modernization of society.[40] In fact, 'they [developing countries] wanted more of it [i.e. of development]'.[41] Its radicalism could only be dissected in what Rajagopal called 'instrument-effects'.[42] The radical demands had a 'paradoxical effect of expanding and strengthening international institution as the apparatuses of management of social reality in the Third World, and, thereby, of international law itself'.[43] Initiating new institutions to respond to the 'resistance of the Third World' not only contributed to containing this 'resistance' but also increased the bureaucratization of international affairs.

From a legal perspective, the assessment of the normative value of the Declaration and the Charter would first depend on subsequent statements and state practice. Some key elements of the NIEO did evolve into one form or another. The primary example is the developments in the trading system, where granting differential and favourable treatment of developing countries became a basic feature of the multilateral trading system.[44] Issues related to a Code of Conduct for Transfer of Technology[45] and a Code of Conduct on Transnational Corporations[46] were followed up as well but eventually were abandoned. A similar fate awaited the issue of stabilization of commodity prices.[47] Additionally, development assistance became the main feature of international cooperation for development as a specialized area of international development law. Initially a transient measure, it has even been given added life in relation to the international engagement towards development, primarily to alleviate poverty. In contrast with international economic law, development assistance rules and procedures, as will be seen in following sections, did not crystallize into a distinguishable set of norms of universal application.

---

40 B. Rajagopal, *International Law from Below: Development, Social Movements and Third World Resistance*, CUP: 2003, pp. 74, 79.

41 *Ibid.*, p. 74.

42 Rajagopal states: 'Third World engagements with international institutions have had a double character: on the one hand, they have radicalised these institutions by converting them into arenas of political and ideological struggle over issues of power, distribution and justice; on the other hand, the most radical strands of Third World critique have also been tamed by being centered on the reform of international institutions.' *Ibid.*, p. 94.

43 *Ibid.*, p. 74.

44 The GSP was put in place within the GATT by the 1971 Protocol on Trade Negotiations Among Developing Countries, and later on, GSP and Special and Differential treatment were formally included into the GATT (Part IV) as part of the Tokyo Round negotiations in 1979 through the adoption of a Framework Agreement including an Enabling Clause, Differential & More Favourable Treatment, Reciprocity & Fuller Participation of Developing Countries.

45 UN GA Resolution 40/184, International Code of Conduct on the Transfer of Technology, UN doc. A/RES/40/184, 17 December 1985.

46 UN GA Resolution 45/186, Code of Conduct on Transnational Corporations, UN doc. A/RES/45/186, 21 December 1990.

47 Agreement on establishing the Common Fund for Commodities was adopted on 27 June 1980; however, after entry into force in 1989, it eventually gave up the objective of regulating prices and sustaining producers' income.

The core of the NIEO strategy lay in its demand for greater equity in economic relations *between* states, and left the issue of equity and justice *within* states as a matter of developing states' prerogative. One can thus observe that the early legal discourse essentially concentrated on the inter-state dimension, which eventually and gradually resulted in reversal in the later stages towards focus on the intra-state dimension. Writing in 1996, the ILA, already discussing the legal aspects of sustainable development, stated that, '[a]s a specialist interest order the NIEO is now widely believed to be defunct'.[48] But to say that the NIEO has long been history means that the underlying NIEO philosophy of order or rule of law in economic relations has ended. Discounting political assessments of the NIEO project, it seems the challenge to the structure of economic relations did not disappear completely. The Seoul Declaration on the Progressive Development of the Principles of Public International Law Relating to a New International Economic Order identified the principle of *the rule of public international law in international economic relations* according to which 'States have a duty to abstain from measures of economic policy, incompatible with their international obligations'.[49]

1.3 Structural adjustments and the post-Washington Consensus era

The NIEO period was followed by the decade known as 'lost development', characterized by the widening gap between the 'rich and poor' and the debt crises of the 1980s.[50] The resultant balance of payment deficits led the IMF to apply the policy of economic adjustments in developing countries. Development assistance became the principal policy instrument, directed mainly by the IFIs.[51] The same period is also known as the so-called 'Washington Consensus era'.[52] To

48 The International Law Association transformed its previous focus from NIEO to Sustainable Development and adopted New Delhi Declaration of Principles of International Law Relating to Sustainable Development, 2 April 2002 during its 70th Conference held in New Delhi, India. ILA, 67 *International Law Association Reports of Conferences* (1996), p. 290.

49 Declaration on the Progressive Development of the Principles of Public International Law Relating to a New International Economic Order, adopted during Plenary Session of Sixty-Second ILA Conference in Seoul in 30 August 1986, ILA, 62 *International Law Association Reports of Conferences* (1986), p. 409ff.

50 Including the Latin American crises experienced in Chile (with foreign debt of 144% of GNP), Mexico (foreign debt of 82%), Argentina (foreign debt of 85% of its GNP) and Bolivia (foreign debt of 166% of GNP).

51 For the development aid, 'this meant that the main focus was moved back to national economic growth, but now connected to a structural transformation of development countries' political economy'. J. Degnbol-Martinussen and P. Engberg-Pedersen, *Aid: Understanding International Development Cooperation*, Zed Books: 2005, p. 27.

52 The consensus's set of economic policy reforms aimed at limiting the state's participation in production sphere, regulatory intervention in private sector and reduction of expenditure in social sector such as health and education formed by the US economic officials, the International Monetary Fund (IMF), and the World Bank in the midst of crisis experienced by of Latin American countries in the 1980s in Joseph Stiglitz, 'More Instruments and Broader Goals: Moving Toward the Post–Washington Consensus', The 1998 WIDER Annual Lecture (Helsinki, Finland), 7 January1998, www.ucm.es/info/eid/pb/Stiglitz98wider.pdf , p. 3.

be eligible for development aid, states had to agree to adjustment programmes restructuring their economies. This first-generation aid conditionality was applied not only by the IFIs but also by all major bilateral donors working within the framework proposed by the IFIs and according to their conditionality rules.[53] It was regarded as a fundamental 'reorientation' of development assistance in the 1980s, to seek to create an enabling environment as opposed to fulfilling basic needs, as earlier promoted by the World Bank.[54] The effects of structural adjustment on human rights have been well analysed. Resistance to adjustment first came from academics, civil society, and later in the 1987 UNICEF landmark study: *Adjustment with a Human Face*.[55]

By the end of the 1990s, criticism of social and economic failures produced by Structural Adjustment Program (SAP) reforms led to a process of reconceptualization of these programmes and reconstruction of principles and modalities of aid conditionality.[56] Political conditionality became more accentuated in this period. Human rights, together with other 'political' concepts such as democracy, good governance and rule of law, entered the development discourse. It would not be entirely fair to attribute the appearance of human rights discourse in the development exclusively to political liberalism. Its initial entry into the scene, although brief, occurred earlier in a different context, in particular in the creation of the UN and the writing of the Charter. Liberalism, however, led to it arriving 'in a more active, systematic, and massive way'.[57]

1.4 Contribution of the UN to development thinking

1.4.1 The early seeds of current policies: United Nations development decades

Resolutions 1710 and 1715 (XVI) in 1961 proclaimed the first UN Development Decade (DDI), recognizing the need for concerted action for the advancement of economically less developed countries.[58] The programme was limited to

53 J. Degnbol-Martinussen and P. Engberg-Pedersen, *Aid: Understanding International Development Cooperation*, Zed Books: 2005, p. 27.
54 O. Stokke, *UN and Development: From Aid to Cooperation, op. cit.*, p. 11.
55 R. Jolly, 'Adjustment with a Human Face: A UNICEF Record and Perspective on 1980s', 19(12) *World Development* (1991), pp. 1807–1821.
56 'The first period, that of "structural adjustment", goes from 1980 to 1990. The second period, which witnesses the emergence of "governance" runs from 1990 to 1999. The last period, from 1999 onward is one of "comprehensive development". Broadly speaking, they encompass the rise and fall of neoliberal thinking, or the so-called Washington Consensus, and the subsequent move to an "enlightened" Washington Consensus, mediated by a decade of profound reforms and severe crisis'. A. Santos, The World Bank's Uses of the "Rule of Law" Promise in Economic Development', in D. Trubek and A. Santos (eds), *The New Law and Economic Development*, CUP: 2006, pp. 253–300, p. 267.
57 O. Stokke, *UN and Development: From Aid to Cooperation, op. cit.*, p. 327.
58 UN GA Resolution 1710(XVI) United Nations Development Decade, A Programme for International Economic Cooperation (I), 19 December 1961.

identifying general directions rather than specific measures or ways. In legal terms, the resolution did not signify anything. From a conceptual point of view, however, it was a silent revolution,[59] setting forth a framework wherein the problem of underdevelopment was presented as a global problem concerning both developed and developing countries. While previously the 'givers' were associated with 'past and present colonial powers and the competing superpowers', this resolution established development as a concern of other developed countries as well.[60]

The DDI formed the basis for establishing institutional machinery for development.[61] Preceded by extensive self-reflection and analysis,[62] the second generation of Development Strategy prioritized more complex issues than merely economic growth.[63] It proclaimed the ultimate purpose of development as 'to provide increasing opportunities *to all people for a better life*', including in areas of education, health, nutrition, housing and social welfare, environment, which were 'determining factors and end-results of development'.[64] The second Development Decade (DDII) strategy set the social objectives on par with the economic, which required 'qualitative and structural changes'.[65] As discussed before, this call for structural changes was covered by ideological confrontation and conflicts of doctrines.

Influenced by the sentiments of the time, the third UN development strategy defined the ultimate aim of development as improving the conditions of all, calling again for 'institutional and structural changes in international economic relations'.[66] The third Development Decade (DDIII) was taken over by CERDS and NIEO thinking[67] in an attempt to reduce the gap between developing and developed countries and 'to promote, if not enforce, a redistribution of wealth and power'.[68] DDIII strategy focused even more strongly on human and social

---

59 M. Virally, 'La 2e décennie des Nations Unies pour le développement – Essai d'interprétation para-juridique', *op. cit.*, p. 10.

60 O. Stokke, *UN and Development: From Aid to Cooperation, op. cit.*, pp. 8, 156.

61 As noted above, UNCTAD, and also UNDP and UNIDO. As a consequence, development aid not only had to be institutionalized but had to be coordinated. See for the list of the early bilateral development agencies in Stokke, *ibid.*, pp. 8–9.

62 See for example Pearson Commission on International Development, Pearson Commission on International Development.

63 UN GA Resolution 2626 (XXV) on International Development Strategy for the Second United Nations Development Decade, UN doc. A/RES/25/2626, 24 October 1970.

64 UN GA Resolution 2626 (XXV), para. 18 (emphasis added).

65 *Ibid.*, para. 18. For a thorough discussion see M. Virally, La 2e décennie des Nations Unies pour le développement – Essai d'interprétation para-juridique, *op. cit.*, pp. 9–33.

66 UN GA Resolution 35/56, International Development Strategy for the Third United Nations Development Decade, UN doc. A/RES/35/56, 5 December 1980.

67 These included South–South 'economic and technical cooperation among developing countries . . . a dynamic and vital part of an effective restructuring of international economic relations'. While developing countries determine 'the main elements of economic and technical cooperation', the international community 'should accord high priority and urgency to supporting the efforts of developing countries to strengthen and implement their programmes of mutual economic and technical cooperation'. UN GA Resolution 35/56, *ibid.*, para. 40.

68 N. Schrijver, 'Agenda for Development', *Max Planck Encyclopaedia of International Law*, www.mpepil.com, para. 5.

development, by prioritizing the goal of poverty alleviation for development assistance and directing the development to promote 'human dignity'.

While there was variation from decade to decade in terms of concretizing the aims and innovations in terms of objectives, there was little progress in developing the normative value of the instruments themselves. By the third decade, international development strategy was rapidly destined to simply form part of the UN panoply.[69] Nonetheless, the importance of fulfilling 'joint responsibility' was repeatedly articulated.[70]

As the idea of NIEO had been completely abandoned, the fourth decade strategy marked the change from a revolutionary to a more moderate approach, not least due to a number of factors present at the time.[71] The predominance of liberalization policies and the importance attached to the market were highlighted by Soviet countries volte-face from planned to market economies, and decreasing references to the need to address structural problems at the international level.[72] The fourth decade announced a new direction for the development cooperation. The signs of the new paradigm already appeared in the text of Resolution A43/554, where 'a *growing convergence of views* is emerging with respect to effective approaches to economic and social development and with regard to the potential contributions to the development process of the private and public sectors, of individuals and enterprises and *of democratic rights and freedoms*'.[73]

The fourth Development Decade (DDIV), while insisting on improving 'human condition' through poverty eradication, voiced the need for due respect to the environment. It also stressed that the prescribed development measures had to take into account 'political freedom, respect for human rights, justice

---

69 UN GA Resolution 35/56, International Development Strategy for the Third United Nations Development Decade, UN doc. A/RES/35/56, 5 December 1980.

70 It was stated that 'however great their efforts [of developing countries], these will not be sufficient to enable them to achieve the desired development goals as expeditiously as they must unless they are assisted through increased financial resources and more favourable economic and commercial policies on the part of developed countries'. UN GA Resolution 2626 (XXV) on International Development Strategy for the Second United Nations Development Decade, UN doc. A/RES/25/2626, 24 October 1970, paras. 7, 11, 12.

71 Partially, it was due to focus of the attention of the international community on the crisis in the Middle East. In addition, the Uruguay Round of negotiations of the GATT turned a new page in the relationship between developing and developed countries and generally contributed to the structural transformation of international relations.

72 As Maurice Flory notes, in the absence of counter-balance, it was the only possible economic model: 'L'une des parties faisant défection, le combat cessait. L'URSS elle-même ne demandait-elle pas son admission au GATT? Et les pays de l'Est ne sollicitaient-ils pas l'aide du FMI et de la Banque Mondiale? Il n'est donc plus question de remettre en cause l'ancien ordre et les institutions qui les caractérisent, mais au contraire de s'y rallier et de demander leur aide pour tenter de sortir de l'endettement, de restructurer l'économie et de trouver les ressources nécessaires au développement.' M. Flory, 'La 4ᵉ Décennie pour le Développement', 36 *Annuaire française de droit international* (1990), pp. 606–613, p. 609.

73 UN GA Resolution 45/199, International Development Strategy for the Fourth United Nations Development Decade, UN doc. A/RES/45/199, 21 December 1990, para. 7, (emphasis added).

and equity', as they 'are all essential and relevant to growth and development'.[74] Much shorter and less radical than its predecessors, DDIV put less emphasis on international economic environment and more focus on internal problems, including barriers to 'market forces': '[n]ational policies must also be directed at . . . taking advantage of the opportunities for trade, investment . . . provided by a changing global economic environment . . . The policy environment should . . . provide scope for the operation of market forces.'[75]

Even though decades of UN strategies in international development have largely been relegated to history, they set in motion several trends. First, they started to develop a consensus on the elements of special treatment of developing countries, which today have received more accommodation, in particular in the trade sector through the establishment of a system of generalized non-reciprocal preferences. Second, the development *problématique* attuned the responsibility of socio-economic development to the notion of 'joint responsibility', despite the repeated affirmation that developing governments bore the main responsibility. In this sense, the practice was set in at least adopting an international program-matic action framework assigning roles and responsibilities to all states. Third, and crucially, the General Assembly resolutions gave important signals on the future directions of development thinking, namely that they regarded the human condition as both an objective and justification of development.

This broader vision, albeit weak in terms of its legal capacity to institute real changes, corresponds to collective practice in development. Last but not least, the strategies of the previous decades provide an insight into development as a concern for the international order as a whole. This is particularly so since global interdependence is not limited to trade and finance alone, as the move-ment of funds, people, ideas – and, most notably, violence, social disorder, and terrorism – are among the many issues that cannot be contained within a coun-try's borders.[76]

1.4.2 The New York dissent: 'Failed' alternative visions

Efforts at the UN to institutionalize a multilateral mechanism to ensure financ-ing of development on a long-term and regular basis[77] in the form of an Interna-tional Development Authority, in light of obligations of UN Member States under

74 *Ibid.*, para. 15.
75 *Ibid.*, para. 25.
76 *Ibid.*, para. 6.
77 In particular, with a view to removing any connection between the government providing funding to the UN and the recipient government. It was proposed that 'the United Nations should establish an International Development Authority to assist the under-developed countries in preparing, co-ordinating and implementing their programmes of economic development; to distribute to under-developed countries grant-in-aid for specific purposes; to verify the proper utilization of such grants; and to study and report on the progress of development programmes'. United Nations, *Measures for the Economic Development of Underdeveloped Countries*, UN DEA: 1951, p. 95.

Articles 55 and 56 of the Charter, did not materialize.[78] The more powerful states did not accept the proposed fund,[79] and instead the 'UN fund for capital assistance' was replaced by the World Bank offering concessionary financial assistance.[80] This affected both the UN as a development institution and its position in coordinating development at a global level. It also, of course, shaped the role of the World Bank in directing the evolution of development, including its priorities and norms.[81] Two different ideologies and practices of development emerged in two institutional settings (opposing value systems) as a result: (i) Bretton Woods, guided by macro-economics, and (ii) the UN, guided by social and human development.

78 UN GA Resolution 520 (VI) on Financing of Economic Development of Under-developed Countries of 12 January 1952 required ECOSOC to submit a detailed plan a special fund for 'grant-in-aid and for low-interest, long-term loans to under-developed countries for the purpose of helping them, at their request, to accelerate their economic development and to finance non-self-liquidating projects which are basic to their economic development'. The idea emerged in the early years of the development thinking of the UN to set up UN Special Fund for Economic Development (SUNFED). The idea was further supported by subsequent GA resolutions, including UN GA Resolution 724B (VIII) Economic develop-ment of under-developed countries, 7 December 1953, where the president of ECOSOC, Mr Raymond Scheyven (Belgium), was asked to examine the comments of the govern-ments and consult with them and to facilitate the establishment of such a fund. The item of SUNFED stayed in the agenda of the GA for quite some time. In 1954, the GA requested a new report from Mr Scheyven on SUNFED, see UN GA Resolution 822 (IX), Question of the Establishment of a Special United Nations Fund for Economic Development, UN doc. A/RES/822(IX), 11 December 1954. In 1955, a new *ad hoc* committee, this time of government representatives, analysed responses of governments on the form, functions, and financial frame of the proposed fund. See UN GA Resolution 923 (X), Question of the Establishment of a Special United Nations Fund for Economic Development, UN doc. A/RES/923(X), 9 December 1955. The *ad hoc* committee reported the written views of the Governments in 1956. See UN GA, Final Report of the *Ad Hoc* Committee on the Question of the Establishment of a Special United Nations Fund for Economic Development Prepared in Accordance with General Assembly Resolution 923(X), *GAOR*, 12th Session, Annexes A/3579 and ADD.1, 16 May 1957.
79 ECOSOC Resolution 662 (XXIV) B, Financing of Economic Development, 31 July 1957 recommended the GA on establishment of fund with the 15 votes for and 3 against including the US, UK and Canada. What happened is that while developing countries were supportive of this initiative, the developed states 'were at best reluctant about a large-scale UN fund for capital assistance' and '[t]he U.S. position had all along been that this role should be assigned to the World Bank'. O. Stokke, *UN and Development: From Aid to Cooperation, op. cit.*, p. 97.
80 This took place through establishment of IFC and integration of IDA – 'the soft window' in 1960. As Stokke remarks: 'The persistence of developing countries, working with the UN Secretariat, pushed the World Bank to expand its engagement with development finance. The first concession of this kind came in 1956 with the establishment of the International Finance Corporation as an affiliate of the IBRD. The other concession – a soft window of the World Bank, the International Development Association – came three years later and became operative in 1960. They were both established as a sort of compensation for the stubborn resistance of the major western powers to the establishment of SUNFED. At the World Bank, Western powers were in full control, in stark contrast to the UN system.' *Ibid.*
81 In his view, '[i]f development funding had been entrusted to a UN agency, they would have been better situated to influence its general direction, norms and priorities'. O. Stokke, *UN and Development: From Aid to Cooperation, op. cit.*, p. 102.

From a legal perspective, this significantly hindered the concretization of general commitments in Articles 55 and 56 of the UN Charter in relation to socio-economic development and, in particular, of the meaning of states' obligations to assist and cooperate and the development of rules in this area. Until the 1990s, the UN continued to form alternative development thinking, owing to its broad participation, in line with its Charter's provisions, thus advancing a normative-based vision of development.[82] From the outset, the main difference of the UN development assistance from other donors was its emphasis on the principle of non-interference and sovereignty of states.[83] It therefore did not attach any conditionality until recent changes.[84] In addition to this, human rights in the UN's vision of development did not appear as part of the package of the neo-liberalism model in tandem with the concepts of good governance, rule of law and democracy. The human rights tradition of the UN stems from the Charter that established it.[85] Human rights are in the DNA of the UN Charter.

The human rights dimension of development had already been included in the 1966 report of the Secretary-General on the progress of the first Development Decade. This was even before links with development and human rights had been officially proclaimed in the Tehran Conference on Human Rights in 1968.[86] In its Resolution 2027(XX), the General Assembly recognized the need for the framework of the Development Decade to 'devote special attention on both the national and international levels to progress in the field of human rights, and to encourage the adoption of measures designed to accelerate the promotion of respect for and observance of human rights and fundamental freedoms'.[87]

---

82 M. Bedjaoui, 'L'humanité en quête de paix et de développement', Cours général de droit international public (2004), *op. cit.*, p. 146ff.
83 See for example UN GA Resolution 1240(XIII) on Establishment of Special Fund, 14 October 1958, among guiding principles articulated: 'In accordance with the principles of the Charter of the United Nations, the assistance furnished by the Special Fund shall *not be a means of foreign economic and political interference in the internal affairs of the country or countries concerned and shall not be accompanied by any conditions of a political nature*' para. I(2)(g) (emphasis added). This 'rule' was repeatedly upheld in the UN International Strategies for Development Decades, and in the Resolution on the Second Development Decade repeated that financial and technical assistance 'should be aimed exclusively at promoting the economic and social progress of developing countries and should not in any way be used by the developed countries to the detriment of the national sovereignty of recipient countries'. Resolution 2626 (XXV) on International Development Strategy for the Second United Nations Development Decade, UN doc. A/RES/25/2626, 24 October 1970, para. 46.
84 In the 1990s, UNDP, based on the philosophy of its human development reports, provided assistance to countries that adhered to the idea of sustainable human development, even though it had been consistently maintained that no conditionality was involved.
85 Although, in the early General Assembly instruments, human rights were not articulated as the objectives of the economic assistance, but, rather, human rights were pursued by separate institutional settings at the UN.
86 Cited in O. Stokke, *UN and Development: From Aid to Cooperation, op. cit.*, p. 153.
87 UN GA Resolution 2027(XX), Measures to accelerate the promotion of respect for human rights and fundamental freedoms, UN doc. A/RES/2027(XX), 18 November 1965.

In this regard, the Resolution urged all Governments 'to make special efforts' and invited them 'to include in their plans for economic and social development measures directed towards the achievement of further progress in the implementation of the human rights and fundamental freedoms' as proclaimed in the Universal Declaration of Human Rights (UDHR) and subsequent instruments. In addition, it called 'the technical assistance authorities of the United Nations and the specialized agencies to give all possible assistance, within the framework of their programmes during the United Nations Development Decade, with a view to achieving progress in the field of human rights'.[88] In response, according to the Secretary-General, 'everything that is being done by the United Nations family of organizations during the Development Decade to promote economic and social development contributes to the implementation of the human rights and fundamental freedoms proclaimed in the Universal Declaration of Human Rights'.[89]

Further, General Assembly Resolution 2081(XX) of 1965 can be seen as one of the first attempts to bring human rights into the plain of socio-economic development and the work of the UN specialized agencies, *inter alia* by requiring the latter to incorporate measures with human rights components into the implementation of the UN Development Decade.[90] Indeed, it is perhaps surprising that the UN development agencies only internalized human rights in their work relatively recently,[91] particularly given the heavy influence the UN agencies have exerted on shaping the ICESCR.[92]

In the last decades, however, the 'New York dissent' (as the UN used to be referred to by some) started to merge with the Washington Consensus. In the mid-1990s, the UN's main technical assistance agency (UNDP) underwent

88 *Ibid.*
89 Cited in O. Stokke, *UN and Development: From Aid to Cooperation, op. cit.*, p. 153.
90 UN GA Resolution 2081(XX), International Year for Human Rights, UN doc. A/RES/2081(XX), 20 December 1965.
91 The UN Statement of Common Understanding on Human Rights-Based Approaches to Development Cooperation and Programming (the Common Understanding) was only adopted by the United Nations Development Group (UNDG) in 2003.
92 The records evidence strong participation of the ILO and WHO in the formulation of articles on International Covenant on Economic, Social and Cultural Rights. ILO, UNESCO, WHO and FAO each contributed to articles relevant to their respective areas of mandate and expertise and even each exerted influence to protect 'its own jurisdiction' – sphere of activity. For an example, see ILO Minutes of the 115th Session of the Governing Body (Sixth sitting, Fourth report) 50 (1951), p. 54, according to which ILO's Governing Body Delegation at the International Organizations Committee had 'deliberately and successfully pressed from the start that the rights which fell within the field of competence of the I.L.O. should be expressed in the shortest and simplest terms possible, because they did not want the United Nations to try to define the meaning of those rights. It was for the I.L.O. itself to define and implement them through its Conventions, its Recommendations and, to some extent, its resolutions.' For a thorough and stimulating discussion see e.g. P. Alston, 'The United Nations' Specialized Agencies and Implementation of the International Covenant on Economic, Social and Cultural Rights', 18 *Columbia Journal of Transnational Law* (1979–1980), pp. 79–118, p. 117.

structural reform and faced changes in policy priorities. First, the UNDP's role was to assist governments ascribing to the sustainable development agenda. Second, the UN's vision of development had to be adapted to the new political context, which included increased cooperation with the IFIs.[93] This led to the cross-fertilization of ideas on development and modes of their implementation.[94] By mid-2000, the General Assembly would ritually invite the UN and IFIs 'to enhance cooperation, collaboration and coordination'.[95] It was at the heart of the multilateral system like the UN that the norms, ideas, objectives and means of development have been developed. The UN had, for instance, significantly contributed to defining the 'human dimension' in the growth-centred vision of development. However, in the last few decades there has been some form of a reversal in development policy: the UN, an organization with a broader ownership and more inclusive policy framework, has merged with the agenda of the development banks and members of the Organization for Economic Cooperation and Development (OECD). This was inevitable, perhaps, as despite its legitimate and normative framework, the UN is less strong in terms of resources and implementation.

1.4.3 Normative framework for development assistance

As a tool of international cooperation for development, initially of a transient nature, development assistance has been sustained over decades. In the UN, early General Assembly Resolutions 198(III) and 200(III) grounded the provision of development assistance on the UN Charter. The resolutions recalled the Charter as binding 'Member States individually and collectively to promote higher

---

93 Strengthening Collaboration between the United Nations Development System and the Bretton Woods Institutions, ECOSOC Resolution 1996/43, 26 July 1996 Triennial Policy Review of Operational Activities for Development of the United Nations System, UN GA Resolution 53/192, UN System: Triennial Policy Review of Operational Activities for Development, UN doc. A/RES/53/192, 15 December 1998.

94 IFIs started to look into the goals and priorities formulated at the UN sponsored conferences and the UN moved in the direction of the IFIs approach in terms of the importance of macro-economics in development. In addition, the GA encouraged: 'greater consistency between the strategic frameworks developed by the United Nations funds, programmes and agencies and the Bretton Woods institutions, and the national poverty reduction strategies, including the poverty reduction strategy papers, where they exist'. UN GA Resolution 56/201, Triennial Policy Review of Operational Activities for Development of the United Nations System, UN doc. A/RES/56/201, 6 March 2002, para. 44.

95 UN GA Resolution 59/250, Triennial Comprehensive Policy Review of Operational Activities for Development of the United Nations System, UN doc. A/RES/59/250, 17 August 2005, para. 52, which in particular recommended cooperation 'including through the *greater harmonization of strategic frameworks, instruments, modalities and partnership arrangements*, in full accordance with the priorities of the recipient Governments, and in this regard emphasizes the importance of ensuring, under the leadership of national authorities, greater consistency between the strategic frameworks developed by the United Nations funds and programmes, agencies and the Bretton Woods institutions' (emphasis added).

standards of living'[96] and hence developed measures 'for the achievement of the objectives set forth in Chapters IX and X'.[97] The idea of fixing a specific target was also conceived at the heart of the UN.[98] This device included all kinds of financial flows, and, more importantly, it 'carried normative influence, emphasizing that a need existed to be met and an obligation to be honoured'.[99]

The origins of aid are manifold. Traces of human rights and humanitarian assistance are least discernible in the origin of aid. Historically, aid, for the most part, served as an ideological tool and was primarily driven by security interest, which appears to still be the case nowadays in relation to certain countries.[100] The first endeavour to confine it within a normative framework came with a proposal to draft a 'Charter for Development'.[101] It was proposed to develop 'guiding legal principles of a promotional nature, the pursuit of which in good faith would be an inescapable duty'.[102] At that time, T.H. Bot, the first Minister for Development Aid of the Netherlands, stated:

> In my view the multitude of declarations, preambles, statements of principles and resolutions has an inflationary effect on the values of our fundamental notions. Indeed, the resolutions and initiatives of the past are like so many trees that obscure the forest of development aid. Sources and documents are now only known to scholars; they have become the secrets of diplomacy in the original sense of the word. What is lacking, however, is a clear and universally accessible document of a higher order, an instrument that world opinion recognizes as giving clear expression to the fundamental rights and duties that must underlie each and every development effort.[103]

96 UN GA Resolution 198(III), Economic Development of Under-developed Countries, UN doc. A/RES/198(III), 4 December 1948.
97 UN GA Resolution 200(III) Technical Assistance for Economic Development, UN doc. A/RES/200(III), 4 December 1948.
98 The idea of 1% of GNI as a target for ODA emerged as a result of the report of Group of Experts appointed by the Secretary-General of the UN; see UN, Measures for the Economic Development of Underdeveloped Countries: Report by a Group of Experts appointed by the Secretary General of the United Nations, NY: United Nations, DEA, May 1951.
99 O. Stokke, *UN and Development: From Aid to Cooperation, op. cit.*, p. 302.
100 The Unites States, for example, pursues aid, despite its previous tradition of striking a moralistic tone in its aid tradition for the security concerns. The US President Bush's pledges at the Monterrey Conference for development emphasized the link between fighting poverty and terrorism. See for more details Press Release 'President Bush, Chirac announce recent increase in Aid at Conference on Financing For Development', International Conference on Financing for Development, 22 March 2002, www.un.org/ffd/pressrel/22b.htm.
101 This initiative is said to have been proposed by the Netherlands. See N. Schrijver, 'A Missionary Burden or Enlightened Self-Interest? International Law In Dutch Foreign Policy', 57 *Netherlands International Law Review* 2010, p. 227.
102 UN GA, 20th Session, Second Committee, 969th meeting, 22 October 1965.
103 UN GA, 21st session, Second Committee, 1036th meeting, 18 October 1966; Ministry of Foreign Affairs publication, no. 83 (The Hague, 1967) p. 218, cited in N. Schrijver, 'A Missionary Burden or Enlightened Self-Interest? International Law in Dutch Foreign Policy', *op. cit.*, p. 228, footnote no. 85.

The proposal for the content of the Charter included a 'well-considered equilibrium of mutual socio-economic and cultural rights and obligations in the field of development'.[104] The proposal, adopted by the General Assembly, recognized that 'the formulation of a consolidated statement of the rights and duties of peoples and nations might sustain and enhance international development efforts and cooperation'.[105] For this purpose, it requested the Secretary-General, in cooperation with the UN 'family', to 'prepare a concise and systematic survey of the various principles, directives and guidelines for action in the field of development, as contained in the resolutions, declarations and similar texts of the United Nations and related agencies and in other relevant sources'.[106] The initiative did not, however, receive much attention. It failed to summon a response from the UN specialized agencies, UN organs and other intergovernmental organizations.[107] Attention was instead being directed towards formulating a strategy for the Second Decade of Development.

In 1971, economic and technical assistance together with rules and measures concerning the regulation and coordination of the economic activities of states and international trade were identified as emerging areas of concern for the development of international law.[108] As noted in the introductory chapter of this book, at the time, the Secretary-General's *Survey of International Law* asked 'whether a body of customary, general law is beginning to emerge'.[109] The reflection on this issue did not produce much comment apart from a conclusion that 'it might be thought that these arrangements – and any resulting substantive obligation – are still at an early stage of their development, and that the time is not yet ripe for any attempt to spell out an obligation in concrete legal terms'.[110]

2 The new discourse and the return of the NIEO?

Since the 1990s, the concept of development has expanded to include human rights, environment, good governance, democracy, and social dimensions. The human dimension of development, often associated with human rights discourse, has brought the focus of development on the individual as an ultimate beneficiary. In this view, development is about choices that an individual can make.[111] This

---

104 *Ibid.*
105 UN GA Resolution 2218 (XXI), United Nations Development Decade, 19 December 1966.
106 UN GA, Twenty-first session, Second Committee, 1036th meeting, 18 October 1966.
107 N. Schrijver, 'A Missionary Burden or Enlightened Self-Interest? International Law in Dutch Foreign Policy', *op. cit.*, p. 228.
108 Survey of International Law – Working Paper prepared by the Secretary-General in the light of the decision of the Commission to review its programme of work, Extract from *the Yearbook of the International Law Commission* 1971, vol. II(2), UN doc. A/CN.4/245 (1971), http://untreaty.un.org/ilc/documentation/english/a_cn4_245.pdf.
109 *Ibid.*, para. 166.
110 *Ibid.*, para. 167.
111 The idea of development as a freedom, or freedom as a premise of economic growth, has come from Amartya Sen. The core of Sen's idea is what he termed a 'capability approach', where the basic function of human development is 'our capability to lead the kind of lives

human dimension of development is often enclosed by other associated but distinct alternative terms such as good governance, understood often as rules on governments' operations. The most striking dimension of development is obviously the link between democracy and development. Since the post-Cold War period, democracy has become an objective in its own right. It was considered (and continues to be) as a necessary ingredient of development. Although variations exist across donors on human rights issues, most often human rights are linked with the democratization process, which at times implies emphasis on some human rights, namely civil and political, rather than the rights more directly implicated by the development process, such as economic, social and cultural rights.

If the first stage of development, regarded as the 'economic modernization' of developing countries, witnessed an impressive proliferation of institutions at the international level, the second period, aimed at constructing or modernizing the developing world 'politically', has also fostered the multiplication of numerous institutions under the 'rubric of democratization and peace maintenance'.[112] Crucially, the integration of the 'political' dimensions to development, such as good governance, democratic processes as well as human rights, also meant that the causes of underdevelopment were *internal*. Therefore, the responses to development had also to focus and be constructed at intra-state level.[113]

From a legal perspective, it is difficult to provide any sound analysis of this new and complex development. The discussions on specific legal issues have become highly idiosyncratic. If a few decades ago legal aspects of development had attracted a lot of attention from scholars, today, as Duncan French points out, '[t]he topic of the international law of development has become both marginalised in light of emerging meta disciplines, such as World Trade Organisation (WTO) or foreign investment law, and subsumed within the day-to-day workings of the World Bank, the International Monetary Fund (IMF) and other international organisations'.[114] While global cooperation for development

---

we have reason to value', rather than the traditional focus on rising GDP, technical progress, or industrialization. A. Sen, *Development as a Freedom*, OUP: 1999, p. 285. The work of Sen has been considered only as a starting point of departure for the interdisciplinary cooperation between ethics and economics. For criticism of Sen's reasoning see B. Fine, 'Economics and ethics: Amartya Sen as point of departure', 1(1) *The New School Economic Review* (2004), pp. 151–162.

112 B. Rajagopal, *International Law from Below: Development, Social Movements and Third World Resistance, op. cit.*, p. 137.

113 On the side of bilateral donors, this stage was associated with the review of aid processes that eventually brought about 'the aid effectiveness' agenda. The substance of the structures created by the adjustment programmes did not change, however. What has changed is the transformation of the donor and recipient relationship which was named 'partnership', as opposed to the 'asymmetrical' relationship predominant before (marking a new configuration of relationships). These predominant issues of current development thinking will be discussed in more details in following sections.

114 D. French, '"From Seoul With Love" – The Continuing Relevance Of The 1986 Seoul ILA Declaration on Progressive Development of Principles of Public International Law Relating to a New International Economic Order', *op. cit.*, p. 17.

occupies a major, if not dominant, concern in the operational work of international and regional organizations, it remains among the least regulated parts of international life.[115]

The doctrinal interest has instead been concentrated on certain aspects such as environment.[116] In theory, the concept of sustainable development was introduced to redefine the concept of development which 'encompassed human rights, international economic order and environmental preservation'.[117] Sustainable development denotes 'above all a programme of global validity, shared by environmentalists, economists and developmentalists, which should be attuned to human and environmental needs alike, anywhere in the world'.[118] Sustainable development is a concept that has been qualified not just as a principle of contemporary international law, but as 'one of the most ancient of ideas in the human heritage'.[119]

In comparison with the demands of the NIEO, sustainable development was relevant to all states alike. First, the issue of intergenerational equity applied to both industrialized as well as developing countries. Second, sustainable development does not question free trade as an instrument for development but seeks to 'harness it for its goals' and accommodate within the terms of a market economy.[120] Third, but less discussed, is the central focus of sustainable development on the issues of poverty, which contrasts with earlier efforts such as the right to development that were primarily sought in terms of 'rights'.[121] Last, the sustainable development concept tries to grapple with and adapt to the institutional changes and shifts in the development paradigm.[122]

---

115 This has led some scholars to conclude that remaining aspects of what once was called development law are now being eroded or 'at risk of fading away due to a lack of relevant practice'. See N. Schrijver, *The Evolution of Sustainable Development in International Law: Inception, Meaning and Status*, Collected Courses of the Hague Academy of International Law, Martinus Nijhoff Publishers: 2008, p. 223.

116 The idea was launched following the Report of the World Commission on Environment and Development under the title 'Our Common Future'. The report included a number of suggestions related to the development of legal principles in the area including drafting of a Universal Declaration and Convention on Environment and Sustainable Development. See also J.E. Viñuales (ed.), *The Rio Declaration on Environment and Development: A Commentary*, OUP: 2015.

117 ILA, Report of the Sixty-Sixth Conference, 66 *International Law Association Reports of Conferences* (1994), p. 137.

118 ILA, Report of the Sixty-Seventh Conference, 67 *International Law Association Reports of Conferences* (1996), p. 290.

119 Separate opinion of the Vice-President Weeramantry in ICJ, *Case Concerning Gabčíkovo-Nagymaros Project (Hungary v. Slovakia)* (1997), ICJ Reports, para. 110.

120 *Ibid.*, p. 291 and see also 1992 Rio Declaration on Environment and Development and the Earth Summit and Agenda 21.

121 T. Karimova and G. Golay, 'Principle 5: Poverty Eradication', in J.E. Viñuales (ed.), *The Rio Declaration on Environment and Development: A Commentary*, OUP: 2015, pp. 181–207.

122 As earlier noted, disintegration of the countries of planned economy, the rallying of Washington consensus, debt crises of 1980s and reliance on market forces reconfigured the development ideology and the vision of causes and solutions to it. Foreign investment

The focus on environment led to the progressive development of a comprehensive body of law. Although the existence of the law on sustainable development is debatable, what is at minimum agreed is the totality of international law that relates to sustainable development. Even though human rights form one of the three pillars (alongside development and environment) upon which the concept of sustainable development is based, in reality, it is not clear at all how these three components have been pursued in a balanced manner. In the view of the ILA's relevant committee, 'developmental concerns were given considerably less weight in politics as well as in academia'.[123]

While follow-up in the field of international environmental law has been viewed as impressive, the progress has been nominal in the field of development.[124] Moreover, there has been little progress in thinking on the interrelationship of sustainable development with the corpus of human rights norms. The few legal rules and principles that have been developed – the principle of participation, the precautionary principle, the principle of common but differentiated responsibilities, and polluter-pays principle – almost entirely deal with the environmental issues and do not apply to the human dimension of development activities. It remains to be seen how the next sustainable development goals will reconcile both the human and sustainable dimensions of development.[125]

The focus on poverty began in the early 1990s. Policy frameworks such as the Millennium Development Goals aim to halve *extreme* poverty. The operational tools of the IFIs aim to reduce poverty (Poverty Reduction Strategies) and deal with the debt problems of the HIPC initiative. Since 1995, the UN has dedicated two decades to the issue of poverty.[126] Development aid *no more follows* the 'modernization' approach but instead is aimed at fighting poverty. Foreign

---

and trade was no more viewed as a threat to the interests of the developing countries but acquired a new role as 'engines' of development. While NIEO did not take into account the role of private actors, they are today given a prominent role in the mobilizing resources for development goals. See below the discussion on Outcome document of the Third International Conference on Financing for Development: Addis Ababa Action Agenda, UN doc. A/CONF.227/L.1, 15 July 2015.

123 ILA, Report of Seventieth Conference, 70 *International Law Association Reports of Conferences* (2002), p. 282.

124 *Ibid.*, p. 283.

125 It is possible that the situation will be reversed. For example, in the framework of current proposals for the SDGs to succeed MDGs through 2030, some critics point out that it is not clear how the new framework will rise to the challenge of integrating sustainability, economic growth and social goals in a balanced way.

126 The UN launched the First United Nations Decade for Eradication of Poverty in 1995, UN GA, UN doc. A/RES/50/107, 20 December 1995; but the commitment to eradicate poverty was already highlighted in the Copenhagen Summit on Social Development, Report of the World Summit for Social Development, UN doc. A/CONF.166/9, 19 April 1995, para. 13; the Copenhagen commitments were reviewed by UN GA, UN doc. A/RES/S-24/2, 15 December 2000, para. 25. The year 2010 was proclaimed as the European Year for Combatting Poverty. A second UN Decade for the Eradication of Poverty 2007–2017 was proclaimed by GA in 2007, UN doc. A/RES/62/205, 10 March 2008.

policies goals are defined in terms of overcoming poverty. The fact that poverty was problematized and became an organizing principle of development was not new; what is thought to be new is its revival as a goal for development.[127]

At the same time, as Jouannet described, the return to the 'poverty' agenda signified a failure of previous development paradigms; 'a crisis of legal policies on global development'.[128] A departure from the structural and systemic transformation to a narrow set of objectives made finding solutions for the development of developing countries impossible.[129] With the global and long-term vision fading away, the turn to poverty in a way embodies 'a sense of helplessness and of the inefficiency of certain legal and economic principles and rules that also led to this focus on poverty alone, and on humanitarian action alone'.[130]

When compared to the formative stages of the international development principles and practices, it becomes clear that the current project of fighting against poverty is consensus-based and, as many scholars point out, is 'much less' revolutionary.[131] The focus is on precisely formulated targets disguising the underlying and systemic factors that contributed to the current persisting inequalities.[132] As has justly been observed:

> Legal policies are ineffective, and the most progressive standards are never adhered to. Some allow the poor states not to founder, others worsen the

---

127 Poverty orientation was already identified in the late 1950s and early 1960s, see Section 1.1.
128 E. Jouannet, 'How to Depart from the Existing Dire Conditions of Development', in A. Cassese (ed.), *Realizing Utopia: The Future of International Law*, OUP: 2012, p. 403.
129 *Ibid.*, p. 402. See also E. Tourme-Jouannet, *What is a Fair International Society? International Law Between Development and Recognition*, Hart Publishing: 2013. But criticism does not come only from 'leftist' academics. See also the Advisory Council on Governmental Policy of the Netherlands, stating: '[h]owever, the MDGs are largely static goals which are strongly oriented around alleviating emergencies. They say nothing of the resources, the strategy and underlying mechanisms required to achieve the goals, nor about the capacities of societies to develop, and from a macroeconomic perspective they are rather vacuous. In that sense they are not very development related. Economic growth is not included as a final or intermediary goal in the MDGs, and important issues like transformation of the productive sectors are not even referred to. Although NDG 8 does refer to the need for a fair trade system, this can only make a very limited contribution to the creation of productive national economic sectors. The MDGs are inspiring but also problematic in that they detract attention away from structural changes and the strengthening and transformation of agriculture and other productive sectors.' Advisory Council on Government Policy (WRR), *Less Pretension, More Ambition; Development Policy in Times of Globalization*, Amsterdam University Press: 2010, p. 110, www.wrr.nl/english/content.jsp?objectid=5516.
130 E. Jouannet, 'How to Depart from the Existing Dire Conditions of Development', *op. cit.*, p. 403.
131 *Ibid.*, p. 407.
132 Saith holds that MDGs are 'a clear shift in the perspective in favour of a narrower frame focusing essentially on absolute aspects of some key measurable facets of poverty and deprivation, and away from a broader, more essentialist rights-based approach'. A. Saith, 'From Universal Values to Millennium Development Goals: Lost in Translation', 37(6) *Development and Change* (2006), p. 1170.

situation. None can be cited as having actually helped to develop a state harmoniously or restrain socio-economic inequalities between states. And yet year after year, decade after decade, numerous standards, rules, and practices relating to an IDL able to save the developing countries are produced. We continue to develop material, that, for decades, has explained that 'the way to go' 'is long' because 'the gap keeps widening' between rich and poor countries; that, however, there 'is progress' or even that 'great progress has been made', that we are going to 'eradicate poverty', because if we recognize the 'failures' we are finally going to 'learn from the past' and 'take up new challenges' with the whole 'international community'. . . . But who can still believe in the enchanted world of UN resolutions, summit declarations, and solemn commitments by states to 'economic', 'human', 'sustainable', or 'social' development? While we continue to proclaim Days and Decades against poverty, disease, and hunger, just as we once multiplied development days and decades, the hollowness of this repetitive rhetoric is in the image of the IDL on the developing countries: it is devoid of meaning.[133]

With recurrent crises and persistent inequalities, the 'new' all-encompassing development has been harshly criticized for the failure to make good on its promises. One reason is that it was built on the preceding premises and assumptions. Instead of dealing with the structural dimension of the development problem, it pursues the agenda of good governance, democracy, and human rights which have further internalized the development *problématique*. These additional layers not only made the development politically interventionist, but have led commentators to qualify the current development praxis as a law of 'dependency'.

The more the ensemble of rules and practices is analysed, the more there is a conviction that the only possible response is to revise the whole spectrum of received development practices. Such is the conclusion of the UN Conference on Trade and Development (UNCTAD), which examined the efficiency of the current development structure under a big question mark. It proposes instead a New International Development Architecture,[134] contending that the existing international economic architecture is not conducive to the development of states. Even if the current – weak in design and implementation – special support measures (aid, debt relief, etc.) are strengthened considerably, they would still be insufficient to promote more sustained development.[135]

Consistent with UNCTAD, scholars suggest that a way to depart from persistent inequities and the crisis of the 'new' politicized forms of development is to return to the NIEO concept, but in its social, human and environmental

133 E. Jouannet, 'How to Depart from Dire Conditions of Development', *op. cit.*, pp. 403–404.
134 UNCTAD, *The Least Developed Countries Report 2010: Towards a New International Development Architecture for LDCs*, New York and Geneva: 2010.
135 *Ibid.*, p. 84 et seq.

dimensions.[136] Such an order should be, first of all, based on the notions of equity and fairness at the international level. While these ideas are slowly emerging, in order to avoid it being just at the rhetoric level, steps need to be taken to define these notions in legal terms.

It is important to situate this broader context within the parameters of our discussion: human rights and development. Human rights, as part of the ensemble of multiple layers interposed on development, have been criticized as politicizing the agenda of development.[137] However, it is too early and simplistic to discount human rights on grounds of the politicization argument. The potential of this corpus of legal norms has already been felt in international economic law.[138] The contribution of human rights to development may lie in introducing legal rules into development practice. This is particularly true when human rights are compared with other principles of development such as governance, democracy and participation, which, as Alston qualifies, 'unless rooted in identified standards their meaning is conveniently open-ended, contingent, and too often subjective'.[139]

Human rights as embodied in international treaties have a fixed normative content addressing all actors of the development process. Obligations are 'the very essence of their "value-added"'.[140] Situated within the development paradigm, one natural question is whether human rights are capable of addressing flaws of the system itself. Can they be an organizing principle of social justice at the international level? Ultimately, this question cannot be answered until the 'uses' of human rights are identified in the current development policy and operational frameworks.

3 Human rights in the development policy framework

The major focus in the debate on human rights and development is on how development actors incorporate the human rights legal framework into their policies. This section demonstrates how human rights have been operationalized in the main development frameworks at both the multilateral and bilateral levels.

---

136 E. Jouannet, 'How to Depart from the Existing Dire Condition of Development', *op. cit.*, pp. 392–417. D. French, '"From Seoul With Love" – The Continuing Relevance Of The 1986 Seoul ILA Declaration on Progressive Development of Principles of Public International Law Relating to a New International Economic Order', *op. cit.*, p. 4.

137 Jouannet, *ibid.*, p. 401.

138 P.-M. Dupuy, E.-U. Petersmann and F. Francioni, *Human Rights in International Investment Law and Arbitration*, OUP: 2009.

139 P. Alston, 'Ships Passing in the Night: The Current State of the Human Rights and Development Debate Seen Through the Lens of the Millennium Development Goals', 27 (3) *Human Rights Quarterly* (2005), pp. 755–829, p. 760.

140 S. McInerney-Lankford, 'International Financial Institutions and Human Rights: Select Perspectives on Legal Obligations', in D.D. Bradlow and D.B. Hunter (eds), *International Financial Institutions and International Law*, Kluwer Law International: 2010, p. 253.

3.1 Global development frameworks: Continuing discrepancy

The starting point for any discussion on the current development agenda is the outcomes of the Millennium Process. The actual scope of the global development agenda is much broader. It includes outcomes of all conferences and summits of the UN since the 1990s, which set out the comprehensive vision and the different dimensions of development.[141] Together they represent 'the United Nations Development Agenda'.[142] This agenda is comprehensive in its scope and degree of incorporation of human rights. It has even been suggested that these fora have been 'the best attempt in the history of the United Nations to give concrete content' to the objectives set in Article 55 of the United Nations Charter.[143]

These conferences were subsequently 'summarized' in the Millennium Declaration, which together with the Monterrey Consensus on Financing for Development,[144] Paris Declaration on Aid Effectiveness, and related instruments, represent the core content of the development cooperation ideology and agenda. They are interrelated operationally and are anchored in technical documents in the management of aid.

3.1.1 Millennium Development Goals

The starting point is the Millennium Declaration, which laid down the agenda of the multilateral cooperation by uniting the key themes and challenges of the new millennium: development and poverty eradication and human rights, democracy, and good governance. The Millennium Declaration states that 'in addition to our separate responsibilities to our individual societies, we have a collective responsibility to uphold the principles of human dignity, equality and equity at the global level'.[145] It further states that 'we are committed to making the right to development a reality for everyone and to freeing the entire human race from want'.[146] While the wording of the Declaration is strong, it seems to exclude any connotation of binding force.

141 Children 1990; Education for All 1990, 2000; Least Developed Countries 1990, 2001; Drug problem 1990, 1998; Food Security 1992, 1996; Sustainable Development 1992, 2002; Human Rights 1993, 2001; Population and Development 1994; Small Island Developing States 1994, 2005; Natural Disaster Reduction 1994, 2005; Women 1995, 2005; Social Development 1995, 2005; Human Settlements 1996, 2001; Youth 1998; Millennium Summit 2000, 2005; HIV/AIDS 2001; Financing for Development 2002; Ageing 2002; Landlocked and Transit Developing Countries 2003; Information Society 2003, 2005.

142 UN DEA, *The United Nations Development Agenda: Development for All: Goals, Commitments and Strategies agreed at the United Nations World Conferences and Summits since 1990*, United Nations, Economic and Social Affairs: 2007, p. 4.

143 *Ibid.*, p. 1.

144 Broadly speaking, the conference outcome, what is known as Monterrey Consensus, deals with the issue of mobilizing funds for development and how to make the most efficient use of the existing ones. ODA constitutes one of the six areas of financing for development.

145 UN GA Resolution 55/2, United Nations Millennium Declaration, 8 September 2000, para. 2.

146 *Ibid.*, para. 11.

Drawing on the scope of commitment reached in the 2000 summit, the *Road Map towards the Implementation of the United Nations Millennium Declaration*[147] was prepared, including detailed plans for implementing the MDGs.[148] The MDGs as adopted reflect many goals that substantively converge with the human rights treaties *ratione materiae*.[149] The last goal, in simplified terms, includes among other things, more generous ODA, an enhanced programme of debt relief, and an open and non-discriminatory trade and finance system.[150] MDGs are in many ways symbolic of a current development policy framework bereft of human rights.[151]

It is difficult to discount the period leading to the MDGs, which had a cumulative impact on their form, content and main drivers. In particular, most of the initiatives, both substantive and procedural, were formulated and driven by the donors.[152] The OECD–DAC's synthesis of the development goals in its publication 'Shaping the 21st Century: The Contribution of Development Cooperation', for instance, is said to have laid the groundwork for the MDGs.[153] Two

147 Report of the Secretary General, Road map towards the implementation of the United Nations Millennium Declaration, UN doc. A/56/326, 6 September 2001. The work carried out by the UN Secretariat in preparation of MDGs was conducted in consultation with the major development institutions, such as the IMF, the World Bank, and the OECD, and the outcome was eight concrete goals with 18 targets and 48 indicators.

148 UN GA Resolution 56/95, Follow-up to the outcome of the Millennium Summit, A/RES/56/95, 30 January 2002, para. 2.

149 The goals include (i) eradicate extreme poverty and hunger; (ii) achieve universal primary education; (iii) empower women and promote gender equality; (iv) reduce child mortality; (v) improve maternal health; (vi) combat HIV/AIDS malaria and other diseases; (vii) ensure environmental sustainability and (viii) develop a global partnership for development.

150 Global Partnership for Development includes 18 targets for its implementation, seven of which pertain to this global compact: developing an open, non-discriminatory trade and finance system that includes good governance, economic development and poverty reduction (target 12); taking into account the special needs of the LDCs (target 13); the special needs of landlocked and small island developing countries (target 14); long-term sustainability of debt management for developing countries through national and international measures (target 15); developing strategies for the creation of decent and productive jobs for young people (target 16); providing access to affordable essential drugs in developing countries (target 17); and transfering new technologies (target 18).

151 Advisory Council on International Affairs writes: '[d]espite the fact that the MDGs were never intended as a one-size-fits-all approach, many-especially in the donor community-have embraced them as a mantra for development, sometimes through lack of a better alternative. The goals have come to be seen in such absolute terms that anything that falls outside them no longer matters.' AIV, *The Post-2015 Development Agenda: The Millennium Development Goals in Perspective*, Report No. 74, The Netherlands: April 2011, p. 40.

152 *Ibid.*, p. 17.

153 *A Better World For All*, paralleling the content of the OECD's 'Shaping 21st Century' jointly endorsed by major actors IMF, OECD, WB and the UN, was taken as a basis for operationalising the poverty reduction component of Millennium Declaration, in the Road Map Towards the Implementation of the United Nations Millennium Declaration. The UN had its own parallel to the OECD's 'Shaping the 21st Century', i.e. *We the Peoples: the Role of the United Nations in the 21st Century* which was launched in the 2000s. In fact, the two publications were two parallel tracks that later were consolidated by a joint IMF, OECD,

goals, Goal 7 (Ensure environmental sustainability) and Goal 8 (Develop global partnership for development), were 'subject to further refinement', as these were the areas that most affected economically advanced countries. Evidently, Goal 8 emerged upon the insistence of the developing countries and differed from the other seven, as its indicators were not time-bound and no quantitative targets were attached.

Commentators have not missed the opportunity to stress that MDGs in effect represent the concept of results-based management that is so intrinsic to the day-to-day workings of the donor organizations. This approach in MDGs 'meant that the MDGs avoided potentially difficult to measure goals like human rights and participation . . . [and consequently] the variety of human development that impacted MDGs was more akin to basic needs than human rights'.[154] Whether this was the main reason or not, it is generally agreed that the process and goals were distanced from human rights. As stressed throughout this chapter, the focus on poverty was not new, nor did the previous development decades lack socio-economic orientation. However, the burgeoning commentary that MDGs have generated emphasize that the MDGs put at the centre stage the socio-economic concerns: an important subset of internationally recognized rights. Perhaps, the major merit of this effort is, indeed, in the catalytic effect it had in generating a political consensus on the need for joint 'responsibility'.

The balance sheet for the achievement of MDGs is rather mixed.[155] Progress achieved in some areas is contrasted with deterioration in other areas.[156] Experts argue that the results, at any rate, need to be put into perspective.[157] In addition,

---

UN, WB document titled '*A Better World For All: Progress towards the international development goals*' that practically leaned towards the OECD document's publication rather than the one produced by the UN.

154 D. Hulme, 'The Making of the Millennium Development Goals: Human Development Meets Results-based Management in an Imperfect World', *Working Paper No. 16*, Brooks World Poverty Institute, December 2007, www.manchester.ac.uk/bwpi, p. 18. Overall, the mechanism attendant to the implementation of the MDGs is also not free of concerns. See A. Saith, 'From Universal Values to Millennium Development Goals: Lost in Translation', *op. cit.*, p. 1170.

155 See UN, The Millennium Development Goals Report 2015, New York 2015, www.un.org/millenniumgoals/2015_MDG_Report/pdf/MDG%202015%20rev%20(July%201).pdf.; UNCTAD, *The Least Developed Countries Report 2014: Growth with Structural Transformation: A Post-2015 Agenda*, UN: 2014; See also WB, *World Development Report 2011: Conflict, Security and Development*, WB: 2011,www.worldbank.org. Little progress has been achieved in the area of sanitation, according to the UN Committee on Economic, Social and Cultural Rights: CESCR, The Statement on the Right to Sanitation, UN doc. E/C.12/201071,19 November 2010.

156 Particularly in the fight against HIV/AIDs see UN, *The Millennium Development Goals Report 2010*, UN: 2010, p. 40.

157 For example, it has been suggested that there are also serious measurement problems related to some of the goals that make the assessment of progress problematic. S. Fukuda-Parr and A.E. Yamin, 'The power of numbers: A critical review of MDG targets for human development and human rights', 56(1) *Development* (2013), pp. 58–65; S. Fukuda-Parr, A.E. Yamin and J. Greenstein, 'The Power of Numbers: A Critical Review of Millennium Development Goal Targets for Human Development and Human Rights', 15(2–3) *Journal of*

gains from some progress in areas of access to markets and efforts on debt relief were compromised by the financial crises. According to the latest reviews, conflict-affected countries are likely not to achieve any of the MDG goals.[158]

The MDG project has generated wide analysis, ranging from an overall positive assessment as to its poverty focus and ability to generate financial aid, to sceptical views questioning the theory behind the MDGs.[159] Critics have pointed to the failure of the goals to grapple with the structural problems generating inequality on the global scale, so much reminiscent of older debates.[160] It has been argued, in particular, that poverty reduction (as an obstacle to 'survival') is about 'lowering of ambitions' as opposed to accepting a broader concept of development.[161] Neither Goal 8 nor subsequent discussions around a new aid paradigm avoided criticism.[162] In human rights circles, the main criticisms concerned the failure to link the goals to human rights treaty obligations, the lack of accountability mechanisms, the failure to deal with the root causes of the poverty, and the like.[163]

Human Development and Capabilities (2014), pp. 105–117; See also T. Pogge, 'The First United Nations Development Goal: A Cause for Celebration', 5(3) *Journal of Human Development and Capabilities* (2004), pp. 337–397.

158 For an updated review see UN, The Millennium Development Goals Report 2015, New York, 2015, www.un.org/millenniumgoals/2015_MDG_Report/pdf/MDG%20 2015%20rev%20(July%201).pdf; But mainly see WB, *World Development Report 2011: Conflict, Security and Development, op. cit.*, in particular pp. 61–63.

159 M. Loewe, 'The Millennium Development Goals: Chances and Risks', *Discussion paper 6/2008*, German Development Institute: 2008; J. Vandemoortele, 'Taking the MDGs Beyond 2015: Hasten Slowly', DSA/EADI/Action Aid Policy Forum, June 2009. See also J. Pronk, 'Collateral Damage or Calculated Default? The Millennium Development Goals and the Politics of Globalisation', Inaugural Address as Professor of the Theory and Practice of International Development at the Institute of Social Studies, The Hague, 11 December 2003.

160 See e.g. UNCTAD, Follow-up to the Millennium Summit and Preparations for High-level Plenary Meeting of the General Assembly on the Millennium Development Goals: New Development Paths. Reconnecting the Millennium Development Goals to the Development Agenda: an UNCTAD Perspective, Geneva, June 2010, www.unctad.org/en/docs/ tdbex49d3_en.pdf.

161 Minority Rights Group, Minority Rights in Development Aid Policies, November 2000, p. 15.

162 Radical criticism is advanced to these goals as being 'cosmetics'. It is said that '[b]y strictly maintaining focus on outcome-type goals and targets, readily justified by the need to think about poverty first, the MDG exercise effectively sweeps a spectrum of concerns over global systemic distortions and deficits under the conference carpet'. A. Saith, 'From Universal Values to Millennium Development Goals: Lost in Translation', *op. cit.*, pp. 1189–1190.

163 P. Alston, 'Ships Passing in the Night: The Current State of the Human Rights and Development Debate Seen Through the Lens of the Millennium Development Goals', *op. cit.*, pp. 755–829; OHCHR, *Claiming the MDGs: A Human Rights Approach*, UN: 2008; P. Nelson, 'Human Rights, The Millennium Development Goals, and the Future of Development Cooperation', 25(12) *World Development* (2007), pp. 2041–2055; S. Fukuda-Parr, 'Are the MDGs Priority in Development Strategies and Aid Programmes? Only Few Are! International Poverty Centre', Working Paper No. 48 (October 2008); T. Pogge, Global Justice and the First U.N. Millennium Development Goal, Evening Address at the University of Oslo Global Justice Symposium (2003), www.etikk.no/globaljustice; P. Nelson and E. Dorsey, New Rights Advocacy: Changing Strategies of Human Rights And Development NGOs, Georgetown University Press/Washington, D.C. (2008).

Clearly, the MDGs did not address central issues to development such as sustainability, inequality, technology, demography, peace and security, infrastructure or, more importantly, human rights.[164] The policy framework did not mention human rights or the relevant human rights treaties despite the substantive overlap of each goal with some economic, social and cultural rights. The central concern to human rights lawyers is that the time-bound partial achievement of the poverty reduction is not compatible with the right of all to a minimum core of all socio-economic and cultural rights as guaranteed by the ICESCR, despite the fact that such rights have been referred to as 'an expression of basic human rights – the rights of all to good health, education and shelter'.[165]

For the purposes of the present discussion, the question is, can any normative value be inferred from these declarations? From a legal perspective, the Millennium Declaration and the follow-up documents are not legally binding. The nature of the instrument, as well as the content of its text, suggests that they are of mere economic and political significance. States supporting or endorsing these declarations would only be making political and moral commitments.

Alston makes a compelling argument to suggest that the fact that states have continuously reiterated their commitment in the decade following the adoption of Millennium Declaration requires that the judgement of the legal significance of Millennium Declaration be nuanced. In his view, '[w]hen large numbers of heads of state or government congregate together, along with foreign ministers and other dignitaries, and solemnly declare their abiding commitment to meet a set of MDGs – as they did in the context of the 2000 Millennium Declaration, and again at both the Johannesburg World Summit on Sustainable Development and the Monterrey Consensus, each in 2002 – there would seem to be good reason to assume that they meant what they said and that they had thereby undertaken a form of obligation that should have some legal consequences.'[166]

Compared to the MDGs, the 2010 Millennium Development Goals Summit Outcome Document[167] represents an important UN policy agreement in terms of the development and human rights nexus. Its significance can be drawn from the perspective of the context and process that generated it.[168] The Outcome Document makes extensive reference to human rights norms, going beyond general

164 C. Gore, 'The Global Development Cycle, MDGs and the Future of Poverty Reduction', 12th EADI General Conference, Geneva, June 2008, www.devstud.org.uk/downloads/4b9e9da140e21_Gore_PAPER.pdf; see for an elaborate discussion on these themes, Advisory Council on International Affairs, *The Post-2015 Development Agenda: The Millennium Development Goals in Perspective*, *op. cit.*

165 UNSG, *'Keeping the Promise; A forward-looking review to promote an agreed action agenda to achieve the Millennium Development Goals by 2015'*, *op. cit.*, para. 2.

166 P. Alston, 'Ships Passing in the Night: The Current State of the Human Rights and Development Debate Seen Through the Lens of the Millennium Development Goals', *op. cit.*, p. 771.

167 UN GA Resolution 65/1, Millennium Development Goals Summit Outcome Document, UN doc. A/RES/65/1, 17 September 2010.

168 In particular, in the 2010 World Summit, the UN Member States took stock of the progress made toward achievement of the Millennium Development Goals.

rhetoric of the commitment to human rights rules and principles and reaffirming the pledge of UN Member States to 'continue to be guided by the purposes and principles of the Charter of the United Nations and with full respect for international law and its principles'.[169]

An explicit recognition that 'respect for all human rights' is essential for achieving Millennium Development Goals and development generally is reiterated in introductory and operative parts.[170] These formulations are remarkable in that not only do they recall the obligations of States, but they link the Millennium Development Goals explicitly to legally binding human rights instruments. This has given rise to hope that '[t]hese provisions provide important milestones and entry points for the more effective positioning of human right in the lead-up to negotiations on the post-2015 development agenda'.[171]

3.1.2 From MDGs to SDGs: Post-2015 development agenda

Despite harsh criticism of the MDGs, the international community renewed its commitment to achieving a cooperative framework to solve economic, social and environmental problems. As the Millennium Development Goals end their cycle in 2015, its 'unfinished work' will be advanced through 2030 within a new set of goals.[172] This framework is intended to be universal, covering both developing and developed states.[173] Moreover, the new goals are expected to transcend some of the limitative features of previous ones and become 'an overarching transformative development agenda'.[174]

---

169 *Ibid.*, para. 2.
170 *Ibid.*, paras. 3, 12, 13. Para. 53 states: 'We recognize that the respect for and promotion and protection of human rights is an integral part of effective work towards achieving the Millennium Development Goals.' Particular focus on gender dimension and rights of women appear in para. 54. Other important references to human rights are included in para. 23, which consists of a long list of good practices in the area of development and includes under section (j) '[r]especting, promoting and protecting all human rights, including the right to development'.
171 M. Darrow, 'The Millennium Development Goals: Milestones or Millstones? Human Rights Priorities for the Post-2015 Development Agenda', 15(1) Yale Human Rights and Development Journal (2012), pp. 55–127, p. 83. Stephen P. Marks's assessment seems to be more sombre, suggesting that the prospects that human rights will be integrated fully in the post-2015 Development Agenda are slim. See S.P. Marks, 'Prospects for Human Rights in the Post-2015 Development Agenda', in J. Kozma, A. Muller-Funk and M. Nowak (eds), *Vienna+20: Advancing the Protection of Human Rights Achievements, Challenges and Perspectives 20 Years After the World Conference*, Ludwig Boltzmann Institute of Human Rights, Studies Series, Vol. 31, Neuer Wissenschaftlicher Verlag: 2014, pp. 291–306.
172 For a full account of preparatory process, see *Intergovernmental Processes of Relevance for Post-2015 UN Development Agenda Preparations*, www.un.org/en/development/desa/policy/untaskteam_undf/post2015_rel_intergov_processes.pdf.
173 In contrast, the MDGs were implemented in developing states only.
174 See *inter alia* Synthesis Report of the Secretary-General on the Post-2015 Sustainable Development Agenda, The Road to Dignity by 2030: Ending Poverty, Transforming All Lives and Protecting the Planet, UN doc. A/69/700, 4 December 2014.

A   POST-2015 PROCESS

The 2010 MDG Summit requested that the UN Secretary-General initiate discussions on an agenda to succeed the Millennium Development Goals. Two years later, the United Nations Conference on Sustainable Development Rio+20 outlined the roadmap to develop sustainable development goals.[175] Thus, there was a consensus that the two processes should converge and translate into a single set of global goals. Consequently, as required by the outcome document of the Rio+20, 'The Future We Want',[176] the UN General Assembly established a 30-member Open Working Group (OWG) on Sustainable Development Goals (SDGs), tasked with preparing a proposal for sustainable development goals for consideration and appropriate action.[177]

Following 13 sessions of discussions, the OWG prepared its report and delivered its proposals to the UN General Assembly in July 2014.[178] The OWG outcome document proposes 17 goals and will serve as a point of departure for the intergovernmental negotiations. The process benefited from 'unprecedented' consultations.[179] It was informed by a number of significant contributions, including the High-level Panel of Eminent Persons on the Post-2015 Development Agenda report,[180] Perspectives from UN Global Compact Participants,[181] the work of the UN System Task Team on the Post-2015 Development Agenda,[182]

---

175 Rio+20 Outcome Document, UN GA Resolution 66/288, 27 July 2012, Annex, The Future We Want.

176 *Ibid.*, para. 248.

177 UN GA Decision 67/555, contained in UN doc. A/67/L.48/Rev.1, 15 January 2013.

178 Report of the Open Working Group of the General Assembly on Sustainable Development Goals, UN doc. A/68/970, 12 August 2014.

179 Initially, the General Assembly Resolution 65/1, 22 September 2010, requested the UN Secretary-General to make recommendations to advance the UN development agenda after 2015. The UN Secretary General subsequently presented his initial recommendations, including a need for an open and inclusive process of consultations on the post-2015 agenda. See Annual report of the Secretary-General, Accelerating Progress towards the Millennium Development Goals: Options for Sustained and Inclusive Growth and Issues for Advancing the United Nations Development Agenda beyond 2015, UN doc. A/66/126, 11 July 2011.

180 The UNSG Ban Ki-moon appointed the 27 members of a High-level Panel to advise on the global development framework beyond 2015. The Panel produced a report entitled A New Global Partnership: Eradicate Poverty And Transform Economies Through Sustainable Development: The Report of the High-Level Panel of Eminent Persons on the Post-2015 Development Agenda, 30 May 2013, www.un.org/sg/management/pdf/HLP_P2015_Report.pdf.

181 UN Global Compact, Corporate Sustainability and the United Nations Post-2015 Development Agenda Perspectives from UN Global Compact Participants on Global Priorities and How to Engage Business Towards Sustainable Development Goals, Report to the UN Secretary-General, 17 June 2013, www.unfoundation.org/assets/pdf/global-compact-report-1.pdf.

182 The UN System Task Team brings together over 60 UN entities and agencies and international organizations, and was established by the UN Secretary-General to support system-wide preparations for the post-2015 development agenda, www.un.org/en/development/desa/policy/untaskteam_undf/.

as well as outreach efforts of civil society groups and global conversations led by the United Nations Development Group.[183]

The next sustainable development agenda through 2030 will be finalized in the framework of high-level international meetings in 2015. The first is the Third International Conference on Financing for Development that already took place in Addis Ababa in July 2015. The second round of negotiations will take place in the summit on sustainable development to be held at the United Nations Headquarters in New York, in September 2015, where it is expected that the new agenda for the next 15 years will be adopted. Finally, the third meeting that will also have an impact on the post-2015 agenda is the twenty-first session of the Conference of the Parties to the United Nations Framework Convention on Climate Change, to be held in Paris in December 2015.

B   THE ROLE OF HUMAN RIGHTS IN THE POST-2015 AGENDA

At the time of writing, the final phase of negotiations on the post-2015 development agenda is yet to take place in the UN Summit in September 2015. From among many contributions, two documents formed the basis for the final outcome of the post-2015 development agenda. These were the OWG outcome document (on sustainable development goals and targets) and the UN Secretary-General Synthesis Report, entitled *The Road to Dignity by 2030: Ending Poverty, Transforming All Lives and Protecting the Planet*.[184]

The consensus opinion, generated by the commentary on these two documents, is that the SDGs go far beyond the MDGs and may eventually, if strengthened and supplied with adequate tools of implementation, represent a real change. Indeed, what emerges from the outcome of the post-2015 processes is that inequality is a common theme and concern to the international community. The proposed sustainable development goals and targets themselves, although not explicitly grounded on human rights, are nonetheless formulated in the terms of *access* – a language mirroring human rights terminology.

The 'Zero Draft' of the Sustainable Development Agenda, entitled *Transforming Our World by 2030: A New Agenda for Global Action*, scheduled for

---

183   One such example is a web platform, www.worldwewant2015.org, co-hosted by civil society and the United Nations as part of the UN global conversations.

184   Report of the Open Working Group of the General Assembly on Sustainable Development Goals, UN doc. A/68/970, 12 August 2014 and Synthesis Report of the Secretary-General on the Post-2015 Sustainable Development Agenda: The road to dignity by 2030: ending poverty, transforming all lives and protecting the planet, UN doc. A/69/700, 4 December 2014. The Secretary-General synthesis report recognizes that human rights must be at the core of the post-2015 agenda and that it 'should also call for full consistency with current political commitments and existing obligations under international law'. It further reinforces that the implementation of the new agenda must ensure that 'all actions respect and advance human rights, in full coherence with international standards'. It also notes that the new agenda 'mirrors the broader international human rights framework, including elements of economic, social, cultural, civil and political rights, as well as the right to development' (see paras. 60, 65, and 83 of the report).

intergovernmental negotiations in June 2015, gives much hope for a real change of course in the area of development. It may be perhaps too early to comment on the SDGs, but the zero draft includes a critical paragraph which, if adopted, will likely pull the next agenda firmly into the international human rights law framework:

> The new Agenda is guided by the purposes and principles of the Charter of the United Nations, including full respect for international law. It is grounded also in the Universal Declaration of Human Rights and other international instruments such as the Declaration on the Right to Development. We reaffirm all the principles of the Rio Declaration on Environment and Development, including, inter alia, the principle of common but differentiated responsibilities.[185]

What is available at this stage is the Addis Ababa Action Agenda (AAAA) – the outcome document of the Third Conference on Financing for Development, held in Addis Ababa in July 2015. This document provides a framework that is considered as to be critical to the implementation of the post-2015 agenda. In contrast with previous financing for development instruments, the AAAA contains a high number of references to 'human rights'.[186] In addition, the AAAA takes up a notion well known to human rights law; that is, the financing of universal basic social services – what the document calls 'a new social compact'. Notwithstanding, even elements such as human rights, gender equality and 'commitment to respect all human rights, including the right to development', despite being expressed in strong language, remain non-operational.

Furthermore, critics point out that the AAAA has been considered somewhat of a regression from pre-existing financing for development commitments as reflected in Monterrey (2002) and Doha Financing for Development Review (2008). Some of the areas highlighted by critics include: a lack of linking the debt sustainability assessment with states' obligation to use resources/finance to meet their human rights commitments (and generally coherence with international human rights standards), a failure to address systemic issues and establish linkages between macroeconomic policies and poverty reduction, a lack of ambitious Official Development Assistance, a lack of an integrated approach to human rights, and a failure to find solutions to the debt problem of developing countries.[187]

Where the 2015 outcome document seemingly makes progress is in its welcoming of 'efforts by new development banks to develop safeguard systems . . . on

185 Of course, the actual formulations of goals and targets should be individually analysed in order to assess their consistency with international human rights standards, as well as the degree of their explicitness. An opening Declaration, Transforming our World by 2030: New Agenda for Global Action, Zero Draft, June 2015.

186 Outcome document of the Third International Conference on Financing for Development: Addis Ababa Action Agenda, UN doc. A/CONF.227/L.1, 15 July 2015.

187 In particular, in integrating developments taking place in the framework of the UN responsible sovereign lending and borrowing, as reflected in the Principles on Responsible Sovereign Lending and Borrowing (PRSLB).

the basis of established international standards' as well as encouragement of 'all development banks to establish or maintain social and environmental safeguards systems, including on human rights, gender equality and women's empowerment'. Progressive as it seems to be, the formulation in the outcome document is not entirely without problem, as it also requires that these safeguards be 'efficient and time-sensitive'.[188]

The majority of critics' opinions would also converge in the contention that AAAA failed to achieve progress on 'classical' financing issues, in other words, underlying structural injustices.[189] As one analysis pointed out, AAAA 'places a strong optimism on the role of the private sector, without evidence to back it up and without parallel recognition of the developmental role of the State and commitments to safeguard States' ability to regulate in the public interest or to protect human rights and the environment'.[190]

3.1.3 Aid effectiveness or effective development cooperation?

Aid effectiveness, one of the main subjects of the development discourse since the 1990s, concerns mostly the management of development assistance (its procedures and standards), rather than issues related to the substance of development. The idea of aid effectiveness, while not new,[191] was given form and content in the context of the MDG 8 on global partnership for development and the subsequent Monterrey Consensus.[192] The Monterrey agreement laid the basis for the discussions in high-level fora convened in Paris (2005), Accra (2008) and Busan (2011).

188 Outcome document of the Third International Conference on Financing for Development: Addis Ababa Action Agenda, UN doc. A/CONF.227/L.1, 15 July 2015, para. 75.
189 Closing Statement on Behalf of the Group of 77 and China by H.E. Ambassador Kingsley Mamabolo, Permanent Representative of the Republic of South Africa to the UN, Chair of the Group of 77 at the Third International Conference on Financing for Development, Addis Ababa, Ethiopia, 16 July 2015, www.g77.org/statement/getstatement.php?id=150716. For civil society position see Third FFD Failing to Finance Development: Civil Society Response to the Addis Ababa Action Agenda on Financing for Development, https://csoforffd.files.wordpress.com/2015/07/cso-response-to-ffd-addis-ababa-action-agenda-16-july-2015.pdf.
190 Rethinking Bretton Woods, FFD 3 Outcome: Fishing for crumbs of hope in a sea of lost ambition, 19 July 2015, https://www.coc.org/rbw/ffd-3-outcome-fishing-crumbs-hope-sea-lost-ambition. See also OHCHR, Key messages on Human Rights and Financing for Development, www.ohchr.org/Documents/Issues/MDGs/Post2015/HRAndFinancing ForDevelopment.pdf.
191 In fact, Article 4.2 of the Declaration on the Right to Development speaks of 'effective international co-operation': 'As a complement to the efforts of developing countries, effective international co-operation is essential in providing these countries with appropriate means and facilities to foster their comprehensive development.'
192 See section D, 'Increasing international financial and technical cooperation for development' (paras. 39–46) of Monterrey Consensus of the International Conference on Financing for Development, Mexico, 2002, where ODA effectiveness is said to depend on effective partnership based on national leadership and ownership of recipients. In the framework of effectiveness, the Consensus also refers to harmonization and triangular cooperation, including countries with economies in transition, and South–South Cooperation (para. 43).

These high-level fora generated a number of non-binding agreements and principles that currently govern the aid relationships and represent altogether what is referred to as the 'aid effectiveness agenda'. Some commentators suggested that the Paris Declaration on Aid Effectiveness, Accra Agenda for Action and the Busan Partnership for Effective Development Cooperation altogether form the corpus of 'development aid law' or form a 'legal regime' governing the provision of official development assistance.[193] Although it is difficult to sustain the argument that these documents in their totality amount to a distinct legal regime,[194] it can nevertheless be conceded that these frameworks make up a branch of institutional law operating in multilevel jurisdictions.[195]

The 2005 Paris Declaration on Aid Effectiveness (Paris Declaration)[196] sets out to harmonize policies and practices to contribute to the achievement of the MDGs.[197] While the Declaration is not legally binding and the sources of international law do not include 'institutionally structured practice',[198] it nonetheless sets five key principles that organize the policy and practice of development: ownership, harmonization, alignment, focus on results, and mutual accountability supported both by donor countries and recipients.

Particularly, country ownership, partnership and participation are perceived and presented in the development discourse as the key components in paradigm shift of the development strategies.[199] They are considered as opposites to the

---

193 P. Dann, 'Accountability in Development Aid Law: the World Bank, UNDP and Emerging Structures of Transnational Oversight', 44 *Archiv des Völkerrechts* (2006), pp. 381–404. P. Dann, *The Law of Development Cooperation: A Comparative Analysis of the World Bank, the EU and Germany*, CUP: 2013.

194 Particularly with the emergence of new actors and approaches, international development standards, actors and institutions are currently undergoing transformations. It is not clear how, for example, the OECD-DAC standards and guidance on ODA can serve as a frame of reference for the new donors.

195 P. Dann, 'Grundfragen eines Entwicklungsverwaltungsrechts', *Working Paper 4/2004*, www.mpil.de/ww/de/pub/organisation/wiss_bereich/pdann.cfm, p. 4.

196 The First High Level Forum on Aid Effectiveness in Rome 2003 and the Marrakech Roundtables on Managing for Development Results in 2004 led to the adoption of Paris Declaration. It has been adopted by the High Level Forum on Aid Effectiveness by the countries members of the OECD. They apply to various participating countries, international organizations, and civil society organizations.

197 The idea of aid effectiveness was shaped as a result of the process of self-reflection. It encompassed three elements: advancement of the economic well-being, social development and ecological sustainability, something that was taken up and shaped in the Millennium Declaration. Second, it brought up the issue of adequate resources for development, also further detailed in the Monterrey Consensus. Judging by the content of 'Shaping the 21st Century', one can clearly see the precursors of the MDGs. OECD, 'Shaping the 21st Century: The Contribution of Development Cooperation' ('S 21'), dating from May 1996 and issued by the DAC, www.oecd.org/dataoecd/23/35/2508761.pdf.

198 P. Dann and L. Vierck, 'Paris Declaration on Aid Effectiveness (2005)/Accra Agenda for Action (2008)', *Max Planck Encyclopaedia of International Law*, www.mpepil.com.

199 For a detailed commentary see R. Bissio, 'The Paris Declaration on Aid Effectiveness', in OHCHR, *Realizing the Right to Development Essays in Commemoration of 25 Years of the United Nations Declaration on the Right to Development*, UN: 2013, pp. 233–247; and

previous practice of 'conditionality' governing the relationship between givers and recipients of development aid.[200] The development of these principles gives the power of decision-making back to the recipient countries. In the legal domain, these principles are rather unclear since they are not anchored in any conventional legal doctrine and essentially stem from the language of development institutions. However, some of them, such as the principle of ownership, may effectively relate to the concept of state sovereignty.[201]

The main intention of the Paris Declaration was to contribute to the achievement of the MDGs, which arguably benefits the achievement of certain components of the socio-economic rights. The principles set by the Paris Declaration are not always depicted as a purely technocratic exercise aimed at improving ODA delivery. Quite on the contrary, it has been suggested that human rights are an essential component of a 'good development result'.[202] The OECD–DAC Action-Oriented Policy Paper on Human Rights (AOPP), stated that:

> The way in which the Declaration's key principles – ownership, alignment, harmonisation, managing for results and mutual accountability – will be put into practice over the coming years and change the ways in which aid is delivered and managed, will have implications for the whole spectrum of substantive development cooperation policy areas, including human rights.[203]

It further reiterated the recurring message that the Paris Declaration and human rights principles and standards could 'reinforce each other'.[204] Furthermore, the

---

P. Dann, *The Law of Development Cooperation: A Comparative Analysis of the World Bank, the EU and Germany*, CUP: 2013, pp. 141–147.

200 137 countries are listed on the OECD website as having adhered to the Paris Declaration and the AAA.

201 Doubts are expressed as to rationality of this principle: first it is questioned how a developing country really can set its own agenda in view of 'internationally agreed development goals' or predominant vehicles of development such as PRSP, and second, similar to first one, whether it is feasible for a state to formulate its own independent development against the background of globalised economic order. UNDP, Staff Opinion, The Paris Declaration and National Ownership: From de Jure to de Facto, 'For example, with so much development policy firmed up at the supra-national level, the realization of national ownership should entail serious capacity development support to partner countries to engage effectively at those levels. Does the Paris Declaration cater to this?', October 2007, No. 1, available at http://204.200.211.80/joomla/attachments/003_staff_opinion_undp_zambia_1.pdf.

202 'Whilst achieving gender equality, human rights and environmental sustainability are worthy goals of development in their own right, each is at the same time functionally essential to achieving the overall goal of the Paris Declaration.' Statement by Richard Carey, Director, Development Cooperation Directorate, OECD, at the Dublin workshop, Workshop on Development Effectiveness in Practice: Applying The Paris Declaration to Advancing Gender Equality, Environmental Sustainability and Human Rights, Dublin, Ireland, 26–27 April 2007, DCD/DAC(2007)40, 28 June 2007, p. 3.

203 OECD, *DAC Action-Oriented Policy Paper on Human Rights and Development (AOPP)*, OECD: 2007, p. 8.

204 *Ibid.*, p. 9.

AOPP added that partnership commitments of the Paris Declaration can help advance human rights 'in a changing context of more aligned and harmonised aid and new aid modalities', while at the same time 'human rights practice *may be* useful in achieving Paris Declaration's partnership commitments'.[205] One cannot help but notice the 'consequentialist' approach to human rights, which we have briefly discussed before. What the Declaration does not say, however, is how the human rights obligations of the partner states apply to the framework of the Paris Declaration. Instead it proposes that '[t]he Paris Declaration principles should be followed in designing and implementing human rights programmes'.[206]

An assessment of the Paris Declaration from the perspective of the right to development has suggested that some of its principles may 'result in a substantial erosion of the right to development'.[207] This is because, to give just a few examples, the 'ownership' is tied to the pre-existing development strategies such as Poverty Reduction Strategies (PRSs), with a target that at least 75% of the 'partner' countries have them in place;[208] or the fact that 'alignment' requires a 'reliable country system', meaning that procurement and financial management must be aligned to donor countries' requirements[209] and the country procurement system must be opened up to foreign firms, etc. All in all, the assessment of the 12 Indicators of Progress and 17 targets have led analysts to conclude that many indicators are related to the sphere of governance, particularly in the area of procurement and financial management.[210]

Human rights considerations have been included in the outcome documents of the High-Level Forum in Accra in 2008, known as the Accra Agenda for Action. This is an oft-quoted document for the human rights community, as

---

205 *Ibid.* (emphasis added).
206 *Ibid.*, p. 8.
207 R. Bissio, Application of the criteria for periodic evaluation of global development partnerships – as defined in Millennium Development Goal 8 – from the right to development perspective: the Paris Declaration on Aid Effectiveness, Paper presented for Eighth session Working Group on the Right to Development High Level Task Force on the implementation of the right to development, UN doc. A/HRC/8/WG.2/TF/CRP.7, 31 December 2007.
208 OECD, Paris Declaration: Indicators of Progress, www.oecd.org/development/aideffectiveness/36080258.pdf.
209 Procurement and financial management system is rated by the World Bank's Country Policy and Institutional Assessment (CPIA) as well as the Public Expenditure and Financial Assistance (PEFA) partnership, which have been criticized for their neo-liberal approaches. See N. Alexander, 'Judge and jury: the World Bank's scorecard for borrowing governments', Social Watch Report 2004, awww.socialwatch.org/en/informeImpreso/pdfs/judgeandjury2004_eng.pdf.
210 Specifically, it was stated that the new aid modalities, as reflected in the Paris Declaration, 'by aligning bilateral and multilateral donors around certain governance requirements might even undermine local democratic processes and the "policy space" that developing country governments need to make their own plans, and in principle work against the RtD [right to development]'. R. Bissio, Application of the criteria for periodic evaluation of global development partnerships – as defined in Millennium Development Goal 8 – from the right to development perspective: the Paris Declaration on Aid Effectiveness, *op. cit.*, para. 83.

it is believed to have endorsed the principle of 'do no harm', by introducing a statement that that both developing and donor countries will ensure that their respective development policies and programmes are 'designed and implemented in ways consistent with their agreed international commitments', among others on human rights.[211]

The latest agreement, the Busan Partnership for Effective Development Co-Operation, while building upon the Paris principles, introduced a few novelties considered as shifts away from the traditional development paradigms.[212] It established a new structure, the Global Partnership for Effective Development Cooperation, which is expected to replace the previous Working Party on Aid Effectiveness which had been in charge of overseeing the implementation of aid effectiveness.

In particular, by recognizing 'more complex architecture for development cooperation', it introduced a principle of inclusive development, aimed at providing a new development platform where 'emerging' donors would be included.[213] In the absence of coordination and some form of common framework (norms and standards) among the new donors, their integration with the aid effectiveness agenda was deemed important. It has been suggested that the current turn to 'policy coherence in development' and 'development effectiveness', particularly on the part of 'traditional donors', is essentially a response to this growing diversification/fragmentation.

Burden-sharing is an additional underlying reason for attempts to include the emerging donors in the current system, an attempt resisted by the emerging economies themselves.[214] The Busan partnership therefore introduced a concept of 'differential commitments', an idea borrowed from the environmental law principle 'common but differentiated responsibility'. In terms of human rights aspects, the chapeau of the principles introduced by the Busan partnership agreement states, '[a]s we embrace the diversity that underpins our partnership and the catalytic role of development co-operation, we share common principles which – consistent with our agreed international commitments on human rights,

---

211 Accra Agenda for Action, 2–4 September 2008, Accra, Ghana, para. 13(b).
212 These are ownership of development priorities (para. 11(a)), focus on results (para. 11(b)), transparency and accountability (para. 11(d)).
213 Paragraph 11(c): 'Inclusive development partnerships: Openness, trust, and mutual respect and learning lie at the core of effective partnerships in support of development goals, recognising the different and complementary roles of all actors.'
214 For an in-depth analysis, see N. Besharati, *South African Development Partnership Agency: Strategic Aid or Development Packages for Africa?*, South African Institute of International Affairs Research Report No. 12, 2013. Besharati quotes South African President Jacob Zuma stating: 'The tendency to attempt to delegate some of these historical responsibilities to new emerging economies in the South is unacceptable and unworkable as such emerging nations have their own historical challenges and backlogs to deal with.' See Statement of the President of the Republic of South Africa, Jacob Zuma, to the General Debate of the 68th Session of the UN General Assembly, UN Headquarters, New York, USA, 24 September 2013.

decent work, gender equality, environmental sustainability and disability – form the foundation of our co-operation for effective development'.[215]

3.2 Operational framework: PRSs and HIPC regimes

Poverty Reduction Strategies (PRSs) are 'a kind of national strategy framework for reducing poverty', which constitute the basis for the International Development Association's (IDA) and IMF's (International Monetary Fund) concessional assistance and debt relief.[216] The importance of PRSs from a human rights perspective lies in the following: first, their focus on the eradication of poverty;[217] second, their status as the main vehicle of the relationship between the IFIs and recipient developing state;[218] and third, their instrumental role in guiding the donor community and/or inter-institutional cooperation in financing development due to their operational link with MDGs.[219] PRSs also, however, reflect a complex mechanism in the institutional structure of development financing. Perhaps the most salient feature of the PRSs is that it is a *magnum opus* instrument in regulating aid distribution for many donors – bilateral and multilateral.

While the principles of national ownership and accountability are stressed throughout the process, analysis of the PRSs shows that the practice differs from the official narrative.[220] PRSs are regarded by analysts as a process where the sovereignty of states and their policy space is considerably circumscribed. The prescriptions under PRSs generally concern economic and social issues but crucially

215 Chapeau of paragraph 11, Busan Partnership for Effective Development Co-Operation.
216 The HIPC initiative its subsequent enhanced HIPC initiative and the Multilateral Debt Relief Initiative (MDRI) were launched in 1996. See IMF, 'Debt Relief Under the Heavily Indebted Poor Countries (HIPC) Initiative: A Factsheet', September 2011, www.imf.org/external/np/exr/facts/pdf/hipc.pdf.
217 For more information see World Bank, The Poverty Reduction Strategy Initiative: an Independent Evaluation of the World Bank's Support Through 2003, Washington, 2004, pp. 2–4.
218 The PRS framework serves as a basis for debt relief under HIPC and MDRI for concessional lending of the IMF.
219 Together with HIPC initiative, these are frameworks serving as a basis for the coordinated financial support on the part of the donors on the basis of harmonization and alignment. IMF, 'Poverty Reduction Strategy Papers: Factsheet', 14 September 2011, www.imf.org/external/np/exr/facts/prsp.htm.
220 IMF and WB, *2005 Review of the Poverty Reduction Strategy Approach: Balancing Accountabilities and Scaling up Results*, 19 September 2005, para. 21. For a critical analysis of the accountability issues as well as the continuity of old style structural adjustments under the new guise of poverty see C. Tan, 'The New Biopower: Poverty Reduction Strategy Papers and The Obfuscation Of International Collective Responsibility', Paper presented at the panel on 'Poverty Reduction as Development Morality: Theory and Practice', Development Studies Association Conference, 5 November 2010, p. 4. K. Jayasuriya, 'Governance, Post Washington Consensus and the New Anti-Politics', Working Paper Series No. 2, Southeast Asia Research Centre: April 2001, p. 1.

reach 'sensitive areas of domestic legislation and state organization which tra-ditionally are protected under public international law through the concept of sovereignty and national self-determination'.[221]

PRSs are intimately linked with the practice of debt relief. The financing of debt relief under HIPC/MDRI (Multilateral Debt Relief Initiative) comes from the creditor/donor countries' ODA budgets 'rather than absorbed as loan losses financed from general budget'.[222] Such a state of affairs has been qualified as shifting the traditional creditor–debtor relationship to 'charity as aid', and is still viewed by the donor countries as discretionary.[223] Such a mixing of regimes is said to prevent discussions on the need for a legal debt resolution framework subject to states' obligations under international law, including both creditor and debtor states' obligations under human rights law.[224]

Human rights are not addressed within poverty-reduction strategies or debt relief, nor do they inform the design process of PRSs. Given that poverty-reduction papers dominate the development policy space of the poor countries as well as serve as a 'main vehicle' for donor financing, such an analysis gives a snapshot

---

221 L. Guder, *The Administration of Debt Relief by the International Financial Institutions A Legal Reconstruction of the HIPC Initiative*, Springer: 2009, p. 261.

222 C. Tan, 'Life, Debt and Human Rights: Contextualising the International Regime for Sovereign Debt Relief', Paper presented at the conference on Poverty and International Economic Legal System: Duties to the World's Poor, Basel, Switzerland, 20–22 October 2011, p. 7. More crucially, as Tan notes, '[t]he relationship between debt relief and aid also meant that HIPC/MDRI initiatives 'played a pivotal part not just in reshaping the sovereign debt regime but also in changing the landscape of development financing', p. 8. Martin notes, 'large amounts of aid are being diverted from bilateral budgets to fund relief by multilateral institutions: over $3.4 billion of OECD aid has been promised to the HIPC Trust Fund or used for bilateral payments of multilateral debt in the HIPC framework; additional contributions to the IMF PRGF-HIPC Trust are $1.5 billion in end-1999 PV terms; and, donors have also funded relief by the IADB separately. Though disbursement of these funds will be spread over several years, there is strong evidence of aid diversion to fund debt relief.' M. Martin, 'Assessing the HIPC Initiative: The Key Policy Debates', in Jan Joost Teunissen and Age Akkerman (eds), *HIPC Debt Relief: Myths and Reality*, The Hague: Forum on Debt and Development: 2004, p. 27.

223 Not least, there is a general sense that debtor and creditor relationship should be separated from development aid/financing characterized as it is by asymmetry of power dynamics, and more towards 'justice and shared state responsibility and the design of an effective international financial architecture based on such principles', or 'debt relief must be located within international law, and situated within a binding international mechanism for collective action'. See C. Tan, 'Life, Debt and Human Rights: Contextualising the International Regime for Sovereign Debt Relief', *op. cit.*, p. 14.

224 E.g. an international regime that secures 'orderly, efficient and fair' resolution of debt problems governed by principles akin to those at the domestic level, in particularly domestic insolvency. An oft-quoted example includes Chapter 9 of the US legal code 'where US law provides for the bankruptcy of governmental organisations, so-called municipalities, under *Chapter 9* of the US legal code'. This law protects government powers in that 'creditors cannot prevent municipalities from carrying out vital services' as well as allows taking into account the interest of individuals. See A. Pettifor, *'Paper 9/11? Resolving International Debt Crises – the Jubilee Framework for International Insolvency'*, Report from the Jubilee Research at the New Economics Foundation, London: 2002.

sufficient to determine the role of human rights in the development cooperation. As noted, in practice, MDGs are operationally linked with the Poverty
Reduction Papers and the debt-relief initiatives. But even at this front, a recent
study demonstrates the relatively partial normative impact of the MDGs on the
PRSPs.[225]

Both PRSs and HIPC initiatives are highly effective despite their non-binding
form. It is a framework that is regarded as a new development in which 'international bureaucracies *control and manage social processes* or assume sovereign
activities'.[226] The way the relationships between recipient and donor countries
are constructed through Poverty Reduction Strategies indicate that compliance
and enforcement of the conditions imposed on the recipient countries derive
not primarily (perhaps not at all) from legal relationships but from the economic
incentives and 'wider economic and geo-political impact of non-compliance'.[227]
'This link between the disbursement of funds and "the implementation of a
desired action of policy" is often the only sanction for non-compliance given the
ambiguous nature of conditionality.'[228]

There are different rationales for the development aid modalities to be bereft
of any legal formulation. First, the reluctance of the IFIs and official aid bodies
(although not exclusively) to confer legal force to their relationship (or to establish binding legal commitment for the substantive content of the programme
itself) on financing, at the outset stems from the political nature of aid. For example, unlike in investment lending, the framework of the World Bank's policy-
based lending 'has been generally regarded as not contractually enforceable
under the legal agreement', as, according to the Bank, '[s]ome of these actions
[e.g. policy and institutional] may entail delicate and sensitive domestic considerations and involve internal decision-making, including parliamentary approval.
It would be unwise and inappropriate for the Bank to be seen as influencing or
interfering with these processes.'[229] As Tan remarks, '[a]ttributing legal force
to policy and institutional reforms which have yet to gain domestic legislative
(or popular) approval may conflict with national constitutional arrangements,

---

225 The study finds that 'the most neglected priorities . . . were hunger, gender equality . . .,
     human rights' and that '[r]arely did the PRSPs give prominence to democratic governance
     and human rights-based participatory approaches: governance was a priority in 17 of them,
     but these focused on decentralization and the rule of law'. S. Fukuda-Parr, 'Are the MDGs
     Priority in Development Strategies and Aid Programmes? Only a Few Are!', *Working Paper
     48*, International Poverty Centre: October 2008, www.ipc-undp.org/pub/IPCWorking
     Paper48.pdf, p. 7.
226 L. Guder, *The Administration of Debt Relief by the International Financial Institutions A
     Legal Reconstruction of the HIPC Initiative, op. cit.*, p. 233 (emphasis added).
227 C. Tan, 'The New Disciplinary Framework: Conditionality, New Aid Architecture and
     Global Economic Governance', in J. Faundez and C. Tan (eds), *International Law, Eco-
     nomic Globalization and Developing Countries*, accessed SSRN, p. 2.
228 *Ibid.*, p. 3.
229 World Bank, 'Review of World Bank Conditionality: Legal Aspects of Conditionality in
     Policy-Based Lending', 29 June 2005, Washington DC: World Bank, paras. 38–39.

making compliance more onerous for the country and enforcement politically difficult for the financier'.[230]

Second, to this adds other considerations such as institutional issues[231] and the reluctance of the IFIs to place disputes with its Member States within the remit of external adjudications. The latter does not hold fully true in relation to bilateral assistance agencies, however, some of which are taking measures going beyond domestic oversight mechanisms.[232] Last, but not least, subjecting terms of development financing to legal norms apart from the corollary necessity to define the details and scope of conditionality 'may expose the IFIs and other donor agencies up to legal challenge on more controversial aspects of their activities'.[233]

Despite these numerous references to human rights *in toto* in these documents, it is not apparent whether human rights constitute an aim in their own right for the development process or are only part of the process towards achieving development goals. From a human rights perspective, clarification of this ambiguity is significant given that development cooperation is omnipresent in virtually all aspects of socio-economic domains of developing states. The other caveat is that the position expressed in the Accra Agenda for Action and Busan Partnership for Effective Development Cooperation, referred to above, is rather occasional without linkages to existing obligations. Moreover, the nature of the instrument itself makes the commitment decidedly 'soft'. Such an outcome can be contrasted with other areas of inter-state cooperation, including in the military sphere such as those on arms transfers, which are increasingly being informed by human rights concerns.[234] The actual impact and implications of including human rights concerns in treaties of this sort is a separate question; however, they go beyond the mere 'alignment of strategies' to human rights but reflect a commonly agreed mutual standard of prioritizing human rights even in areas of high sensitivity to states' sovereignty, such as national security and defence.

These developments clearly highlight an increasing evolution in making human rights an imperative in states' external activities, and that inter-state cooperation cannot be guided only by economic or commercial interests but should be balanced and in compliance with states' international obligations, in particular in the field of human rights.[235]

---

230 C. Tan, 'The New Disciplinary Framework: Conditionality, New Aid Architecture and Global Economic Governance', *op. cit.*, p. 4.

231 For example in the case of IMF, L. Guder, *The Administration of Debt Relief by the International Financial Institutions A Legal Reconstruction of the HIPC Initiative*, *op. cit.*

232 See e.g. the new Human Rights German Ministry for Development Cooperation (BMZ), Human Rights in German Development Policy Strategy 4, 2011, p. 21, where the is considering setting up a human rights complaint mechanism.

233 C. Tan, 'The New Disciplinary Framework: Conditionality, New Aid Architecture and Global Economic Governance', *op. cit.*, p. 5.

234 See, for example, Articles 6 and 7 of the Arms Trade Treaty.

235 This discussion leads us to having a closer look at the international assistance and cooperation provision of the Covenant on ESC rights, to which development cooperation is linked, to see if the current mismatch of normative provision with the application in practice have anything to do with the provision itself. See Chapter IV.

3.3 'Human rights-based approaches' to development

One of the practical elements that emerged from the human rights and development discourse is human rights based approaches to development (HRBA). Normatively the rights-based approaches to development can be linked to the Declaration on the Right to Development.[236] The term has been in use since early 1990s by development agencies and has since become a growing area of study by academics and practitioners.[237] Like other ideas, set out in previous sections, the concept emerged during the era where human rights gained prominence in the international scene and in response to the development discontents following structural adjustments. The use of the concept of a 'human rights based approach' is not particular only to the development sphere.[238]

Within the UN system, the HRBA was especially given visibility at the institutional level, through the process of UN reform.[239] Under this reform, human rights were integrated at a structural level as a cross-cutting issue for UN system activities, including development. The Millennium Declaration of 2000 and the Secretary-General's 2002 reform programme provided additional impetus to the HRBA.[240] The latter led to development and implementation of a plan of action for strengthening the UN human rights actions at the country level.[241] The call of the UN Secretary-General to mainstream human rights in the UN activities resulted in the Stamford Statement, entitled 'The Human Rights Based Approach to Development Cooperation – Towards a Common Understanding among UN Agencies'.[242]

---

236 See Chapter III for a thorough discussion.

237 A. Frankovits, 'Introduction: A Rights-Based Approach to Development and the Right to Development', 3 *Human Rights and Development Yearbook* (2002), p. 4

238 The concept has gained following in the other areas, for example, see the work of the International Law Commission on the Protection of Persons in the Event of Disasters, where the expression HRBA has primarily a meaning of putting an individual (and/or his rights) at the focus of the rules.

239 Human rights has become a central theme or cross-cutting issue in four areas of the UN activity, namely: peace and security; economic and social affairs; development cooperation; and humanitarian affairs. See Secretary General's Report, Renewing the United Nations: a Programme for Reform, A/51/950, 14 July 1997. It should be noted, however, that the United Nations Children's Fund (UNICEF) had been developing its programming approach designed in accordance with principles and standards in the Convention on the Rights of Child (CRC) much earlier, prior to 1997.

240 For a thorough chronology within the UN, see in particular UNESCO, *The Human Rights Based Approach and the United Nations System*, Desk Study Prepared by A. Frankovits, UNESCO: 2006.

241 Plan of Action entitled 'Action 2 Initiative' stems from the report of the Secretary-General, *Strengthening of the United Nations: an Agenda for Further Change*, UN doc. A/57/387, 9 September 2002.

242 United Nations, The Human Rights Based Approach to Development Cooperation – Towards a Common Understanding Among UN Agencies (the 'Stamford Statement'), adopted at a meeting which was held at Stamford, Connecticut, 3–5 May 2003, www.undg.org/index.cfm?P=221.

There has been a great deal of discussion on what a human rights based approach actually is, in view of its diverse conception and means of application in practice.[243] There is, however, no single definition or explanation of the approach, and conceptual obscurity has not prevented a proliferation of 'rights-based approach' thinking and their diverse modes of application.[244] This is not surprising as the concept means different things to different people, 'depending upon thematic focus, disciplinary bias, agency profile, and the external political, social, and cultural environment'.[245] Consequently, the UN agencies, funds and programmes, development agencies and NGOs have been developing and operationalizing a wide range of rights-based models to development programming, driven, as Darrow and Tomas write, 'by various blends of personal or corporate conviction'.[246]

At its core, the concept is (or should be) an operational expression of inclusion of human rights in development policy and practice.[247] In other words, the HRBA is itself an approach, a method, a tool, to incorporate human rights into development.[248] What does a HRBA mean? Does it mean ensuring that development goals and targets respect human rights? Or does it mean formulating goals and targets in human rights terms? Boesen and Sano define human rights based approaches

---

243 For a stocktaking of various experiences of rights-based approaches in development see S. Hickey and D. Mitlin (eds), *Human Rights-Based Approaches to Development*, Kumarian Press: 2009. A critical assessment stems from a more dated research by C. Nyamu-Musembi and A. Cornwall, *What is the 'Rights-Based Approach' All About? Perspectives from International Development Agencies*, IDS Working Paper 234, November 2004.

244 There have been different takes on categorizing essential elements common to HRBAs. See e.g. J.K. Boesen and H.-O. Sano, 'The Implications and Value Added of a Human Rights-Based Approach', in B.A. Andreassen and S.P. Marks (eds), *Development as a Human Right: Legal, Political and Economic Dimensions*, 2nd edition, Intersentia: 2010, pp. 45–64; OHCHR, *Human Rights and Poverty Reduction: A Conceptual Framework*, UN: 2004.

245 M. Darrow and A. Tomas, 'Power, Capture, and Conflict: A Call for Human Rights Accountability in Development Cooperation', 27(2) *Human Rights Quarterly*, 2005, pp. 471–538, p. 483.

246 *Ibid.*, p. 479.

247 Mary Robinson, United Nations High Commissioner for Human Rights, Development and Rights: the Undeniable Nexus, UN General Assembly Special Session on the Implementation of the Outcome of the World Summit for Social Development, Geneva (26 June 2000), www.unhchr.ch/huricane/huricane.nsf/0/F31C625AA489D31BC125690A005 3C8DE?opendocument.

248 One study documents several 'approaches' to integrate human rights into development: (i) a human rights based approach (HRBA); (ii) human rights mainstreaming; (iii) dialogue and conditionality; (iv) projects or global initiatives; and (v) implicit human rights work. World Bank and Organisation for Economic Co-operation and Development, *Integrating Human Rights into Development: Donor Approaches, Experiences, and Challenges*, 2nd edition, World Bank and the OECD: 2013, p. 23. It must be noted that distinguishing HRBA from human rights mainstreaming may not be that easy to do. Compare, for example, with UNDG, *Human Rights Mainstreaming Mechanism: Operational Plan 2011–2013*, November 2011, https://undg.org/wp-content/uploads/2015/04/UNDG-HRM-Operational-Plan-Nov-20-2011.pdf.

as an approach 'in which goals and processes of international assistance reflect the principles and norms embodied in the international human rights instruments'.[249] For the Office of High Commissioner for Human Rights (OHCHR):

> A human rights-based approach is a conceptual framework for the process of human development that is normatively based on international human rights standards and operationally directed to promoting and protecting human rights.[250]

Furthermore, as the OHCHR explains, under a human rights based approach, 'the plans, policies and processes of development are anchored in a system of rights and corresponding obligations established by international law. This helps to promote the sustainability of development work, empowering people themselves – especially the most marginalized – to participate in policy formulation and hold accountable those who have a duty to act.'[251] From this perspective, HRBA is often portrayed as the strongest articulation of commitment by a development actor, since HRBAs situate 'human rights' as an objective of all development interventions.

Another approach to HRBA is defined as the integration of human rights principles into development processes. For example, the Food and Agriculture Organization (FAO) has developed its human rights based approach to food, called the PANTHER framework, which requires decision-making processes (from policy formulation to law-making, down to administrative acts) to comply with seven principles: participation, accountability, non-discrimination, transparency, human dignity, empowerment and rule of law.[252] In a similar vein, the OHCHR's framework on poverty reduction emphasizes the importance of these principles.[253]

Hans-Otto Sano rightly observes a strong overlap between some of these principles, such as principles of participation and accountability with governance criteria (also applied in development practice).[254] One could also add that principles

249 J.K. Boesen and H.-O. Sano, 'The Implications and Value Added of a Human Rights-Based Approach', in B.A. Andreassen and S.P. Marks, *Development as a Human Right: Legal, Political and Economic Dimensions, op. cit.*, p. 45.

250 OHCHR, *Frequently Asked Questions on a Human Rights-Based Approach to Development Cooperation*, UN: 2006, p. 15, www.ohchr.org/Documents/Publications/FAQen.pdf.

251 *Ibid.*

252 FAO, Human Rights Principles: PANTHER, www.fao.org/righttofood/about-right-to-food/human-right-principles-panther/ru/.

253 OHCHR, *Human Rights and Poverty Reduction: A Conceptual Framework*, UN: 2004.

254 H.-O. Sano, 'The Drivers of Human Rights Change in Development', in P. Gready and W. Vandenhole (eds), *Human Rights and Development in the New Millennium: Towards a Theory of Change,* Routledge: 2014, pp. 29–49, p. 30. OHCHR website, with reference to the Commission on Human Rights Resolution 2000/64 (on the role of good governance in the promotion of human rights), defines key attributes of good governance as transparency, responsibility, accountability, participation and responsiveness (to the needs of the people). See www.ohchr.org/EN/Issues/Development/GoodGovernance/Pages/GoodGovernanceIndex.aspx.

of empowerment and the rule of law similarly resemble good governance agenda integrated into development. There is, therefore, a risk that focusing exclusively on these governance and rule of law related dimensions may dilute the logic of a human rights based approach. The main criticism, however, is that the development actors, while visualizing individuals in recipient development states as rights bearers, do not see themselves as bearing any responsibility.[255] Thus, 'the problem in integrating human rights into sustainable human development is that the normative framework for imposing responsibilities on development institutions is underdeveloped'.[256]

In view of these ambiguities, it is suggested that, recently, a more coherent and normative formulation of human rights based approaches has been advanced by human rights treaty bodies. In particular, the Committee on Economic, Social and Cultural Rights has suggested to states engaged in international development a number of parameters that would constitute a rights-based approach. Thus, a rights-based approach to international development would include: (i) undertaking a systematic and independent human rights impact assessment prior to making funding decisions; (ii) establishing an effective monitoring mechanism to regularly assess the human rights impact of policies and projects in the receiving countries and to take remedial measures when required; and (iii) ensuring that there is an accessible complaint mechanism for human rights violations in receiving states.[257]

To date, the record of implementation of HRBA remains unclear. The conclusion that can be reached at this stage is that, currently, the HRBA as a concept has no normative bearing on the underlying issues of the 'human rights in development' debate. It may nonetheless serve as a litmus test of the extent to which human rights obligations have been taken seriously in development policies and practices. The next section will take a closer look at the way in which a select number of states have integrated human rights into their development activities, viz. the essence of their human rights based approach.

---

255 For example, a Norwegian White Paper defines human rights based approach as follows: 'A human rights-based approach to development cooperation builds on individual rights set by the human rights commitments and obligations of the countries concerned.' Norwegian Ministry of Foreign Affairs, Opportunities for All: Human Rights in Norway's Foreign Policy and Development Cooperation, Meld. St. 10 (2014–2015) Report to the Storting (white paper), p. 55.

256 B. Rajagopal, *International Law from Below: Development, Social Movements and Third World Resistance*, CUP: 2003, p. 230.

257 This wording has been adopted in two of the concluding observations of the CESCR, viz. Austria and China. See CESCR, Concluding Observations: China, UN doc. E/C.12/CHN/CO/2, 13 June 2014, para. 12; CESCR, Concluding Observations: Austria, UN doc. E/C.12/AUT/CO/4, 29 November 2013, para. 11; CEDAW Committee adopted a similar approach to cooperation programming with the only difference being focus on women's rights and adopting a gender sensitive approach. CEDAW: Concluding observations: India, UN doc. CEDAW/C/IND/CO4, 24 July 2014, para. 15.

3.4 *Variations across the spectrum: The practice of individual states*

Scarce reference to a legally binding human rights framework raises the question of whether development cooperation has anything to do with the normative framework of rights, standards and obligations as prescribed by the human rights treaties.[258] Notwithstanding universal consensuses and enhanced aid-harmonization schemes, individual donors continue to manage their own separate policies and activities.[259] This raises interesting questions regarding states' own interpretations of human rights obligations in the context of development cooperation. After all, the states are addressees of the legal rules and it is the state practice that can give us an idea about the extent to which human rights international standards are invoked in the context of development.

Donor policies in relation to human rights vary in time and between donors. Unsurprisingly, they are rarely viewed by international lawyers as an appropriate 'raw' material or of any normative value. Nonetheless, it is suggested they are not overlooked. On the one hand, the divergence of bilateral approaches from global frameworks strengthens the general conception that this area continues to be characterized by ambiguity, and the existence of such diversity indicates we are far from consolidating norms or even having a universal interpretation of existing ones. On the other hand, it is indicative of the fact that universal policy frameworks discussed in the previous sections are only part of the picture.

Generally, there appears to be a trend among donors towards legislated mandates for the provision of development assistance. Such legislation embeds poverty reduction as the core focus of development aid. The new generation of these laws[260] attempts to legally standardize issues such as 'objectives' to ensure a 'pro-poor' focus, 'accountability' issues[261] and, paradoxically, even to make achievement of the 'development targets' a legal obligation. An example of the latter is the recent UK International Development (Official Development Assistance Target) Act 2015, which makes a binding legislative requirement for the UK government to allocate 0.7% of GNI (Gross National Income) to development assistance.[262] The legislation is an interesting example, particularly because it

---

258 One assessment pointed out '[t]he weak linkage of specific human rights to legally binding international instruments and standards means that recognition of specific human rights is not linked to recognition that these entail obligations for the state'. T. O'Neil, M. Foresti, T. Braunholtz and B. Sharma, *DFID's Human Rights Policy: Scoping Study*, ODI: 2007, p. 5.

259 Relevant policy documents include those of Canada, Finland, Denmark, Germany, Netherlands, Norway, Sweden, Switzerland and the UK.

260 The relevant legislation reviewed includes laws of Austria, Belgium, Canada, Denmark, Italy, Luxembourg, Spain, Switzerland and UK.

261 Canada's Official Development Assistance Accountability Act, Bill C-293 (S.C. 2008, c. 17), www.canlii.org/en/ca/laws/stat/sc-2008-c-17/latest/sc-2008-c-17.html; UK's International Development (Reporting and Transparency) Act 2006, /www.legislation.gov.uk/ukpga/2006/31/pdfs/ukpga_20060031_en.pdf.

262 UK International Development (Official Development Assistance Target) Act 2015, www.legislation.gov.uk/ukpga/2015/12/contents/enacted.

raises a question whether the UK has come to accept the aid target of 0.7% as an obligation within the broader question of the existence of a duty to internationally assist and cooperate for development.[263]

While a number of countries have adopted legislation related to development cooperation, which refer to varying degrees to human rights,[264] a more detailed view of human rights can be gleaned through examining internal policies, statements, guidelines and tools available in the depository of the donors. These policies may shed light on a variety of issues: donors' position vis-à-vis human rights, the definitions of human rights, the concept and implications of human rights based development; the relationship of poverty and human rights; the role of economic, social, and cultural rights in development policies; and the relationship between human rights and other concepts such as good governance, democracy, and the rule of law. In what follows, only two questions of a general nature shall be discussed: one on the integration of human rights as a matter of legal obligation and the other on the use of human rights.[265]

As far as the new donors are concerned, to date, in view of an evidentiary deficit regarding the aid provided by the South–South cooperation, it is difficult to assess the contribution of the emerging donors to development outcomes.[266] What is clear, however, is that today's dominant development ideologies, practices

263 See particularly the wording of Section 1: 'It is the duty of the Secretary of State to ensure that the target for official development assistance (referred to in this Act as "ODA") to amount to 0.7% of gross national income (in this Act referred to as "the 0.7% target") is met by the United Kingdom in the year 2015 and each subsequent calendar year.'

264 References to human right and/or human rights standards can be found in the legislation of the following countries: Switzerland: Article 5(1), Loi fédérale sur la coopération au développement et l'aide humanitaire international) 19 March 1976 (Etat le 1er juin 2007) and Article 4, Loi fédérale sur la coopération avec les Etats d'Europe de l'Est of 24 March 2006 ; UK: Part 1(1) of the International Development Act 2002 of the UK; Denmark: Section I of the International Development Cooperation Act, *cf. Consolidated Act no. 541 of 10 July 1998*; Luxemburg : Article 1, Loi du 6 janvier 1996 sur la coopération au développement; Italy: Article 1(1), Legge 26 febbraio 1987. N. 49 'Nuova disciplina della cooperazione dell'italia con i paesi in via di sviluppo'; Spain: Artículo 1, Ley 23/1998, de 7 de julio, de Cooperación Internacional para el Desarrollo; Belgium: Article 2 and 3, the Law on Belgian International Cooperation of 25 May 1999; Canada: Section 2 of the Official Development Assistance Accountability Act, Bill C-293 (S.C. 2008, c. 17); Austria: Section I(3), Austria, Federal Act on Development Cooperation (2002), including its Amendment (2003). From among these national legislation, Italy, Switzerland, Spain and Austria explicitly define human rights as a core component of development.

265 Bilateral agencies examined include those of Canada, Finland, Denmark, Germany, Netherlands, Norway, Sweden, Switzerland and the UK. The selection of policies is not entirely representative, only agencies that have adopted human rights policies have been examined.

266 N. Besharati, *South African Development Partnership Agency: Strategic Aid or Development Packages for Africa?*, South African Institute of International Affairs Research Report No. 12, 2013, p. 21. As the author explains, evaluation of the South–South Cooperation would require application of common definitions and interpretations, common measurement and reporting standards. In addition, institutions responsible for managing development cooperation are weakly developed and consequently eschew minimal coordination and common framework.

and funding, particularly standards of democracy, human rights and good governance, are weakly incorporated into South–South development cooperation
policies and programmes.[267]

3.4.1 The position on human rights obligations

Virtually all traditional donor states recognize the importance of human rights.
Various rationales are invoked: national interests, peace, security, development and
stability. However, the question remains: how do they relate to their legally binding
obligations under human rights treaties? According to an OECD report examining the question of human rights among the donors, their involvement in human
rights is driven by two reasons.[268] The first is the intrinsic reason which includes the
legal obligations stemming from common binding commitments as a goal in their
own right, and the second concerns instrumental rationale arguing that a focus on
human rights can improve development aid. Without going into details of the specific cases, the report concludes: '[n]ot all aid agencies accept that they are under a
legal obligation to promote and respect human rights through their assistance.'[269]

   A closer inspection of specific examples is therefore in order. According to the
German Federal Ministry for Economic Cooperation and Development Strategy
paper of 2011, '[h]uman rights are a guiding principle for German development
policy. They play a key role in shaping Germany's development policy objectives,
programmes and approaches in cooperation with partner countries and at international level.'[270] The rationale for this approach lies in the fact that 'Germany and the
majority of its development partners have ratified the international human rights
conventions and have *thus recognized the implementation of these conventions as a
legally binding obligation*', which provides 'the binding frame of reference for Germany's development cooperation'.[271] Along similar lines, Finland also seems to view
its human rights priorities in development cooperation as deriving from Finland's
and its partner countries' ratification of human rights conventions. Finland refers
to its constitution as the basis for the objectives of its development cooperation.[272]

---

267 For the full analysis see E. Mawdsley, 'Human Rights and South-South Development
     Cooperation: Reflections on the "Rising Powers" as International Development Actors',
     36(3) *Human Rights Quarterly* (2014), pp. 630–652.
268 OECD, *Integrating Human Rights into Development: Donor Approaches, Experiences and
     Challenges*, Paris: 2006, pp. 28–30. World Bank and Organisation for Economic Co-operation
     and Development, *Integrating Human Rights into Development: Donor Approaches, Experi-
     ences, and Challenges*, 2nd edition, World Bank and the OECD: 2013, pp. 8–11.
269 The report continues: 'ethical arguments thus drive a positive association between human
     rights and aid, centered around human dignity and the need to combat poverty'. *Ibid.*, p. 9.
270 BMZ of Germany, *Human Rights in German Development Policy*, BMZ Strategy Paper 4,
     BMZ: 2011e., p. 3.
271 *Ibid.* (emphasis added).
272 See also Section 1 of Chapter 1 of the Constitution, which states that 'Finland participates
     in international cooperation for the protection of peace and human rights and for the devel-
     opment of society.' Constitution of Finland, adopted 11 June 1999, www.finlex.fi/fi/laki/

While a 2011 evaluation report of the Norwegian Development Cooperation considered Norway's membership to international human rights treaties as a justification for its efforts to promote human rights worldwide,[273] a recently published white paper is not explicit on the legal basis for Norway's engagement with human rights outside of its territory. Rather, the focus is on the 'commitments and obligations' of the state recipient of international development.[274] This change of heart stands in contrast with the previous statement emphasizing that '[s]ince all UN Member States have legally undertaken to fulfil the obligations set out in one or more international human rights treaties, it is everyone's interest to respect and protect human rights in the best possible way'.[275]

In any event, it is not clear whether these statements imply that these international treaties apply to the activities of the donors, whether this framework gives rise to a legal basis to work on human rights in the framework of development activities, or both. Judging by references to a common normative framework for donors and recipients alike, one is inclined to interpret that some donors acknowledge themselves as acting as contracting states having a common interest for all to accomplish purposes set out in the human rights treaties.

This is further strengthened by a recurrent idea emerging from some of the policy instruments, that assistance is directed towards the efforts of the recipient states in order to discharge their obligations under human rights treaties. For instance, Denmark renders its assistance in 'developing the capacity and ability of

---

kaannokset/1999/en19990731. MFA of Finland, *The Instruction on Cross-cutting themes in the Development Policy Programme of the Government of Finland*, MFA: 18 June 2009. See also Finland's Development Policy Programme Government Decision-in-Principle, 16 February 2012, which seems to entirely focus on human rights obligations of a recipient of aid, while another document entitled 'Cross-cutting objectives in the Development Policy Programme of the Government of Finland; Guidelines' (Document ref. HEL 7215–63 of 16 August 2012) states that '[c]ross-cutting objectives have been derived from international human rights and environmental conventions, which the Government of Finland has ratified or which reflect international political commitments considered specifically important by the Government'.

273 E.g. 'It is the universal character of human rights, based on international legally binding conventions making all state parties to these conventions the primary duty bearers, that is the main justification for Norway's international efforts to promote and contribute to protect human rights worldwide and in other countries.' Norway, Evaluation Department, *Evaluation of Norwegian Development Cooperation to Promote Human Rights*, Report 7/2011 – Evaluation, NORAD: September 2011, p. 14. See also Report on the Role of Human Rights in Norwegian Foreign and Development Policy, MFA: June 2009, p. 7; Report 21 (1999–2000) to the Storting, *A Plan of Action for Human Rights: Focus on Human Dignity*, is said to have had significant implications: 'The Plan of Action led to a significant upgrading of human rights as a policy issue. The Minister of Development Cooperation took the official name 'Minister of Development and Human Rights'.

274 Norwegian Ministry of Foreign Affairs, Opportunities for All: Human Rights in Norway's Foreign Policy and Development Cooperation, Meld. St. 10 (2014–2015) Report to the Storting (white paper).

275 NORAD, Evaluation Department, *Evaluation of Norwegian Development Cooperation to Promote Human Rights, op. cit.*, p. 52.

the countries to fulfil' their responsibility of protecting individuals from infringe-ments and violations.[276] Norway makes it more explicit by stating that its devel-opment cooperation is aimed at strengthening developing countries' abilities to fulfil the human rights obligations they have undertaken.[277] The use of formulas such as 'rendering assistance' or 'supporting' the fulfilment of rights reproduces the notion of assistance and cooperation for the achievement of rights as embed-ded in human rights treaties.[278]

Inconsistencies seem to appear when, in addition to engaging statements, pov-erty reduction is depicted only as a 'joint responsibility' and human rights are 'fundamental values and goals' of development cooperation.[279] Donors' policies and statements carefully avoid any formulations explicitly referring to 'obliga-tion'. German policy may, however, be deemed an exception. While acknowl-edging that MDGs do not make any reference to binding human rights norms, German policy seeks to establish normative links between each development goal and corresponding human rights obligations.[280]

In this context, a question arises regarding the relationship between the state-donor and individuals in the third countries. Yet again, this issue is touched upon in passing in the German policy document. The Strategy specifies that 'human rights impose obligations on states not only within their own territory but also in relation to their actions in international organizations and in other countries' and acknowledges the presence of a debate of extraterritorial obligations in relation to human rights implementation.[281]

---

276 Denmark, *International Human Rights Cooperation: Strategy for Government's Approach*, MFA: 2009, p. 12.
277 Norwegian Ministry of Foreign Affairs, Opportunities for All: Human Rights in Norway's Foreign Policy and Development Cooperation, Meld. St. 10 (2014–2015) Report to the Storting (white paper).
278 Foreign and Commonwealth Office, Human Rights and Democracy: The 2014 Foreign & Commonwealth Office Report. At the same time, a dated UK policy statement explicitly denies any links to the relevant debate on the duty to provide assistance. DFID's Human Rights Policy Study, recalling the debate on Article 2(1) of the ICESCR, states: 'The UK government has consistently taken the position in international discussions that it does not accept a legal obligation to provide development assistance. It is believed that moving away from this position would constrain the ability of the UK government, and DFID in particular, to set its own policy in these matters.' T. O'Neil, M. Foresti, T. Braunholtz and B. Sharma, *DFID's Human Rights Policy – Scoping Study*, DFID: 2007, p. 12.
279 DANIDA, The Right to a Better Life Strategy for Denmark's Development Cooperation, August 2012.
280 BMZ of Germany, *Human Rights in German Development Policy, op. cit.*, p. 10.
281 In comparison, a report commissioned by the UK's DFID pre-emptively rejects any impli-cation that the UK can have obligations vis-à-vis the human rights of people living outside its jurisdiction by virtue of its ratification of human right treaties. The report states: 'The UK has not accepted that it exercises effective control/jurisdiction in either Afghanistan or Iraq and therefore has stated that CAT does not have extraterritorial application in these cases (Response to Committee Against Torture, November 2004). The UK government may review its position on extraterritorial application of the core international human rights treaties as a result of the House of Lords judgment on the *Al Skeini* case related to the extraterritorial application Human Rights Act (HRA). However, even if this happens, it is

On balance, notwithstanding references made in relation to a common international legal framework as the basis of the work of donors as well as their 'contribution' to the fulfilment of the obligations of the recipient states, the majority of policy frameworks remain very general. The suggestion is that anchorage of commitments in the context of development to internationally binding treaties may leave states little room for political consideration. This may explain, therefore, the preference of the majority of donors to phrase their 'interest' or 'concerns' in the language of political documents, such as various poverty-related proclamations. Bearing this in mind, one cannot help but pay a tribute to inspiring pledges that leave very little to be desired:

> It is our obligation to enable people all over the world to live in dignity and at the same time it is one of the great challenges facing us today and for the near future.[282]

3.4.2 Definition of human rights: ESC rights in development policies

It is not enough to state that human rights are integrated into the practice of development. This raises a basic question as to the content of human rights referred to in the policy and practice. Back in 1993, Tomasevski qualified the approach of donors in relation to favouring one set of rights over the other as a 'food *versus* freedom' debate. According to her, most of the donors resolved this by saying 'no freedom without food, but freedom comes first'.[283] At the principle level, economic and social rights are equally important as civil and political rights. At the policy level, however, some donors use the human rights agenda to focus on civil and political rights, institutions, procedures and actors of democracy and the rule of law, highlighting that these create preconditions for the fulfilment of other rights.[284]

---

difficult to imagine circumstances in which DFID's obligations would be engaged overseas, because the House of Lords confirmed the Court of Appeal's finding of an extremely narrow basis for extraterritorial application of the HRA/ECHR, i.e. circumstances where the UK has 'effective control' of a territory or exercises all or some of the public powers normally exercised by the government or the UK exercises authority over an individual (e.g. in a detention centre).' T. O'Neil, M. Foresti, T. Braunholtz and B. Sharma, *DFID's Human Rights Policy: Scoping Study, op. cit.*, p. 13.

282 Foreword by Federal Minister for European and International Affairs and State Secretary at the Federal Ministry for European and International Affairs Three-Year Programme on Austrian Development Policy 2013–2015 (pursuant to Section 23 of the Federal Development Cooperation Act 2002 as amended in the Federal Law Gazette I No. 65/2003).

283 K. Tomasevski, *Development Aid and Human Rights Revisited*, 2nd edition, Pinter Publishers: 1993, p. 86.

284 For example, DANIDA, The Right to a Better Life Strategy for Denmark's Development Cooperation, August 2012; Norwegian Ministry of Foreign Affairs, Opportunities for All: Human Rights in Norway's Foreign Policy and Development Cooperation, Meld. St. 10 (2014–2015) Report to the Storting (white paper); Sweden, Aid policy framework – the direction of Swedish aid, Government Communication 2013/14:131, 13 March 2014. and also UK Foreign and Commonwealth Office, Policy paper 2010 to 2015 government policy: human rights internationally, 8 May 2015.

An overview of the human rights portfolios of many development cooperation agencies reveals a concentration on civil and political aspects. Human rights writ large are conceived of and centre on the notion of the participation of the poor in decision-making processes that affect their lives, and their right to be heard and to be able to hold their governments to account. Such development cooperation therefore focuses on the individual's relationship with its own government rather than the donor's own obligations to honour commitments under human rights treaties. Emphasis on the political dimension is evidenced further by the fact that the extent of a state's respect for human rights is measured often on the basis of a government's respect of political rights and civil liberties.[285] In cases where a general rights-based approach is adopted, it seems that socio-economic rights are protected. Alternatively, in certain instances, economic and social rights may be seen as implicit in development activities:

> Development cooperation, at the heart of which is poverty reduction, is a major instrument for achieving ESC rights and goes beyond only achieving a certain level of socioeconomic development. Fair distribution of wealth, social justice, and non-discrimination are all equally important. It is essential for members of the public to have a say about development in their country.[286]

However, it generally appears from donors' policy documents that socio-economic aspects of improving better standards of living are considered an aspect of development rather than a matter of human rights obligations.

3.4.3 Assessment

One certainly needs to be careful not to draw rapid conclusions from donor policies. The shift in individual donors' development thinking and conception of human rights does not automatically translate into a shift in their programmes or projects. Moreover, it is a separate endeavour to measure the actual performance against the standards set out in the official documents.[287]

The general tendency has been 'to integrate human rights in principles, perspectives or considerations rather than obligations, and to leave them without

285 E. Neumayer, 'Do Human Rights Matter in Bilateral Aid Allocation? A Quantitative Analysis of 21 Donor Countries', 84(3) *Social Science Quarterly* (2003), p. 651.
286 MFA of the Netherlands, *Dutch Human Rights Policy*, www.minbuza.nl/en/key-topics/human-rights/dutch-human-rights-policy/dutch-human-rights-policy.html.
287 Uncertain relationships between donors' official policy goals with the facts continue to sustain highly polarized view on aid and its effectiveness, and nurtures the scepticism that their goals are nothing but political rhetoric of altruism. One study concluded that: 'If donors want to appear less hypocritical about their commitment to the pursuit of human rights, our analysis suggests that they still have a long way to go.' E. Neumayer, 'Do Human Rights Matter in Bilateral Aid Allocation? A Quantitative Analysis of 21 Donor Countries', 84(3) *Social Science Quarterly* (2003), p. 665.

specific anchorage in laws and treaties'.[288] Therefore, the point of departure for the section on individual donors' policies was to arrive at a conclusion whether the approach to human rights as formulated in multilateral development frameworks is a general rule. It appears that human rights commitments in the practice of individual states are more pronounced. There is a visible trend indicative of an increasingly normative approach to development, but incomplete as it were. As noted before, the practice is far from being evenly applied. Where human rights are incorporated nominally, it is difficult to draw conclusions as to whether they are mainly addressed to recipient countries or equally apply to the donor states.

What is not ubiquitous in the practice of states is the manner in which human rights are integrated, particularly their specific and explicit linkages with the *international legal framework*. References to human rights do not always translate into increased use of human rights treaties. In extremely limited cases, the use of human rights also meant that human rights norms and concepts have also been integrated in the conceptualization of development policy. They may evidence a small but visible recognition that 'rights and responsibilities have to be approached in their inter-related and mutual perspective'.[289] The case of the positive examples also 'point to ways in which the work of international human rights bodies could be put to use in development activities, and where the accumulated wisdom of states' experience as parties to international conventions could be brought to bear in particular circumstances where human rights have a direct and obvious bearing'.[290]

Conclusion

The traditional analysis of the development and human rights *rapprochement* tends to depict this historical configuration as a consequence of a linear, evolutionary process. A more textured narrative of development reveals many ideologies behind the concept. Development discourse 'constituted a complex space in which power and justice and security and humanitarianism functioned in contradictory and complementary ways'.[291] All these factors, in intricate and interpenetrative ways, played a crucial role in the formation of the different dimensions of development discourse, including its human rights aspects.[292]

---

288 S. McInerney-Lankford, 'Human Rights and Development: a Comment on Challenges and Opportunities from a Legal Perspective', 1(1) *Journal of Human Rights Practice* (2009), pp. 51–82, at 71.

289 T. Van Boven, 'Is There an Emerging Right to Good Governance?', 3 *Netherlands Quarterly on Human Rights* (1995), pp. 304–310, p. 304.

290 S. McInerney-Lankford, 'Human Rights and Development: a Comment on Challenges and Opportunities from a Legal Perspective', *op. cit.*, p. 68.

291 Rajagopal further argues that '[t]his idea of "development," . . . was not merely a rational response to the problems of the Third World but a specific exercise of power that was constituted in the complex struggle between the West and the non-West, and whose most concrete manifestations were to be found in international institutions'. B. Rajagopal, *International Law from Below: Development, Social Movements and Third World Resistance, op. cit.*, p. 108.

292 *Ibid.*, p. 112.

The combination of the phrases 'human rights' and 'development' can only be discussed under a big question mark. Analysis of the history of human rights in development policy reveals a discursive practice both in their definition and application. When integration of human rights remains at the rhetorical level, it becomes clear that human rights may not live up to their promises and unique contribution to development, since the sources of human rights and the obligations they imply remain unclear.

There is one important lesson that can be drawn from the absence of references to a human rights legal framework in major development policies and operational frameworks. Integration of a legal dimension of human rights, like integration of any legal rule, carries with it normative force – i.e. concrete rules of application, monitoring and enforcement. Human rights treaties, as legally binding international commitments, compared to other development dimensions (be it democracy, good governance), have a fixed normative content. They provide a normative foundation determining possible risks to human rights and provide a framework to prevent and redress negative impacts of development interventions. In addition to defining the limits of development interventions, they also identify ways in which development instruments can be put in practice.

By integrating the legal dimension, the development agencies may have to take into account not only the obligations of the recipient governments but also their own obligations under international treaties, which already seems like a serious possibility for certain bilateral agencies.[293] Put in these 'legal' terms, the 'value-added' of human rights may be in instilling the role of law into development, which has been to date 'insufficiently legalized' and has been described in terms of ethical obligations rather than legal.

---

293 'Mechanisms of accountability which can be accessed by individuals or groups if they consider that their human rights have been infringed play an important role in human rights implementation . . . For that reason, . . . the possibility of setting up a human rights complaints mechanism is being considered by BMZ [Federal Ministry for Economic and Development].' BMZ of Germany, *Human Rights in German Development Policy, op. cit.*, p. 21.

III The right to development

Introduction

The 'right to development' is a concretization of a broader human rights and development debate. Historically it precedes all the current efforts to integrate human rights into a development paradigm. According to Donnelly, '[t]he quite proper, even essential, desire to link human rights and development clearly lies at the heart of the appeal of the idea of a human right to development'.[1]

The changes the international society has undergone since the adoption of the Declaration on the Right to Development lead many to question the validity of the concept today, in this 'era of post-development and of hyperglobalization'.[2] It seems erroneous to sidestep completely the right to development in contemporary thinking. It is true, however, that the issue is more in the agenda of the human rights community than major development institutions. The work of the High-Level Task Force on the Right to Development, the mandates of the Office of the High Commissioner for Human Rights and the UN Human Rights Council, as well as pledges by states at the Millennium Summit to make the right to development 'a reality for all', demonstrate the attempts to revitalize the concept (or at least to signal that it is not entirely obsolete). It is, though, far from certain that frequent incantations in international discourse are sufficient evidence of the existence of a global norm.

Although more than 30 years have passed since the most prominent analyses were undertaken, notably by Georges Abi-Saab, Mohamed Bedjaoui and Philip Alston, there is little new substance to add today. Therefore, this chapter is not so much about seeking to settle the many controversies about the right

1 J. Donnelly, 'In Search of the Unicorn: The Jurisprudence and Politics of the Right to Development', 15 *California Western International Law Journal* (1985), pp. 473–509, p. 478.
2 U. Baxi, 'Normative Content of a Treaty as Opposed to the Declaration on the Right to Development: Marginal Observations', in S.P. Marks (ed.), *Implementing the Right to Development: the Role of International Law*, Friedrich Ebert Stiftung: 2008, pp. 47–52. Some authors even question whether the international system, after the dissolution of the Eastern bloc and the age of trade and financial liberalization, even constitutes an environment suitable for the right to development debate. See e.g. A. Orford, 'Globalization and the Right to Development', in P. Alston (ed.), *Peoples' Rights*, OUP: 2005, pp. 127–185.

to development as about reviewing the debates as to its definition, legal value, and content. The aim of the chapter is to examine the utility of the concept, in particular if the concept of the right to development can help to construct an understanding and interpretation of human rights obligations in the area of development. Rather than being an independent legal rule or a principle, I will argue that the right to development is an interpretation of existing development-oriented human rights.

1 Genesis of the concept of the right to development: A structural approach to human rights?

The background and relevant development discourse were provided in Chapter II. Suffice here to reiterate that the possibility for a right to development was offered by the political and economic situation that existed at the time. Norberto Bobbio, when explaining his historical approach to human rights, stated that human rights 'come into existence, when their existence is either essential or possible'.[3] The formation of the concept of the right to development was made both important and possible during earlier decades that bristled with new ideas and the founding of the notions of self-determination and the rights of peoples.[4]

The situation in which the newly independent states found themselves served as a basis to question the abstract notion of legal equality and sovereignty upon which international relations were based. The difference in economic position of states (or level of development) was introduced as a criterion in analysis of relations between them. This approach gave rise to the school of thought – '*droit de développement*' – shaped doctrinally by francophone legal literature in the 1960s, with Michel Virally as its main proponent.[5] In its broadest definition, it includes the totality of rules of international law in relation to economic relations between North–South and South–South.[6] Although chronologically these rules appeared earlier than the concept of right to development, according to Georges

---

3 He further states that 'human rights however fundamental are historical rights and therefore arise from specific conditions characterized by the embattled defense of new freedoms against old powers'. N. Bobbio, *The Age of Rights*, Polity Press: 2005 Reprint, p. x.

4 Added to this, the past colonial relationships parsed the debate and 'the assumption that reparations were payable was never far below the surface'. P. Alston, 'Revitalising United Nations Work on Human Rights and Development', 18 *Melbourne University Law Review* (1991), p. 218.

5 The concept and the expression 'international law of development' is attributed to André Philip, 'who, in 1965, on the eve of the first meeting of the United Nations Conference on Trade and Development (UNCTAD), appealed to industrialized countries to take action to establish such law'. See A. Mahiou, 'International Law of Development', *Max Planck Encyclopedia of Public International Law*, www.mpepil.com. However, inaugural juridical enquiry into the law of development has been attributed to Michel Virally, 'Vers un droit international du développement', 11 *Annuaire français de droit international* (1965), pp. 3–12.

6 G. Abi-Saab, 'Le droit au développement', 44 *Annuaire suisse de droit international* (1988), p. 9–24.

Abi-Saab, they can only find their ultimate justification in the underlying right to development.[7]

It was sought to concretize the body of ideas and concepts comprising policy measures prescribed by the New International Economic Order in two areas,[8] one of which was human rights.[9] This attempt did not meet easy success, as will be seen later. In the area of human rights, the idea or concept of a 'right to development' was born. The formulation of *'droit au développement'* is traditionally attributed to Keba M'baye, however the concept existed much earlier than the terminology.[10] Reference to the idea was already made in the Declaration of Philadelphia (Concerning the Aims and Purposes of the ILO) of 10 May 1944. It was also planned to become part of the UDHR, but ultimately did not find its way into the Declaration as adopted.

Ascribing the emergence of the notion solely to the claims of the developing countries would, though, be too restrictive.[11] Other factors played an important role. Namely, the distinction prevalent at the time between economic, social and cultural rights on the one hand, and civil and political rights on the other, made a significant contribution in the formation of the right to development.[12] Another important factor in constructing the genesis of the right to development is the continued persistence in limiting human rights obligations within the confines of national borders, considered by some as a failure to recognize the international dimension of human rights obligations.[13] The doctrine explains that conceptually the origins of the formation of a right to development can be traced back to the two streams of work at the heart of the UN, one of which, in the early days of the

---

7 *Ibid.,* p. 11.
8 However, the introduction of an equity factor did not happen in a systematic and integrated manner. Special treatment in terms of transfer of resources was not deemed sufficient, and in the view of the Third World countries, the entire system of rules needed to be changed. As illustrated in Chapter II, efforts to address issues of development in the framework of the international economic institutions did not succeed.
9 A. Cassese, *International Law in a Divided World*, Clarendon Press: 1986, p. 368
10 K. M'Baye, 'Le droit au développement comme un droit de l'homme', 5 *Revue des droits de l'homme* (1972), pp. 503–534.
11 See generally R. Rich, 'The Right to Development as an Emerging Human Right', 23 *Virginia Journal of International Law* (1982–1983), pp. 287–328; A. Sengupta, 'The Human Right to Development', in B.A. Andreassen and S.P. Marks (eds), *Development as a Human Right: Legal, Political and Economic Dimensions*, Intersentia: 2010, p. 13.
12 P. Alston, 'Revitalising United Nations Work on Human Rights and Development', *op. cit.*, pp. 218–219.
13 Alston made the following suggestion in framing the debate on the right to development: 'Thus, it is only in the light of growing recognition of the need for (1) more attention to economic rights, (2) greater recognition of the international implications of a national commitment to human rights and (3) a less atomistic approach, that the full significance of the right to development can be appreciated.' P. Alston, 'Shortcomings of a Garfield the Cat Approach to the Right to Development', 15 *California Western International Law Journal* (1985), p. 516. See also P. Alston, 'Revitalising United Nations Work on Human Rights and Development', *op. cit.*, p. 220.

institution, focused on developing the normative landscape of human rights.[14] The elaboration of human rights in two covenants, according to Abi-Saab,

> témoignent d'une approche formelle, purement normativiste, atomiste et procédurale des droits de l'homme. Il s'agit de standards de traitement, définis abstraitement, qui constituent des droits pour les individus et des obligations de faire, mais surtout de ne pas faire, à la charge des gouvernement, et dont le respect ou la violation se constate en mesurant chaque comportement par ces standards abstraits, pris isolément, et *en faisant abstraction du contexte global environnant.*[15]

Although the UN Charter's well-known provisions set a broader context and link the promotion of human rights with peace and economic and social progress, it is the Covenant on Economic, Social and Cultural Rights and its subsequent interpretations that are more explicit in making development a *conditio sine qua non* for socio-economic human rights. In this sense, the Covenant takes into account the context, by integrating economic conditionality under Article 2(1). However, 'cette prise en considération des conditions environnantes a pour but, limité, de placer le niveau de la prestation sur une échelle variable, en fonction des capacités matérielles des gouvernements, et non pas de peser sur les facteurs positifs et négatifs qui déterminent ces capacités'.[16]

Indeed, Article 2(1) of the Covenant inserts a degree of differentiation in terms of obligations, by linking the obligations of states to realize the rights embedded in the treaty by taking steps 'to the maximum available resources', with their implementation 'through international assistance and cooperation'.[17] At the same time, it is not clear how Article 2(1), despite some indications given by the Committee on Economic, Social and Cultural Rights, resolves the issue of a state's capacity to fulfil the human rights of persons under its jurisdiction in view of the dramatic impact external economic processes have on national efforts.[18]

Situating human rights in a broader context led to the formulation of express linkages between the economic development and human rights. The 1968

---

14 G. Abi-Saab, 'Le droit au développement', *op. cit.*, p. 11; P. Alston, 'Making Space for New Human Rights: The Case of the Right to Development', 1 *Harvard Human Rights Yearbook* (1988), p. 8; P. Alston, 'Human Rights and the New International Development Strategy', 10(3) *Bulletin of Peace Proposals* (1979), pp. 281–290.
15 G. Abi-Saab, 'Le droit au développement', *op. cit.*, p. 11 (emphasis added).
16 *Ibid.*
17 See *inter alia* the Convention on the Rights of a Child, Convention on the Rights of Persons with Disabilities.
18 See Chapter VI. Only recently, the doctrine of the socio-economic rights has started to read within the notion of 'maximum available resources' the question of economic capacity situated within the broader global economic context. M. Dowell Jones, *Contextualising the International Covenant on Economic, Social and Cultural Rights: Assessing the Economic Deficit*, Martinus Nijhoff Publishers: 2004.

Proclamation of Teheran declared that '[t]he achievement of lasting progress in the implementation of human rights is dependent upon sound and effective national and international policies of economic and social development',[19] characterizing a structural approach and going beyond the normative aspects in dealing with human rights problems.[20] Realization of human rights was placed in the context of peace, self-determination of peoples, and development.

This consideration of structural aspects of the enjoyment of human rights became the second stream of thinking that eventually led to the formulation of the concept of the right to development, and also to the awareness and recognition of moving beyond normative articulation to practical implementation of human rights. In the debates of the ILA, it was mentioned that the right to development 'constitutes, therefore, an opportunity for a conceptual overcoming of the artificial division between human rights and economic and social development'[21] and that realization of human rights through principles as reflected in the NIEO, 'gives the area of human rights a new dynamism – and above all makes this subject much more realistic'.[22]

More concrete elements of the right to development can be already traced in the Declaration on Social Progress and Development proclaimed by UN GA Resolution 24/2542 of 11 December 1969. The UN General Assembly's Report of the Secretary-General on the International Dimension of the Right to Development as a Human Right of 1969 called for: 'promotion of respect for human rights in general including the human right to development . . . [which] . . . should be part of a new international development strategy'. The concept itself was formally endorsed by the Human Rights Commission in its Resolution 4(XXXIII) of 1977[23] and was soon after included in two declarations, the Declaration on the Preparation of Societies for Life in Peace, adopted as General Assembly Resolution 33/73, and the UNESCO Declaration on Race and Racial Prejudice. Following that resolution, the Secretary-General issued a Report on the International Dimension of the Right to Development as a Human Right.[24]

---

19 Proclamation of Teheran, Final Act of the International Conference on Human Rights, Tehran, 22 April to 13 May 1968, UN Doc. A/CONF. 32/41 at 3 (1968), para. 13.
20 G. Abi-Saab, 'Le droit au développement', *op. cit.*, p. 12.
21 ILA, Report of the Sixty-First Conference, 61 *International Law Association Reports of Conferences*, para. 142.
22 *Ibid.*
23 Commission on Human Rights, Report on the Thirty-Third Session, 62 UN ESCOR Supp. (No. 6), UN doc. E/5927 (1978), para. 4, which stipulated: '*Recommends* to the Economic and Social Council to invite the Secretary-General, in cooperation with UNESCO and the other competent specialized agencies, to undertake a study on "The international dimensions of the right to development as a human right in relation with other human rights based on international cooperation, including the right to peace, taking into account the requirements of the New International Economic Order and the fundamental human needs".' The resolution called for study to be made available for consideration by the Commission on Human Rights at its 35th session.
24 Report of the Secretary-General, The International Dimensions of the Right to Development as a Human Right in relation with other Human Rights based on International Cooperation,

The Commission on Human Rights reiterated that the right to development is a human right in Resolution 5 (XXXV) of 2 March 1979.

The UN General Assembly recognized the right to development in Resolution 34/46 on 23 November 1979, under the title 'Alternative approaches and ways and means within the United Nations system for improvising the effective enjoyment of human rights and fundamental freedoms'. The right to development was subsequently reiterated and discussed in successive resolutions of both the Commission and the General Assembly. Initially, a degree of convergence on some basic tenets of the concept was sought, but by the time the actual drafting of the Declaration commenced in the Commission, the political and ideological climate was not conducive to producing a consensus on the outcome.[25] The existence of the right culminated with the proclamation of the Declaration on the Right to Development (DRD) in UN General Assembly Resolution 41/128 of 4 December 1986. The right to development found further recognition in the 1993 World Conference on Human Rights.[26] While the right may have received political recognition, the same cannot be said to apply to its legal value and content.[27]

2 The right to development: A contentious concept

To date, academic and intergovernmental processes have not achieved consensus on key issues, including the content of the right to development. Debate has revolved around the capacity of the concept to be integrated into international law, its foundation in international law, and its legitimacy, coherence and ability to be translated into concrete obligations. Other concerns include its 'juridical utility' (i.e. the added value of the concept within the confines of international

---

including the Right to Peace, taking into account the Requirements of the New International Economic Order and the Fundamental Human Needs, UN doc. E/CN.4/1334, 2 January 1979.

25 'While it would be both inaccurate and unfair to lay all of the blame for the controversy that surrounded the Working Group's negotiations at the door of the Reagan Administration, its coming to office was nevertheless one of the key factors in shaping the 1980s debate over the right to development. Other factors were also important. They included: the enthusiasm with which the Eastern Europeans embraced the concept – thus adding an overlay of East–West rivalry to existing North–South tensions; the increased East–West antipathy in response to the suppression of the Solidarity trade union movement in Poland; the worldwide recession of the early 1980s; the escalating Third World debt crisis; and the generally poor international relations climate, in which human rights initiatives were, almost by definition, contentious.' P. Alston, 'Revitalising United Nations Work on Human Rights and Development', *op. cit.*, pp. 219–220.

26 UN GA, Vienna Declaration and Programme of Action, UN doc. A/CONF.157/23, 12 July 1993, paras. 10, 11, 72, 73.

27 According to Abi-Saab, the Declaration on the Right to Development 'loin d'être une transcription juridique complète et cohérente du droit au développement, n'énonce – un consensus oblige- qu'une série fragmentaire et non structurée de propositions, portent avantage sur le thème des "droits de l'homme dans le processus du développement" que sur le droit au développement en tant que tel, et laisse sans réponse les questions conceptuelles et techniques les épineuse soulevées par ce droit'. G. Abi-Saab, 'Le droit au développement', *op. cit.*, p. 13.

law) and what is, was, or will be its course from the world of ideas and social values towards that of law.[28] More recently, however, critical questions have centred on the practicality of the original concept in the current economic conditions, as manifested by an integrated market, a multiplicity of actors and privatization of the development paradigm itself.[29]

The concept gives rise to a number of controversies. Politically, the concept was not acceptable to some, as it placed responsibility for the problems of the development at the international level. The focus of the Declaration on the Right to Development on 'effective cooperation' in providing developing countries 'with appropriate means and facilities to foster their comprehensive development' was clearly seen as an obligation for resource transfers.[30] Given the potential inter-state implications of the right to development, industrialized states did not support the juridical existence of the right to development in the first place and, even if it did exist, then only in an individual dimension. This meant that it was nothing but a synthesis of the existing socio-economic and civil and political rights.[31] In this case, these rights: 'ne dépend pas de préalables tels qu'un NOEI, et qui trouve sa justification dans la même impérative moral que les autres droits de l'homme'.[32] Developing countries, in contrast, took a contrary position, asserting the collective dimension of a right to development which depended on the rule of law in international economic relations, hence the emphasis on the obligations of the international community.

If, for developed states, it was (and is) aspects such as an obligation to provide development aid, as well as broader reforms needed in the international economy, that made the concept as a whole barely acceptable to them, in academic circles great scepticism was expressed as to the legal foundation of the concept.[33] The main argument advanced was that there is no 'solid' legal ground on which a right to development can be based. In effect, the right to development does not have any formal legal status. Rather, the Declaration on the Right to Development draws its constituent components from the provisions of the UN Charter and the ICESCR. In sum, it provides a framework for interpretation of 'development-oriented rights provisions of both covenants [ICCPR and

28 *Ibid.*, p. 10.
29 See U. Baxi, 'Normative Content of a Treaty as Opposed to the Declaration on the Right to Development: Marginal Observations', *op. cit.*, p. 47–52.
30 Article 4(2), Declaration on the Right to Development.
31 It is interesting to note that for Socialist countries, the Right to Development also signified a collective right; however, when it came to specific commitment in terms of legally binding obligation to support developing countries in their economic endeavours, the Socialist countries denied such an obligation on the basis that it only applied to those industrialized countries with colonial past and that such an obligation would be based on the one related to reparation for colonial damage.
32 G. Abi-Saab, 'Le droit au développement', *op. cit.*, p. 13.
33 See for a comprehensive critique J. Donnelly, 'In Search of the Unicorn: The Jurisprudence and Politics of the Right to Development', *op. cit.*; Y. Ghai, 'Human Rights and Governance: The Asia Debate', 15 *Australia Yearbook of International Law* (1994).

ICESCR]', none of which refers to the right as such explicitly.[34] The question is how the right to development can be legally conceptualized.

The issue covers a wide range of opinions. At one end of the spectrum, there are scholars who are deeply sceptical at a theoretical level as to whether it is adequate to transpose a 'human rights' framework into the area of development.[35] In the opinion of Cassese, for example, 'the need to impose upon industrialized countries the duty to promote the economic advancement of poor nations' from a human rights perspective is wrong, as the right to development is not susceptible to translation into legal terms as a human right.[36] As a right, development could only benefit states. His position is that the right in question can only be a right of developing states. As such, instead of trying to translate development concerns through human rights, focus needed to be on translation of the principles of the NIEO into binding rules, thus 'turning the principle of cooperation, in its significance as "postulate of international solidarity", into operational standards of behaviour'. Donnelly also found that the right to development was misleading at the conceptual level. In his view, proponents of the right confused two different ideas: a right and righteousness. Importantly, he asserted that 'a right-holder is not merely a passive beneficiary of someone else's obligation, but an active participant in a relationship that in large measure he controls'.[37]

Nearer the middle of the spectrum, a second category of thought proposes defining the right to development within the confines of the traditional human rights paradigm. In this view, the right to development 'remains squarely within mainstream thinking of international human rights law'.[38] The existence and value-added of the right to development are assessed against basic mainstream human rights' premises, such as the individualism of human rights, understood as rights claimed against the nation state. In this conception, the substance of the concept is no different from the sum of existing civil and political, and social, economic and cultural rights. One of the advantages of this modest form of the concept is political acceptability. However, it raises questions as to its utility from a legal point of view.

---

34 B. Ibhawoh, 'The Right to Development: The Politics and Polemics of Power and Resistance', 33(1) *Human Rights Quarterly* (2011), pp. 76–104, p. 82.

35 Rosas stated: 'The right to development should, perhaps, be seen as an umbrella concept and programme rather than a specific human right.' A. Rosas, 'The Right to Development', in A. Eide, C. Krause and A. Rosas (eds), *Economic, Social and Cultural Rights. A Textbook*, Martinus Nijhoff Publishers: 1995, pp. 254–255; P. de Waart proposed: 'The ongoing discussion on the right to development shows that indeed the term principle is more appropriate. There is no question of an absolute legal State right or human right to development.' P. de Waart, 'State Rights and Human Rights as Two Sides of One Principle of International Law: the Right to Development', in P. de Waart, P. Peters and E. Denters (eds), *International Law and Development*, Martinus Nijhoff Publishers: 1988, p. 397.

36 A. Cassese, *International Law in a Divided World*, Clarendon Press: 1986, p. 369.

37 J. Donnelly, 'In Search of the Unicorn: The Jurisprudence and Politics of the Right to Development' *op. cit.*, p. 490.

38 W. Vandenhole, 'The Human Right to Development as a Paradox', 36(3) *Verfassung und Recht in Übersee. Law and Politics in Africa, Asia and Latin America* (2003), pp. 377–404, p. 380.

Finally, at the other end of the spectrum, there are authors who regard the right to development expansively. In this vision, the right encompasses different metrics under one umbrella concept. First, it integrates into the equation the international dimension of human rights obligations, enlarging the circle of duty-bearers beyond the state primarily responsible for human rights. Second, and related to the first, is the all-encompassing nature of right to development that includes realization of a full set of human rights 'as an integrated whole',[39] but also in this notion 'the operational space covered by the right is vast, potentially encompassing all of national and international economic and social policy on the one hand and all of international human rights standards and practice on the other'.[40] The right to development in this form casts more broadly and sharply in terms of subjects and content. Legally innovative in this form, the right can hardly be acceptable at political level.[41] There is no settled view on these questions. To answer the question as to how to legally construct the right to development, it is necessary to look at its basic elements such as the subjects (holders of rights and obligations) and the content.

3 Basic elements of the right to development

3.1 Subjects of the right to development

The question of who are active and passive subjects of the right to development does not seem to draw much attention in contemporary academic literature.[42] This approach in the UN intergovernmental fora is understandable on the basis

---

39 See A. Sengupta, Independent Expert on Right to Development, First report: UN doc. E/CN.4/1999/WG.18/2, 27 July 1999; Second report: UN doc. A/55/306, 17 August 2000; Third report: UN doc. E/ CN.4/2001/WG.18/2, 2 January 2001; Fourth report: UN doc. E/CN.4/2002/WG.18/2, 2 March 2002; Fifth report: UN doc. E/CN.4/2002/WG.18/6, 16 September 2002; Sixth report: UN doc. E/CN.4/2004/WG.18/2, 17 February 2004; Country study: UN doc. E/CN.4/2004/WG.18/3, 23 January 2004, and the Preliminary study UN doc. E/CN.4/2003/WG.18/2, 27 January 2003. See also S. Osmani, who suggests that 'the right to development is the right of everyone to enjoy the full array of socio-economic-cultural rights as well as civil-political rights equitably and sustainably and through a process that satisfies the principle of participation, non-discrimination, transparency, and accountability'. S. Osmani, 'Some Thoughts on the Right to Development', in Franciscans International, *The Right to Development: Reflections on the Right to Development – Reflections on the First Four Reports of the Independent Expert on the Right to Development*, Franciscans International: 2003, pp. 34–45.
40 M. Green and S. Randolph, Consultant report – Right to development criteria and corresponding operational sub-criteria (Bringing Theory into Practice: Operational Criteria for Assessing Implementation of the International Right to Development), UN doc. A/HRC/15/WG.2/TF/CRP.5, 14 January 2010, para. 60.
41 W. Vandenhole, 'The Human Right to Development as a Paradox', *op. cit.*, pp. 377–404.
42 Nowadays the issue is placed under the rubric of 'general principles of implementation'. For that reason, one gets an impression of its rather lesser degree of importance to the substance of the debate. Much focus is instead on the 'specific normative content' of the right. See e.g. M. Green and S. Randolph, Consultant report – Right to development criteria and corresponding operational sub-criteria, *op. cit.*, pp. 17–18.

that the issue of 'duty-bearers' is a subject of difficult negotiation and strong political undertones. It is suggested here to proceed with the classical analysis, as it illustrates important nuances of the entire concept.

The subjects of the right to development vary, depending on which dimension of the right is being invoked: individual or collective. In its individual dimension, the right to development is nothing more than a synthesis of all existing human rights: civil and political, as well as economic, social and cultural rights. Conceived of as an individual human right, the right to development does not result in controversies as to its passive and active subjects or its content. Even if it is considered as a right of an individual to develop, the point of reference is still human rights, as the specific legal criteria of what personal development might entail can only be sought in human rights standards.[43] On this ground, it is questioned whether, as a purely individual right (e.g. an aggregate of all existing human rights), the right to development offers any added value.[44]

Since the very nature of underdevelopment is underpinned by 'structural phenomenon linked to a given model of international economic order', and 'negative effects of the international factors', a collective approach for solutions is required.[45] According to Abi-Saab, some legal substance can be inferred from the right to development if it is regarded as a collective right.[46] In effect, the entire debate on the collective dimension of the right to development is closely linked with the issue of the external dimension of the concept, i.e. all provisions related to issues going beyond the jurisdiction of the state concerned.

Taken as a collective right, the passive subject of the right, i.e. its beneficiary, is the collectivity. In the context of the right to development, the distinction between people and the state is less visible than with the right to self-determination. On the international plane, such a collectivity is represented by a state that meets the criteria of being in need, i.e. by extension a developing country. By this logic, who else at the international level would claim the right to development on behalf of peoples, other than a state? Here, the state serves as a *relais* between the international community and an individual. In this case, the most immediate identifiable subject bearing duties is the international community as a whole, in particular those of its members that are in possession of means to achieve development.

43 Compare with Articles 22, 26, and 29, UDHR.
44 On the other hand, some authors do not seem to have a problem with the version of right to development as a synthesis right as '[it] helps to emphasize the dynamism of existing rights'. P. Alston, *Development and Rule of Law: Prevention versus Cure as a Human Rights Strategy*, International Commission of Jurists: 1981, p. 104.
45 M. Bedjaoui, 'Some Unorthodox Reflections on "the Right to Development"', in Snyder F. and Slinn P. (eds), *International Law of Development: Comparative Perspectives*, Professional Books: 1987, pp. 90–92.
46 In other words, we can 'consider the right to development as the aggregate of the social, economic and cultural rights not of each individual, but of all the individuals constituting a collectivity'. G. Abi-Saab, 'The Legal Formulation of the Right to Development', in R-J Dupuy (ed.), *The Right to Development at the International Level*, The Hague Academy of International Law: 1980, p. 164.

But how do we make sure that the benefits of measures to promote development reach the individuals and not political and economic elites of the developing countries?[47] This link to translating measures aiming to ensure peoples their right to development into the right of individuals to benefit from basic social services is what Abi-Saab calls the 'chaînon manquant' that could serve the purpose of 'transformateur ou desagregateur du droit collectif en plus de prestations individuelles'.[48] Put in these terms, the utility of recognition of a right to development as an individual right becomes apparent. Thus, the right to development is both a collective right and an individual right: 'il s'agit d'un droit collectif à la finalité individuelle, d'un droit de l'homme au second degré'.[49] This missing link or 'interpreter' of a collective right to an individual one can be found in the Declaration on the Right to Development. The Declaration seems to have an inbuilt mechanism in the form of a requirement of a procedural nature, namely the principle of participation in development process.

Article 1(1) of the Declaration on the Right to Development defines the right to development as:

> The right to development is an inalienable human right by virtue of which every *human person* and all *peoples* are entitled to participate in, contribute to, and enjoy economic, social, cultural and political development, in which all human rights and fundamental freedoms can be fully realized.[50]

It appears that the text identifies the right to development as both an individual and collective right, i.e. its *version mixte*.[51] Nonetheless, there seems to be an array of different interpretations of the provision. For example, despite the lack of an explicit reference to states as subjects of the right to development, some authors mistakenly refer to Article 2(3) of the Declaration[52] as a basis for

47 According to Ghai, '[i]t is implied that economic development may well require restrictions on human rights, both to provide a secure political framework in which it can be pursued and to remove obstacles in its way'. By means of the right to development, 'Asian governments seek to promote the ideology of developmentalism which justifies repression at home and the evasion of responsibility abroad.' Y. Ghai, 'Human Rights and Governance: The Asia Debate', 15 *Australia Yearbook of International Law* (1994), pp. 9–10.
48 G. Abi-Saab, 'Le droit au développement', *op. cit.*, p. 20.
49 *Ibid.*, p. 19.
50 Emphasis added.
51 The UN Report (1979) stated: 'It would be a mistake, however, to view the right to development as necessarily attaching only at one level or the other. Indeed there seems no reason to assume that the interests of the individuals and those of the collectivist will necessarily be in conflict.' Report of the Secretary-General, The International Dimensions of the Right to Development as a Human Right in relation with other Human Rights based on International Cooperation, including the Right to Peace, taking into account the Requirements of the New International Economic Order and the Fundamental Human Needs, *op. cit.*, 2 January 1979, para. 85.
52 Article 2(3) stipulates: 'States have the right and the duty to formulate appropriate national development policies that aim at the constant improvement of the well-being of the entire

considering the right to development as the right of states.[53] Such a meaning has been attached to the concept mainly in light of the claims of developing states during the heyday of the redistributionist claims under the NIEO. A closer reading of the provision reveals that nowhere does it contain a reference to a right as such.

Instead, it merely specifies that states have a right and a duty to formulate appropriate national development policies with a view to facilitating implementation of the right to development, but not a right to development as defined in Article 1(1). Here, in the provision as well as in the rest of the Declaration, references to states are made in the context of their various obligations only. Even where the following paragraph of Article 4(2) recognizes the special character of developing countries, by requiring 'sustained action' to promote their more rapid development, the formulation avoids the usage of a right granted to developing countries.[54] This interpretation of the right to development is therefore inconsistent with the Declaration. The right is articulated in much the same way as the right to self-determination, or the right to full sovereignty over natural wealth and resources – that is, as rights of peoples. The argument that the right to development gives entitlements to states can only be advanced through the notion of peoples as mentioned in the definition of the right.

For James Crawford, for example, the cumulative readings of relevant provisions of the Declaration 'stop short of stating that the right to development is a collective right, or a right of peoples'.[55] He points to differences of language between 'a human right to development' as articulated in Article 1(1) and the reference to two peoples' rights as provided in Article 1(2).[56] Although the right

---

population and of all individuals, on the basis of their active, free and meaningful participation in development and in the fair distribution of the benefits resulting therefrom.'

53 See e.g. A. Orford, 'Globalization and the Right to Development', *op. cit.*, p. 137. Some authors conclude that 'an analysis of the *travaux préparatoires* and the Declaration itself leaves no doubt that the State is a subject of the right to development'. Assistance to such an interpretation has been found in the preamble of the Declaration which states that 'equality of opportunity for development is a prerogative both of nations and of individuals who make up nations'. See M.M. Kenig-Witkowska, 'The UN Declaration on the Right to Development in Light of Its Travaux Preparatoires', in P. J.I.M. de Waart, Paul Peters and Erik Denters (eds), *International law and development*, Martinus Nijhoff Publishers: 1988, p. 382.

54 Article 4(2) of DRD: 'Sustained action is required to promote more rapid development of developing countries. As a complement to the efforts of developing countries, effective international cooperation is essential in providing these countries with appropriate means and facilities to foster their comprehensive development.' M.M. Kenig-Witkowska, 'The UN Declaration on the Right to Development in Light of Its Travaux Preparatoires', *op. cit.*, p. 382.

55 J. Crawford, 'The Rights of Peoples: "Peoples" or "Governments"?' in J. Crawford (ed.), *The Rights of Peoples*, Clarendon Press: 1988, p. 55 text of footnote 20.

56 Article 1(2) of the DRD states: 'The human right to development also implies the full realization of the right of peoples to self-determination, which includes, subject to the relevant provisions of both International Covenants on Human Rights, the exercise of their inalienable right to full sovereignty over all their natural wealth and resources.'

to development is linked further with the rights of peoples in Article 5,[57] Crawford concludes that the rest of the text reveals no implication that development is a collective or peoples' right.[58] Since, in the context of development, collective rights of peoples are coextensive with states' rights (although this point is also arguable), and given that '[s]o far as States are concerned, the notion that "peoples" have a right to development does not appear to differ from the proposition that States have such a right', Crawford concludes that the Declaration limits itself to recognizing only the individual dimension of the right.

One cannot dismiss the interpretation of Crawford lightly, not only from an analytical point of view, but also from the perspective of current debates. As already conceded, the formulations are too vague and too complex to supply any straightforward answer. The definition of the right as supplied by Article 1(1) recognizes peoples as subjects entitled to development. Yet, one cannot help but notice that the Vienna Declaration, as adopted by the World Conference on Human Rights, and which is often quoted as a source for global endorsement of the right,[59] omits any reference to *peoples* in the context of the right to development.[60]

The question whether the right to development concept retains its collective dimension cannot be answered in isolation from consideration of the place of 'peoples' rights' in general in international law. The right to development not only shares the general feature of a peoples' right to self-determination, but is regarded otherwise as its key element, 'built-in' and 'inextricably enshrined' in the right to self-determination.[61]

---

57 Article 5 of the DRD: 'States shall take resolute steps to eliminate the massive and flagrant violations of the human rights of peoples and human beings affected by situations such as those resulting from apartheid, all forms of racism and racial discrimination, colonialism, foreign interference and threats against national sovereignty, national unity and territorial integrity, threats of war and refusal to recognize the fundamental right of peoples to self-determination.'

58 J. Crawford, 'The Rights of Peoples: "Peoples" or "Governments"?', *op. cit.*, p. 55, note 20.

59 The Vienna Declaration is a major point of reference to infer on the existence of a consensus on the right to development, by virtue of its support by virtually all states, both from developing and developed countries, including the US.

60 Paragraph 10 of the Vienna Declaration proclaims: 'The World Conference on Human Rights reaffirms the right to development, as established in the Declaration on the Right to Development, as a universal and inalienable right and an integral part of fundamental human rights', para. 10. B. Rudolf who argues that 'this wording cannot be interpreted as ruling out a collective dimension for two reasons. First, the Vienna Declaration speaks of a "universal and inalienable right," thus does not limit it to individuals. Second, it considers the RTD as an integral part of "human rights," and it is generally recognized that this category not only encompasses individual rights, but also collective rights.' B. Rudolf, 'The Relation of the Right to Development to Existing Substantive Treaty Regimes', in S. Marks, *Implementing the Right to Development: the Role of International Law*, Friedrich Ebert Stiftung: 2008, p. 108.

61 More specifically, 'right of every nation to freely adopt its own economic and social system, without outside interference or compulsion of any kind, and to choose its own development model with the same degree of freedom, a right to development a sine qua non of the sovereignty'. *Ibid.*, p. 94.

From this perspective, a crucial point is in order. There is an overall trend indicative of a change in the perception of human rights with collective dimensions. In particular, in the context of the right to self-determination, '[t]he balance began to swing in relation to the long-standing distinction between internal and external self-determination, in favour of the former, although not in the way that might have been expected'.[62] Outside the context of decolonization, the modern conception of the right to self-determination concentrates on the internal dimension, which is expressed in the notions of the 'right to democratic governance' within a nation state.[63]

This overall trend has also influenced the debates on the collective dimension of the right to development. Generally, the collective dimension is not brought sharp into the open in the debates over the right in intergovernmental fora:

> while the discourse of peoples' rights continues to thrive in a few settings, the situation in both law and practice today, is characterized by a systematic reluctance on the part of the governments to attach any significance to this dimension of human rights. This might not be unduly problematic were it not for the fact that most other actors in human rights field have also adopted a comparable approach.[64]

It is highlighted that 'the prospect of this particular peoples' right seem to depend significantly on eliminating for practical purposes the collective rights dimension and of defining the concept in such a way that it blends seamless into mainstream human rights analysis'.[65] Notably, if within the self-determination debate the inclination towards the internal dimension of the right manifested itself in greater support for a right to democratic governance in the context of a right to development, a similar trend is manifested in greater emphasis on the rule of law, transparency, corruption and accountability – all issues concerning the proper functioning of state apparatus. But a conception of human rights 'which has banished all dimensions of group and peoples' rights will be a greatly impoverished one and one which is ill-equipped to deal with some of the major challenges that are certain to confront it in the years ahead'.[66]

Paradoxically, in the current context of interdependence, responsibility for questions of development is located within a state, rather the opposite to an assumption promulgated in the early days of the right to development movement.

62 P. Alston, 'The Peoples' Rights: Their Rise and Fall', in P. Alston (ed.), *Peoples' Rights*, OUP: 2005, pp. 270, 289.
63 T.M. Franck, 'The Emerging Right to Democratic Governance', 86 *American Journal of International Law* (1992), pp. 46–91; T. Van Boven, 'Is There an Emerging Right to Good Governance?', 3 *Netherlands Quarterly on Human Rights* (1995), pp. 304–310, p. 304.
64 P. Alston, 'The Peoples' Rights: Their Rise and Fall', *op. cit.*, p. 289.
65 *Ibid.*, p. 283.
66 *Ibid.*, p. 292.

3.2 The content of the right to development

The text of the Declaration on the Right to Development does not unequivocally specify obligations flowing from the right to development. In literature, the following elements of the concept of the right to development seem to have solicited a general acceptance: the individual or human person is the centre of development;[67] development is a particular process aiming for the full realization of all human rights (e.g. civil and political, and economic and social);[68] participation as a key principle,[69] with an emphasis on the duty of states to ensure participation of women;[70] the requirement that development contributes to social justice;[71] and that development presupposes structural conditions both at national and at international levels.

Some of these elements, such as participation, a human-centric vision of development, and development as a process based on human rights *grosso modo*, are less contested than others and have acquired following in practice, sometimes in the form of human rights-based approaches, as we saw in Chapter II. In this section, it is suggested to analyse in detail three particular elements of the right to development: as a right to a particular process and result, the international dimension of the right, and, finally, the definition of development it provides.

3.2.1 Right to development as a right to a particular process

The Declaration requires that the development process should be respectful of human rights and be a process in which all human rights and fundamental freedoms are realized.[72] Failure to observe human rights, both civil and political, and economic, social and cultural, constitutes an obstacle to development.[73] Drawing

---

67 According to Article 2, the human person is the central subject of development and should be the active participant and beneficiary of the right to development.
68 The Declaration also attempts to negate the traditional division between civil and political on one hand and economic, social and cultural rights on the other. The concept considers all human rights as indivisible and interdependent.
69 Article 1(1) (cited above); Article 2(3): 'States have the right and the duty to formulate appropriate national development policies that aim at the constant improvement of the well-being of the entire population and of all individuals, on the basis of their active, free and meaningful participation in development', and Article 8(2): 'States should encourage popular participation in all spheres as an important factor in development and in the full realization of all human rights.'
70 Article 8(1): 'Effective measures should be undertaken to ensure that women have an active role in the development process.'
71 Article 8(1) refers to appropriate economic and social reforms to be carried out with a view to eradicating all social injustices. The Declaration also refers to 'fair distribution of benefits' of development for individuals (Article 2(3), including equality of opportunity for all in their access to basic resources, education, health services, food, housing, employment and the fair distribution of income (Article 8(1)).
72 Article 1(1), DRD.
73 Article 6(3) of the DRD states: 'States should take steps to eliminate obstacles to development resulting from failure to observe civil and political rights, as well as economic, social and cultural rights.'

on his reports, Arjun Sengupta, the former Independent Expert on the Right to Development, provided the following definition of the right to development, which according to him is based on different articles of the DRD, namely Article 1 and the Preamble (defining development):[74]

> The Right to Development, which is an inalienable human right, is the right to a particular process of development in which all human rights and fundamental freedoms can be fully and progressively realized.

Underlining that development according to the DRD is a complex process and includes non-economic parameters, the Independent Expert reminds us that the process of development should be participatory, with a fair and equal distribution, these two elements constituting the core of a rights-based approach.[75] Five principles characterize rights-based development – equity, non-discrimination, participation, accountability and transparency – 'all of which contribute to making the process consistent with human rights'.[76] These principles have been internalized by most of the development agencies as part of their governance agenda.[77]

It follows from the reasoning of the former Independent Expert that the right to development is a right to a particular process of economic, social, cultural and political development, in which all human rights and fundamental freedoms can be fully realized. However, he maintains that rights-based development is not coextensive with the right to development.[78] The difference in his view is that when a rights-based process can be claimed as a right, it can be and is the object of a right to development: '[i]t would follow from Article 1 of the Declaration that, among the different rights-based processes which "aims at and realizes all human rights and fundamental freedoms" qualifies to be regarded as the object of claim as the right to development'.[79] One has to agree with Alston's

---

74 Paragraph 2 of Preamble of Declaration on the Right to Development states: 'Recognizing that development is a comprehensive economic, social, cultural and political process, which aims at the constant improvement of the well-being of the entire population and of all individuals on the basis of their active, free and meaningful participation in development and in the fair distribution of benefits resulting therefrom.'
75 A. Sengupta, 'The Human Right to Development', *op. cit.*, p. 16.
76 *Ibid.*
77 References in Chapter II were made to the new aid modalities, one of which includes the principle of partnership. According to this approach, developed and developing countries have shared responsibilities and mutual commitments towards each other on the issues of development. However, this partnership does not consider either human rights as a centre of development process nor does it recognize development as a human right. L.H. Piron, *The Right to Development: A Review of the Current State of the Debate*, ODI: 2002.
78 Sengupta states: 'However, the human rights approach to development is not the same thing as realizing the right to development.' Report of the independent expert on the right to development, Arjun Sengupta, pursuant to General Assembly Resolution 54/175 and Commission on Human Rights Resolution 2000/5, UN doc. A/55/306, 17 August 2000, para. 21.
79 A. Sengupta, 'The Human Right to Development', *op. cit.*, p. 16.

assessment that 'his analysis seems to tie them [rights-based development and right to development] together to the point where the distinction between them becomes rather difficult to maintain'.[80]

It is suggested here that the reading of Articles 1 and 6 of the DRD can, in effect, be said to represent an explicit pronouncement of a legal requirement according to which the development process would be regulated by human rights norms. All development interventions would have to go beyond the confines of econometrics focused on the economic growth and follow the priorities set by human rights.[81] This interpretation has been followed by the UNDP, which has relied upon the right to development as a legal framework for integrating human rights in the development process. The discourse on rights-based approaches would move beyond the question of added value (instrumentality) of human rights towards an intrinsic conception of human rights in the development process.

3.2.2 *International dimension of the right to development (ensuring an enabling environment at the international level)*

The tapestry of development in any given country consists of diverse threads of national and international origin. It is, therefore, difficult to detach the national context from the international one.[82] Globalization has, of course, contributed to blurring the distinction between the two.[83] As a result, creating conditions conducive to the realization of the right to development only at national level are not sufficient in themselves to achieve development. Such a conception has been supported by development and economic theories. For example, development theories have singled out categories of obstacles to development, or put forward 'enabling factors' involving international support measures, such as (i) aid, debt, technology transfers, (ii) international trade regime, (iii) asymmetries in global governance, in particular as regards multilateral financial and monetary institutions, and (iv) broader issues related to peace, security and disarmament.[84] These potentially umbrella categories have been reflected in the Declaration, which proposes a range of relevant duties/measures.

---

80 P. Alston, 'The Peoples' Rights: Their Rise and Fall', *op. cit.*, p. 285.

81 B. Rudolf, 'The Relation of the Right to Development to Existing Substantive Treaty Regimes', *op. cit.*, p.107.

82 The Report of the Secretary General also draws attention to: 'In view of growing inter-relationship between "national" and "international" aspects of development it may not always be possible to draw a workable distinction between what constitutes the "international" as opposed to the "national" dimensions of particular issues.' Report of the Secretary-General, The International Dimensions of the Right to Development as a Human Right in relation with other Human Rights based on International Cooperation, including the Right to Peace, taking into account the Requirements of the New International Economic Order and the Fundamental Human Needs, *op. cit.*, para. 37.

83 R. Malhotra, Implementing the Right to Development — A Review of the Task Force Criteria and Some Options, UN doc. A/HRC/12/WG.2/TF/CRP.6, para. 24.

84 *Ibid.*, para. 16.

The text of the DRD makes reference to, (i) full respect for the principles of international law concerning friendly relations and cooperation in accordance with the UN Charter,[85] (ii) the duty to create international conditions favourable to realization of right to development (Article 3(1)); (iii) the duty to cooperate to eliminate 'obstacles' to development (Article 3(3)); and (iv) the duty to take steps to formulate international development policies with a view to facilitating the right to development, which comprises a full range of rights recognized in international Covenants (Article 4(1)). Furthermore, Article 4(2) emphasizes *effective* international cooperation as essential, '[a]s a *complement* to the efforts of developing countries [and] in providing these countries with appropriate means and facilities to foster their comprehensive development'.[86]

Two further references to the international dimension of the duties are reflected in Article 6(1), which calls upon states to cooperate in promoting, encouraging and strengthening universal respect for human rights and fundamental freedoms for all, and Article 10, which calls for 'steps to ensure the full exercise and progressive enhancement of the right through the formulation, adoption and implementation of policy, legislative and other measures'.[87] These provisions provide, in a more or less detailed manner, an interpretation of what the concept of international assistance and cooperation would imply in relation to the fulfilment of human rights.

The provisions of the Declaration do not prescribe any specific course of action by which 'conditions conducive to the fulfilment of human person' are created. The Declaration employs the terminology of the time of its conclusion, i.e. efforts to establish a New International Economic Order as a supplement to international action to promote and protect human rights.[88] The 'bundle of policy measures' prescribed under the NIEO would proceed 'as a blueprint' for creating conditions necessary to realize the right to development.[89] Since, 'at each stage of the evolution of ideas we can identify certain policy measures over which there exists a large though not necessarily complete, consensus opinion as being the necessary conditions for achieving global development',[90] a present-day consensus can be found in the totality of the legal and policy measures discussed in

---

85 Very briefly, these principles include (i) prohibition of the use or threat or use of force against the territorial integrity or political independence of any State, (ii) peaceful settlement of disputes, (iii) principle of non-intervention in matters within the domestic jurisdiction of any State, in accordance with the Charter, (iv) the duty of States to co-operate with one another in accordance with the Charter, (v) the principle of equal rights and self-determination of peoples, (vi) the principle of sovereign equality of States, (vii) the principle that States shall fulfill in good faith the obligations assumed by them in accordance with the Charter.

86 Article 4(2), Declaration on the Right to Development.

87 Article 10, Declaration on the Right to Development.

88 A preambular paragraph proclaims: 'Aware that efforts at the international level to promote and protect human rights should be accompanied by efforts to establish a new international economic order.'

89 G. Abi-Saab, 'The Legal Formulation of the Right to Development', *op. cit.*, p. 167.

90 *Ibid,*. p. 164.

Chapter II. As noted earlier, many of the claims of developing states have been deradicalized subsequent to the NIEO movement, and the current project focusing on poverty eradication is far more consensual but does not generally question the underlying logic of the established international economic order.[91]

3.2.3 Definition of development

It is commonly agreed that development is 'multidimensional', 'a shifting concept' and generally 'an unsettled, or relative idea, varying according to the different societies to which it applies'.[92] But the question is what definition of development one can find in the context of the right to development. While remaining at the level of generality, the Declaration ties it closely to the human-centric definition of development, and essentially makes development itself a human right.[93]

This human-centric definition of development has undergone transformation, informed by growing understanding of the environmental concerns. Principle 3 of the Rio Declaration on Environment and Development (1992) adds a contextual nuance in that it stipulates that the right to development should be fulfilled in a way that equitably meets 'developmental and environmental needs of present and future generations'. From this point onwards, environmental concerns form an integral part of the development processes. Principle 5 of the Rio Declaration further specified that all states and all peoples 'shall cooperate in the essential task of eradicating poverty as an indispensable requirement for sustainable development, in order to decrease the disparities in standards of living and better meet the needs of the majority of the people of the world'.[94] Similarly, the Vienna Declaration links the right to development with sustainability.[95]

In a way, due to the global endorsement of development in its sustainable dimension and the emphasis of the sustainable development concept as an

---

91 In terms of policy measures required to attain the objective of poverty reduction, the consensus reached is reflected in the Monterrey Consensus on Financing for Development. The outcome produced six areas of financing for development, whereby the development cooperation is only one of the components: (i) mobilizing domestic financial resources; (ii) mobilizing international resources: foreign direct investment and private financial flows; (iii) international trade as an engine of development; (iv) increasing international financial and technical cooperation for development (ODA); (v) sustainable debt financing and external debt relief, and (vi) addressing the structural issues, namely enhancing the coherence and consistency of the international monetary, financial and trading systems.

92 A. Pellet, 'The Functions of the Right to Development: A Right to Self-Realisation', 3 *Third World Legal Studies* (1984), p. 129.

93 S. Marks, 'Human rights and Development', in Sarah Joseph and Adam McBeth (eds), *Research Handbook on International Human Rights Law*, Edward Elgar Publishing: 2010.

94 T. Karimova and C. Golay, 'Principle 5: Poverty Eradication', in J.E. Vinuales, *The Rio Declaraiton on Environment and Development: A Commentary*, OUP: 2015, pp. 181–206.

95 Paragraph 11 of the Vienna Declaration states: 'The right to development should be fulfilled so as to meet equitably the developmental and environmental needs of present and future generations.'

'essential task' of *poverty eradication*, one can conclude that the right to development and concomitant state obligations is reduced to the goal of reduction of poverty, as supported by state practice.[96] Reducing the scope of right to development to poverty reduction is, however, somewhat different from the content of the Declaration, which requires that the outcome of the development process must lead to realization of all human rights – economic, social, and cultural and civil and political rights.[97] The Declaration speaks of the duty 'to formulate appropriate national development policies that aim at the constant improvement of the well-being of the entire population and of all individuals'.[98] While there may not be major inconsistencies between the notion of constant improvement of well-being and poverty eradication or sustainable development, potential tensions between the two have not yet been adequately reflected.

4 Current debates and practical measures to implement the right to development

4.1 Measures to give binding force to the right to development

Lately, efforts in implementing the right to development included 'consideration of an international standard of a binding nature' with the support of Non-Aligned Movement (NAM) Member States.[99] First, the UN Commission on Human Rights, in its resolution 2003/83, requested the Sub-Commission on the Promotion and Protection of Human Rights to 'prepare a concept document establishing options for the implementation of the right to development and their feasibility, *inter alia*, an international legal standard of a binding nature . . . for submission to the Commission at its sixty-first session for consideration and determination of the feasibility of those options'.[100] The resolution was adopted with the support of 47 countries, with the negative votes of the US, Australia and Japan, and 12 abstentions.

The subsequent working paper did not substantially pursue the issue of the legally binding standard, noting, *inter alia*, 'strong differences of opinion among

---

96 See e.g. Principle 2 of the ILA New Delhi Declaration of Principles of International Law Relating to Sustainable Development, 2 April 2002, http://cisdl.org/tribunals/pdf/NewDelhiDeclaration.pdf.
97 See e.g. reports produced by the Independent Expert on the Right to Development, *op. cit.*
98 Article 2(3), DRD.
99 Final Document, 14th Summit Conference of Heads of State or Government of Non-Aligned Movement, Havana, Cuba, 11–16 September 2006, Doc. NAM2006/Doc.1/Rev.3 (16 September 2006). Subsequently reaffirmed in XV Summit of Heads of State and Government of the Non-Aligned Movement, Sharm el Sheikh, Egypt, 11–16 July 2009, Final Document, NAM2009/FD/Doc.1, 16 July 2009. See also the latest resolutions on the topic, including: UN GA Resolution 68/158, The right to development, UN doc. A/RES/68/158, 18 December 2013; UN GA Resolution 69/181, The right to development, UN A/RES/69/181, 18 December 2014.
100 Commission on Human Rights Resolution 2003/83: The Right to Development, UN doc. E/CN.4/RES/2003/8325 April 2003, para. 2.

legal luminaries as to whether the right to development can be placed within a legally binding framework' and that '[t]he view that human rights instruments address the obligations of a State to its citizens and not obligations between States seems to be in ascendancy'.[101] Instead, the author of the document suggested that '[i]n view of the ongoing discussions among duty bearers, partners and stakeholders, I am of the view that the successful identification of ways to infuse human rights values and principles into the development process would better serve the realization of the right'.[102] The concept document concluded that '[i]t would seem that the development of binding legal standards is premature at this time'.[103]

However, the UN Human Rights Council, in its resolutions 4/4 and 9/3, endorsed the work of the High-Level Task Force on the Implementation of the Right to Development (HLTF) to develop a set of criteria for the periodic evaluation of global partnerships as identified in Millennium Development Goal 8. It noted that 'the above criteria, once considered, revised and endorsed by the Working Group, should be used, as appropriate, in the elaboration of *a comprehensive and coherent set of standards for the implementation of the right to development*'.[104] The High-Level Task Force completed its mandate in 2010 with a submission of the criteria and operational sub-criteria on the implementation of the right to development, initially designed to be applied to Global Partnership for Implementation of MDG 8, with an objective of translating the right to development from political commitment to development practice.[105] The criteria and operational sub-criteria as they stand now would require a lot of refinement to be translated into an international legal standard of a binding nature.[106]

In its more recent resolution of 19 September 2014, the Human Rights Council confirmed its previous pronouncements, and reiterated that

> the Working Group on the Right to Development shall take appropriate steps to ensure respect for and practical application of the above-mentioned

---

101 Sub-Commission on the Promotion and Protection of Human Rights, Concept Document on the Right to Development, Working Paper submitted by Florizelle O'Connor, UN doc. E/CN.4/Sub.2/2005/23, 24 June 2005, para. 14.

102 *Ibid.*, para. 18.

103 *Ibid.*, para. 69.

104 See Human Rights Council Resolution 4/4, adopted 30 March 2007 and Resolution 9/3, adopted 17 September 2008, both containing the same formulae above (emphasis added). This decision has been reiterated in the latest Human Rights Council Resolution on the subject; see Human Rights Council Resolution 27/2, The Right to Development, UN Doc. A/HRC/RES/27/2, 19 September 2014.

105 Report of the high-level task force on the implementation of the right to development on its sixth session, Addendum: Right to development criteria and operational sub-criteria, UN doc. A/HRC/15/WG.2/TF/2/Add.2, 8 March 2010.

106 For an analysis of the issue, see S.P. Marks, B. Rudolf, K. De Feyter and N. Schrijver, 'The Role of International Law' in OHCHR, *Realizing the Right to Development Essays in Commemoration of 25 Years of the United Nations Declaration on the Right to Development*, UN: 2013, pp. 445–468.

standards, which could take various forms, including guidelines on the implementation of the right to development, and *evolve into a basis for consideration of an international legal standard of a binding nature through a collaborative process of engagement.*[107]

Thus, the possibility of the right to development evolving into a legal standard of a binding nature remains in the balance. The perspective of elaborating legally binding standards did not find support from developed states,[108] in part due to their argument that the requirement to create an enabling environment cannot be translated into binding obligations.[109] Since the locus of responsibility is instead situated within domestic jurisdictions, the Working Group was, rather, advised to focus 'on best practices, practical measures, implementation, and strengthening existing initiatives, particularly at the national and sub-national levels, rather than *focussing on the impact of the international system on the right to development*'.[110]

While the European Union (EU) was in favour of, and committed to, many efforts in relation to development and promoting human rights, it restated that it was not in favour of elaborating an international legal standard of a binding nature, because it did not believe it was 'the most appropriate instrument to operationalize the right to development'.[111] Furthermore, comment was made in relation to the three levels of responsibilities identified by the HLTF, namely that responsibilities towards the right to development existed at the level of (i) states acting collectively in global and regional partnerships; (ii) states acting individually as they adopt and implement policies that affect persons not strictly within their jurisdiction; and (iii) states acting individually as they formulate national development policies and programmes affecting persons within their jurisdiction.[112] The EU has sought clarification, as it was of the view that 'International

---

107   Human Rights Council Resolution 27/2, The Right to Development, UN doc. A/HRC/RES/27/2, 19 September 2014, para. 11(c) (emphasis added).
108   Canada stated that it did not support 'the desire of some to see a legally binding instrument on the right to development, but rather favours more action-oriented and practical approaches'. Canada, Submission in follow-up to Human Rights Council Resolution 15/25 'The Right to Development', p.1. In the same vein, the UK and Portugal did not see the possibility of its support, while Japan was 'concerned about the elaboration of a legally-binding instrument and believes it is necessary to seek other options including guidelines'. Japan, Submission in follow-up to Human Rights Council Resolution 15/25 'The Right to Development', para. 1.
109   The Netherlands, Submission in follow-up to Human Rights Council Resolution 15/25 'The Right to Development', p. 2.
110   Canada, Submission in follow-up to Human Rights Council Resolution 15/25 'The Right to Development', p.1 (emphasis added).
111   EU, Submission in follow-up to Human Rights Council Resolution 15/25 'The Right to Development', www.ohchr.org/EN/Issues/Development/Pages/HighLevelTaskForceWrittenContributions.aspx, para. 7; and EU, Submission in follow-up to Human Rights Council Resolution 19/34 'The right to development', www.ohchr.org/Documents/Issues/Development/HRCPanel/2012–2013/EU.pdf.
112   *Ibid.*

Human Rights law only recognizes clearly that States have legally binding obligations with regard to persons falling under their national jurisdiction'.[113] In addition, the Netherlands posed questions regarding the legal basis for such responsibilities, their order, and relationship.[114]

As for the view of the NAM, it felt that the international dimension for creating an enabling environment has been lost.[115] The Movement held that the work of the HLTF presented the right to development criteria that 'do not reflect adequately, in addition to the role of Governments at the national level, the dimension of international cooperation, as well as the international responsibility for creating an enabling environment for the realization of the right to development'. The NAM was of view that

> [c]ontrary to the spirit and content of the Declaration on the Right to Development, the criteria shifted the focus towards the state responsibility to create a national environment conducive to the realization of the right to development, without addressing the global obstacles that go beyond the ability of a state to tackle on its own and thereby requiring a recognition of the notion of the collective responsibility and the state duty to cooperate and fulfil the principle of international cooperation in the field of human rights.[116]

On balance, the right to development clearly lacks consensus to be acceptable as an interpretation of the implementation of human rights, particularly in its

---

113 EU, Submission in follow-up to Human Rights Council Resolution 15/25 'The Right to Development', www.ohchr.org/EN/Issues/Development/Pages/HighLevelTaskForce WrittenContributions.aspx, para. 16.

114 The Netherlands, Submission in follow-up to Human Rights Council Resolution 15/25 'The Right to Development', p. 1.

115 'The Movement disagrees with the reformulation of the scope and content of the right to development, and specially the overemphasis on national responsibilities, in neglect of the basic notion of international cooperation, for the purposes of creating an enabling environment. The task force went beyond its mandate in redefining the right to development, with a focus on some of its elements and leaving out others as they came in the UN Declaration on the Right to Development.' 'The right to development criteria presented for consideration do not reflect adequately, in addition to the role of Governments at the national level, the dimension of international cooperation, as well as the international responsibility for creating an enabling environment for the realization of the right to development'. Egypt on behalf of the Non-Aligned Movement (NAM), Submission in follow-up to Human Rights Council Resolution 15/25 'The Right to development', /www.ohchr.org/Documents/ Issues/Development/Session12/NAM.pdf, p. 2. Compare with the position of Canada, who is of view that 'Canada stresses the importance of underscoring that the primary responsibility of States to ensure the fulfilment of the right to development is within their jurisdictions. In this regard, and in the context of creating enabling environments for the realization of this right, we believe that the focus on the national dimension must remain central, taking into account international dimensions as appropriate'. Canada, www.ohchr. org/Documents/Issues/Development/Session12/Canada.pdf.

116 Submission in follow-up to Human Rights Council Resolution 15/25 'The Right to development', Egypt on behalf of the Non-Aligned Movement (NAM), Comment (A), www. ohchr.org/Documents/Issues/Development/Session12/NAM.pdf.

international dimension. These accounts demonstrate that there is no general political will to pursue the idea. Neither position is immune from stricture. If the attempts of the developed world to confine the problem of development within the borders of poor states is conflicting with the idea of interdependence and their increasing influence in shaping the economic and social structures of the developing world, the approach of the developing countries can also be criticized for taking lightly and at times disregarding completely the internal dimension of the right to development.[117] In any event, neither of the groups of states wants 'one-sided obligations'. Stephen Marks appropriately describes the political context behind the right to development discourse:

> In the current political climate, governments that pay a relatively high percentage of their gross domestic product (GDP) in official development assistance (ODA), most developing countries, many international agencies, and most non-governmental organizations (NGOs) support the concept of the right to development without being explicit about the nature of the reciprocal responsibilities involved.[118]

He further notes that '[c]ountries that spend considerable amounts of their taxpayers' money on development in line with the right to development do not welcome being told that they have a legal obligation to do so. Several delegations have mentioned "shared responsibilities", which avoids forcing the issue of legal vs. moral obligations.'[119] At the same time, developments in the area of international policy-making are clearly leaning towards formulation of the core content of human development needs that demand a shared responsibility. Consensus exists in relation to the fact that there is a minimum so absolute that efforts beyond domestic measures are required to address them. However, there is no consensus as yet in terms of the specific means necessary, and that are readily agreed upon to operationalize the goal.

---

117 Ibhawoh describes the contradictions of the use of rights talk by the South as follows: 'The paradox of the right to development talk coming from the South is that it is at once deployed to demand radical change in the international economic order and to resist change in the national political order. When Chinese officials invoke the right to development to demand more favorable trade terms or when the Ugandan government invokes it to push for more development assistance from the West, the emphasis is often on challenging a hegemonic international economic system with a view to changing the status quo. Yet, when China invokes the right to development to deflect criticism of its human rights record, or to resist pressure to cap environmental emissions, the intent is clearly to maintain the domestic economic order and preserve the political status quo.' B. Ibhawoh, 'The Right to Development: The Politics and Polemics of Power and Resistance', *op. cit.*, p. 78–79.
118 S. Marks, 'Obligations to Implement the Right to Development: Philosophical, Political and Legal Rationales', in B.A. Andreassen and S.P. Marks (eds), *Development as a Human Right: Legal, Political and Economic Dimensions*, Intersentia: 2010, p. 86.
119 *Ibid.*, p. 89.

4.2 Measures to implement the right to development

The UN Human Rights Commission endeavoured to develop a clear understanding of the concept through the establishment of the Intergovernmental Working Group on the Right to Development, which has so far served as a principal intergovernmental process in search of a consensus on the right to development and its practical implementation.[120] In 1998, the UN Commission on Human Rights appointed an Independent Expert on the Right to Development, Arjun Sengupta, who produced eight reports that tried to steer a middle path between the different groups of states.

The Independent Expert focused on identifying measures that would render the right operational. He suggested development compacts as a method to implement the right to development.[121] Sengupta proposed that international cooperation could take the form of a 'voluntary and consensual' compact between donor nations, financial institutions and developing countries to realize three basic rights (the right to food, the right to primary education and the right to primary health care).[122] The process of working out a development compact would have to be 'fully satisfactory and democratic' and developing countries 'should be able to negotiate on an equal footing' with the developed countries and the IFIs.[123] Once the compact is negotiated:

> there will be an agreement about what the States would be expected to do in pursuance of the right to development, in clearly determined phases. The representatives of the international community would then enter into an assurance that they would provide the resources and other means of international cooperation, as determined in the assessment of the requirements for the arrangements. The compact is essentially the acceptance of a mutual obligation. If the developing countries concerned follow fully the obligations of realizing these rights, in accordance with the arrangements worked out with their full participation, the international community, the donors and the financial institutions will meet their part of the obligation by providing the necessary financial, technical and other assistance.[124]

120 The Working Group was established by the Commission on Human Rights in its Resolution 1998/72, 22 April 1998, and by the Economic and Social Council in its Decision 1998/269, The right to development, 30 July 1998.

121 He introduced the idea of development compacts in his first report (E/CN.4/1999/WG.18/2 of 27 July 1999) and further developed in more details in his fourth report (E/CN.4/2002/WG.18/2 of 20 December 2001).

122 Study on the current state of progress in the implementation of the right to development submitted by Mr Arjun K. Sengupta, independent expert, pursuant to Commission Resolution 1998/72 and General Assembly Resolution 53/155, E/CN.4/1999/WG.18/2 of 27 July 1999, paras. 70 and 71.

123 Commission on Human Rights, Study on the current state of progress in the implementation of the right to development, by Mr Arjun K. Sengupta, independent expert, UN doc. E/CN.4/1999/WG.18/2, 27 July 1999, para. 74.

124 *Ibid.*

The idea of compacts developed by the Independent Expert has been innovative both in its form and approach.[125] In particular, his idea was considered as a way to expand the circle of duty-bearers that would also include developed states and international financial institutions. At the same time, the arrangement proposed by the Independent Expert, as the above passages indicate, would have to be negotiated and mutually agreed upon. In other words, 'the mutual obligations', referred to in the development compact concept, will not stem directly from the right to development itself. Wouter Vandenhole made an important point: 'The legal basis for the mutual obligations is not the human right to development, but an internationally agreed plan of action freely entered into. Therefore, the obligations would at best be contractual obligations, and any rights arising from it would be contractual rights.'[126] He further argued that the compacts would create rights for states and not for individuals, and '[c]onsequently, development compacts rightly bring back the issue of the right to development to the realm to which it belongs, namely that of interstate rights'.[127]

From 2004 to date, the international efforts moved towards practical realization of the Right to Development (RtD). From 2005 to 2010, the process was led by the High-Level Task Force on the Implementation of the Right to Development of the Intergovernmental Working Group on the Right to Development under the former Commission on human rights.[128] Currently, the Working Group continues to discharge its mandate, including, in particular, by considering, revising and refining the draft right to development criteria and its corresponding operational sub-criteria, as proposed by the final report of the High-Level Task Force on the Implementation of the Right to Development.[129]

To date, the Declaration has not 'made any difference in the behaviour of governments or the improvement of conditions'.[130] The main development and economic fora rarely mention the right to development and, even if they do,

---

125 As the Independent Expert argued, the proposal provided opportunity for cooperative relationship on 'basis of partnership rather than the confrontation of earlier years'. Fourth report, UN doc. E/CN.4/2002/WG.18/2, 20 December 2001, p. 45.
126 W. Vandenhole, 'The Human Right to Development as a Paradox', *op. cit.*, p. 402.
127 *Ibid.*, pp. 402–403.
128 The Task Force included experts in areas such as international development, finance and trade, with an aim to formulate and include recommendations for including the right to development into the existing policies and practices within aid, trade, debt relief, technology transfer, private sector and global governance.
129 The High-Level Task Force initially reviewed a range of topics, including obstacles and challenges to the implementation of MDGs and social impact assessments in the areas of trade and development. Subsequently, the Task Force focused on the MDG 8 'Global Partnership for Development', which then led to periodic evaluation, on a pilot basis (from 2007–2009), of global partnerships according to adopted criteria from the right to development perspective. Eventually, these criteria contributed to development of the draft right to development criteria on the implementation of the right to development.
130 O. Schachter, 'Implementing the Right to Development: Programme of Action', in S.R. Chowdhury, E.M.G. Denters and P. J.I.M. de Waart (eds), *The Right to Development in International Law*, Martinus Nijhoff Publishers: 1992, p. 27.

it is only in a generic and preambular way.[131] Nor did the concept attract any follow-up in the practice of the IFIs.[132] The right to development rarely informs mainstream development or human rights NGOs and remains entirely outside of development thinking. Its role, rather, has been confined to platitudinous wording in the declarations, action plans and other outcome documents adopted in the framework of financing for development conferences.[133] At the same time, linkages between human rights in general and the work of the World Bank have received some attention in research. What has been internalized by the practice of the IFIs, and bilateral and multilateral donors in some way, is the internal aspects of development, e.g. those principles and measures that tackle the problem of development within a state. The inter-state dimension of the content of the right to development is notoriously missing in practice.[134]

The only clearly identifiable practical measure implementing RtD is an agreement between the European Economic Community (EEC) and African, Caribbean and Pacific (ACP) countries, also known as the EEC–ACP Lomé Conventions (from 1974 to 2000). This arrangement is considered to encapsulate some aspects of the RtD in that they enshrine the principles of equality, solidarity, cooperation and partnership in development and are by far the framework in which human rights are most integrated as an essential component.[135] The new aid modalities, as reflected in my introduction, introduce the concept of partnership, reflecting the idea that both donor and recipient states' aid relationships are based on shared responsibilities and mutual commitments. The only practice relevant to the concept of the right to development is the adoption of human rights based approaches to development by an increasing number of donor states. This practice is also inconsistent, and approaches to understanding rights-based development and its implications vary across donors and international organizations.

---

131 The Millennium Declaration equally endorsed components of the right to development where states pledged to make 'the right to development a reality for all persons and freeing the human race from want'. However, it did not deal with the concept of right to development in a substantive manner, even if the HLTF on the implementation of the right to development is of view that 'Millennium Development Goal 8, with its focus on international cooperation, is a framework consistent with international responsibilities outlined in the Declaration on the Right to Development'. Consolidation of findings of the High-level Task Force on the Implementation of the Right to Development, 25 March 2010, UN doc. A/HRC/15/WG.2/TF/2/Add.1, para. 20.
132 A. Orford, 'Globalization and the Right to Development', *op. cit.*, pp. 127–185.
133 For further discussion see Chapter II.
134 Since the adoption of the DRD, very little evidence exists as to its implementation. At the same time, from a purely pragmatic perspective, it is impossible to discuss here all the advances made and the challenges remaining in the practical implementation of the full range of issues, at the international level only, which were raised in the Declaration on the Right to Development.
135 From 2000, the new round of the Cotonou Agreements replacing the Lomé Conventions has, in contrast, been criticized for having departed from the initial equality of states towards conditionality for developing countries.

5 The right to development: The added value of the concept?

What is the utility of the right to development? Is it a concept-symbol of resistance to the negative effects of economic structures? Or is it, as Brownlie described, a product of 'the enthusiastic legal literature to develop an isolated genre, with the select few repetitiously citing one another and the same materials, completely outside the main stream of diplomacy and international law'?[136] Does the right to development still have any legal and practical implications to the issue of human rights and development? May the right to development be just an additional layer to the existing and generally accepted principles? The principal question might rather be: is the right to development filling the 'gap' in human rights treaty commitments, such as the requirement to integrate standards stipulated by both Covenants into a development process that is indispensable to the effectiveness of human rights law? What no one really wants to answer is whether those principles from which the right to development derives its normative force, namely the 'international assistance and cooperation' provisions of the UN Charter and human rights treaties, are not in themselves sufficient to be pursued in the way the RtD framework proposes.

In the discussions of an expert consultation on the criteria and operational sub-criteria for the implementation of the right to development in the framework of the HLTF on the Implementation of the Right to Development, it was stated that the Covenant on Economic, Social and Cultural Rights, while broadly accepted, has 'not been mainstreamed into development practice', and that:

> [the] Covenant does not exhaust the international normative space concerning human rights relevant to development. The criteria under present review will therefore provide an important new basis for furthering these rights.[137]

Along similar lines, the right to development provides 'additional normative support for integrating human development approach into mainstream economics at both national and international levels'.[138] The contribution of the concept is that it 'seeks to bring a new approach to development thinking, policy making and, in particular, to development cooperation'. According to Sengupta, the difference of the right to development from other individual rights includes its focus on 'coordinated policy and resources'. In other words, specific individual rights, when treated as a component of the right to development, 'must include policies

---

136 I. Brownlie, 'The Rights of Peoples in Modern International Law', in J. Crawford (ed.), *The Rights of Peoples*, Clarendon Press: 1988, p. 14.
137 Human Rights Council, Working Group on the Right to Development, Report on Expert Consultation, The criteria and operational sub-criteria for the implementation of the right to development UN doc. A/HRC/15/WG/2/TF/CRP/4, 18 January 2010, para. 16.
138 *Ibid.* See M. Green and S. Randolph, Consultant report – Right to development criteria and corresponding operational sub-criteria, *op. cit.*, para. 79; S. Marks, 'Human rights and Development', *op. cit.*, p. 168.

to expand resources as well as institutions over time, taking into account compet-ing claims of other rights'.[139] This approach 'might imply a much larger claim on resources and much greater inputs from international cooperation' than would be the case for the fulfilment of human rights separately.[140]

Another approach, in supporting the legally distinct function of the right to development from other individual human rights, is that it provides a legal frame-work for international cooperation for 'the creation of a structural environment favourable to realization of basic human rights, for everyone'.[141] Thus the locus of these arguments rest with the idea of international cooperation to provide assistance not only in meeting human rights obligations, but also in creating favourable conditions at the global level. The Declaration on the Right to Devel-opment thus provides a particular articulation of a set of obligations, or, put otherwise, a comprehensive articulation of the obligations in the development setting.[142] Finally, it has been argued that as human rights treaties focus only on the individual as a bearer of rights, the collective dimension of the right to devel-opment is its added value.[143]

As one tries to parse out the normative value of the right to development, it is useful to recall two factors within which Alston suggested the right to develop-ment discourse ought to be framed. First, one has to situate the concept within the 'current' human rights debate on socio-economic rights.[144] The second fac-tor concerns the international dimension of the obligations on human rights. Assessment of the 'value-added' nature of the concept may depend on the assess-ment of these two factors.

It has already been mentioned that socio-economic human rights are concep-tually and operationally linked to socio-economic development. Their realization is tied to international cooperation and hence factored into enabling structures at national and international levels. Since the adoption of the Declaration on Right to Development in 1986, the landscape in human rights and development has undergone considerable change. The shift is discernible not only in the inter-national economic relations, theories, and practice of development, but also in development-oriented provisions of human rights standards.

From the time when the concept of the right to development was formulated, several instruments, such as the Convention on the Rights of the Child and the Convention on the Rights of Persons with Disabilities, have integrated provisions

139 A. Sengupta, 'Preface', in S.P. Marks (ed.), *Implementing the Right to Development: the Role of International Law*, Friedrich-Ebert Stiftung: 2008, p. 9.
140 *Ibid.*
141 M. Salomon, 'Legal Cosmopolitanism and the Normative Contribution of the Right to Development', in S.P. Marks (ed.), *Implementing the Right to Development: the Role of International Law*, Friedrich Ebert Stiftung: 2008, p. 17.
142 S. Marks, 'Human rights and Development', *op. cit.,* p. 168.
143 B. Rudolf, 'The Relation of the Right to Development to Existing Substantive Treaty Regimes', *op. cit.*, p. 109.
144 P. Alston, 'Shortcomings of a Garfield the Cat Approach to the Right to Development', *op. cit.*, p. 516.

on international assistance and cooperation with a focus on the needs of developing countries. More importantly, if the Declaration at the time tried to articulate the international dimension of obligations in relation to human rights in a detailed and subtle way, the theory and practice of protection of socio-economic rights evolved considerably and include a number of indicators tackling the human rights and development intersection. To a certain extent, socio-economic rights are beginning to acquire dynamism. Thus, the concept of the right to development 'exists within a complex structure of contemporary international human rights law, theory and practice'.[145]

In the statement on the occasion of the 25th Anniversary of the DRD, the Committee on Economic, Social and Cultural Rights identified a lot of 'complementarity' between the Declaration and ESC rights. According to the Committee on Economic Social and Cultural Rights (CESCR) there is a 'correspondence between articles 3 and 4 of the Declaration on the Right to Development relating to national and international responsibilities and article 2 of the Covenant on the obligations of States parties, including the duty to provide international assistance and cooperation'.[146] Furthermore, the Committee drew attention to several general comments and statements that it adopted, which 'not only complement the substance of the right to development but also indicate the ways and means of implementing the fundamental elements of the right to development'.[147] The Committee also considered that:

> the right to development, through the *systematic application* of the core principles of equality, non-discrimination, participation, transparency and accountability, at both the national and international levels, establishes *a*

---

145 M. Green and S. Randolph, Consultant report – Right to development criteria and corresponding operational sub-criteria, *op. cit.*

146 In its recent statement on the 25th anniversary of the DRD, the CESCR wished 'to emphasize the close relationship and the complementarity existing between the International Covenant on Economic, Social and Cultural Rights (the Covenant) and the Declaration'. Furthermore, the Committee has identified a complementarity that exists between Article 8, para. 1 of the DRD and the relevant provisions of the Covenant, in particular those provisions 'relating to, for example, ensuring the empowerment and active participation of women, disadvantaged and marginalized individuals and groups; employment; basic resources and fair distribution of income; eradication of poverty; the provision of an adequate standard of living, including food and housing; health services; education; and enjoyment of culture'. CESCR, Statement on the importance and relevance of the right to development, UN doc. E/C.12/2011/2, 13 July 2011, para. 5.

147 *Ibid.*, para. 6. 'These include general comment No. 3 (1990) on the nature of States parties' obligations and its statements on globalization (15 May 1998), poverty (4 May 2001), and the Millennium Development Goals (September 2010). Moreover, in its dialogue with States parties the Committee also consistently recalls the commitment of developed countries to provide at least 0.7 per cent of gross national product as official development assistance, and the duty incumbent on all States to cooperate in the promotion of development and respect for all human rights and fundamental freedoms, in accordance with the Charter of the United Nations.'

specific framework within which the duty to provide international cooperation and assistance has to be implemented.[148]

Apart from the CESCR, a number of UN experts and bodies in the area of debt relief, extreme poverty, international solidarity and individual human rights (including the right to food, the right to education and the right to health, among others) contribute to the body of thought on development-related aspects of human rights, specifying normative and practical understanding of various treaty provisions, including the obligations of states towards persons outside their jurisdiction.[149] These developments are not to be attributed solely to the 'rise' of socio-economic rights in human rights theory and practice. More recently, the question of international cooperation for the promotion and realization of human rights is taking shape as a distinct area of inquiry in the work of the UN human rights bodies and also in expanding academic literature. Areas such as trade and investment, development aid, climate change, business, and non-state actors experience a degree of influence by rules and principles of human rights law.

As far as the collective nature of the right is concerned, few human rights are collective in nature, although, from a conceptual point of view, it can be said that socio-economic rights have both individual and collective components. Louis Henkin observed that ESC rights 'tend to be collective' both in their outcome, and in their need for national planning and policies.[150] The

---

148 *Ibid.*, para. 5ff (emphasis added).
149 See e.g. the recent CESCR, Statement of the Committee on Economic, Social and Cultural Rights in the context of the Rio+ 20 Conference (June 2012) on 'The Green Economy in the Context of Sustainable Development and Poverty Eradication', UN doc. E/C.12/2012/1, 18 May 2012; In the High-level Plenary Meeting of the General Assembly on the Millennium Development Goals, the Chairpersons of the UN human rights treaty bodies urged Member States 'to be guided by human rights in finalizing the Summit Outcome Document'. The appellation of the members of human rights treaty bodies hinged on the argument that human rights are of legally binding nature. Joint statement of the Chairpersons of the United Nations human rights treaty bodies, presented at the High-level Plenary Meeting of the General Assembly on the Millennium Development Goals, New York, 20–22 September 2010, www.ohchr.org/en/NewsEvents/Pages/DisplayNews.aspx?NewsID=10329&LangID=E. The statement also states: 'Adhering to international human rights standards, including to the principles of non-discrimination, meaningful participation and accountability, *can accomplish* an accelerated progress towards achieving the MDGs' or 'Realizing all human rights for all is therefore a goal in itself, a goal that is one of the three fundamental pillars of the United Nations, and *should be seen* independently from the goal of generating global economic growth.' (Emphasis added).
150 L. Henkin, 'International Human Rights as "Rights"', 1 *Cardozo Law Review* (1979), pp. 425–447, p. 437. In contrast, Donnelly held that '[t]he fact that collective action is required to realize a right in no way suggests that the right is a collective right . . . No human rights are secure-not even civil rights are likely to be securely maintained-in the absence of collective action and social and political exertion, which will always involve at least opportunity costs, and usually substantial direct costs as well.' J. Donnelly, 'In Search of the Unicorn: The Jurisprudence and Politics of the Right to Development', *op. cit.*, pp. 496–497.

CESCR, in interpreting the normative content of the ESC rights, has, for example, elaborated on the availability and accessibility of certain rights (e.g. right to education or right to health). These parameters clearly require collective arrangements such as education or health care, which need to be in place as a system for individuals to benefit from them.[151] The Committee on ESC rights pledged to contribute to the realization of elements of the right to development by stating that:

> [i]n doing so, the Committee will, in its examination of the reports of States parties and in its dialogue with them, continue to address the eradication of poverty and underdevelopment and the creation of conditions for achieving economic and social progress and development for all, including for disadvantaged and marginalized individuals and groups.[152]

In view of this progress (sufficient or not), one has to ask whether we are witnessing the whole of the right to development emerging from diverse parts – through elaboration of its constituent elements – following Abi-Saab's prophecy, who long ago claimed that:

> it is very unlikely that the right to development will emerge exclusively through the spontaneous process of custom formation, or out of *one legal instrument* which covers all its facets and provides it with the necessary legal sanction. Rather the whole will gradually emerge from its part . . . But if the negotiations on the parts produce different types of legal instruments with varying legal nature and effect, the right to development is emerging from them through the process of custom-formation. For it is through the cumulative effect of these policy measures, legal instruments and underlying principles that the right to development is slowly but surely taking shape and asserting itself.[153]

Therefore, it could be there is no requisite to seek an added value of the concept of the right to development. Rather, the right to development, 'relie toutes ces questions ensemble, leur sert de cadre conceptuel et de principe unificateur et leur fournit une justification et une finalité commun en termes de droit'.[154]

---

151 There are many other examples of interaction between individual and collective dimensions of rights, such as a right to form a trade union, which, although formulated as an individual right, cannot be satisfied other than by a collective action.

152 CESCR, Statement on the importance and relevance of the right to development, adopted on the occasion of the twenty-fifth anniversary of the Declaration on the Right to Development, UN doc. E/C.12/2011/2, 13 July 2011, para. 7.

153 G. Abi-Saab, 'The Legal Formulation of the Right to Development', *op. cit.*, p. 168 (emphasis added).

154 G. Abi-Saab, 'Le droit au développement', *op. cit.,* p. 23.

Conclusion

The right to development has been described in various ways, such as an 'enabling right',[155] 'a crossroad right',[156] a meta-right[157] or a right as a means of achieving other human rights. The different terminologies conceal the many facets of the concept that try to depart from traditional approaches in human rights law in particular and international law generally. Despite countless efforts to come up with a settled analysis, many issues related to the concept remain ambiguous, including the use of terminology of 'rights' in the context of development.

This unease with terming the right to development as a proper right is due to the dual nature that the concept purports to encapsulate: the rights and obligations of states in relation to each other on the one hand, and the rights and obligations of states in relation to the individual on the other. Although the dual premise produces a different set of legal consequences, they are inextricably linked. The Declaration placed the right to development within the framework of international human rights order but linked the realization of this right to inter-state solutions of an economic and social character. This two-dimensional premise is not new in international law, but is missing in parsing the relevant issues concerning the right to development.[158] When posing the question in these terms, it becomes apparent that, while to some extent progress has been made regarding the individual dimension of the right to development, such as the right to participation in the development process as supported by regional human rights bodies, as was demonstrated above, the inter-state dimension of the right to development lacks any measure of consensus.[159]

Taken as a whole, as both an individual and collective right, the right to development is yet to attain the status of *lex lata*, despite the true nobility of its purpose.[160] Having said that, in view of the sources of international law from which the right to development draws its legal force, another approach to see the utility

155 The credit for this entitlement has been attributed to G. Abi-Saab, in M.E. Salomon, 'Legal Cosmopolitanism and the Normative Contribution of the Right to Development', *op. cit.*, p. 17.
156 A. Pellet, 'The Functions of the Right to Development: A Right to Self-Realisation', *op. cit.*, p. 129.
157 A. Sengupta, 'The Human Right to Development', *op. cit.*, pp. 13–45.
158 See ICJ, *LaGrand Case (Germany v. United States of America)*, Judgment, ICJ Reports 2001, p. 466, para. 89; ICJ, *Case concerning Avena and other Mexican Nationals (Mexico v. United States)*, Judgment, ICJ Reports 2004, p. 12, paras. 121–122.
159 AComHPR, *Centre for Minority Rights Development (Kenya) and Minority Rights Group (on behalf of Endorois Welfare Council) v. Kenya*, Case 276/03, 27th Activity Report: Jun 2009 – Nov 2009, para. 125, where the African Commission found a violation of the right to development 'as a result of the Respondent State's failure to adequately involve the Endorois in the development process and the failure to ensure the continued improvement of the Endorois community's well-being'.
160 R. Rich, 'The Right to Development: A Right of Peoples?', *op. cit.*, p. 40. I. Brownlie, *Human Right in Development*, Commonwealth Secretariat Human Rights Unit Occasional Paper, London 1989, p. 14.

of the concept is to consider it both as structuring the legal requirement to integrate human rights into development processes at national and international
levels in a narrow sense, and, broadly, as an interpretation of the international
dimension of human rights obligations, including in the development context.
Thus, the right to development appears more as a totality of the means which will
make economic and social rights effective.[161]

A few important parameters of the right to development, such as the duties
incumbent upon states to cooperate and assist each other, are being built within
the confines of existing human rights treaties concerning ESC rights. There are
discernible elements contributing to the formation of a doctrine on the international dimensions of obligations under the International Covenant on Economic,
Social and Cultural Rights. But even if we construct the concept as an interpretation of the existing body of the law of human rights, it remains to be seen
whether such an interpretation is supported by the actors to whom the rules are
addressed, namely states.[162]

For the time being, the role assigned to the concept of the right to development is its moral and political force.[163] But even this role needs to be redefined
in terms of new realities and new emerging trends. One has to be aware that the
right to development's emergence in a specific historical juncture carries with it
an engrained tendency to be confined to problems of developing countries solely,
while the potential the concept carries with it is much larger. As Roberto Ago has
described, the right to development is:

> un droit à mettre dans les conditions nécessaires pour lui [l'être humaine]
> permettre d'atteindre l'épanouissement le plus complet de sa personnalité
> dans tous les domaines: la santé, l'instruction, les libertés civiques et poli-
> tiques, le bien-être économique, etc.[164]

New dynamics, such as the flaws of current economic policies, felt ever more
strongly in recent and often recurring economic crises, could serve as a paradigm
shift moment to consider the rule of law in financial and economic relations and
thus give new impetus to the notion of the right to development.

---

161 J. Rivero, 'Sur le droit au développement', Paper SS-78/CONF.630/2, p. 3 cited in the
    Secretary-General Report, UN doc. E/CN.4/1334, 2 January 1979, para. 65.
162 See further below Chapter IV.
163 As Alston points out, 'what is probably the single most significant feature of the right to
    development: its potential mobilizing power; its instinctive appeal to a wide range of people
    for whom development (in its comprehensive sense) is a matter of the utmost priority'.
    P. Alston, 'Shortcomings of a Garfield the Cat Approach to the Right to Development', *op.
    cit.*, p. 51.
164 R. Ago, 'Opening Statement', in R-J Dupuy (ed.), *The Right to Development at the Inter-
    national Level*, The Hague Academy of International Law: 1980, p. 7.

IV The obligation of international assistance and cooperation

Introduction

This chapter addresses the notion of international assistance and cooperation for human rights and the existence of an international legal obligation to provide such support. The notion, as encapsulated in Articles 55 and 56 of the UN Charter and Article 2(1) of the ICESCR, was a principal legal basis to argue for the existence of the international dimension of the right to development. These provisions languished for a long time in the shadow of the right to development discourse. Recent attempts to give more visibility to economic, social and cultural rights in human rights debates, as well as the drafting of the Optional Protocol to the ICESCR, have renewed the interest in the UN Charter provisions and Article 2(1), and in their potential. They are also increasingly used as legal justification to a variety of claims relevant to 'external context', including social or distributive justice at the international level, obligations to address systemic causes of violations of human rights, global obligations to address poverty and so on. Although the obligation to cooperate for human rights is legally well founded, it is far from being understood as such in practice.

A number of questions will help to frame the *problèmatique*. Does this duty to cooperate for human rights constitute a hard law obligation, or does it just broaden the scope of possibilities for action on the international scene? What is the scope of any obligation and the content of a duty to cooperate both under general international law and under express obligations undertaken in human rights treaties? Moreover, if states have an obligation to promote human rights in other states, does this imply a legal obligation to provide development assistance? What would the implications be for multilateral or bilateral relations?

In examining the duty to cooperate, the present chapter will focus primarily on legal regimes that cover economic, social and cultural rights. The reason for this is twofold. First, these rights concern the areas traditionally dealt with by development cooperation, such as education, health, living standards and poverty reduction.[1] Second, although, the duty to cooperate for human rights is an

---

1 Certainly, poverty, although considered a massive 'systemic breach' of socio-economic rights, is not coextensive with them, but it closely relates to the normative content of these rights by virtue of the existence of people who lack access to health, clean water, food, literacy and who

all-encompassing concept, the normative articulation of this obligation is found in treaties providing for socio-economic rights. Prior to the analysis, however, I will analyse whether it is possible for the international legal order to accommodate the idea of an obligation to cooperate. Furthermore, in order to understand in full the implications of the obligations of international assistance and cooperation, it is important to introduce basic elements of the context in which they operate.

1 Obligations of international cooperation in international law

Edward McWhinney observes that as a term of art of international law, 'cooperation' emerged after World War II.[2] No treaty or international decision defines the notion or the term 'cooperation', though. Wolfrum defines cooperation as 'the voluntary coordinated action of two or more States which takes place under a legal régime and serves a specific objective' and to 'this extent marks the effort of States to accomplish an object by joint action, where the activity of a single State cannot achieve the same result' or mutual benefit.[3] What follows is that the duty to cooperate would lead to an obligation to enter into such an action to achieve a specific goal. In terms of substance, cooperation *per se* has no independent content;[4] it must be tied to a specific area to acquire a specific meaning.

Although the concept of international cooperation should not be reduced to being understood only in a 'development paradigm', traditionally the obligation to cooperate was associated with economic and social spheres, i.e. development.[5] Cooperation should not, however, be amalgamated with the notions of

---

are also poor. The UN Committee on Economic and Social Rights provided the following definition: 'In the light of the International Bill of Human Rights, poverty may be defined as a human condition characterised by the sustained or chronic deprivation of the resources, capabilities, choices, security and power necessary for the enjoyment of an adequate standard of living and other civil, cultural, economic, political and social rights.' CESCR, Statement on Poverty and the International Covenant on Economic, Social and Cultural Rights, UN doc. E/C.12/2001/10, para. 8.

2 He also refers to international cooperation 'in larger, generic terms, as a special body of international law in its own right'. E. McWhinney, 'The Concept of Cooperation', in M. Bedjaoui (ed.), *International Law: Achievements and Perspectives*, Martinus Nijhoff Publishers: 1991, pp. 424–436, p. 424.

3 R. Wolfrum, 'International Law of Cooperation', EPIL Vol. II, Elsevier, 1995, pp. 1242–1247, p. 1242.

4 *Ibid.*

5 See e.g. Commentary by R. Wolfrum, 'Article 55', in B. Simma et al. (eds), *The Charter of the United Nations. A Commentary*, 2nd edition, pp. 897–917; Commentary by E. Riedel, 'Article 55 (c)', in B. Simma et al. (eds), *The Charter of the United Nations. A Commentary*, 2nd edition, pp. 918–941; and R. Wolfrum, 'Article 56', in B. Simma et al. (eds), *The Charter of the United Nations. A Commentary*, 2nd edition, pp. 941–944. See also Human Rights Council Advisory Committee, Study on the Enhancement of International cooperation in the field of human rights, pursuant to Human Rights Council Resolution 13/23, UN doc. A/

interdependence and solidarity. Interdependence depicts a material fact (a factual situation) among states that may give rise to legal consequences but does not connote rights and/or obligations of parties.[6] Solidarity, although closely associated, differs from cooperation. If cooperation stems from a cooperative agreement whereby all parties are expected to benefit from such a relationship, in a relationship based on solidarity, 'providers of solidarity are not expected to concretely benefit from their implication'.[7] Solidarity can, however, contribute to the intensification of cooperation.

1.1 Cooperation as the basis of modern international law

In legal doctrine, cooperation is defined as the underlying logic of the present international legal order. This idea was captured by Wolfgang Friedman's distinction between the 'law of cooperation' and the 'law of coexistence'[8] and later theorized by Georges Abi-Saab.[9] As Abi-Saab explains, these are not two distinct branches of law, but merely represent two different types of legal regulation.[10] In essence, the 'law of cooperation' is premised on a critical and fundamental presumption of the existence of a community of interests or values which 'cannot be protected or promoted unilaterally, but only by a common effort'.[11] This community of interest 'must be verified not only from the factual point of view,

---

HRC/19/74, 29 February 2012, para. 34. For Wolfrum, however, '[t]he term "cooperation" used in the context of the law of cooperation therefore means cooperation among States for the purposes of development to increase the social welfare of the world community'. R. Wolfrum, 'International Law of Cooperation', *Max Planck Encyclopaedia of International Law*, www.mpepil.com.

6 Judge Alvarez expanded the idea of 'international law of cooperation' by stating that 'States no longer have an absolute sovereignty but are interdependent, they have not only rights but duties towards each other and this society', terming this 'new law' 'the law of social interdependence'. ICJ, *Admission of a State to the United Nations (Charter, Art. 4)*, Advisory Opinion: ICJ Reports 1948, p. 57; Individual Opinion of Judge Alvarez, p. 15.

7 See generally on distinction between the two, R. Wolfrum, 'International Law of Cooperation' and D. Campanelli, 'Principle of Solidarity', both in *Max Planck Encyclopaedia of International Law*, www.mpepil.com.

8 The concept 'law of cooperation' was introduced as a counterpart to the term 'law of coexistence' by Wolfgang Friedmann as one of the key developments of the post-World War II international law. See W. Friedmann, *The Changing Structure of International Law*, Columbia University Press: 1964, pp. 10, 63. According to McWhinney, cooperation is the product of a historical-dialectical process of law-making based on the old classic law concepts of (prohibition of) abuse of rights and good neighbourliness, and involved their analogical extension under the influence of general legal ideas of justice and equity to new problem situations, growing into a larger body of principles and rules of a still evolving international law of cooperation. E. McWhinney, 'The Concept of Cooperation', *op. cit.*, p. 430.

9 See generally G. Abi-Saab, 'Cours général de droit international public', 207 *Recueil des Cours* (1987).

10 *Ibid.*, p. 320 and for the distinction between the two, p. 321ff.

11 G. Abi-Saab, 'Wither the International Community?', 9(2) *European Journal of International Law* (1998), pp. 248–265, p. 251.

but above all from the point of view of the awareness among the subjects concerned of the common need, value or interest involved and of the appropriate solutions'.[12] In international law, traces of the 'law of cooperation' approach can be visible in some areas, while other areas can still be governed by the logic of coexistence, which aims, as is widely known, at ensuring a minimum of order between states. This is because the existence of a 'community' of interest may be felt in one area but not necessarily in another.[13]

The foundation of such an international law is the obligation of states to cooperate with each other.[14] In this respect, obligations require more than abstention, but also positive duties to achieve a common objective.[15] In the framework of the 'law of cooperation', equality between states means participation, with tasks apportioned to each according to the states' abilities and needs.[16] In other words, the international law of cooperation is required to take into consideration the real situation of states, and to provide a division of labour among them based on their capacities and needs, i.e. 'dose their rights and obligations to their specific situations'.[17] Even if the principle of sovereign equality figures as the main principle of the structure of international law, it is relativized by other principles such as the duty to cooperate.[18] In 'the absence of an embryonic international community, it is Member States that assume responsibility, jointly and severally'.[19]

Emmanuelle Jouannet makes a further distinction, between the rules of cooperation and the rules of assistance. For her, the former are still driven by liberal rather than 'welfarist' motives. Cooperation rules are based on the specific interest of each contracting state, which, through a cooperation framework, engages in a joint action that would be beneficial to it individually.[20] Assistance and rules pertaining to it, in contrast, are something more than mere 'cooperation'. In contrast to cooperation where all parties to a cooperative agreement would benefit from the result of common effort, the rules on assistance are intended for the

12 *Ibid.*, p. 440.
13 'La communauté est donc un phénomène parcellaire et quand on dit que la réglementation juridique procède de la présomption de l'existence d'une communauté, cela ne veut pas dire qu'elle existe de la même manière et avec la même intensité partout et par rapport à tous les sujets'. G. Abi-Saab, 'Cours général de droit international public', 207 *Recueil des Cours* (1987), p. 321.
14 R. Wolfrum, 'International Law of Cooperation', *op. cit.*.
15 See also Human Rights Council Advisory Committee, Study of the Enhancement of International cooperation in the field of human rights, *op. cit.*, para. 37.
16 G. Abi-Saab, *ibid.*, p. 261.
17 Report of the Secretary General, Progressive Development of the Principles and Norms of International Law Relating to the New International Economic Order, UN doc. A/39/504/Add.1, 23 October 1984, para. 124.
18 G. Abi-Saab, 'Whither the International Community?', *op. cit.*, p. 261.
19 HRC Advisory Committee, Report on Enhancement of International Cooperation in the Field of Human Rights, *op. cit.*
20 E. Jouannet, *The Liberal-Welfarist Law of Nations: A History of International Law*, CUP: 2012, p. 77.

good of others.[21] These rules of assistance were at the core of legal thinking from much further back than conventionally suggested.

Ever since international law has emerged as a body of law, the question of a 'legal obligation to assist' preoccupied not only legal minds but also 'rulers', all of whom needed to know whether they, (i) had legal obligations, and (ii) what the foundations of any obligation to aid 'a neighbouring nation in distress' would be when there was no self-interest in doing so.[22] This is a very real question to date for areas of law governing situations of armed conflict, protection of persons in the event of disaster, and, undoubtedly, also development. Conceptually, rules of assistance, although part of the larger genus of 'cooperation', are dealt with separately, as will be seen below in the framework of interpretation of the International Covenant on Economic, Social and Cultural Rights.

Human rights and the environment are two prominent examples of areas permeated by the logic of the law of cooperation and rules of assistance. The same could be said in relation to the field of development, which is a key element in the promotion of both peace and human rights. However, even with a global awareness of a need to address hunger, malnutrition, exploitation and disease, whether these issues represent 'a common concern' is far from certain. The requisite awareness of common need, interest and solutions to socio-economic grievances is still evolving.[23] What follows is an analysis of the classic examples of the 'law of cooperation' approach, namely Articles 55–56 of the UN Charter.

1.2 UN Charter as a legal basis for the obligation to cooperate

The obligation to cooperate can be said to constitute one of the basic premises of the UN Charter. Chapter I of the UN Charter (Purposes and Principles) in Article 1(3) establishes as one of the purposes of the United Nations:

> international cooperation in solving international problems of an economic, social, cultural, or humanitarian character, and in promoting and encouraging respect for human rights and for fundamental freedoms for all without distinction as to race, sex, language or religion.

---

21 *Ibid.*
22 *Ibid.*, p. 79.
23 The famous 'financial transaction tax' (FTT), better known as Tobin tax, has been proposed regularly by the UN as a device to generate financing for development (see United Nations, High-Level Panel on Financing for Development, 2001, reproduced in Letter dated 25 June 2001 from the Secretary-General to the President of the General Assembly, UN doc. A/55/1000, 21 June 2001). The idea is being currently pursued in the EU among a limited number of states (despite opposition within other EU members), as a measure in response to the economic crisis and as well as a source to generate revenue. Ultimately, the FTT is said to encourage responsible financing. As for the current discussion on the universal agenda for development post-2015, although the goals formulated evidence of community interests, the means of implementation agreed in the 2015 Addis Ababa outcome document are deficient of this awareness. For discussion see Chapter II.

Analysis of the nature of Article 1 reveals that the provision contains certain elements that are binding under customary international law.[24] Among the essential purposes articulated by Article 1, the objective of 'maintenance of peace and security' (paragraph 1) is singled out as one of a customary nature. It has been also argued that the aspirations as specified by paragraph 3 (i.e. cooperation in socio-economic areas and promotion of human rights) are a purpose in their own right too. These aims are further linked to international peace in a broader sense, where solving the problems in enumerated areas contributes to maintenance of peace and security.[25] The purposes of peace and security, economic development and human rights are thus interdependent.

On several occasions, the General Assembly has referred to Article 1(3) in the context of economic development and cooperation.[26] The provision has served as a basis for relief action, financing for economic development,[27] for formulation of fundamental principles of economic relations[28] and in establishing mechanisms for economic development.[29] Equally, as far as the protection of human rights is concerned, Article 1(3) has been invoked on many occasions in relation to human rights within the UN, for example as a basis for drafting instruments, strengthening the rule of law, eliminating discrimination and so on.[30]

It is notable that the purpose set out in Article 1(3) pertains only to the UN itself and not as a charge on its Member States. The duty imposed on Member States can be derived from the operative chapters to which Article 1(3) refers, namely Chapters IX and X. Article 55 of Chapter IX on International Economic and Social Cooperation[31] implements and reinforces Article 1(3) and additionally

---

24 Commentary by R. Wolfrum, 'Article 1', in B. Simma et al. (eds), *The Charter of the United Nations. A Commentary*, 2nd edition, pp. 39–47, p. 40.
25 See Chapter II, on the contribution of the UN to the development thinking.
26 For example, in UN GA Resolution 2152 (XXI), 17 November 1966, the GA Stated that the purpose of UNIDO should be 'to promote industrial development, in accordance with Article 1 para. 3, and Articles 55 and 56 of the Charter'.
27 UN GA Resolutions: 48 (I), 11 December 1946; 400 (V), 20 November 1950 (financing of economic development of developing countries); 410 A (V), 1 December 1950 (relief and rehabilitation of Korea).
28 UN GA Resolutions: 626 (VII), 21 December 1952 (right to exploit freely natural wealth and resources); 1803 (XVII), 14 December 1962; 2158 (XXI), 25 November 1966 (permanent sovereignty over natural resources).
29 UN GA Resolutions: 923 (X), 9 December 1955 (establishment of a special United Nations Fund for Economic Development); 1423 (XIV), 5 December1959; 2152 (XXI), 17 November 1966 (purpose of the United Nations Industrial Development Organization).
30 For a recent example see the Resolution of the Human Rights Council 13/23 on Enhancement of international cooperation in the field of human rights, UN doc. A/HRC/13/L.7, 19 March 2010.
31 The Covenant for the League of Nations did not set up the foundation for the connection between economic and social stability with the maintenance of peace and security internationally. The provisions of the Covenant in economic and social areas were of a more restricted nature embracing labour rights.

stresses the internal coherence between the principles and purposes of the UN.[32] Article 55 of the UN Charter reads:

> With a view to the creation of conditions of stability and well-being which are necessary for peaceful and friendly relations among nations based on respect for the principle of equal rights and self-determination of peoples, the United Nations shall promote:
>
> a   higher standards of living, full employment, and conditions of economic and social progress and development;
> b   solutions of international economic, social, health, and related problems; and international cultural and educational cooperation; and
> c   universal respect for, and observance of, human rights and fundamental freedoms for all without distinction as to race, sex, language, or religion.[33]

Article 55 hence defines the scope of cooperation in the areas of economic and social welfare and human rights by developing the conceptual construct envisaged in the preamble of the Charter. This determines reaffirmation in human rights, the goal of 'social progress and better standards of life in larger freedom'[34] and determines for these ends 'to employ international machinery for the promotion of the economic and social advancement of all peoples'.[35] It therefore becomes quite clear that there is a strong correlation between socio-economic progress and human rights. Furthermore, these two objectives are closely tied to peace and security, as the text of Article 55 links them with 'necessary conditions of stability and well-being', thereby reflecting a positive conception of peace.[36]

In practice, Article 55 has served as a platform for General Assembly activities and efforts to restructure international economic relations.[37] Section (c) of Article 55 contains a 'human rights clause', included in the provision on universal respect for, and observance of, human rights and fundamental freedoms for all, without distinction as to race, sex, language or religion. The interpretation of

---

32   See UN GA Resolution 47/120B, An Agenda for Peace, 20 September 1993, which establishes linkages between peace and security as well as underscoring the need for cooperative efforts in economic, social and humanitarian areas to promote durable foundation for peace.

33   Paragraph (a) of Article 55 is construed as specification of paragraph (b), Article 55, and eventually has acquired less usage, since promotion of 'solutions of international economic, social, health, and related problems' has taken a prevailing form of all UN actions in the area of development encompassing all areas. R. Wolfrum, 'Article 55', in B. Simma et al. (eds), *The Charter of the United Nations. A Commentary*, 2nd edition, pp. 897–917, p. 901.

34   Paras. 2 and 4, the Preamble of the UN Charter.

35   Para. 8, the Preamble of the UN Charter.

36   See D.L. Tehindrazanarivelo and R. Kolb, 'International Protection of the Right to Peace', *Max Planck Encyclopaedia of International Law*, available at www.mpepil.com.

37   R. Wolfrum, 'Article 55', *op. cit.*, p. 906.

Article 55(c) in conjunction with Article 56 is maintained as creating basic obligations that all members must fulfil in good faith. Article 56 reads:

> All members pledge themselves to take joint and separate action in co-operation with the Organization for the achievement of the purposes set forth in Article 55.

Article 56 is interpreted as a means of achieving an objective rather than a purpose in itself.[38] To an extent, Article 56 restates the requirement of Article 2(2) of the Charter[39] and parallels Article 25,[40] albeit without 'creating a comparably strong obligation upon member States'.[41] Article 56 contains three elements: joint action, separate action and cooperation (with the UN) in relation to obligations laid down by Article 55.[42] Some uncertainty persisted as to whether Article 56 created an obligation for Member States to act independently outside the UN framework in order to fulfil the pledges undertaken.[43] Despite controversies, a common reading is that the pledges encompass both a separate commitment, understood as 'independent, separate and national', and a joint meaning of 'any conduct by two or more members'.[44]

It is on the basis of Article 56 that a general obligation of cooperation can be construed in the economic, social and cultural fields, as well as in the field of human rights.[45] At the same time, there is a sense of ambiguity regarding the legal consequences stemming from Article 56. The commentaries on Article 56 provide a reading according to which:

> States are only under an obligation to give, jointly or separately, such support to the UN to achieve the purposes delineated in Art. 55 as they see fit. Article 56 neither specifies the ways and means of this envisaged cooperation

---

38 *Ibid.*, p. 900.

39 Article 2(2) stipulates: 'All Members, in order to ensure to all of them the rights and benefits resulting from membership, shall fulfill in good faith the obligations assumed by them in accordance with the present Charter.'

40 Article 25: 'The Members of the United Nations agree to accept and carry out the decisions of the Security Council in accordance with the present Charter.'

41 R. Wolfrum, 'Article 56', in B. Simma et al. (eds), *The Charter of the United Nations. A Commentary*, 2nd edition, pp. 941–944, p. 942.

42 *Ibid.*

43 Legislative history reveals that the provision was a compromise wording. On the one hand, the Australian delegation's proposal envisaged the duty of states to take measures nationally and internationally and, on the other, the US concern that separate action meant something more than cooperation but, rather, intervention into domestic affairs. Therefore, '[i]t was understood that "separate" action would reflect the Australian proposal whereas the reference to cooperation "with the organization" took care of the concerns of the United States, because the wording could be read in a way that only covered actions taken in cooperation with the Organization.' See P.T. Stoll, 'Article 56', in B. Simma, D.-E. Khan, G. Nolte and A. Paulus (eds), *The Charter of the United Nations. A Commentary*, 3rd edition, OUP: 2013, para. 3, p.1604.

44 *Ibid.*, para. 7.

45 Report of the Secretary General, Progressive Development of the Principles and Norms of International Law Relating to the New International Economic Order, UN doc. A/39/504/Add.1, 23 October 1984, para. 129.

between the Organization and its member States, nor vests the Organization with power to require specific forms of cooperation.[46]

The UN Charter commentary asserts that the obligatory nature of Article 56 is rather weak, since the provision refers to Article 55 which sets 'purposes' and not substantive obligations: '[t]o this extent, Article 56 can thus only create substantive obligations (as opposed to procedural obligations) in so far as Article 55 contains a corresponding basis in that respect'.[47]

In relation to human rights, Wolfrum in the commentary on Article 56 states that '[a]lthough the "universal respect for, and observance of, human rights and fundamental freedoms" have been formulated as an objective, the additional words "without discrimination as to race, sex, language, or religion" already circumscribe a fixed and directly executable legal obligation'.[48] Such a conclusion is supported by an argument that the General Assembly has often made reference to the pledges of states in the context of the discrimination based on race, sex, language or religion.[49] A more plausible reading is provided by Schachter, who clarifies that '[t]he language is that of obligation, but the contents of the obligation are not specified except for the general non-discrimination requirement'.[50]

In the early days of the UN Charter, doctrine was also divided on whether these provisions were creating legal obligations for Member States. Some scholars saw human rights clauses in the Charter as being limited to setting out a programme of action rather than creating a binding obligation.[51] Others, such as Lauterpacht, did not support the view that the Charter provisions on the issue

---

46 Wolfrum, 'Article 56', *op. cit.*, p. 974.
47 R. Wolfrum, 'Article 56', *op. cit.*, p. 943.
48 *Ibid.*
49 See UN GA Resolutions: 616 B (VII), 5 December 1952; 917 A (X), 6 December 1955; 1178 (XII), 26 November 1957; 1248 (XIII), 30 October 1958.
50 O. Schachter, 'International Law in Theory and Practice: General Course in Public International Law', 178 *Recueil des Cours* (1982), pp. 332–333.
51 In the work of the ILC on the draft Declaration on the Rights and Duties of States, in 1949, the Chairman, M.O. Hudson, stated that 'whenever the question of respect for human rights appeared in the Charter, it was as an aim to be achieved (Articles 1. 3, 13.1b, 55 c, 62.2 and 76 c). The conclusion had been drawn that the Charter did not in any way impose on the Members of the United Nations a legal obligation to respect human rights and fundamental freedoms.' Yearbook of the International Law Commission 1949, Summary Records and Documents of the First Session including the report of the Commission to the General Assembly, 25th Meeting, New York: 1956, p. 178, p. 6. Kelsen, also analysing various inconsistencies related to human rights provisions of the UN Charter, noted, 'the Charter does not impose upon the Members a strict obligation to grant to their subjects the rights and freedoms mentioned in the Preamble or in the text of the Charter. The language used by the Charter in this respect does not allow the interpretation that the Members are under legal obligations regarding the rights and freedoms of their subjects . . . Besides, the Charter does in no way specify the rights and freedoms to which it refers. Legal obligations of the Members in this respect can be established only by an amendment to the Charter or by a convention . . . ratified by the Members.' H. Kelsen, *The Law of the United Nations: A Critical Analysis of Its Fundamental Problems*, The Lawbook Exchange: 1950, pp. 29–32.

were devoid of any element of legal obligation. For Lauterpacht, 'the provisions of the Charter on the subject figure prominently in the statement of the Purposes of the United Nations. Members of the United Nations are under a legal obligation to act in accordance with these purposes. It is their legal duty *to respect* and *observe* fundamental human rights and freedoms.' He also said that:

> There is a distinct element of legal duty in the undertaking expressed in Article 56 in which 'All Members pledge themselves to take joint and separate action in cooperation with the Organization for the achievement of the purposes set forth in Article 55'. The cumulative legal result of all these pronouncements cannot be ignored . . . Any construction of the Charter according to which Members of the United Nations are, in law, entitled to disregard – and to violate – human rights and fundamental freedoms is destructive of both the legal and the moral authority of the Charter as a whole.[52]

Although the wording in relevant provisions of the Charter appears to require states only to 'promote' or 'encourage' universal respect for, and observance of, human rights, for Lauterpacht as well as other scholars, this 'detail' did not carry weight in arriving at the conclusion that the Charter created obligations *to respect* and *observe* human rights.[53] At any rate, the International Court of Justice put to rest many ambiguities in regard to human rights clauses of the Charter, in the *Namibia* case. Here, the Court, first, mentioned the pledge of states to observe and respect human rights and fundamental freedoms (omitting the word 'promote'), and second, qualified the denial of human rights as a violation of the Charter.[54]

The political and judicial organs of the UN have consistently interpreted Article 55(c), addressed to the UN, and Article 56, involving its members, as a general framework for a range of issues falling in the human rights domain.[55] There is therefore, at a minimum, a consensus that Article 56, together with Article 55,

---

52 H. Lauterpacht, *International Law and Human Rights*, Stevens & Sons: 1950, pp. 147–149. See also Lauterpacht's report on 'Human Rights' in ILA, Report of the 43rd Conference (Brussels), 43 *International Law Association Reports of Conferences* (1948), pp. 29–154.

53 See Q. Wright, 'National Courts and Human Rights – The *Fujii* Case', 45 *American Journal of International Law* (1951), pp. 62–82, p. 73; E. Schwelb, 'The International Court of Justice and the Human Rights Clauses of the Charter', 66 *American Journal of International Law* (1972), pp. 337–351, p. 340; E. Shwelb, 'The Law of Treaties and Human Rights' in W.M. Reisman and B.H. Weston (eds), *Towards the World Order and Human Dignity: Essays in Honour of Myres S. McDougal*, Free Press:1976, p. 256.

54 ICJ, *Legal Consequences for States of the Continued Presence of South Africa in Namibia (South West Africa) notwithstanding Security Council Resolution 276 (1970)*, Advisory Opinion, ICJ Reports 1971, para. 131 See also infra, Chapter VI.

55 E. Riedel, 'Article 55 (c)', in B. Simma et al. (eds), *The Charter of the United Nations. A Commentary*, 2nd edition, pp. 918–941, p. 923.

creates legal obligations for states to cooperate 'both one with another' and with the United Nations, to achieve the purposes set.[56] A French-language commentary on the UN Charter not only makes an explicit reference to the duty to cooperate for human rights as a legally binding duty, but also links it to the existence of a customary rule in that matter.[57]

The only caveat, as highlighted before, is that the provisions are not specific enough, and they set the 'obligation' of states to cooperate in rather broad, generic terms, with little interpretation as to the scope of the obligations that these articles give rise to. In contrast to human rights clauses, as the UN Charter commentaries make clear, Articles 55 and 56 are 'rarely mentioned in regard to the issues addressed in Art. 55(a) and (b)', that is, in the economic and social fields.[58] In effect, the majority of references to Article 56 and the debates surrounding the import of the provision relate to the question of human rights. One explanation states as follows:

> the lack of explicit reference might also be due to the limited normative value of the provisions. It neither envisages that the UN be a strong forum in international economic relations, nor does it contain any strong mandate in the area of social justice. More than once, States have chosen to deal with economic matters outside the UN in other multilateral forums – like the WTO – in small groups – such as the G-20 – and at the regional or bilateral levels. Also, they were always reluctant to contribute to the implementation of the many declarations and work programmes adopted and to furnish the UN with the means and funds necessary to

56 As suggested also by Commentaries to Article 56, '[r]eferences to Article 56 . . . have been made primarily in connection with human rights provisions, and only to a lesser degree with economic and social provisions of Article 55'. R. Wolfrum, 'Article 56', *op. cit.*, p. 943. References to Article 56 are also made in the context of a right to development. The duty of the international community to cooperate for the right to development, as provided for in 1986 Declaration on the Right to Development and 1993 Vienna Declaration and Programme of Action, was grounded on Articles 56 and 57 of the UN Charter. Arjun Sengupta, Report of the Independent Expert on the Right to Development, UN doc. E/CN.4/2000/WG.18/CRP.1, 11 September 2000, para. 11.

57 'On avait bien pris soin de souligner que l'Organisation et les Etats qui la composent s'étaient engagés à réaliser les buts fixés à l'article 56 et que cette tâche n'est pas seulement pour chaque Etat une question d'intérêt national mais qu'elle constitue aussi, et dirions-nous surtout, une obligation internationale. Cette obligation est d'autant plus importante qu'elle est assumée de façon formelle par les Etats membres en vertu de la Charte. En réalité, la Charte ne fait que codifier une règle d'origine coutumière tout au moins en ce qui concerne la dimension "droits de l'homme", identifiés aux droits fondamentaux.' L. Bouony, Article 56, in J.-P. Cot and A. Pellet (eds), *La Charte des Nations Unies: commentaire article par article*, 3rd edition, Economica & Bruylant: 2005, p. 1508.

58 P.T. Stoll, 'Article 55 (a) and (b)', in B. Simma, D.-E. Khan, G. Nolte and A. Paulus (eds), *The Charter of the United Nations A Commentary*, 3rd edition, OUP, para. 29, p. 1543. Stoll, at the same time, states that since Article 55 (a) and (b) 'is very broad and abstract, however, such use of the terms of the provision is not very significant in legal terms'.

play a stronger role in this regard. *The shortcomings of a law of cooperation become obvious at this very point.*[59]

Unlike in the area of peace and security, the cooperation to be achieved with respect to both human rights and socio-economic development is decentralized. In particular, efforts to create centralized schemes to deal with socio-economic problems faced resistance within the UN and therefore developed outside, as we saw in Chapter II.[60] On the other hand, the debate is hardly exhausted. The question of cooperation had been brought up more than once: in the process of codification of basic rules of international law and in specific human rights treaty regimes.

1.3 Obligation to cooperate for development

There is considerable uncertainty as to whether, outside of express obligations under the UN Charter, there is a legally binding obligation on states to cooperate. Normatively, attempts to answer this question have been addressed in the realm of the 1970 Declaration on Principles of International Law Concerning Friendly Relations and Cooperation among States, the 1974 Declaration on the Establishment of a New International Economic Order, the 1974 Charter of Economic Rights and Duties of States[61] and the 1990 Declaration on International Economic Cooperation, in particular the Revitalization of Economic Growth and Development of the Developing Countries.[62]

Among the instruments enumerated above, the Declaration on Friendly Relations and Cooperation among States is the only instrument the International Court of Justice has noted as containing evidence of *opinio juris* of customary international law.[63] Whether the duty to cooperate is considered as a principle of the UN

---

59 T. Stoll, 'Article 55 (a) and (b)', in B. Simma, D.-E. Khan, G. Nolte and A. Paulus (eds), *The Charter of the United Nations A Commentary*, 3rd edition, OUP, para. 29, paras. 31, 106 (emphasis added).
60 Chapter II, Section 1.4.
61 Article 17 of the Charter provides that international cooperation for development is the shared goal and common duty of all states. UN GA Resolution 3281 (XXIX), Charter of Economic Rights and Duties of States, 12 December 1974.
62 While the legally binding nature of these instruments has been contested, Wolfrum has opined that such an outcome does not 'preclude the use of individual provisions of these instruments as evidence of the existence of corresponding rules of international law'. Commentary by R. Wolfrum, 'Article 55', *op.cit.*, p. 907.
63 In the *Nicaragua* case, the International Court of Justice, in analysing the significance of some General Assembly Resolutions, referred to the Declaration on Principles of International Law concerning Friendly Relations and Cooperation among States, and more specifically qualified the nature of this Resolution as 'an acceptance of the validity of the rule or set of rules'. Although these references in pronouncement were concentrated on the principles of non-intervention and prohibition of the use of force, in a later passage the Court held that 'texts like this' contain customary content with regard to certain provisions. ICJ, *Military and Paramilitary Activities in and Against Nicaragua (Nicaragua v. US)*, Judgment of 27 June 1986, ICJ Reports 14, paras. 99–100.

Charter or a principle of general international law does not produce a difference in the legal consequences, since the addressees of such an obligation in both cases are the same.[64] Rather, the main question revolves around the content of such an obligation. It is here that the Declaration provides a more nuanced understanding. The relevant section of the Declaration, entitled 'The duty of States to cooperate with one another in accordance with the Charter', specifies that:

> States have the duty to co-operate with one another, irrespective of the differences in their political, economic and social systems, in the various spheres of international relations, in order to maintain international peace and security and to promote international economic stability and progress, the general welfare of nations and international cooperation free from discrimination based on such differences.[65]

The origin of the wording 'the duty to co-operate . . . in the various spheres' is a reflection of the negotiating process, wherein Western states opposed the *opinio juris* of the developing countries and the socialist states, concerning the existence of a general legal obligation of cooperation.[66] But this carefully circumscribed formulation can be contrasted with subsection (a) of the Declaration, which, in relation to peace and security, uses the word 'shall'.[67] Equally, the Declaration stipulates that:

> States *shall* co-operate in the promotion of universal respect for, and observance of, human rights and fundamental freedoms for all, and in the elimination of all forms of racial discrimination and all forms of religious intolerance.

For socio-economic development, the relevant passage chooses a softer wording:

> States *should* co-operate in the economic, social and cultural fields as well as in the field of science and technology and for the promotion of international cultural and educational progress. States should co-operate in die promotion of economic growth throughout the world, especially that of the developing countries.[68]

The text of the Declaration endorses the obligation to cooperate for 'universal respect for, and observance of, human rights' as a statement of a binding rule.

64 G. Abi-Saab, 'Cours général de droit international public', *op.cit.*, p. 453.
65 Declaration on Principles of International Law Concerning Friendly Relations and Cooperation among States in accordance with the Charter of the United Nations, UNGA Resolution 2625, Annex, 25 UN GAOR, Supp. (No. 28), UN doc. A/5217 at 121 (1970), 24 October 1970.
66 R. Wolfrum, 'International Law of Cooperation', *Max Planck Encyclopaedia of International Law*, www.mpepil.com.
67 The full text of the subsection (a) reads: 'States shall co-operate with other States in the maintenance of international peace and security.'
68 Emphasis added.

However, the way the text is formulated in relation to socio-economic development has led commentators to conclude that the Declaration falls short of establishing a 'general legal obligation to cooperate' for development.[69] The Declaration 'appears . . . as a meagre and ineloquent contribution to those immense and urgent problems of the developing world'.[70] In light of the above, the conclusion has been reached that no general customary law-based duty to cooperate for development has emerged;[71] an obligation exists only where an international agreement specifies so.

1.4 Assessment

The basic coordinates of the post-war legal order bear witness to an order designed to induce welfare for everyone, that is, a world in which mankind would be free from hunger, poverty, fear and insecurity. As Jouannet reminds us, '[t]he evils that the great instigators of the UN Charter were to address on a worldwide basis were the same as those in their democracies and that, in their view, had fostered the advent of fascism in Europe: poverty, unemployment, disease and ignorance'.[72] Although the recognition in the rhetoric of the relationship between peace, human rights and development is a recent advent,[73] freedom from want, as a constituent component of international peace, was declared already in 1941.[74] These ideals concerned all states, and not only developing nations.

---

69 H. Neuhold, 'Discussions', in J. Delbruck (ed.), *International Law of Cooperation and State Sovereignty: Proceedings of an International Symposium of the Kiel Walther-Shucking-Institute of International Law, May 23–26, 2001,* Dunker and Humbold: 2001, p. 96; See also G. Arangio-Ruiz, *The UN Declaration on Friendly Relations and the System of the Sources of International Law,* Sijthoff & Noordhoff: 1979, p. 144; and R. Wolfrum, 'International Law of Cooperation', *Max Planck Encyclopaedia of International Law,* www.mpepil.com, para. 17.

70 G. Arangio-Ruiz, *The UN Declaration on Friendly Relations and the System of the Sources of International Law,* Sijthoff & Noordhoff: 1979, p. 144.

71 See R. Wolfrum, 'International Law of Cooperation', in R. Bernhard (ed.), *EPIL* Vol. 2, 1242–1247; J. Delbruck, 'The International Obligation to Co-operate-An Empty Shell or A Hard Law Principle of International Law? – A Critical Look at A Much Debated Paradigm of Modern International Law', in H.P. Hestermeyer et al. (eds), *Coexistence, Cooperation and Solidarity: Liber Amicorum Rudiger Wolfrum,* Vol. 1, Martinus Nijhoff Publishers: 2011, pp. 3–16.

72 E. Jouannet, *The Liberal-Welfarist Law of Nations: A History of International Law, op. cit.,* p. 259.

73 UNSG K. Annan, In Larger Freedom: Towards Development, Security and Human Rights for All, UN doc. A/59/2005, 21 March 2005; UN GA Resolution 60/1, 2005 World Summit Outcome, 16 October 2005.

74 Some of the common principles included in the Atlantic Charter of 1941, on which hopes for a better future of the world were based, were 'to bring about the fullest collaboration between all nations in the economic field with the object of securing, for all, improved labor standards, economic advancement and social security' and 'a peace which will afford to all nations the means of dwelling in safety within their own boundaries, and which will afford assurance that all the men in all lands may live out their lives in freedom from fear and want'.

The UN Charter was thus clearly devised by its founders in the spirit of the law of cooperation, including its elevation of human rights and socio-economic issues to the level of common objectives. Both are written into the purposes of the organization. The pursuit of these objectives will therefore require common action, since it is in the interest of all that these objectives be attained. This being said, 'notwithstanding the validity of these very general postulates and the apparent suitability of international law as a means to pursue them, there is little consensus on how to use the law to this effect'.[75]

The grand legal objectives defined in the UN Charter remain so general and abstract that they are capable of engendering goal conflicts and definitional problems. The survey of UN Charter provisions so far did not provide any straightforward answers to questions raised in the introductory part of this chapter. Furthermore, compared to the socio-economic development, human rights have been confirmed and reconfirmed as constituting the core of the international community's values and interests.[76] The requisite of collective action for the realization of human rights has been reflected in the body of instruments on the subject. In the words of Antonio Cassese:

[H]uman rights doctrine has operated as a potent leaven, contributing to shift the world community from reciprocity-based bundle of legal relations, geared to the 'private' pursuit of self-interest, and ultimately blind to collective needs, to a community hinging on a core of fundamental values, strengthened by the emergence of community obligations and community rights and the gradual shaping of public interest.[77]

Two conclusions can therefore be inferred from this general discussion. First, that the UN Charter, as well as the General Assembly Declaration on Friendly Relations, ascribe the obligation to cooperate to both human rights and development. Second, the obligation to cooperate for development has been contested and has never crystallized into a binding norm, hence the need or search for another source of law.[78] The same cannot be said of human rights, however,

---

75 E. Jouannet, 'What Is The Use Of International Law? International Law as a 21st Century Guardian of Welfare', 28 *Michigan Journal of International Law* (2006–2007), p. 817. Particularly in the area of development, there are disagreements, as mentioned elsewhere in this book, whether 'law' should be used, and if so, to what extent. M. Bothe, 'Environment, Development, Resources', 318 *Recueil des Cours* (2005), p. 352.

76 See ICJ, *Reservations to the Convention on the Prevention and Punishment of the Crime of Genocide*, Advisory Opinion, ICJ Reports, 1951, 14, p. 23; *Barcelona Traction, Light and Power Company Limited (Second Phase) (Belgium v. Spain)*, ICJ Reports 1970, 3, paras. 33–34; *Legality of the Threat or Use of Nuclear Weapons*, Advisory Opinion, ICJ Reports 1996, 226, para. 76; *Democratic Republic of the Congo v. Uganda*, ICJ Reports 2005, para. 64; *Legal Consequences of the Construction of a Wall in the Occupied Palestinian Territory*, Advisory Opinion, ICJ Reports 2004, para. 157.

77 A. Cassese, *International Law*, 2nd edition, OUP: 2005, p. 396.

78 G. Abi-Saab, 'Cours général de droit international public', *op.cit.*, p. 454.

where an obligation to cooperate to that effect is a position endorsed by *communis opinio*. While both goals, human rights and development, are of equal rank, it is human rights that is a leading idea of our time, capable of soliciting universal and unconditional support in the international community.[79] This dividing line between human rights and development at the level of obligations becomes blurred when socio-economic human rights treaties require states, to use the wording of the UN Charter, 'to employ international machinery for the promotion of the economic and social advancement' and the fulfilment of their obligations.

2 Human rights and international cooperation

2.1 General observations

Before analysing the concept of international cooperation within the confines of a specific treaty framework, it is useful to make some observations on the meaning of international cooperation for human rights generally, as understood in practice. The UN Charter does not provide any indication as to the concrete meaning and implications of cooperation in promoting and encouraging respect for human rights and fundamental freedoms. A cursory review of instruments of a binding and non-binding nature reveals a host of meanings attached to the notion of cooperation in the context of human rights. In treaty-making practice, international cooperation sometimes has a general connotation;[80] in certain cases, cooperation may or may not include development-related aspects, while in others, specific reference is made to cooperation for development.[81]

There are instances where the concept of international cooperation is used as a way to give effect to a treaty.[82] Article 37 of the Convention on the Rights of

---

79 M. Ragazzi, *The Concept of International Obligations Erga Omnes*, OUP: 2000, p. 135.

80 See, for example, Article 23(4) of the Convention on the Rights of the Child (CRC): 'States Parties shall promote, *in the spirit of international cooperation*, the exchange of appropriate information . . ., with the aim of enabling States Parties to improve their capabilities and skills and to widen their experience in these areas. In this regard, particular account shall be taken of the needs of developing countries' (emphasis added).

81 Paragraph 3 of Article 10 of the Optional Protocol to the Child's Rights Convention on the sale of children, child prostitution and child pornography requires that 'States Parties *shall promote the strengthening of international cooperation* in order to address the root causes, such as poverty and underdevelopment, contributing to the vulnerability of children to the sale of children, child prostitution, child pornography and child sex tourism' and in paragraph 4 specifies 'States Parties in a position to do so shall provide financial, technical or other assistance through existing multilateral, regional, bilateral or other programmes' (emphasis added).

82 1977 Additional Protocol I (AP1) to 1949 Geneva Conventions further contains an article called 'Cooperation', according to which 'the High Contracting Parties undertake to act jointly or individually, in cooperation with the United Nations' in situations of serious violations of any of the four Geneva Conventions and Protocol I. The 1998 Rome Statute of the International Criminal Court also contains reference to 'international cooperation' in the preamble, and

Persons with Disabilities (CRPD), for example, stipulates that '[e]ach State Party shall cooperate with the Committee and assist its members in the fulfilment of their mandate'. Other examples of such use can be observed in a number of other human rights treaties. The preamble of the 1948 Genocide Convention refers to the need for international cooperation 'in order to liberate mankind from such an odious scourge'.[83] Accordingly, one form of obligation to cooperate implies a duty to 'comply' with the treaty.[84] From this perspective, 'cooperation', in a very abstract sense, can be a factual precondition for the operation of international treaties. This has led some scholars to conclude that international cooperation is a 'metalegal factual basis' or a *sine qua non* of international law.[85]

Sometimes international cooperation, in the sense of socio-economic cooperation through technical assistance, is made explicit by reference to the needs of developing countries. Article 28(3) of the Convention on the Rights of the Child (CRC) is an example:

> States Parties shall promote and encourage international cooperation in matters relating to education, in particular with a view to contributing to the elimination of ignorance and illiteracy throughout the world and facilitating access to scientific and technical knowledge and modern teaching methods. In this regard, particular account shall be taken of the needs of developing countries.

The most prominent human rights provision containing a reference to international assistance and cooperation is Article 2(1) of the Covenant on Economic, Social and Cultural Rights (examined in more detail further below). Its broad and all-encompassing nature and close linkage with treaty implementation has been interpreted as intending to refer to cooperation for development.

2.2 UN practice

International cooperation in relation to human rights has often been invoked in the practice of the UN General Assembly. The Assembly has regularly endorsed resolutions on the topics of '[e]nhancement of international cooperation in the

---

includes Article 86, prescribing a 'general obligation to cooperate' for States Parties to the Statute, with a comprehensive regulation of the issues of cooperation under Part 9, including cooperation for purposes of investigation and prosecution of crimes within the jurisdiction of the Court.

83 The 1951 Convention Relating to the Status of Refugees and the Protocol Relating to the Status of Refugees both specify undertakings 'to co-operate with the Office of the United Nations High Commissioner for Refugees' and in particular to 'facilitate its duty of supervising the application of the provisions' of the treaties.

84 Klein, in J. Delbruck (ed.), *International Law of Cooperation and State Sovereignty: Proceedings of an International Symposium of the Kiel Walther-Shucking-Institute of International Law, May 23–26, 2001*, Dunker and Humbold, Berlin: 2001, p. 67.

85 Dicke, *ibid.*, p. 101.

field of human rights',[86] '[r]espect for the purposes and principles contained in the
Charter of the United Nations to achieve international cooperation in promoting
and encouraging respect for human rights and for fundamental freedoms and in
solving international problems of a humanitarian character',[87] and on the subject
of '[s]trengthening United Nations action in the field of human rights through
the promotion of international cooperation and the importance of non-selectivity,
impartiality and objectivity'.[88] The latter category incorporates principles that were
already present in the Vienna Declaration and Programme of Action, but their significance and implications have rarely, if ever, been discussed in the literature.[89]

This triad of resolutions is controversial, to say the least. Overall, little detail
can be inferred from records of the context of resolutions. Nor is there any
proper analysis in the literature of the significance of the concepts these documents propagate. What is deducible is that, traditionally, the resolutions were
introduced at the initiative of Cuba and sponsored by members of a non-Western
group of countries.

The first and third groups of resolutions refer only to Article 1(3) as the legal
basis of international cooperation for human rights under the Charter of the UN.[90]
These resolutions underline the collective responsibility of states to uphold 'human
dignity', stressing also that the promotion of human rights should conform to the
purposes and principles of the Charter and, particularly, that they should be guided
by principles of universality, objectivity, non-selectivity and transparency.[91]

86 UN GA Resolutions on 'Enhancement of International Cooperation in the Field of Human
Rights' include UN docs. A/RES/58/170, 9 March 2004; A/RES/59/187, 10 March 2005;
A/RES/60/156, 23 February 2006; A/RES/63/180, 26 March 2009; A/RES/64/171,
24 March 2010, and the series of latest ones include UN docs. A/RES/67/169, March
2013, A/RES/68/160, 21 February 2014, A/RES/69/179, 28 January 2015.
87 UN GA Resolutions under the title 'Respect for the purposes and principles contained in
the Charter of the United Nations to achieve international cooperation in promoting and
encouraging respect for human rights and for fundamental freedoms and in solving international problems of a humanitarian character' include: A/RES/56/152, 13 February 2002;
A/RES/57/217, 27 February 2003; A/RES/59/204, 23 March 2005; A/RES/62/166,
20 March 2008.
88 UN GA Resolutions under the title 'Strengthening United Nations action in the field of
human rights through the promotion of international cooperation and the importance of
non-selectivity, impartiality and objectivity' include: A/RES/59/190, 15 March 2005; A/
RES/62/165, 20 March 2008; A/RES/64/158, 10 March 2010; A/RES/66/157,
20 March 2012; A/RES/68/176, 16 January 2014.
89 Paragraph 32 stipulates: 'The World Conference on Human Rights reaffirms the importance
of ensuring the universality, objectivity and non-selectivity of the consideration of human
rights issues.'
90 The second group of resolutions (e.g. Respect for the purposes and principles contained in
the Charter of the United Nations to achieve international cooperation in promoting and
encouraging respect for human rights and for fundamental freedoms and in solving international problems of a humanitarian character) does not avoid making references to Articles 55
and 56 of the UN Charter since their 'purpose' is to appeal on the contrary to cooperation in
promoting and encouraging respect for human rights and in solving international problems.
91 For example, UN GA Resolution on Enhancement of International Cooperation in the Field
of Human Rights, UN doc. A/RES/64/171, 24 March 2010, paras. 2, 6, and 7.

The key theme dominating their origin has sometimes been associated with the question of human rights and non-interference in internal affairs. In this context, the terms 'non-selectivity', 'impartiality' and 'objectivity', which may resemble some of the core principles of humanitarian assistance, were used as an express opposite to the use of 'selective' protection of human rights for political ends.[92] Therefore, the resolutions call for a 'genuine' cooperation which should be oriented towards an 'unbiased and fair approach to human rights'.[93]

In its Resolution 63/180 on enhancement of cooperation in the field of human rights, the General Assembly requested the Secretary-General of the UN, in collaboration with the High Commissioner on Human Rights, to consult with states and inter- and non-governmental organizations, on 'ways and means to enhance international cooperation and dialogue in the United Nations human rights machinery, including the Human Rights Council'.[94] The same request was reiterated in the context of 'strengthening of United Nations action in the field of human rights, through the promotion of international cooperation based on the principles of non-selectivity, impartiality and objectivity'.[95] These requests, articulated time after time, seem to have evoked only marginal attention among Member States, with a few exceptions.

The initiatives taken in the General Assembly have been paralleled in the work of the UN human rights bodies, where the question of international cooperation has figured under the similar rubric of 'enhancement of cooperation in the field of human rights'.[96] These resolutions also incorporate the principle that cooperation

---

92 Kamminga, for example, provides a brief background on Resolution Strengthening United Nations action in the field of human rights through the promotion of international cooperation and the importance of non-selectivity, impartiality and objectivity, at the origin of which lay the draft resolution entitled 'Inadmissibility of exploitation or distortion of human rights issues for interference in the internal affairs of States'. M. Kamminga, *Inter-state Accountability for Violations of Human Rights*, University of Pennsylvania Press: 1992, pp. x–xi. The resolutions on 'Strengthening United Nations action in the field of human rights through the promotion of international cooperation and the importance of non-selectivity, impartiality and objectivity' fall short of articulating the principle of non-interference, however. Rather, they call for a 'cooperative' approach in dealing with human rights issues.
93 See e.g. UN doc. A/RES/64/158, 10 March 2010, para. 7.
94 The latest UN GA Resolution, Enhancement of international cooperation in the field of human rights, UN doc. A/RES/65/218, 31 March 2011.
95 UN GA Resolution, Strengthening United Nations action in the field of human rights through the promotion of international cooperation and the importance of non-selectivity, impartiality and objectivity, UN doc. A/RES/64/158, 10 March 2010.
96 UN Human Rights Council Resolutions on 'Enhancement of international cooperation in the field of human rights': E/CN.4/RES/1998/81, 24 April 1998; E/CN.4/RES/1999/68, 28 April 1999; E/CN.4/RES/2001/67, 25 April 2001; E/CN.4/RES/2002/86, 26 April 2002; Commission on Human Rights, Resolution 2003/60 on Enhancement of international cooperation in the field of human rights, UN doc. E/CN.4/RES/2003/60, 24 April 2003; Resolution 2004/63, UN doc. E/CN.4/RES/2004/63, 21 April 2004; Resolution 2005/54, UN doc. E/CN.4/RES/2005/54, 20 April 2005; Human Rights Council Resolution 7/3, UN doc. A/HRC/RES/7/3, 27 March 2008; Human Rights Council Resolution 13/23, UN doc. A/HRC/RES/13/23, 26 March 2010; Resolution 19/33,

should be based on universality, objectivity and non-selectivity in consideration of human rights issues.[97] Human Rights Council Resolution 13/23 provided the Human Rights Council Advisory Committee with a mandate to explore ways and means to enhance cooperation in the field of human rights, taking into account the views of states and relevant stakeholders. For this purpose, the Advisory Committee set up a drafting group to prepare a report on the topic, and to highlight, among other things, the legal basis of international cooperation in the field of human rights.[98] In surveying the legal dimensions of international cooperation in the UN Charter, the report concludes that:

> the field of international cooperation is much broader than that of human rights, *stricto sensu*, and, at the same time, that this broad vision of 'economic and social cooperation' clearly encompasses human rights. Hence, there is a need for an ongoing dialectic between solving 'international problems of an economic, social, cultural, or humanitarian character' and strengthening human rights, but also between political cooperation and the 'progressive development of international law', including the codification of international human rights law. Similarly, the link between culture, education and human rights must be emphasized. This multifaceted form of cooperation reinforces and includes the human rights dimension, which is an element, not to say a condition, of that cooperation.[99]

The report acknowledges that there are two important dimensions of the topic: the first is cooperation in the field of human rights, and the second concerns human rights as a cross-cutting issue in different areas of inter-state cooperation. The report focuses only on the first issue, aiming to clarify 'the legal framework for cooperation in the United Nations system'.[100] It tries to grapple with the complex issues surrounding the question of international cooperation, identifying different levels of cooperation, as well as the multiplicity of actors, which various cooperative schemes entail.[101]

UN doc. A/HRC/RES/19/33, 18 April 2012; Resolution 22/116, UN doc. A/HRC/DEC/22/116, 15 April 2013; Resolution 23/3, UN doc. A/HRC/RES/23/3, 21 June 2013; Resolution 25/3, UN doc. A/HRC/RES/25/3, 10 April 2014; Resolution 28/2, UN doc. A/HRC/RES/28/2, 1 April 2015.

97 Commission on Human Rights Resolution 1998/81, UN doc. E/CN.4/RES/1998/81; Resolution 1999/68, UN doc. E/CN.4/RES/1999/68; Resolution 2000/70, UN doc E/CN.4/RES/2000/70; Resolution 2001/67, UN doc. E/CN.4/RES/2001/67; Resolution 2003/60 UN doc. E/CN.4/RES/2003/60, 24 April 2003; Resolution 2004/63, UN doc. E/CN.4/RES/2004/63, 21 April 2004; Resolution 2005/54, UN doc. E/CN.4/RES/2005/54, 20 April 2005; Human Rights Council: Resolution 7/3, UN doc. A/HRC/RES/7/3, 27 March 2008; Resolution 13/23, UN doc. A/HRC/RES/13/23, 26 March 2010; Resolution 16/22, UN doc. A/HRC/RES/16/22, 25 March 2011.

98 Human Rights Council Advisory Committee, Report on Enhancement of International Cooperation in the Field of Human Rights, *op.cit.*

99 *Ibid.*, para. 10.

100 *Ibid.*

101 *Ibid.*, paras. 28–32.

While acknowledging the very different use of the concept of cooperation, and despite the claim that it is 'too soon to set up a typology', the report suggests developing a systematic framework that allows all relevant parameters to be taken into consideration.[102] It is fair to say that the report reduced analysis of the concept of cooperation to exploring its forms, dimensions and manifestations in the human rights field, rather than looking into ways the normative framework it identifies has been interpreted and implemented in practice. Nonetheless, it represents perhaps the first systematic analysis of 'cooperation' as a self-standing topic, expanding beyond its traditional confinement to development-related concerns.

Under the concept/heading of '*international cooperation in the field of human rights*', the report considers issues such as ratification of human rights instruments,[103] dialogue with states to persuade them to withdraw their reservations,[104] enhancing the capacity of states nationally to enable them effectively to apply human rights treaties,[105] coordination, information-sharing between global, regional, and national human rights monitoring bodies,[106] cooperation of states with the human rights monitoring bodies,[107] follow-up with the recommendations of these bodies and technical and financial assistance mechanisms to facilitate implementation of the recommendations, strengthening the role of the NGOs, and international cooperation in the framework of international criminal justice (as discussed above). There is obviously a wide range of possibilities of action that could be covered by such a notion.[108] Generally speaking, almost

---

102 *Ibid.*, para. 26.
103 *Ibid.*, para. 40.
104 *Ibid.*, para. 41.
105 *Ibid.*, para. 42.
106 *Ibid.*, para. 43.
107 *Ibid.*, para. 44.
108 See for an example of different senses in which the term 'cooperation' could be used in the field of human rights protection, the work of L. Fisler Damrosch, according to whom, 'cooperation of human rights' may take the following forms: (i) quiet diplomacy: 'cooperation to resolve a given problem on a non-confrontational basis, perhaps in a package so that neither side losses face nor each side can claim benefits'; (ii) constructive engagement: 'cooperation across a range of activities, with human rights improvements as potential by-product'; (iii) negative cooperation: 'action to withhold certain benefits or transactions from a human rights violator, in order to ensure that the cooperating entity does not become complicit in or otherwise facilitate another State's violations . . . Other variants would be withdrawal of various forms of support for regimes that seriously violate human rights, as with the spectrum of measures against the former apartheid regimes in Southern Rhodesia and South Africa'; (iv) transnational cooperation: 'cooperation to solve a problem that requires action across national boundaries', and an example would be extradition and/or judicial assistance to make possible the prosecution of an individual accused of a serious violation of human rights, such as torture; (v) technical assistance: '[c]ooperation to offer expertise or assistance toward mitigating violations or enhancing compliance'; (vi) foreign aid (wealth transfer): '[i]nternational cooperation in support of human rights could take the form of foreign assistance or other forms of resource transfer, with human rights improvements as a potential byproduct'; and (vii) institutional cooperation: 'while all the foregoing modes involve government-to-government relationship, cooperation can also take place within the framework of an international human rights institutions – e.g.

any human rights activity pursued through an international organization reflects some form of institutional cooperation.

The Human Rights Council Advisory Committee stipulated that human rights in all areas where international cooperation takes place should be examined through a cross-cutting approach: '[t]he centrality of human rights in international cooperation must be reaffirmed through the mainstreaming of human rights issues in all cooperation policies'.[109] In this respect, the negative impact of sanctions, structural adjustment policies and 'certain forms of conditionality' are given as examples of possible areas where human rights issues come to the fore. Sustainable development, immigration, the right to development and the need to foster the emergence of conditions favourable to development, as well as 'a need for clearer delineation of the relationship between human security and international cooperation in relation to confidence-building, security measures, arms controls, the implementation of humanitarian law and the workings of the criminal justice system', are all mentioned in the continuum between human rights and international cooperation.[110]

3 International covenant on economic, social and cultural rights

It falls now to be examined whether the International Covenant on Economic, Social and Cultural Rights (ICESCR) can provide a concrete normative content beyond the minimum statement of principle found in Articles 55 and 56 of the UN Charter. In particular, what is the relationship of the ICESCR with development (cooperation)? The ICESCR is an example of a human rights treaty that ties

---

institutional cooperation'. L. Fisler Damrosch, 'Obligation of Cooperation in the International Protection of Human Rights', pp. 15–45 in J. Delbruck (ed.), *International Law of Cooperation and State Sovereignty: Proceedings of an International Symposium of the Kiel Walther-Shucking-Institute of International Law, May 23–26, 2001*, Dunker and Humbold: 2001, pp. 25–28.

109 Human Rights Council Advisory Committee, Report on Enhancement of International Cooperation in the Field of Human Rights, *op. cit.* The version as submitted to the HRC is under A/HRC/19/74, 29 February 2012, para. 51.

110 As a follow-up to the Advisory Committee's Study, the Human Rights Council Resolution 19/33 requested an organization of a seminar to discuss enhancement of cooperation in the field of human rights building on the findings and recommendations of the study. The participants of the seminar (see the report in UN doc. A/HRC/23/20, 23 April 2013), while noting the difficulty of formulating a general definition of international cooperation, in particular in the field of human rights, nevertheless concluded that an operational definition of the term would be needed. Substantively, the discussion on international cooperation for human rights revolved around a number of topics including cooperation for development (thus for realization of human rights), integration of human rights in various fields of inter-state cooperation, cooperation of states in prevention of gross violations of human rights and the dialogue between states on human rights in inter-governmental forums (such as Universal Periodic Review). From a quantitative perspective, ample focus was put on international cooperation and the impact thereof on economic, social and cultural rights.

together the general notion of the obligation to cooperate for human rights and the notion of cooperation in the area of development.[111] From a legal perspective, it can be argued that the ICESCR, to a certain extent, absorbs 'cooperation for development', qualifies it and complements it with additional elements.

3.1 The normative content of 'international assistance and cooperation' under article 2(1) of ICESCR

3.1.1 Basic tenets and contentions over the notion of 'international assistance and cooperation'

Reference to international cooperation is found in Articles 2(1), 11(1), 11(2), 15(4), 22 and 23 of the International Covenant on Economic, Social and Cultural Rights.[112] Article 2(1) of the Covenant provides an 'umbrella' obligation on States Parties' obligations, reading as follows:

> Each State Party to the present Covenant undertakes to take steps, *individually and through international assistance and co-operation*, especially economic and technical, to the maximum of its available resources with a view to achieving progressively the full realization of the rights recognized in the presented Covenant.[113]

The fundamental aspects of 'international assistance and cooperation' were raised in the process of drafting ICESCR, but remained unsettled in the final text as adopted. Questions thus remain; namely, what is the legal nature of 'international assistance and cooperation'? Does it imply a duty to provide international assistance and cooperation? If there is an obligation, what are the consequences for its violation? As the treaty concerns individual rights, do the obligations of states *inter se* automatically translate into the right of individuals to receive assistance? And, if so, what would be the means for enforcing such a right? What is the import of 'international assistance and cooperation' given the fact that it is

---

111 The Human Rights Council Advisory Committee Report on the Enhancement of Cooperation in the Field of Human Rights, having noted that the wording of international assistance and cooperation does not figure in the Covenant on Civil and Political Rights, raises a question: 'should not all human rights be promoted through international cooperation, starting with legal cooperation and technical assistance in the area of education and vocational training of public officials?' The report importantly stresses that it is 'only when the two covenants are taken together that the full extent of the commitment to cooperation for the promotion of human rights is made clear'. *Ibid.*, paras. 14–15.

112 Provision on international cooperation and assistance is included in: Article 4 of Convention on the Rights of the Child; Articles 4 and 32 of Convention on the Rights of Persons with Disabilities; Article 26 of the American Convention on Human Rights and in Article 1 of the Additional Protocol to the American Convention on Human Rights in the Area of Economic, Social and Cultural Rights (Protocol of San Salvador).

113 Emphasis added.

placed in the main 'covering provision' stipulating States Parties' obligations?[114] What are the specific means to implement such a duty?

It is difficult to address all of these questions and to identify the content of the provisions in light of the ordinary meaning of Articles 2(1), 11(1), 11(2), 15(4), 22 and 23,[115] or through the ICESCR's context and its object and purpose, as the Vienna Convention on the Law of Treaties (VCLT) would require.[116] While the CESCR has provided useful guidance, it has not yet systematically clarified these aspects so as to enable their uniform application in any given situation. It has, however, established a basic element of the notion clarifying that:

> [I]n accordance with Articles 55 and 56 of the Charter of the United Nations, with well-established principles of international law, and with the provisions of the Covenant itself, international cooperation for development and thus for the realization of economic, social and cultural rights is an obligation of all States. It is particularly incumbent upon those States which are in a position to assist others in this regard. The Committee notes in particular the importance of the Declaration on the Right to Development adopted by the General Assembly in its resolution 41/128 of 4 December 1986 and the need for States parties to take full account of all of the principles recognized therein. It emphasizes that, in the absence of an active programme of international assistance and cooperation on the part of all those States that are in a position to undertake one, the full realization of economic, social and cultural rights will remain an unfulfilled aspiration in many countries.[117]

Yet, the requirement of realizing ESC rights *through* international assistance and cooperation means different things for states in a position to provide assistance, on the one hand, and those who are in need of it, on the other.[118] The

---

114 The Committee on Economic, Social and Cultural Rights describes the role of this provision as having a dynamic relationship with all of the other provisions of the CESCR. This provision read together with each and every provision defines the scope and nature of obligations. See CESCR, General Comment No. 3, The Nature of States Parties' Obligations, UN doc. E/1991/23, 14 December 1990, para. 1.

115 Importance of international cooperation was underlined in Articles 11, 15, 22 and 23 of the Covenant on Economic, Social and Cultural Rights. Article 11(1), on the right to food, reaffirms the necessity of international cooperation, and in paragraph 2 stipulates that states 'shall take, individually and through international cooperation, measures'. Article 15(4), on cultural rights, makes use of the term 'cooperation'.

116 Article 31(1), Vienna Convention on the Law of the Treaties.

117 CESCR, General Comment No. 3, The Nature of States Parties' Obligations, UN doc. E/1991/23, 14 December 1990, para. 14.

118 Report of the Open-ended Working Group to Consider Options Regarding the Elaboration of an Optional Protocol to the International Covenant on Economic, Social and Cultural Rights on its Third Session, 2006, UN doc. E/CN.4/2006/47. While the developing states held the view that the obligation of international assistance and cooperation was a legally binding duty, developed states doubted this position and some even deemed it merely a moral obligation.

former group of states has consistently rejected the existence of any legal obligation in this regard.[119] The focus in the debates on the existence of an obligation for resource transfers indicates that states see the provision as requiring mainly positive obligations; a narrow, 'resource-based' action. To that end, it is not clear whether international cooperation and assistance is controversial in its entirety or only regarding one of its elements, namely development assistance.[120] Consequently, the general perception that international cooperation and assistance provisions are resolutely 'soft', and therefore lacking legal quality, requires a more nuanced assessment.

References to the UN Charter and the Declaration on the Right to Development by the Committee are not very helpful in determining implications of such an obligation.[121] During debates in the *travaux préparatoires* of the ICESCR, the idea of international assistance and cooperation being mandatory was not supported, since it was held that the legal obligation would serve as an excuse for countries to evade any obligation on the basis of inadequacy of international assistance.[122]

The records of, and comments on, the drafting history of Article 2 do not allow for the attribution of an obligation to provide assistance to either cooperation or assistance. More precisely, if, for example, a 'duty to cooperate' existed separately from a 'duty to assist', could the latter be covered by the former, or is the element of a duty to assist attributable to both? Discussions took place to identify the meaning of 'international assistance and cooperation' and, more specifically, whether it was confined to technical assistance only.[123]

---

119 The debates surrounding the issue in the negotiation of the Optional Protocol to the ICESCR demonstrate that developed states considered that international cooperation provisions lack a binding force. Report of the Open-ended Working Group to Consider Options Regarding the Elaboration of an Optional Protocol to the International Covenant on Economic, Social and Cultural Rights on its Second Session, UN doc. E/CN.4/2005/52, paragraph 76, according to which, '[i]n relation to article 2 (1), the discussions focused on the reference to international assistance and cooperation. The representatives of the United Kingdom, the Czech Republic, Canada, France and Portugal believed that international cooperation and assistance was an important moral obligation but not a legal entitlement, and did not interpret the Covenant to impose a legal obligation to provide development assistance or give a legal title to receive such aid.'

120 On general issues related to the international cooperation in the field of human rights see the Report of the Human Rights Council's Advisory Committee, Report on Enhancement of International Cooperation in the Field of Human Rights, *op. cit.*

121 See the discussion in Chapter III.

122 P. Alston and G. Quinn, 'The Nature and Scope of States Parties' Obligations under the International Covenant on Economic, Social and Cultural Rights', *9 Human Rights Quarterly* (1987) pp. 156–229, p. 189.

123 In fact, the earlier draft of the provision referred only to 'cooperation', therefore it can be interpreted that assistance was inserted to underline its importance as a form of cooperation. The 1952 draft of Article 2(1) reads: 'Each State Party hereto undertakes to take steps, individually and through international cooperation, to the maximum of available resources, with a view to achieving progressively the full realisation of the rights recognised in this Covenant by legislative as well as other means.' Commission on Human Rights, Report

As for development assistance specifically, 'there did not seem to be a clear view as to whether States facing resource shortages would have a duty to try to obtain resources from wealthier States, or whether wealthier States had a duty to provide such assistance' and that '[b]oth views were voiced, and no substantial discussions as to either way of addressing these things seems to have taken place'.[124]

Reference can also be made to the provisions of other treaties on socio-economic rights that contain similar provisions on international assistance and cooperation (Article 4 of the CRC[125] and Article 4(2) of the CRPD). These treaties were adopted in different historical timeframes. As such, a comparison of the nature of the meaning attached to the term 'international cooperation' in each treaty may reveal a progressive understanding of the notion and the degree of legal force assigned to it.[126] Article 4 of the CRC lacks reference to 'assistance', adopting instead a broader term: 'international cooperation'.[127] In Articles 4,[128] 23(4), 24(4) and 28(3), international cooperation is linked

---

of the Eighth Session (14 April to 14 June 1952), ECOSOC Official Records Fourteenth Session, Suppl. No. 4, Annex I. The same wording was contained in the draft which the Human Rights Commission handed over to the General Assembly in 1954, and which was then further discussed in the Third Committee of the General Assembly between December 1954 and December 1966.

124 S. Skogly, *Beyond National Borders: States' Human Rights Obligations in International Cooperation*, Intersentia: 2006, p. 85.

125 The wording of the CRC on international obligations differs. Article 4 of the Convention on the Rights of the Child stipulates: 'States Parties shall undertake all appropriate legislative, administrative, and other measures for the implementation of the rights recognized in the present Convention. With regard to economic, social and cultural rights, States Parties shall undertake such measures to the maximum extent of their available resources and, where needed, within the framework of international cooperation.' According to the commentaries, they are not as explicit as ICESCR. See M. Rishmawi, *A Commentary on the United Nations Convention on the Rights of the Child, Article 4 – The Nature of States Parties' Obligations*, Martinus Nijhoff Publishers: 2006, p. 7. The comparison with the Child's Rights Covenant shows, that unlike in CESCR, 'full realisation' of the ESC rights of children is not made explicit.

126 W. Vandenhole, 'Economic, Social and Cultural Rights in the CRC: Is There a Legal Obligation to Cooperate Internationally for Development?', 17 *International Journal of Children's Rights* (2009), pp. 23–63, p. 25.

127 CRC, General Comment No. 5 (2003), General Measures of Implementation of the Convention on the Rights of the Child (Articles 4, 42 and 44, para. 6), UN doc. CRC/GC/2003/5, 27 November 2003, also see CRC, Seventh Session, Overview of the Reporting Procedures, UN doc. CRC/C/33, 24 October 1994. See also S. Detrick, *Commentary on the United Nations Convention on the Rights of the Child*, Kluwer International: 1999, p. 109.

128 Article 4 of the CRC: 'States Parties shall undertake all appropriate legislative, administrative, and other measures for the implementation of the rights recognized in the present Convention. With regard to economic, social and cultural rights, States Parties shall undertake such measures to the maximum extent of their available resources and, where needed, *within the framework of international cooperation*' (emphasis added).

to the 'needs of developing countries'.[129] International cooperation featured prominently in the adoption of the Optional Protocol to the Convention on the Rights of the Child on the Involvement of Children in Armed Conflict.[130] In its General Comment on the Implementation of the Convention, the Committee on the Rights of the Child pointed out that: '[w]hen States ratify the Convention, they take upon themselves obligations not only to implement it within their jurisdiction, but also to contribute, through international cooperation, to global implementation'.[131] The CRC underscored the implementation of the Convention as 'a cooperative exercise for the States of the world'.[132] On another occasion, the Committee, in light of the conflicting views on the meaning of references to international cooperation, indicated that it 'believes

129 Article 23(4) CRC: 'States Parties shall promote, in the spirit of international cooperation, the exchange of appropriate information in the field of preventive health care and of medical, psychological and functional treatment of disabled children, including dissemination of and access to information concerning methods of rehabilitation, education and vocational services, with the aim of enabling States Parties to improve their capabilities and skills and to widen their experience in these areas. In this regard, particular account shall be taken of the needs of developing countries.' Article 24 of CRC concerns the right to health, and paragraph 4 reads: 'States Parties undertake to promote and encourage international cooperation with a view to achieving progressively the full realization of the right recognized in the present article. In this regard, particular account shall be taken of the needs of developing countries.' Article 28(3) of the CRC reads: 'States Parties shall promote and encourage international cooperation in matters relating to education, in particular with a view to contributing to the elimination of ignorance and illiteracy throughout the world and facilitating access to scientific and technical knowledge and modern teaching methods. In this regard, particular account shall be taken of the needs of developing countries.'

130 International assistance and cooperation was included as one of the nine main areas and, in fact, as voiced by representative of the Indian delegation, 'it did raise standards in a real and substantive manner over the existing norms in its various provisions including those on international cooperation'. Report of the working group on a draft optional protocol to the Convention on the Rights of the Child on involvement of children in armed conflicts on its sixth session, UN doc. E/CN.4/2000/74, para. 145. Discussions that took place in the drafting process of the Optional Protocol indicate the importance attached to international cooperation; moreover, it was articulated by the US that '[s]tates can and should assist in bringing an end to this tragedy through international cooperation and assistance'. See Report of the working group on a draft optional protocol to the Convention on the Rights of the Child on involvement of children in armed conflicts on its sixth session GE.00–12043 (E), UN doc. E/CN.4/2000/74, para. 145. Inter-sessional open-ended working group on a draft optional protocol to the Convention on the Rights of the Child on involvement of children in armed conflicts Comments on the Report of the Working Group, UN doc. E/CN.4/2000/WG.13/2/Add.1, paras. 18–20. The position of the US was interpreted as acceptance of the human rights obligation to cooperate for the rehabilitation and integration of child soldiers. W. Vandenhole, 'Economic, Social and Cultural Rights in the CRC: Is There a Legal Obligation to Cooperate Internationally for Development?', *op. cit.*, p. 39.

131 CRC, General Comment No. 5 (2003) General measures of implementation of the Convention on the Rights of the Child (Articles 4, 42 and 44, para. 6), para. 7.

132 *Ibid.*, para. 60.

that children's rights are a shared responsibility between the developed and the developing countries'.[133]

Akin to the CESCR, the Committee on the Rights of the Child closely links the international assistance and cooperation provision to the issues of cooperation for development.[134] The CRC, in the first place, advised States Parties to approach the Convention on the Rights of the Child as a legal basis for international development assistance.[135] Second, the Committee stressed that development programmes and policies should be based on the rights contained therein.[136] Third, the Committee advised donors to meet the target for international development assistance. Fourth, it was of the view that the UN and UN-related agencies should be guided by the Convention and mainstream children's rights in their activities. In addition:

> [t]hey should seek to ensure within their influence that international cooperation is targeted at supporting States to fulfil their obligations under the Convention. Similarly the World Bank Group, the International Monetary Fund and World Trade Organization should ensure that their activities related to international cooperation and economic development give primary consideration to the best interests of children and promote full implementation of the Convention.[137]

References to international cooperation in the CRPD are contained in the preamble, Article 4(2)[138] on state obligations, and in Article 32, specifically dealing

---

133 The Committee also stressed that: 'State parties must respect and protect economic, social and cultural rights of children in all countries with no exceptions, and take all possible measures to fulfil these rights – whenever they are in a position to do so – through development cooperation.' CRC, General Discussion on 'Resources for the Rights of the Child-Responsibility of States', 46th Session, 21 September 2007, paras. 50–51.

134 In this context, it recalls the UN Charter's provisions and pledges of states in economic and social cooperation as well as the UN Millennium Declaration, where states have 'pledged themselves, in particular, to international cooperation to eliminate poverty'. CRC, General Comment no. 5 (2003) General measures of implementation of the Convention on the Rights of the Child (Articles 4, 42 and 44, para. 6), para. 60.

135 It 'urges States to meet internationally agreed targets, including the United Nations target for international development assistance of 0.7 per cent of gross domestic product'. See CRC, General Comment no. 5 (2003) General measures of implementation of the Convention on the Rights of the Child (Articles 4, 42 and 44, para. 6), para. 60. In paragraph 64, the CRC stated that States Parties recipients of international aid are asked to apportion 'substantive part of that aid' to children.

136 The CRC in particular urges that PRSP and sector-wide approaches to development (SWAps) should reflect children's rights principles. *Ibid.*, para. 62.

137 CRC, General Comment no. 5 (2003) General measures of implementation of the Convention on the Rights of the Child (Articles 4, 42 and 44, para. 6), para. 64.

138 Article 4(2) of the CRPD: 'With regard to economic, social and cultural rights, each State Party undertakes to take measures to the maximum of its available resources and, where needed, within the framework of international cooperation, with a view to achieving progressively the full realization of these rights, without prejudice to those obligations contained in the present Convention that are immediately applicable according to international law.'

with international cooperation[139] and acknowledging 'the importance' of coop-eration. As already mentioned, the Convention presents an interesting case for review in terms of debates concerning 'international cooperation' and its implica-tions for the present understanding of the meaning and scope of the concept. The records of the drafting history indicate that although importance was attached to the imperative of cooperation, it remained a difficult subject matter to reach consensus on.[140]

A summary of the debates on the question is illuminating:

> Some members expressed particular concern about creating international obli-gations with regard to international cooperation, development aid or assis-tance in the context of a binding instrument, although they actively engaged in international cooperation. Other members considered that the issue should not be interpreted as imposing obligations beyond any other existing model of international cooperation.[141]

Objections to inclusion of a specific provision on international cooperation were grounded on the fact that the Disability Convention, as a human rights

---

139 Article 32 of the CRPD reads as follows:

'1 States Parties recognize the importance of international cooperation and its promo-tion, in support of national efforts for the realization of the purpose and objectives of the present Convention, and will undertake appropriate and effective measures in this regard, between and among States and, as appropriate, in partnership with relevant international and regional organizations and civil society, in particular organizations of persons with disabilities. Such measures could include, inter alia:

   a Ensuring that international cooperation, including international development pro-grammes, is inclusive of and accessible to persons with disabilities;
   b Facilitating and supporting capacity-building, including through the exchange and sharing of information, experiences, training programmes and best practices;
   c Facilitating cooperation in research and access to scientific and technical knowledge;
   d Providing, as appropriate, technical and economic assistance, including by facilitat-ing access to and sharing of accessible and assistive technologies, and through the transfer of technologies.

2 The provisions of this article are without prejudice to the obligations of each State Party to fulfil its obligations under the present Convention.'

140 The discussions in the drafting process underscored that implementation of the Convention will be primarily a national responsibility and that compliance with the Convention should not be conditional on receiving international development aid or assistance. Another view held that international cooperation was an important means to support national efforts for the realization of goals and objectives of the Convention, and even though it was agreed that primary responsibility for implementation will rest upon states domestically, there was a shared responsibility, and international cooperation is to complement national efforts. As seen from the records of the discussions, the issue of shared responsibility was later seen with regard to the allocated resources (once development assistance is provided by the donor-state to the recipient-state), e.g. how they are used.

141 Annex II, Summary of the discussions held regarding the issue of international cooperation to be considered by the *Ad Hoc* Committee, UN doc. A/AC.265/2004/WG/1, paras. 2, 3, 5.

treaty, involved rights of individuals as opposed to international cooperation, which was not a 'specific' human right. Furthermore, the EU was of view that insertion of an international cooperation provision would make the Convention deal with states' obligations towards other states.[142] In negotiations at a later stage, it was the general framework for cooperation that was supported, rather than international cooperation, understood as development assistance.[143]

3.1.2 Contrasting various approaches to the definition of international assistance and cooperation

The legal nature and meaning of 'international assistance and cooperation', as it appears in the ICESCR, continue to remain highly contested and, as a consequence, its implications for the role of development cooperation in the implementation of ESC rights are rather unclear. Neither the CESCR nor doctrine seem to have consistently theorized the concrete implications of the requirement of 'international assistance and cooperation'.[144]

Scholarly writings often focus on states' extraterritorial obligations under the ICESCR, building on Article 2(1) of the Covenant's prescription on international assistance and cooperation.[145] Applying the framework of tripartite obligations to analyse state obligations under various rights to 'international assistance and cooperation',[146] the leading texts on ESC rights allude to the existence of

142 Daily summary of discussion at the sixth session 1 August 2005, Vol. 7, No. 1 of 1 August 2005, www.un.org/esa/socdev/enable/rights/ahc6sum1Aug.htm.

143 W. Vandenhole, 'Economic, Social and Cultural Rights in the CRC: Is There a Legal Obligation to Cooperate Internationally for Development?', *op. cit*, pp. 23–63, p. 59.

144 For a critique of the CESCR's treatment on the issue, see K. Mechlem, 'Treaty Bodies and the Interpretation of Human Rights', 42 *Vanderbilt Journal of Transnational Law* (2009), pp. 907–947, p. 934, who opined in this regard that '[w]ith every new General Comment the scope of such obligations seems either to expand or to shrink again'.

145 F. Coomans and M.T. Kamminga, *Extraterritorial Application of Human Rights Treaties*, Intersentia: 2004; M. Gibney, K. Tomasevski and J. Vedsted-Hansen, 'Transnational State Responsibility for Violations of Human Rights', 12 *Harvard International Law Journal* (1999), pp. 267–295; M.T. Kamminga, *Inter-state Accountability for Violations of Human Rights, op. cit.*; S. Narula, 'The Right to Food: Holding Global Actors Accountable Under International Law', 44 *Columbia Journal of Transnational Law* (2006), pp. 691–800; M. Sepúlveda Carmona, 'Obligations of "International Assistance and Cooperation" in an Optional Protocol to the International Covenant on Economic, Social and Cultural Rights,' 24 *Netherlands Quarterly of Human Rights* (2006), pp. 271–303; S.I. Skogly, *Beyond National Borders: States' Human Rights Obligations in International Cooperation*, Intersentia: 2006; J.B. de Mesquita, *International Covenant on Economic, Social and Cultural Rights: Obligations of International Assistance and Cooperation*, Human Rights Centre, University of Essex: 2002; M. Gibney and S. Skogly (eds), *Universal Human Rights and Extraterritorial Obligations*, University of Pennsylvania Press: 2010.

146 The levels of obligations have been elaborated on the basis of works of H. Shue, *Basic Rights: Subsistence, Affluence, and U.S. Foreign Policy*, 2nd edition, Princeton University Press: 1996; and A. Eide, The Right to Adequate Food as a Human Right, UN Commission on Human Rights, Report on the Right to Adequate Food by A. Eide, Special Rapporteur, UN doc. E/CN.4/Sub.2/1987/23, 7 July 1987. See Maastricht Guidelines (No. 6) for the description of the obligations.

three distinct obligations to respect, protect and fulfil ESC rights with an international dimension (i.e. with respect to individuals in other states).[147] According to this logic, States Parties are 'to avoid measures that hinder or prevent the enjoyment of the Covenant's rights in another State', 'to take measures to prevent that non-State entities under their jurisdiction interfere with the enjoyment of the Covenant's rights abroad', and to provide assistance for 'satisfaction of rights' of individuals in other states.[148]

More theorists find that from among these obligations, only those of a negative nature (obligations to respect, viz. not to do) are well established at the international level. Such theorists arrive at a conclusion that positive duties (such as the obligation to fulfil) are the least settled.[149] In contrast, previous debate on the issue generally understood the concept of international assistance and cooperation as primarily (but not exclusively) linked to such positive obligations, more specifically, positive obligations as specified broadly by the notion of a right to development and the related principles and norms related to inter-state cooperation in socio-economic matters, including official development assistance.[150]

The current overwhelming view seems to have largely transformed this debate. There is, however, a non-negligible counter-perspective to this interpretation in the doctrine. According to one view, international assistance and cooperation is not a self-standing, independent obligation that is incumbent upon the States Parties at all times and in all circumstances.[151] Pisillo Mazzeschi argues that international assistance and cooperation 'font seulement partie de l'éventail

---

147 Report of the Special Rapporteur on the Right to Food: The Way Forward, UN doc. A/HRC/28/65, 12 January 2015, para. 41ff; General principles 1(3), Maastricht Principles on Extraterritorial Obligations of States in the Area of Economic, Social and Cultural Rights; Craven earlier suggested that: 'the obligations to respect, protect, and ensure operate at the international level just as they do at the national level. Thus States could be said to have an initial duty to restrain themselves from any action that might impede the realization of economic, social and cultural rights in other countries.' M. Craven, *The International Covenant on Economic, Social and Cultural Rights: A Perspective on Its Development*, OUP: 1995, p. 147. For examples of analysis of international assistance and cooperation by reference to the tripartite obligations: M. Sepúlveda Carmona, 'Obligations of "international assistance and cooperation" in an Optional Protocol to the International Covenant on Economic, Social and Cultural Rights', 24(2) *Netherlands Quarterly of Human Rights* (2006), pp. 271–305; J. Tobin, *The Right to Health in International Law*, OUP: 2012, pp. 325–370.
148 Sepúlveda Carmona, *ibid.*, pp. 280–289.
149 International Council on Human Rights Policy, *Duties sans frontières: Human Rights and Global Social Justice*, International Council on Human Rights Policy: 2003; M. Sepúlveda Carmona, 'Obligations of "international assistance and cooperation" in an Optional Protocol to the International Covenant on Economic, Social and Cultural Rights', *op. cit.*, pp. 271–305; W. Vandenhole, 'Economic, Social and Cultural Rights in the CRC: Is There a Legal Obligation to Cooperate Internationally for Development?', *op. cit.*, pp. 23–63.
150 On the existence of a positive obligation to provide assistance, see M. Flory, *Droit International du Développement*, Presses Univertaires de France: 1977.
151 R. Pisillo Mazzeschi, Responsabilité de l'état pour violation des obligations positives relatives aux droits de l'homme, 333 *Recueil des Cours* (2008), p. 456.

des mesures "appropriées" possibles visées à l'article 2 paragraphe 1, du Pacte'.[152] His interpretation is based on the fact that the commitment to assist and cooperate is too vague to translate into true legally binding obligations. He stresses that Article 2(1) of ICESCR 'ne considère pas la coopération et l'assistance comme des obligations séparées et autonomes, mais seulement comme l'un des moyens possibles par lesquels les Etats peuvent agir en vue d'assurer progressivement l'exercice des droits reconnus dans le Pacte'.[153] For one thing, the provision speaks of international assistance and cooperation, especially *economic and technical*.[154] More fundamentally, in referring to Article 11 of the ICESCR (the right of everyone to an adequate standard of living), which makes international cooperation conditional upon the state recipient's consent, Mazzeschi usefully points out that the Committee itself has never expressly asserted a violation of the obligation of cooperation in the examination of states' reports.[155]

Undeniably, the argument that international cooperation as such is not a self-standing obligation can be further supported by the wording of Article 4 of the CRC, which indicates that in order to fulfil the rights secured in the Convention, states are to 'undertake such measures to the maximum extent of their available resources and, *where needed*, within the framework of international cooperation'. The CRPD reproduces almost *verbatim* the provision of the CRC, similarly limiting the international cooperation to situations where it is *needed*. Given that the CRPD is a recent treaty, one has to ask whether states have actually transformed their understanding of the notion of 'cooperation' to a more complex, all-encompassing one, as proposed by the current analysis.

The nature of the notion of international assistance and cooperation as a *measure* rather than an independent obligation can be further contrasted by reference to regional human rights instruments. The Additional Protocol to the American Convention on Human Rights in the Area of Economic, Social and Cultural Rights, provides that:

> [t]he States Parties to this Additional Protocol to the American Convention on Human Rights undertake to adopt the necessary measures, both domestically and through international cooperation, especially economic and technical, to the extent allowed by their available resources, and taking

---

152   *Ibid.*

153   *Ibid.*, p. 457.

154   As Craven notes, 'it is not clear whether the terms "assistance" and "cooperation" have discrete meanings. Neither is it obvious whether the terms "economic and technical" refer to both forms of international action or merely to "cooperation"'. M. Craven, *The International Covenant on Economic, Social and Cultural Rights: A Perspective on Its Development, op. cit.*, p. 147.

155   Article 11(1) reads as follows: 'The States Parties to the present Covenant recognize the right of everyone to an adequate standard of living for himself and his family, including adequate food, clothing and housing, and to the continuous improvement of living conditions. The States Parties will take appropriate steps to ensure the realization of this right, recognizing to this effect the essential importance of international cooperation based *on free consent*' (emphasis added).

into account their degree of development, for the purpose of achieving progressively and pursuant to their internal legislations, the full observance of the rights recognized in this Protocol.[156]

In light of this legal situation, it is possible to conclude that the requirement of Article 2(1) of the ICESCR on assistance and cooperation is not a substantive legal provision requiring States Parties to abstain from or perform certain actions. The provision does not lay out what States Parties are to do or not do in relation to a specific question; rather, it creates a legal obligation on *how* all the obligations contained in substantive provisions of the ICESCR are to be discharged. In this context, an obligation of assistance and cooperation can only be a rule of secondary nature, specifying means by which obligations under specific rights are to be achieved.[157] If such an interpretation is accepted, it will be difficult to extrapolate, on the basis of international assistance and cooperation *only* (Article 2(1)), concrete obligations that potentially cover all acts and omissions that may have an impact on the ESC rights of persons in third states.

A further question is whether international assistance and cooperation denotes a comprehensive concept or, rather, is to be reduced to resources, that is, development aid *stricto sensu*. A systematic analysis of Article 2(1), as well as its different manifestations in other articles of the ICESCR, points towards a notion going beyond the issue of provision of material assistance. This is mainly because the text of the ICESCR itself seems to be in favour of an extensive approach to the concept. The provision leaves the list of (international) means and measures open, specifying only some forms such as economic and technical measures. This *ratio legis* can be found in paragraph 2 of Article 11 of the ICESCR, dealing with the fundamental right of everyone to be free from hunger, which requires states *individually and through international cooperation* to take measures 'to ensure an equitable distribution of world food supplies in relation to need', taking into account 'the problems of both food-importing and food-exporting countries'.[158]

---

156 Article 1, Additional Protocol to the American Convention on Human Rights in the Area of Economic, Social and Cultural Rights. See also for a discussion on the meaning of international cooperation in the context of the OAS Charter, D.M. Negro, 'Article 17 and Chapter VII of the Revised OAS Charter and Relevant Experience of OAS Institutions', in S. P.Marks (ed.), *Implementing the Right to Development: the Role of International Law*, Friedrich Ebert Stiftung: 2008, pp. 64–72.

157 The formulation of this paragraph is inspired by the analysis of Article 1 of Geneva Conventions of 1949 in A. Cassese, *International Law*, 2nd edition, OUP: 2005, p. 18.

158 For Alston, the meaning of the provision implies a duty to avoid depriving and duties to protect from deprivation. The obligation to avoid depriving may imply: '1. The duty to avoid international policies and practices which deprive other states of their means of subsistence or which promote an inequitable distribution of world food supplies. 2. The duty to mitigate national policies which have the effect of promoting an inequitable distribution of world food supplies. 3. The duty not to use food as an international sanction.' P. Alston, 'International Law and the Human Rights to Food', in P. Alston and K. Tomasevski (eds), *The Right to Food: Towards a System for Supervising States' Compliance with the Right to Food*, Martinus Nijhoff Publishers: 1984, p. 44.

Indeed, to reduce international cooperation and assistance to mere development assistance would be an unduly narrow approach to the framework of rights that are posited on international action, the enjoyment of which is inevitably contingent upon external socio-economic processes. This scholarly consensus, to visualize international assistance and cooperation expansively, can be attributed to the changes of perception in relation to ESC rights generally. For a long time, the normative essence of ESC rights was conceived as being based on a different logic.[159] In particular, the obligations of States Parties to the Covenant, when analysed through the standard of 'maximum available resources', has carried forward an idea that compliance is not an important concern: 'States wish to comply and will do so if they have the necessary resources.'[160] By extension, the debates at the international level revolved around issues of resource generation and redistribution, and thus also the importance of technical and financial transfers (in form of official development assistance), investment, etc., rather than focusing on developing rules and legal principles on prevention, or ensuring that various processes, including development itself, are not harmful to individual rights.

As is well known, long-established perceptions have gradually changed. The CESCR, in a number of general comments, has pronounced that certain ESC rights require immediate performance. The obligation to respect ESC rights, similar to civil and political rights, obliges States Parties to avoid depriving someone of a right he or she already has. The contents of ESC rights and their corresponding obligations have been developed in various general comments, supplemented by documents produced by experts defining the nature and scope of obligations arising from the ESC rights at national and international levels.[161] These efforts to define the international dimension of obligations are significant in that they attempt to respond to exogenous causes of the systematic denial of

159 O. Schachter, 'International Law in Theory and Practice: general course in public international law', *op. cit.*, p. 346.
160 L. Henkin, 'International Law: Politics, Values and Functions', 216 *Recueil des Cours* (1989), p. 270.
161 The 1986 Limburg Principles on the Implementation of the International Covenant on Economic, Social and Cultural Rights, contained in UN Commission on Human Rights, Note verbale dated 86/12/05 from the Permanent Mission of the Netherlands at the United Nations Office at Geneva addressed to the Centre for Human Rights ('Limburg Principles'), 8 January 1987, UN doc. E/CN.4/1987/17; International Commission of Jurists, Maastricht Guidelines on Violations of Economic, Social and Cultural Rights, 26 January 1997; International Commission of Jurists, The Bangalore Declaration and Plan of Action, Bangalore, India, in 23–25 October 1995; Quito Declaration on the Enforcement and Realization of Economic, Social, and Cultural Rights in Latin America and the Caribbean, 24 July 1998; Maastricht Principles on Extraterritorial Obligations of States in the area of Economic, Social and Cultural Rights, and the Commentary by O. De Schutter, A. Eide, A. Khalfan, M. Orellana, M. Salomon and I. Seiderman, www.icj.org/dwn/database/Maastricht%20ETO%20Principles%20-%20FINAL.pdf.

basic subsistence rights to a large majority of individuals, and to the deterioration of standards of living due to crises of an external nature.[162]

Proponents of the expansive reading of 'international assistance and cooperation' find ample assistance in the views of the CESCR to support their arguments.[163] In fact, the CESCR has not been conceptually clear on what is meant by 'international assistance and cooperation' and what purpose such references ought to serve. Occasionally, the Committee has opted for a resource-based construction of international assistance and cooperation, stressing that it is incumbent on states in a position to assist, '*to provide* "international assistance and cooperation, especially economic and technical"',[164] referring to 'an active programme of international assistance and cooperation',[165] and requiring states to 'seek international cooperation and assistance' in the context of means of implementation.[166]

On a closer look, however, it becomes apparent that when shedding light upon the obligations of states at the international level, the Committee does not rely exclusively on the provision on 'international assistance and cooperation' as a basis to clarify the substantive obligations of States Parties. For example, in certain instances, the Committee reads international assistance and cooperation in conjunction with 'the spirit' of Article 56 of the Charter of the United Nations, the specific provisions contained in Articles 11 and 23 of the ICESCR and, sometimes, global policy statements, such as, for example, the Rome Declaration of the World Food Summit. The UN Charter and other provisions of the ICESCR are altogether framed as '*international obligations*' in relation to the right to food requiring that:

> States parties should recognize the essential role of international cooperation and comply with their commitment to take joint and separate action to

---

162 International welfare inducing law 'can also be used as a means of obtaining international aid, despite the fact that the sharp rise in poverty and famine over recent years has actually been due to negligence, blind collectivism, terror, or civil war'. E. Jouannet, 'What is the Use of International Law? International Law as a 21st Century Guardian of Welfare', *op. cit*, p. 853.

163 See e.g. M. Sepúlveda Carmona, 'Obligations of "International Assistance and Cooperation" in an Optional Protocol to the International Covenant on Economic, Social and Cultural Rights', *op. cit*, pp. 271–303, p. 278, who supports her approach to develop states' obligations at international level by reference to the CESCR which 'itself applies the "tripartite typology" to analyse international obligations'.

164 CESCR, General Comment No. 14, The Right to the Highest Attainable Standard of Health, UN doc. E/C.12/2000/4, 11 August 2000, para. 45 (emphasis added).

165 CESCR, General Comment No. 3, The Nature of States Parties' Obligations, UN doc. E/1991/23, 14 December 1990, para. 14.

166 CESCR, General Comment No. 4, The Right to Adequate Housing, contained in UN doc. E/1992/23, 13 December 1991, para. 10; CESCR, General Comment No. 5, Persons with Disabilities, contained in UN doc. E/1995/22, 12 September 1994, para. 13. CESCR, General comment No. 6, The Economic, Social and Cultural Rights of Older Persons, contained in UN doc. E/1996/22, 12 August 1995, para. 18.

achieve the full realization of the right to adequate food. In implementing this commitment, States parties should take steps to respect the enjoyment of the right to food in other countries, to protect that right, to facilitate access to food and to provide the necessary aid when required.[167]

Similarly, in relation to the right to education, the Committee has relied upon the UN Charter and relevant commitments expressed in the policy statements, which 'all reinforce the obligation of States Parties in relation to the provision of international assistance and cooperation for the full realization of the right to education'.[168] In relation to the right to health, however, the CESCR defines international obligations to respect the enjoyment of the right to health in other countries and to prevent third parties from violating that right, by reference to the UN Charter and *applicable international law*. Only in relation to the fulfilment of core obligations does the CESCR express in explicit and exclusive terms the obligation to provide 'international assistance and cooperation, especially economic and technical'.[169]

Two conceptions of international assistance and cooperation therefore can be deduced from the practice of the Committee on Economic, Social and Cultural Rights. One is international assistance and cooperation in the narrow sense, i.e. 'as means of implementation', meaning primarily technical and financial assistance. The second expansive construction of the notion, which tends to be identified under the umbrella concept of 'cooperation', is interpreted broadly in light of the obligations of states under the UN Charter. The Committee clearly makes this distinction between the two when it states: '[*i*]*nternational cooperation requires States parties to refrain from actions that interfere, directly or indirectly, with the enjoyment of the right to water in other countries*'.[170]

The assumption here, as distinct from the approach of many authors, is that obligations to respect and protect socio-economic rights in other states (crucial in the context of development cooperation) are *more composite*. On numerous occasions, the CESCR referred to a number of legal sources such as the UN Charter, and albeit in a much more ambiguous manner to '*applicable international law*', in order to construe an argument that states are to abstain from interfering directly or indirectly with ESC rights of individuals in other countries. A more complex analysis in search of this 'applicable law' is therefore in order.[171]

167 CESCR, General Comment No. 12, The Right to Adequate Food, UN doc. E/CN.12/1999/5, 12 May 1999, para. 36.
168 CESCR, General Comment No. 13, The Right to Education, UN doc. E/C.12/1999/10, 8 December 1999, para. 56.
169 CESCR, General Comment No. 14, The Right to the Highest Attainable Standard of Health, UN doc. E/C.12/2000/4, 11 August 2000, para. 39.
170 CESCR, General Comment No. 15, The Right to Water, UN doc. E/C.12/2002/11, 20 January 2003, para. 31 (emphasis added).
171 See Chapter VI.

3.1.3 The relationship of ICESCR with 'cooperation for development'

As discussed earlier, the ICESCR, perhaps in line with its genuine essence, absorbs the cooperation for development construct, *in toto* or in part, by designating it as one of the means of implementation of socio-economic rights. By doing so, it also incorporates a highly contentious element of inter-state economic relations, namely development assistance, or cooperation as it is increasingly now termed.[172] Development assistance (in its all forms: financial, technical, etc.), as a permanent feature of the relationship between developing and developed states, has over the years determined its own field of reality. Its controversial aspects will not be examined here. The more fundamental question is whether, considering the consistent and continued practice of providing development assistance to developing states, it can be defined in terms of rights and obligations.[173]

Despite the existence of the 'regularity of flows of assistance' between developed and developing countries for an extended period of time, as indicated by Georges Abi-Saab long ago, it is 'difficult to maintain that they have given place to a concrete normative proposition, specific as to their content (level) or individualized as to their destination (or beneficiaries)'.[174] The difficulty in maintaining the existence of donor states' obligations to transfer official development assistance with a corresponding right in favour of developing states is the absence of a 'direct legal link . . . between the members of the two categories of State considered individually'.[175] While development assistance is perfectly compatible and naturally allies with the 'law of cooperation' logic, as a right, if there is one in the first place, it can only be directed towards the international community. Equally, if there is a corresponding obligation on the part of the developed countries, it would have to be also towards the international community. In the absence of the independent resources necessary for fulfilling its obligation of assistance, the international community will have to rely on those of its members that have a capacity to do so.[176]

For the general principle of the obligation to provide assistance to become operational, 'not only does its content need to be specified, but so do also the parties to the legal relations deriving therefrom and the institutional arrangements which relate them to each other'.[177] Although this observation is made in relation to the issue of development assistance generally, it remains valid for the

---

172 As suggested throughout this book, ODA is not always automatically linked with compliance with the Covenant's obligations, but rather is channelled for the purposes of development.

173 Development assistance is a permanent item of the budgets of both developed and developing countries, and one of the main features of international organizations.

174 Report of the Secretary General, Progressive Development of the Principles and Norms of International Law Relating to the New International Economic Order, UN doc. A/39/504/Add.1, 23 October 1984, para. 179.

175 *Ibid.*

176 *Ibid.*

177 *Ibid.*, para. 180.

legal situation of international assistance and cooperation under the ICESCR, to the extent that the legal weight of Article 2(1) is questioned. If, however, one considers 'international cooperation' under Article 2(1) as providing sufficient legal justification for developing and developed states to assist each other in terms of financial and technical resources, then an institutional framework of implementation is required in order for it to become an operational legal principle.[178]

A shift in this direction would move development assistance towards a more objective regime and would make the assertion of development assistance as a legal obligation or entitlement possible. Institutionalization will also address challenges of the current development architecture, such as the lack of objective rules and standard criteria governing the flows of resources and their ultimate destination or the lack of objective criteria, specific as to the need, level and time development assistance is provided.[179] There is, of course, no shortage of multilateral institutional frameworks for this purpose. The problem, however, is that states still favour providing assistance bilaterally.[180]

Would it be possible to devise an adequate institutional framework for international assistance and cooperation under the ICESCR? In effect, this is not a theoretical question. The readiness of the states to accept a specific, as well as 'compelled', cooperation can be inferred from the drafting history of the Optional Protocol to the ICESCR. The Optional Protocol contains Article 14 on international assistance and cooperation, which provides for, *inter alia*, the establishment of a trust fund. The purpose of this fund is to 'enhance implementation of the rights' contained in the ICESCR and to help build national capacities of states in the area of ESC rights. The provision caused much debate in the drafting of the Optional Protocol, but in the end was accepted, as it is based on voluntary contributions.[181]

Similarly, commitments as formulated in the global pledges to eradicate poverty and promising development remain resolutely voluntary. Some transient contractual proposals have been designed since the 1990s, though without much success, as the logic of such approaches is a shared responsibility. No serious follow-up ensued to the undertakings such as the 20/20 initiative 'to ensure that all people have access to basic social services' suggested by the World Social Summit of 1998,[182] or even the pledge for World Solidarity Fund in the

178 *Ibid.*, para. 31.
179 *Ibid.*, para. 124.
180 According to one estimate only 29% of development assistance is channelled through multilateral institutions, a share of which is earmarked, thus undermining freedom of programming by multilateral institutions and ownership by programme countries. See Report of Secretary General on Trends and Progress in International Development Cooperation, UN doc. E/2010/93, 10 June 2010, para. 52.
181 E. Riedel, 'New Bearings in Social Rights? The Communications Procedure Under the ICESCR', in U. Fastenrath et al. (eds), *From Bilateralism to Community Interest: Essays in Honour of Bruno Simma*, OUP: 2011, pp. 575–589, p. 587.
182 The Copenhagen Declaration and Programme of Action 1995, Report of the World Summit for Social Development (Copenhagen, 6–12 March 1995), UN doc. A/CONF.166/9,

Summit Outcome of 2005.[183] The latest idea in this regard is a so-called 'new social compact' envisaged by the Addis Ababa Action Agenda (AAAA) of the Third International Conference on Financing for Development.[184] Presented as a novelty rather than a reaffirmation of pre-existing obligations under human rights treaties, the social compact is to fund essential public services for all (such as healthcare, education, etc.). It is now to be seen how the UN Member States will fulfil their pledges for a 'strong international support for these efforts' and their commitment to explore 'coherent funding modalities to mobilize additional resources'.[185]

The ICESCR has only defined the objective of the obligation to cooperate and assist, in general, for the full realization of economic, social and cultural rights. This would imply that the first responsibility of States Parties to ICESCR is to negotiate further *with a view to articulating* more precisely the obligations incumbent upon them and the means of achieving them.[186] In the absence of this definition agreed by States Parties, treaty bodies and particularly the Committees on Economic Social and Cultural Rights, and on the Rights of the Child, have (rightly or wrongly), where appropriate, referred to state pledges for development cooperation in outcome documents of UN summits.[187] The CESCR has consistently requested states to report on their efforts on the ODA target of 0.7%, the volume of aid defined as a standard of achievement (as opposed to a legal obligation) in the area of development. While the primary obligation rests

---

para. 88; The Beijing Declaration and Platform for Action 1995, Report of the Fourth World Conference on Women, UN doc. A/CONF.177/20, 17 October 1995, paras. 353 and 358 requiring allocation of 20% of ODA and 20% of national budgets, respectively, for basic social programmes.

183 Paragraph 24 of the 2005 World Summit Outcome Document endorsed UN GA Resolution 57/265 on Establishment of the World Solidarity Fund, UN doc. A/RES/57/265, 28 February 2003.

184 UN GA Resolution 69/313, Addis Ababa Action Agenda of the Third International Conference on Financing for Development (Addis Ababa Action Agenda), UN doc. A/RES/69/313, 17 August 2015, para. 12.

185 *Ibid.*

186 Similarly, the Report on the Secretary General on Progressive Development of the Principles and Norms of International Law Relating to the New International Economic Order suggested that the normative prescription of the duty to cooperate 'can at most, in addition to defining the objective in general, create a duty or an obligation to negotiate with a view to defining more precisely the targets to be reached and the ways and means of reaching them'. However, as the Report admits, 'such a normative prescription is not sufficient by itself to constitute a normative proposition. In other words, the purely normative approach reaches its limits in the context of the international law of cooperation, which, by modulating the legal regulation closely to its subject-matter, is rich in specific applications that do not, or not yet, led themselves to normative generalizations.' UN doc. A/39/504/Add.1, 23 October 1984, paras. 134–135.

187 The CESCR has made references to the agreements reached at Rome Declaration of the World Food Summit, the Alma-Ata Declaration on Primary Health Care, and CRC has made references to the Millennium Development Goals.

with the domestic state,[188] states have an obligation to seek assistance and cooperation, where needed.[189] Hence, international assistance, depending on the circumstances, may either be subsidiary (the most common case) or concurrent.[190] On one occasion, the CESCR clarified that when a state is *clearly lacking* in financial or technical resources, 'the international community has a clear obligation to assist'.[191]

One reading of the international assistance and cooperation provision by the treaty-monitoring bodies comes very close to the essence of the right to development, particularly in linking Article 2(1) with cooperation for development. It is useful to iterate the view of the CESCR in this regard: 'international cooperation *for development and thus for the realization of economic, social and cultural rights is an obligation for all States*'.[192] Perhaps a somewhat far-fetched and strained, though nonetheless theoretically possible, argument can be made for the existence of an obligation to cooperate for development *via* human rights. This could be developed on the basis of the UN Charter and interpretations given to the provisions of the ICESCR and the CRC.[193] This understanding, however, is to be construed as only one component of a greater and far more expansive conception of 'international assistance and cooperation', as discussed in the previous section.

In view of the many ambiguities and inconsistencies emanating from the drafting history of the ICESCR and OP-ICESCR,[194] and the practice in the area of

---

188 See CESCR, General Comment No. 3, para. 11. Similarly, '[w]hile development facilitates the enjoyment of all human rights, the lack of development may not be invoked to justify the abridgement of internationally recognized human rights'. UN GA, *Vienna Declaration and Programme of Action*, UN doc. A/CONF.157/23, 12 July 1993, para. 10.

189 See e.g. CESCR Statement: An evaluation of the obligation to take steps to the 'Maximum of available resources' under an optional protocol to the Covenant, UN doc. E/C.12/2007/1, 10 May 2007, para. 10.

190 For instance, in the context of the right to food, the CESCR clarified that states 'have a joint and individual responsibility, in accordance with the Charter of the United Nations, to cooperate in providing disaster relief and humanitarian assistance in times of emergency, including assistance to refugees and internally displaced persons'. CESCR, General Comment No. 12, The Right to Adequate Food, UN doc. E/CN.12/1999/5, 12 May 1999, para. 38.

191 CESCR, General Comment No. 11, Plans of action for primary education, UN doc. E/C.12/1999/4, 10 May 1999, para. 9.

192 Emphasis added. The Committee repeated its position regarding an obligation to cooperate for development in General comment No. 17, The right of everyone to benefit from the protection of the moral and material interests resulting from any scientific, literary or artistic production of which he or she is the author (Article 15), UN doc. E/C.12/GC/17, 12 January 2006, para. 37.

193 Louis Henkin suggests: 'The Covenant serves as justification for demands for international economic change . . . and for assistance from international institutions and from other States.' L. Henkin, 'International Law: Politics, Values and Functions', *op. cit.*, p. 270.

194 In the discussion of the Draft Resolution concerning the right to food in the UN Commission on Human Rights, the US representative while supporting the 'progressive realization' of the right to food emphasized 'categorically' that such a right 'did not give rise to international obligations'. See Williamson (USA), UN doc. E/CN.4/2004/SR.51, p. 16, para. 84, Comments made in respect of the Draft resolution concerning Right to Food (UN doc. E/CN.4/2004/L.24).

'development', some scholars have assumed the absence of a legal duty in relation to assistance and cooperation.[195] What is often omitted in the debates, however, is the fact that assistance and cooperation have been included in the provision that is fundamental for the definition of states' obligations in relation to ESC rights. This alone suggests that it was the intention of the framers of the ICESCR to envisage international (or external) support as a means of rendering the rights effective.

More fundamentally, the position taken by the Committee on Economic, Social and Cultural Rights, as well as the existence of the debate on the nature of the provision, make it difficult to sustain the position that there is no obligation of assistance and cooperation, even where it concerns a resources dimension. As Marco Sassòli observed, '[t]he mere fact that the addressees of a rule consider that in a certain situation that rule is inadequate to what they perceive as the normative needs cannot make the rule disappear, in particular as long as no consensus on a new desirable rule exists'.[196] Challenges involved in setting up a 'cooperative' framework, bringing together all parties (developing and developed states), should not diminish the validity of the CESCR's interpretation of the relationship between development cooperation and the ICESCR.

In the final analysis, these broad assumptions should be verified by recourse to the interpretative scheme devised by the VCLT under Article 31. This method will first allow constructing a more complex investigation of the subject. Second, the rule of interpretation may direct us to a number of so-far neglected avenues where answers can be sought. More importantly, the rule of interpretation can help us to identify the type of 'legal material' that may be relevant as an interpretative guide. Finally, the VCLT's framework will take the analysis beyond the narrow confines of the socio-economic rights and development debate, to a broader environment, allowing for the consideration of other rules of international law.

3.1.4 Subsequent practice in the application of the ICESCR

The starting point in our analysis is that, to date, no agreement has been reached between the parties to the ICESCR in connection with the conclusion of the Covenant,[197] nor is there any subsequent agreement regarding the interpretation or the

195 International Council on Human Rights Policy, *Duties sans frontières: Human Rights and Global Social Justice*, International Council on Human Rights Policy: 2003; M. Sepúlveda Carmona, 'Obligations of "international assistance and cooperation" in an Optional Protocol to the International Covenant on Economic, Social and Cultural Rights', *op. cit.*, pp. 271–305; W. Vandenhole, 'Economic, Social and Cultural Rights in the CRC: Is There a Legal Obligation to Cooperate Internationally for Development?', *op. cit*, pp. 23–63.
196 M. Sassòli, 'The Role of Human Rights and International Humanitarian Law in New Types of Armed Conflicts', in O. Ben-Naftali (ed.), *International Humanitarian Law and International Human Rights Law*, OUP: 2011, pp. 47–48.
197 Article 31(2)(a), VCLT.

application of its provisions.[198] The successive step suggested by the rule of interpretation is to ascertain whether the words of the ICESCR are given meaning by states' deeds.[199] According to the International Law Commission (ILC), the importance of practice, 'as an element of interpretation, is obvious; for it constitutes objective evidence of the understanding of the parties as to the meaning of the treaty'.[200]

Recourse to practice can indeed parse out more carefully various meanings of international cooperation, given that it serves as a permanent function of all donor and recipient countries and is one of the main objectives of the United Nations.[201] The main problem is that establishing a required practice expressing an agreement is a complex undertaking.[202] If Article 2(1) of the ICESCR itself did not render a precise result, one has to admit that the resultant practice is also difficult to reconcile. Assessment of conduct[203] possibly meeting the requirement of subsequent practice also has to satisfy two criteria: first, that the practice is 'in

---

198 Article 31(3)(a), VCLT.
199 Inspiration to this formulation is taken from a similar quote, 'words are given meaning by deeds', from R. Gardiner, *Treaty Interpretation*, OUP: 2008, p. 225.
200 Yearbook of International Law Commission, Vol. II, 1966, p. 221, para. 15.
201 Article 31(3)(b) of VCLT stipulates 'any subsequent practice in the application of the treaty which establishes the agreement of the parties regarding its interpretation'. For subsequent practice for the purposes of the interpretation of 'international assistance and cooperation', imply answers to questions such as the type of conduct, who 'must engage in the conduct for it to count', which parties need to participate in the practice and what it is that constitutes an interpretative agreement. J. Arato, 'Subsequent Practice and Evolutive Interpretation: Techniques of Treaty Interpretation over Time and their Diverse Consequences', 9 (3) *The Law and Practice of International Courts and Tribunals* (2010), p. 459.
202 The report of Special Rapporteur Mr Georg Nolte on the work of the ILC on 'Subsequent agreements and subsequent practice in relation to the interpretation of treaties' informs that '[t]he jurisprudence of international courts and tribunals, including the Dispute Settlement Body of WTO, recognizes that not only "subsequent practice in the application of a treaty which establishes the agreement of the parties regarding its interpretation" may be relevant for the purpose of interpretation, but possibly also other subsequent practice which does not reflect an agreement on interpretation by all the parties. The concept of "subsequent practice" should therefore be defined broadly. A narrow definition . . . may be helpful in identifying a fully agreed and authentic interpretation of a treaty in the sense of article 31 (3)(b) of the Vienna Convention. The taking into account of other treaty practice by States for the purpose of interpretation should not be excluded at the outset since it may in some situations serve as a supplementary means of interpretation in the sense of article 32 of the Vienna Convention. Such use of subsequent practice (in a broad sense) must, however, always remain within the limit of the rule that treaty interpretation is not self-judging and that "the view of one State does not make international law".' See ILC, First report on subsequent agreements and subsequent practice in relation to treaty interpretation by Georg Nolte, Special Rapporteur, UN doc. A/CN.4/660, 19 March 2013, para. 107.
203 See the list of material sources often referred to as evidence of international custom as provided by Brownlie: 'diplomatic correspondence, policy statements, press releases, the opinions of legal advisers, official manuals on legal questions, e.g. manuals of military law, executive decisions and practices, orders to naval forces etc., comments by governments produced by International Law Commission, State legislation, international and national judicial decisions, recitals in treaties and other international instruments, a pattern of treaties in the same form, the practice of international organs, and resolutions relating to legal questions in the United Nations General Assembly'. I. Brownlie, *Principles of Public International Law*, 6th edition, OUP: 2003, p. 6.

application of the treaty' and, second, that it 'establishes the agreement of the parties regarding its interpretation'.[204]

A PRACTICE OF STATES ACTING INDIVIDUALLY

In the beginning of our analysis, references were made to the opinion of states. To the extent that the opinions and reactions of states on the issue is relevant 'practice', a few observations are in order. The position of developed states expressed in the latest negotiations of human rights treaties has sometimes been regarded as reflecting the interpretation of international assistance and cooperation.[205] The opinion of donor states of course is not *the* interpretation of the provision but, rather, is *one* of its possible interpretations. This is particularly so, first, given that the position of developed states is contradicted by others.[206] Considering that the ICESCR is a multilateral treaty and donor states represent only some of the States Parties, their position is insufficient to be regarded as the only interpretation of Article 2(1) of the ICESCR. Of course, Article 31(3)(b) of the VCLT does not require that the practice be performed by all the parties; what it requires is that the agreement be that of all parties.[207] Therefore, the equally important counterweight position of developing states will have to be factored in the final analysis.

The position of donor states themselves is also not coherent on the issue. As far as the obligation of cooperation and assistance under Article 2(1) is concerned, the overall impression is rather mixed. A sample analysis of the CESCR's dialogue with States Parties, in the framework of state reporting, shows that the Committee has systematically raised the issue of compliance with Article 2(1).[208] The CESCR required reporting on three points: (i) provision of development assistance, (ii) on the way the development policies of the State concerned contributed to the realization of ESC rights in developing countries, and (iii) measures states take as members of international financial institutions to ensure their policies are in compliance with the Covenant.[209]

---

204 See also ICJ, *Kasikili/Sedudu Island (Botswana/Namibia)*, Judgment 13 December 1999, ICJ Reports 1999, p. 1094, para. 74, where the Court, in the assessment of the meaning of 'subsequent practice' clarified that two criteria have to be met: first, that the conduct 'was linked to a belief' on the part of the authors of the conduct as reflecting the interpretation of the treaty and, second, that the other party to the treaty 'were fully aware of and accepted this as a confirmation of the Treaty boundary'.
205 Particularly the OP-ICESCR and CPRD.
206 China, Egypt and Congo attributed legal title to the obligation of assistance and cooperation. See Report of the open-ended working group to consider options regarding the elaboration of an Optional Protocol to the International Covenant on Economic, Social and Cultural Rights on its second session, UN doc. E/CN.4/2005/52, para. 77.
207 R. Gardiner, *Treaty Interpretation, op. cit.*, p. 235.
208 The analysis covers the period from 2004 to 2012 and covers examination of state reports, list of issues and summary records of considerations of States Parties' reports.
209 It needs to be observed that the Committee does not take up these questions in relation to all state reports in a uniform manner. The CESCR raised one, both or all three issues above in relation to Italy, Austria, Finland, Netherlands, Belgium, France, Sweden, UK, Australia, Switzerland, New Zealand and Spain reports.

The majority of states in their response to CESCR's questions reported with varying degrees of detail on measures undertaken, including their current and planned volumes of ODA, contributions to development and poverty reduction, etc.[210] Their attitude raises a question as to whether their positive response and absence of refutation in the process of international monitoring of compliance with international treaty obligations amounts to endorsement of the existence of an obligation to cooperate and provide assistance. The plausibility of such an interpretation is further supported by the fact that only one state, in the period under review, clarified that its development cooperation efforts 'stem from a strong and solid political commitment, *rather than from its obligations under the Covenant*'.[211]

Other relevant material for our analysis is the practice of individual donor states, some aspects of which have already been discussed.[212] By way of summary, the policy statements of governments are very ambiguous and constantly shifting. It is not possible to identify a straightforward and explicit answer to the question of whether 'international assistance and cooperation' is understood as legally binding or not. For one thing, the language of obligation is generally carefully avoided in policy statements. Some examples, however, are suggestive and come close to the type of element that could be relevant for the purpose of constructing 'subsequent practice'. Consider, for instance, the following development policy on human rights:

> Germany and the majority of its development partners have ratified the international human rights conventions and have thus recognized the implementation of these conventions as a legally binding obligation. This also provides the binding frame of reference for Germany's development cooperation with partner countries.

Furthermore, defining the MDG 8 (Global partnership for development), the same policy document states:

> This MDG relates to the establishment of a global partnership for development. Besides the UN Charter (Articles 1, 55 and 56), the human rights treaties (including Article 2(1) ICESCR, Article 4 of the Convention on the Rights of the Child, and Article 32 of the Convention on the Rights of

---

210 Italy (UN doc. HR/CESCR/NONE/2004/3), Finland (UN doc. E/C.12/FIN/Q/5/Add.1), Netherlands (UN doc. E/C.12/NLD/Q/3/Add.1), Belgium (UN doc. E/C.12/BEL/Q/3/Add.1), Sweden (UN doc. E/C.12/SWE/Q/5/Add.1), UK (UN doc. E/C.12/GBR/Q/5/Add.1), Australia (UN doc. E/C.12/AUS/Q/4/Add.1), Switzerland (UN doc. E/C.12/CHE/Q/2–3/Add.1), New Zealand (UN doc. E/C.12/NZL/Q/3/Add.1), Spain (UN doc. E/C.12/ESP/Q/5/Add.1).
211 See the response of Sweden to the list of issues, UN doc. E/C.12/SWE/Q/5/Add.1, para. 48 (emphasis added).
212 See the discussion in Chapter II.

Persons with Disabilities) contain binding provisions for international cooperation that is aimed at the realization of human rights. For example, developing countries are required to use the maximum of their available resources,
including funds from international cooperation, for the implementation of
human rights obligations and hence, inter alia, for the attainment of the
MDGs. The targets defined for MDG 8 give rise to human rights-related
obligations for the donor countries as well. These include, for example, their
participation in further developing an open, rule-based, predictable, non-
discriminatory trading and financial system and providing access to affordable essential drugs in developing countries.[213]

This policy statement contains at least three useful elements: (i) the legal
sources cited are legally binding, (ii) indirect reference to the international assistance as part of resources devoted to the fulfilment of human rights (i.e. linking
cooperation for development with human rights), and (iii) some further indicia
interpreting possible action flowing from the legal obligation to cooperate, such
as measures to create an enabling environment. All these issues have been already
raised in the examination of the nature and scope of 'international assistance
and cooperation'. Other examples of state practice are less explicit and informa-
tive on these issues. The Canadian Official Development Assistance Accountability Act specifies that all Canadian official development assistance is provided
'with a central focus on poverty reduction and in a manner that is consistent
with . . . democracy promotion and that promotes international human rights
standards'.[214]
Iceland's legislation on the subject matter provides that 'Iceland's international development cooperation shall be based on the Charter of the United
Nations and other international conventions on development cooperation that
the Icelandic Government has undertaken to comply with'.[215] Luxembourg's
strategy, entitled 'Gouvernance pour le développement', stipulates that '[e]n tant
que signataire, le Luxembourg s'engage à respecter et à faire respecter les droits
fondamentaux contenus dans ce document. En outre le Luxembourg a *pris des
engagements internationaux* en ratifiant les textes relatifs à la gouvernance suiv-
ants' and lists among others the ICCPR and ICESCR.[216] The Spanish Law on
International Cooperation for Development pledges that Spanish cooperation
aims at contributing, among others, to development and respect and protection

213 BMZ of Germany, *Human Rights in German Development Policy*, BMZ Strategy Paper 4,
    BMZ: 2011e., p. 12.
214 Article 2(1), Official Development Assistance Accountability Act S.C. 2008, c. 17, Canada,
    http://laws-lois.justice.gc.ca/eng/acts/O-2.8/page-1.html.
215 Act No. 121/2008 on Iceland's International Development Cooperation amended with
    Act No. 126/2008, www.iceida.is/english/iceida/iceida-act/.
216 *Gouvernance pour le développement*, Ministère des Affaires étrangères, Direction de la coo-
    pération au développement, p. 5, www.mae.lu (emphasis added).

of human rights, fundamental freedoms and sustainability in countries with a high levels of poverty.[217]

From the above passages it is not evident whether donor states themselves are beginning to accept that they are under a human rights obligation to provide development cooperation and contribute to the 'fulfil' aspect of ESC rights obligations, or whether their concern is to ensure that the manner in which they conduct their cooperation is consistent with their human rights obligations (e.g. focusing on their obligation to respect ESC rights). All in all, these statements confirm a lack of convergence in the practice of states at the moment. At the same time, these examples, in comparison with multilateral frameworks (as will be seen below), illustrate that the activities of states may be close to meeting evidentiary standards as required by the 'subsequent practice' doctrine, and, in particular, they may have more resonance to what one can describe as a belief reflecting relevant authorities' position 'in application of the treaty'.[218] The only caveat is that such a practice is not sufficiently developed and, more importantly, does not yet represent the agreement of the parties (i.e. all parties) regarding *the* interpretation of the Covenant.[219]

B　PRACTICE OF STATES AT MULTILATERAL LEVEL

What is to be made of the wealth of practice taking place in the multilateral fora and day-to-day workings of international institutions? Can they provide key ingredients to construct an interpretation of Article 2(1) of ICESCR? Are they legally relevant for the purposes of interpretation? Whether the legal regimes of the development institutions (i.e. the World Bank, the European Commission and bilateral donors) or recent international declarations dealing with development cooperation (such as the UN Millennium Declaration (2000), the Monterrey Consensus of the International Conference on Financing Development (2002), recent Addis Ababa Action Agenda (2015), Paris Declaration on Aid Effectiveness (2005), the Accra Agenda for Action (2008) and Busan Partnership for Effective Development Cooperation (2011)) can be qualified as expressing state practice is a judgement to be made on the basis of a number of factors.

---

217 Artículo 1. Objeto de la Ley y ámbito de aplicación: '1. . . . . La cooperación española impulsará procesos de desarrollo que atiendan a la defensa y protección de los Derechos humanos y las libertades fundamentales, las necesidades de bienestar económico y social, la sostenibilidad y regeneración del medio ambiente, en los países que tienen elevados niveles de pobreza y en aquellos que se encuentran en transición hacia la plena consolidación de sus instituciones democráticas y su inserción en la economía internacional.' Ley 23/1998, de 7 de julio, de Cooperación Internacional para el Desarrollo, www.boe.es/aeboe/con sultas/bases_datos/act.php?id=BOE-A-1998-16303.

218 This is not, however, limited to a conduct referable to a particular treaty, but applies to the treaty as a whole. R. Gardiner, *Treaty Interpretation, op. cit*, p. 232.

219 *Ibid.*, p. 236

As far as the practices of international organizations are concerned, first, the Vienna Convention on the Law of Treaties bears upon the practice of states, and not of international organizations, although it allows its application to a treaty that is a constituent instrument of an international organization.[220] Second, distinction should be drawn between the practice of international organizations in relation to the treaty establishing them, and the practice of international organizations in relation to a treaty other than their constituent instrument. A more cautious approach should thus be taken in choosing what is relevant when establishing 'subsequent practice'.[221]

Assessment of the repertory of the practice of UN organs reveals that development cooperation and financing for development, as subject matters, are dealt with entirely in relation to Article 55(a) and (b) of the Charter.[222] More precisely, the vast body of practice relating to development cooperation by the UN's principal bodies, such as ECOSOC and the General Assembly, is barely addressed with respect to or within the purview of Article 55(c), despite the convergence of subject matter. A large proportion of UN practice dealing with the matters under Article 55(a) and (b) falls squarely within the domain of economic, social and cultural rights, where the relevance of the ICESCR is most 'immediate and direct'. In sum, the views and concerns expressed by the CESCR in General Comment No. 2 on Article 22 of the Covenant dealing with the state of ESC rights in development cooperation within the UN system remain largely valid even today.[223]

As for the international declarations listed above and, as previously noted, the important characteristics of subsequent practice are that it be '*in the application of the treaty*'. None of these documents, however, were adopted in application of the ICESCR, nor does any use the language of the ICESCR.[224] Despite significant progress in past decades, ESC rights have been largely neglected in the UN-sponsored social, economic or sustainable development conferences at the global level.[225] The Committee on Economic, Social and Cultural Rights has

---

220 Article 5, VCLT.
221 In the latter case, subsequent practice will derive primarily from international courts and tribunals, which in the present subject is almost non-existent. In the former case, where states 'by treaty entrust performance of activities to an organization, how these activities are conducted can constitute practice under the treaty', although whether such practice establishes agreement of the parties regarding the treaty's interpretation requires consideration of the powers of the organ acting on the issues, the way in which States Parties to the treaty participate in the activities of the organization, etc. R. Gardiner, *Treaty Interpretation, op. cit*, p. 246.
222 See Repertory of Practice of the United Nations Organs, www.un.org/law/repertory/.
223 CESCR, General Comment No. 2, International Technical Assistance Measures, UN doc. E/1990/23, 2 February 1990.
224 Conversely, the human rights treaty and charter bodies have integrated the aforementioned development frameworks extensively in their work.
225 See e.g. Statements of the Committee on Economic, Social and Cultural Rights: Statement of the Committee to the Commission on Sustainable Development acting as the Preparatory Committee for the World Summit for Sustainable Development, Bali, Indonesia, 27 May–7 June 2002, Twenty-eighth session, UN doc. E/2003/22-E/C.12/2002/13, annex VI; The World Summit for Social Development and the International Covenant on

repeatedly called for inclusion of references to ESC rights in those fora that were, in the opinion of the Committee, contexts which 'could give content and effect to those norms', and that '[u]pholding and invoking relevant international human rights instruments in general, and the Covenant in particular, will provide a solid legal basis for international cooperation and a sense of duty to demonstrate the seriousness of the efforts'.[226] In the words of the Committee itself, ESC rights are 'systematically downgraded to be covered by terms which have no specific normative content, such as "basic needs", "human needs", "equal opportunity", "the eradication of poverty" . . . etc.', and 'it would appear that these open-ended terms are used primarily because they do not recall any legal obligations for States' arising out of human rights treaties affirming obligations on ESC rights.[227]

These accounts are relevant to current negotiations, practice and behaviour of states in the context of socio-economic development. Deriving elements relevant for the purpose of establishing practice is difficult in the absence of any link with the ICESCR or any ESC rights' legal standards under other treaties. In fact, as Chapter II demonstrated, the Millennium Development Goals, which for the last 15 years represented a blueprint for the international community's development cooperation framework, lacks reference to human rights obligations. It is questionable, then, whether it has any relevance for translating 'international assistance and cooperation' for the fulfilment of ESC rights in practice.[228] A change of *status quo* can still be possible, however, with the adoption of the Sustainable Development Goals.[229]

Relatively recent developments forge a more optimistic view about the future direction of the obligation to assist and cooperate. An example of this is the Food Assistance Convention adopted 25 April 2012.[230] It is perhaps the only legally binding treaty that requires donors to make a 'minimum annual commitment' at the international level, to assist states in need and to progressively discharge

---

Economic, Social and Cultural Rights: Statement of the Committee, Tenth session, UN doc. E/1995/22-E/C.12/1994/20 and Corr. 1, annex V; Economic, social and cultural rights in the context of the World Summit for Social Development: Statement of the Committee, Eleventh session, UN doc. E/1995/22-E/C.12/1994/20 and Corr. 1, annex VI.

226 Statement of the Committee to the Commission on Sustainable Development acting as the Preparatory Committee for the World Summit for Sustainable Development, Bali, Indonesia, 27 May–7 June 2002, Twenty-eighth session, UN doc. E/2003/22-E/C.12/2002/13, annex VI, para. 4.

227 Economic, social and cultural rights in the context of the World Summit for Social Development: Statement of the Committee, Eleventh session, UN doc. E/1995/22-E/C.12/1994/20 and Corr. 1, annex VI, paras. 2, 3.

228 The Office of the High Commissioner for Human Rights, however, closely relates the MDGs with human rights.

229 See Chapter II for discussion.

230 Food Assistance Convention, adopted on 25 April 2012, in London, UK. The text of the treaty is available at http://treaties.un.org/doc/source/signature/2012/CTC_XIX-48.pdf. The Convention entered into force 1 January 2013. As of today, there are 14 State Parties to the treaty.

their obligations under the right to adequate food.[231] Perhaps it can be said that the rules on assistance in the area of food have arrived at a 'concrete normative proposition', as Georges Abi-Saab would term it, since they are specific as to their content and as to their destination.[232] This example demonstrates that it is probably through a situation-specific agreement that it is possible to transcribe the broadly formulated provisions of the ICESCR on assistance and cooperation.[233]

By way of conclusion, evidentiary standards for establishing subsequent practice are not always clear-cut. What is settled, however, is that subsequent practice should at least be 'consisting of non-isolated actions, committed consistently in application of the treaty, reflecting a position on interpretation, and engaged in or legitimately acquiesced by all of the parties'.[234] The actual practice may have little bearing in generating relevant principles, since diverse practices do not converge satisfactorily in language, rationale or result. That being said, there is clearly a need for more reputable studies to be undertaken so as to evaluate whether the emerging practice of individual states can meet the test of Article 31(3)(b) of the VCLT; often the failure of development cooperation to comply with human rights obligations is well documented, while positive achievements are rarely recorded or analysed. Self-assessments by the donors themselves could also contribute to such an undertaking, if only they were carried out from the perspective of human rights legal standards.

3.1.5 *International assistance and cooperation: Its different levels and cases of application under other 'relevant rules of international law'*

Progressing from the analysis of the ICESCR's text, through from its context to subsequent practice, Article 31 of the VCLT suggests recourse to the relevant

231 The Convention contains few progressive elements that may usefully inspire future directions of 'international assistance and cooperation' for the realization of human rights and of development generally. First, as commentators point out, the change of the name of the instrument from 'aid' to 'assistance' is a positive development. Second, the Convention provides that food assistance is to be based on the principles of upholding the dignity of beneficiaries of food assistance, to be provided in accordance with the food and nutrition needs of the most vulnerable, and to meet specific criteria of quality and acceptability (Article 2). Third, the Convention requires that the food assistance 'is not tied directly or indirectly, formally or informally, explicitly or implicitly, to commercial exports of agricultural products or other goods and services to recipient countries' (Article 5(9)). Finally, the Convention introduces principle of food assistance accountability (Article 2).

232 Report of the Secretary General, Progressive Development of the Principles and Norms of International Law Relating to the New International Economic Order, UN doc. A/39/504/Add.1, 23 October 1984, para. 179.

233 As discussed in the previous chapter, it was also one of the ideas by the Independent Expert on the Right to Development, who proposed the concept of 'Development Compacts' as a framework to implement the right to development. See Report of the Independent Expert on the Right to Development, Dr Arjun Sengupta, pursuant to General Assembly Resolution 54/175 and Commission on Human Rights Resolution E/CN.4/RES/2000/5, UN doc. E/CN.4/2000/WG.18/CRP.1, 11 September 2000.

234 J. Arato, 'Subsequent Practice and Evolutive Interpretation: Techniques of Treaty Interpretation over Time and their Diverse Consequences', *op. cit*, p. 461.

rules of international law.[235] At the origin of Article 31(3)(c), which is a legislative expression of a broader principle of systemic integration, is the idea that, regardless of their subject matter, treaties are all nevertheless part of the international legal system.[236] The importance of the last element stipulated by Article 31(3) is clear, as 'an international instrument has to be interpreted and applied within the framework of the entire legal system prevailing at the time of the interpretation'.[237]

Consistent with this principle of *systemic integration*, inquiry into the concept of international assistance and cooperation can be usefully inspired by principles of cooperation and assistance in parallel treaty provisions and as understood in other areas of international law.[238] In this regard, international humanitarian law and the ongoing work of the ILC on legal aspects of the protection of persons in the event of disasters can be deemed relevant, given that these fields of international law are also based on the notions of obligations of international cooperation, human dignity and solidarity. It is suggested that parallels found in these two bodies of law may provide 'a rich source of comparative understanding on generic issues' such as assistance and cooperation.[239]

A   INTERNATIONAL HUMANITARIAN LAW

International humanitarian law is directly relevant to the subject of our inquiry, not only in terms of regulation of issues concerning assistance but also because its normative content overlaps with material provisions of human rights treaties on ESC rights, in particular those that govern basic needs essential to the survival of civilians.[240] These humanitarian law rules prescribe humanitarian assistance as an unconditional obligation so as to ensure protection of survival rights, which 'shall, to the fullest extent of the means available', be provided.[241] The relevant

---

235 Article 31(3)(c) of the VCLT stipulates that, together with the context, 'any relevant rules of international law applicable in the relations between the parties' shall be taken into account.

236 C. McLachlan, 'The Principle of Systemic Integration and Article 31(3)(c) of the Vienna Convention', 54 *International Comparative Law Quarterly* (2005), pp. 279–320, p. 280.

237 ICJ, *Legal Consequences for States of the continued presence of South Africa in Namibia (South West Africa), notwithstanding Security Council Resolution 276 (1970)*, Advisory Opinion, ICJ Reports 16, 1971, para. 53.

238 R. Gardiner, *Treaty Interpretation, op. cit.*, p. 260.

239 C. McLachlan, 'The Principle of Systemic Integration and Article 31(3)(c) of the Vienna Convention', *op. cit.*, p. 286.

240 The rules govern the scope of 'basic needs', including food and medical supplies, clothing, bedding, means of shelter, other supplies essential to the survival of the civilian population and objects necessary for religious worship. See e.g. Article 55 Geneva Convention IV, and Article 69 of the Additional Protocol I.

241 Commentary to Geneva Convention IV, 1958, p. 320. It is argued that in the context of humanitarian assistance, 'it is rather the rights to emergency medical and health care and life-sustaining services that are at stake, as opposed to the more long-term aims of an adequate standard of living', comprising a group of so-called 'survival rights' which can be

rules of international humanitarian law leave open the question of who is to provide relief assistance to civilians: national or international providers. In most cases, the text of the provisions applicable to both international and non-international armed conflict only specify that relief actions 'shall be undertaken' when a civilian population 'is not adequately provided' (in the case of international armed conflicts)[242] or 'is suffering undue hardship' (in the context of internal armed conflicts), with the supplies essential for its survival, subject to the consent of the party concerned in the relief action.[243]

When these preconditions exist, the formula employed (i.e. 'shall be undertaken') seems to refer to both internal and external humanitarian assistance.[244] International humanitarian law explicitly envisages the duty to ensure that civilians have access to humanitarian assistance as resting with the party controlling the area. In this sense, both humanitarian law and human rights law coincide in designating external assistance to function as a subsidiary duty.

There is a widely supported proposition that obligations relating to humanitarian assistance should be read in conjunction with Article 1 of the Geneva Conventions that provides a system of collective responsibility, requiring all States Parties 'to respect and to ensure respect' for the Conventions and the Protocol I 'in all circumstances'.[245] Article 1 reflects the principle that each state 'contracts obligations vis-à-vis itself and at the same time vis-à-vis the others'.[246] The *Nicaragua*

related also to the minimum core of the economic, social and cultural rights. M. Sandvik-Nylund, *Caught in conflicts: civilian victims, humanitarian assistance and international law*, 2nd revised edition – Turku; Abo Academy University, Institute for human rights: 2003 – VIII, p. 54.

242 Article 70, Additional Protocol I, and Article 18, Additional Protocol II to the 1949 Geneva Conventions.

243 It is said that the rules found in the Geneva Conventions and Protocol I reflect to a greater degree the rules of customary international law. See Rule 55: 'The parties to the conflict must allow and facilitate rapid and unimpeded passage of humanitarian relief for civilians in need, which is impartial in character and conducted without any adverse distinction, subject to their right of control.' J.-M. Henkaerts and L. Doswald-Beck, *Customary Rules of International Humanitarian Law*, ICRC Study (Vol. I and II), CUP: 2005, pp. 193–200.

244 M. Sandvik-Nylund, *Caught in conflicts: civilian victims, humanitarian assistance and international law, op. cit.*, p. 31.

245 L. Boisson de Chazournes and L. Condorelli, 'Common Article 1 of the Geneva Conventions revisited: Protecting Collective interests', 887 *The International Review of the Red Cross*, pp. 67–87; L. Boisson de Chazournes and L. Condorelli, 'Quelles perspectives pour la responsabilité de protéger?' in A. Auer , A. Flückiger and M. Hottelier (eds), *Les droits de l'homme et la constitution : études en l'honneur du Professeur Giorgio Malinverni*, Schulthess : 2007. The ICTY stated that these norms 'do not pose synallagmatic obligations, i.e. obligations of a State vis-à-vis another State. Rather . . . they lay down obligations towards the international community as a whole, with the consequence that each and every member of the international community has a "legal interest" in their observance and consequently a legal entitlement to demand respect for such obligations.' *Prosecutor v. Zoran Kupreskic and others*, ICTY Trial Chamber, Judgment, The Hague, 14 January 2000, Case No. IT-95–16-T, para. 519.

246 See J.S. Pictet, *The Geneva Conventions of 12 August 1949*, Commentary, Fourth Geneva Convention Relative to the Treatment of Civilian Persons in Time of War, ICRC, 1958, p. 26.

case confirmed that the obligation to respect and ensure respect, derived from general principles of international humanitarian law and in relation to humanitarian assistance, would result in the duty of all parties to respect and ensure respect for guaranteeing supplies essential for the survival of civilians.[247]

At the same time, international humanitarian law does not specify what measures should be undertaken to implement the obligation to ensure respect, in particular when it comes to providing assistance to civilians.[248] More fundamentally, what does it say in relation to the duties of third states, that is, states not parties to the conflict?[249] There is no established view in the doctrine on the interpretation of the obligation to ensure respect and the extent to which it imposes individual obligations on third states.[250] Ensuring respect requires positive actions, and it was questioned 'what kind of positive actions resulting from this obligation . . . may be expected from individual States, apart from diplomatic demarches'.[251] In the same way, the International Committee of the Red Cross's study of customary international humanitarian law did not deal with the scope of obligations of third states.[252]

247 ICJ, *Military and Paramilitary Activities in and against Nicaragua (Nicaragua v. United States of America)*, Judgment, ICJ Reports 1986, para. 220. In the *Wall* opinion, ICJ held that 'Article 1 of the Fourth Geneva Convention, a provision common to the four Geneva Conventions, provides that "The High Contracting Parties undertake to respect and to ensure respect for the present Convention in all circumstances." It follows from that provision that every State Party to that Convention, whether or not it is a party to a specific conflict, is under an obligation to ensure that the requirements of the instruments in question are complied with.' ICJ, *Legal Consequences of the Construction of a Wall in the Occupied Palestinian Territory*, Advisory Opinion, ICJ Reports, pp. 199–200, para. 158. It is also argued that the notion of *erga omnes* is expressed in Article 1 of the Geneva Conventions and Additional Protocol I, and since humanitarian assistance is based on the principles and rules concerning the basic rights of human persons as pronounced in the dictum of ICJ in the *Barcelona Traction*, obligations related to assistance are *erga omnes* obligations.

248 References to possible measures include Article 7 and Article 89 Additional Protocol I, e.g. meetings of the High Contracting Parties and cooperation with the United Nations in situations of severe violations respectively. This can include means such as diplomacy, on-site missions, specific counter-measures, deployment of UN peace operations and including the role of judicial mechanisms such as the ICC in repression of crimes.

249 'Third states' in this context is used to connote states not parties to the conflict.

250 ICJ, *Legal Consequences of the Construction of a Wall in the Occupied Palestinian Territory*, Advisory Opinion, ICJ Reports, pp. 199–200, Separate Opinion of Judge Higgins, para. 39.

251 *Ibid*, Separate Opinion of Judge Kooijmans, para. 50.

252 Dieter Fleck notes that ICRC study 'takes a rather cautious approach, in relating this obligation of a State only to "its armed forces and other persons or groups acting in fact on its instructions, or under its direction or control." With this approach, methods and means of influencing the conduct of other States, groups or individuals remain unexplored. It would be worthwhile to go beyond the practice of parties to an armed conflict and explore the practice of third States and legal doctrine in this context.' D. Fleck, 'International Accountability for Violations of the *Ius in Bello*: The Impact of the ICRC Study on Customary International Humanitarian Law', 11(2) *Journal of Conflict & Security Law* (2006), p. 182. See also J.-M. Henckaerts and L. Doswald-Beck, *Customary International Humanitarian Law*, Vol. I: Rules, ICRC: 2006, Rule 144.

B   ILC'S DRAFT ARTICLES ON PROTECTION OF PERSONS IN THE EVENT OF DISASTERS

The work of the ILC on the draft articles on legal aspects of the protection of persons in the event of disasters, although still not finalized, provides contemporary thinking on efforts to articulate norms on the role of assistance and cooperation and the scope of rights and duties of the affected state and other relevant actors in disaster situations.[253] It has even been suggested that dealing with these aspects could help to articulate the content of *erga omnes* obligations.[254]

Taking the rights of individuals as an overall approach to the question of protection of persons,[255] the Commission adopted a dual-axis analysis, by which it decided to examine rights and obligations of states vis-à-vis each other first, and only thereafter the rights and obligations of states towards individuals.[256] The latter, referred to as a 'rights-based' approach, was deemed not without problems. This is because individual rights would invoke fundamental questions about consequences that 'would flow from a rights-based approach, in particular whether such an approach would also require addressing questions on how such rights would be enforced'.[257]

Furthermore, the work of the Commission recognized the difficulties inherent in the topic, in particular, as far as determining the rights and obligations of the assisting actor and those of the affected State are involved. It therefore decided not to invoke concepts such as the 'responsibility to protect' in the study, since it would have raised possible complex questions on the extent of these obligations for third parties, their content, the circumstances to trigger those obligations, and whether they will be singular or collective.[258]

253 See UN GA 46/182, Strengthening of the coordination of humanitarian emergency assistance of the United Nations, UN doc. A/RES/46/182, 19 December 1991, where linkages are established among relief, rehabilitation and development.

254 International Law Commission, Report on the work of its sixtieth session (5 May to 6 June and 7 July to 8 August 2008), GAOR Sixty-third Session Supplement No. 10, UN doc. A/63/10, para. 231.

255 Current draft articles include two provisions on the subject: Article 5[7] on Human dignity ('In responding to disasters, States, competent intergovernmental organizations and relevant non-governmental organizations shall respect and protect the inherent dignity of the human person') and Article 6 [8] on Human rights ('Persons affected by disasters are entitled to respect for their human rights'). ICL, Report on the work of the sixty-sixth session (2014), UN doc. A/69/10, p. 87. China expressed doubts about the viability of a rights-based approach, as it would imply 'that individuals were in a position to appeal for international disaster relief'. UN GA, Sixth Committee, Summary record of the 20th meeting, UN doc. A/C.6/64/SR.20, para. 21.

256 See International Law Commission, Second report on the protection of persons in the event of disasters, by Eduardo Valencia-Ospina, Special Rapporteur, UN doc. A/CN.4/615, paras. 20, 21.

257 International Law Commission, Report on the work of its sixtieth session (5 May to 6 June and 7 July to 8 August 2008), GAOR Sixty-third Session Supplement No. 10, UN doc. A/63/10, para. 229.

258 International Law Commission, Preliminary report on the protection of persons in the event of disasters, by Mr Eduardo Valencia-Ospina, Special Rapporteur, UN doc. A/CN.4/598, para. 55.

From a state-to-state perspective, a draft article on a 'duty to cooperate' was formulated providing that states 'shall cooperate among themselves' and when appropriate, with the UN, etc. The draft article received wide support in the Sixth Committee of the General Assembly, with states noting 'that cooperation was a central principle of international law'.[259] Commentary to the draft articles stipulate that the 'duty to cooperate is well established as a principle of international law and can be found in numerous international instruments', citing, among the many sources discussed in this book, the Covenant on Economic, Social and Cultural Rights.[260]

There was no dispute on the status of a 'duty to cooperate' for the respect and observance of human dignity. This well-established principle of international law should not, however, 'be interpreted as diminishing the prerogatives of a sovereign State within the limits of international law', as '[c]ooperation complements the primary duty of States'.[261] The principles of sovereignty and non-intervention would interpret the scope of duty to cooperate.[262] Since the draft article on the duty to cooperate at this level of abstraction remained unclear,[263] an article clarifying the primary responsibility of the affected state was drafted.[264]

Despite the careful approach taken by the ILC, the view was expressed that it 'leant too much in favour of the traditional view of international law', relying on sovereignty and the consent of States, without adequately taking into account the contemporary understanding of State sovereignty.[265] To balance (i) the interests

---

259 International Law Commission, Third report on the protection of persons in the event of disasters, by Eduardo Valencia-Ospina, Special Rapporteur, UN doc. A/CN.4/629, para. 12.

260 Report on the work of the sixty-sixth session (2014), UN doc. A/69/10, p. 106.

261 It was, however, recalled that 'the principles of sovereignty and non-intervention were a point of departure and not a point of conclusion, and implied both rights and obligations'. See A/65/10, para. 307.

262 This would include elements such as imposition of obligation on the part of disaster-affected states to accept relief or on the part of states providing relief to satisfy requests for assistance, since that depended on their capacity. International Law Commission, Second report on the protection of persons in the event of disasters, by Eduardo Valencia-Ospina, Special Rapporteur, UN doc. A/CN.4/615, paras. 63, 65. See also UN GA Resolution 46/182, Annexed Guiding Principles, Principle 3.

263 Austria, UN GA, Sixth Committee, Summary record of the 20th meeting, UN doc. A/C.6/64/SR.20, para. 17; See International Law Commission, Third report on the protection of persons in the event of disasters, by Eduardo Valencia-Ospina, Special Rapporteur, UN doc. A/CN.4/629, para. 12.

264 Draft Article 8 on Primary Responsibility of Affected State reads as follows:

'1 The affected State has the primary responsibility for the protection of persons and provision of humanitarian assistance on its territory. The State retains the right, under its national law, to direct, control, coordinate and supervise such assistance within its territory.

2 External assistance may be provided only with the consent of the affected State.'

265 International Law Commission, Report on the work of its sixty-second session (3 May to 4 June and 5 July to 6 August 2010), GAOR Sixty-fifth Session, Supplement No. 10, UN doc. A/65/10, para. 316.

of the international community in the protection of persons in the event of disasters with (ii) the sovereignty of the affected state, a special provision has been formulated, complementary to the provision on the primary responsibility of the concerned state, which stipulates the right to 'offer' assistance. There is a nuanced distinction from the wording 'right to provide', as merely 'offering' is in line with the prerogative of the sovereign states.[266]

Draft provisions establishing a duty to cooperate and the right to offer assistance operating together would put states and other actors under some pressure to offer assistance.[267] However, the role of the international community in offering assistance should not be interpreted as an 'assertion of rights', but rather be based on the principles of cooperation and solidarity. Further, the precise relationship between the duty to cooperate and the principles of sovereignty and non-intervention, as well as possible derogations therefrom, remains to be defined.[268]

Bearing in mind the very delicate nature of the questions at stake, the Commission decided to raise the issue of interrelationship between the legal obligations established under articles on the duty to cooperate and the duty of the affected state to seek assistance, by putting a blunt question to states:[269]

> The Commission has taken the view that States have a duty to cooperate with the affected State in disaster relief matters. Does this duty to cooperate include a duty on States to provide assistance when requested by the affected State?[270]

States did not provide written replies but expressed their views in negative terms in response to the question. There was no such basis under existing international law, customary law, or practice.[271] One view was that 'duty to cooperate' in effect expressed the duty to 'consider' requests for assistance.[272] Another view,

---

266 Draft Article 12 of the Draft Rules on the Protection of Persons in the Event of Disasters.
267 International Law Commission, Fifth Report on the Protection of Persons in the Event of Disasters, by Special Rapporteur E. Valencia-Ospina, UN doc. A/CN.4/652, 9 April 2012, para. 44.
268 *Ibid.*, para. 37.
269 *Ibid.*, paras. 55, 56.
270 International Law Commission, Report on the work of its sixty-third session (26 April to 3 June and 4 July to 12 August 2011), GAOR Sixty-sixth Session, Supplement No. 10, UN doc. A/66/10 and Add.1.
271 Mexico (A/C.6/66/SR.18, para. 55, and A/C.6/66/SR.22, para. 21), Slovenia (A/C.6/66/SR.20, para. 12), Singapore (A/C.6/66/SR.21, para. 76), Italy (A/C.6/66/SR.21, para. 91), Colombia (A/C.6/66/SR.22, para. 28), Austria (A/C.6/66/SR.23, para. 23), Germany (A/C.6/66/SR.23, para. 28), United Kingdom (A/C.6/66/SR.23, para. 45), Netherlands (A/C.6/66/SR.23, para. 48), Spain (A/C.6/66/SR.23, para. 50), Hungary (A/C.6/66/SR.24, para. 59), Malaysia (A/C.6/66/SR.24, para. 120), Republic of Korea (A/C.6/66/SR.24, paras. 120 and 121), Ireland (A/C.6/66/SR.25, para. 21).
272 Mexico (A/C.6/66/SR.18, para. 55).

in contrast, felt 'sympathetic' to the idea of duty to provide assistance; however, it suggested formulating the duty to provide assistance, rather, as 'a strong recommendation or as an example, using wording that took into account the capacities of the States to which requests were made'.[273]

All these discussions demonstrate the *adagium* of the subsidiarity principle of international efforts to protect persons and the primary role of the affected state.[274] However, the aspects of the ILC work which *could* and *should* be transposed to the area of development cooperation are the inclusion of a number of core principles of international law, such as humanity, neutrality and impartiality, deriving from a body of soft-law rules in disaster relief and well established in humanitarian law, all seen within the scope of protection of the individual.[275]

C IS THERE AN INDIVIDUAL RIGHT TO RECEIVE ASSISTANCE IN TIMES OF CONFLICT, IN POVERTY OR IN THE EVENT OF DISASTERS?

Does the provision on international assistance and cooperation under the ICESCR automatically translate into the right of individuals to receive assistance? The discussions within humanitarian law and rules on disaster response provide proof that such a right is very controversial.[276] International humanitarian law lays down a strong legal construct guaranteeing assistance to civilians, but does not automatically confer rights upon individuals or private actors to receive assistance, nor does it provide the recipient State with any corresponding rights to receive such assistance from other High Contracting Parties.

In the context of rules on protection of persons in disaster situations, the ILC confirmed there was no specific instrument supporting the existence of such a right and that it could only be implicit in international human rights law.[277] The

---

273 Hungary (A/C.6/66/SR.24, para. 59).
274 International Law Commission, Report on the work of its sixtieth session (5 May to 6 June and 7 July to 8 August 2008), GAOR Sixty-third Session Supplement No. 10, UN doc. A/63/10, para. 228.
275 These principles are 'core principles regularly recognized as foundational to humanitarian assistance efforts generally' in Protection of Persons in the Event of Disasters, Memorandum prepared by the Secretariat, Doc. A/CN.4/590, 11 December 2007, para. 11. Current Article 7 [6] on Humanitarian principles, Report on the work of the sixty-sixth session (2014), UN doc. A/69/10, p. 87.
276 International Law Commission, Report on the work of its sixtieth session (5 May to 6 June and 7 July to 8 August 2008), GAOR Sixty-third Session Supplement No. 10, UN doc. A/63/10, paras. 241–246.
277 For Nigel Rodley it is clear that 'there is no right to humanitarian assistance or that, even if there ought to be one and if there were in fact one, it would not be a human right', further arguing that 'human rights have already been flouted when a person is in this situation. And it hardly seems useful . . . to suggest that another human right has been violated, namely, the right to receive assistance' in '*Le droit à l'assistance humanitaire: actes du Colloque international organisé par l'Unesco*', UNESCO, SHS-95/CONF.805/3 p. 146. See also ILC, Protection of persons in the event of disasters: Memorandum by the Secretariat, UN doc. A/CN.4/590, para. 244. Compare also with the Preamble of the European Union's Council Regulation No. 1257/96 concerning humanitarian aid, which stated: 'people in

resolution adopted by the Institut de Droit International states that 'leaving the victims of disaster without humanitarian assistance constitutes a threat to human life and an offence to human dignity and therefore a violation of fundamental human rights. The victims of disaster are entitled to request and receive humanitarian assistance.'[278]

It is true that the nature of such a right is unclear and would raise a number of questions: '[w]ould it be a human right or just a right of those affected by a disaster [*or armed conflict or even poverty*], or [w]ould it be an individual right or a collective right? Against whom, if at all, would it be enforceable?'[279] Importantly, all these questions preoccupying the legal minds recall uncertainties surrounding the ICESCR provision on the same subject. For the time being, the ILC has suggested:

> instead of considering the right to humanitarian assistance as 'a right to impose assistance', it was more appropriate to envisage it as a 'right to provide assistance'; such an approach would be in line with the reasoning of the International Court of Justice in the *Nicaragua* case. The point was also made that if an affected State cannot discharge its obligation to provide timely relief to its people in distress it must have an obligation to seek outside assistance.[280]

3.1.6 *International assistance and cooperation: In search of common ground among the rules of international law*

International humanitarian law, rules on protection of persons in the event of disasters, and the ICESCR essentially deal with a common general norm – the obligation to assist and cooperate and its different levels and cases of application, i.e. in armed conflict, disasters and in the area of development. Fundamentally, all of these rules overlap with each other on the core content of socio-economic rights, although the ICESCR sets a higher standard of achievement for international cooperation of states, namely the 'full realization of ESC rights'.

None of the rules examined provides unconditional support for a conclusion that there is a duty incumbent upon the international community to offer for the protection of persons, whether in the context of armed conflict or disaster

---

distress, victims of natural disasters, wars and outbreaks of fighting, or other comparable exceptional circumstances have a right to international humanitarian assistance where their own authorities prove unable to provide effective relief'. Council Regulation (EC) No. 1257/96 of 20 June 1996 Concerning Humanitarian Aid.

278 Institut de Droit International Resolution of 2003 on Humanitarian Assistance, Bruge Session, Sect. II, paras. 1 and 2.

279 International Law Commission, Preliminary report of the Special Rapporteur, Mr Eduardo Valencia-Ospina, UN doc. A/CN.4/598, para. 54.

280 International Law Commission, Report on the work of its sixtieth session (5 May to 6 June and 7 July to 8 August 2008), GAOR Sixty-third Session Supplement No. 10, UN doc. A/63/10, para. 243.

events.[281] Specific positive obligations to provide assistance would have to be in the form of separate agreements. Examples of such a practice include the Food Assistance Convention of 2012, discussed earlier, whereby donor states pledge to provide specified minimum amounts of food aid to those developing nations with the greatest needs. Accordingly, there is a consensus that there is a duty for a state to protect and take care of persons in its territory and where needed to *seek assistance*.[282] Such a right to seek assistance is affirmed especially if directed towards the international community.

The CESCR takes the same position with regards to the primary obligation of the state, although this is somewhat different from the accepted view in humanitarian law and the disaster relief framework.[283] The Committee is of the opinion that 'States have a joint and individual responsibility, to cooperate in providing disaster relief and humanitarian assistance in times of emergency.'[284] In contrast to the language of duties, states have a *right to offer* assistance which is predicated upon the inability or unwillingness of the primary duty-bearer.[285]

Corollary to the right to offer assistance is the duty of the state not to arbitrarily reject the offer. This element is clearly elucidated both in IHL and in the current project of draft articles on protection of persons in the event of disasters. In relation to disaster response, it has been said that a 'more definitive obligation' to provide assistance has been ascribed to international organizations, which is mainly due to their mandate to provide assistance and cooperation.[286] It is suggested that the same approach can and should be adopted in the context of ESC

---

281 In the framework of disaster response, Memorandum of Secretariat concluded that 'while most agreements and instruments deal explicitly with requests, few provide guidance on offers'. Protection of Persons in the Event of Disasters, Memorandum prepared by the Secretariat, Doc. A/CN.4/590, 11 December 2007, para. 60.

282 Institut de Droit International, Resolution of 2003 on Humanitarian Assistance, Bruge Session, Section II (2) and Section III (3). At the same time, states in at the Sixty-forth session of the International Law Commission (7 May – 1 June, and 2 July – 3 August 2012), commenting on the Draft Article of the obligation to seek assistance in the event of disasters, stated that such a duty will be contrary to sovereignty and it had no legal basis in current international law. It was hence proposed to change 'duty to seek assistance' with a hortatory wording 'should' seek assistance. See UN doc. A/CN.4/652, para. 28 and UN Doc. A/C.6/66/SR.23 and A/C.6/66/SR.24 for the separate opinions of the opposing states.

283 CESCR, General Comment No. 3: 'The Committee wishes to emphasize, however, that even where the available resources are demonstrably inadequate, the obligation remains for a State party to strive to ensure the widest possible enjoyment of the relevant rights under the prevailing circumstances.'

284 CESCR, General Comment No. 12, The Right to Adequate Food, UN doc. E/CN.12/1999/5, 12 May 1999 and General Comment No. 14, The Right to the Highest Attainable Standard of Health, UN doc. E/C.12/2000/4, 11 August 2000, specifically refer to the general framework of 'obligation to cooperate' and make it explicit that states should cooperate in providing disaster relief and humanitarian assistance for the rights in question.

285 Institut de Droit International, Resolution of 2003 on Humanitarian Assistance, Bruge Session, Section IV (1).

286 *Ibid.*, Section V (2).

rights in relation to organizations in the UN system entrusted with a mandate that covers a wide spectrum of socio-economic rights.

Further, international humanitarian law and international disaster-response rules provide certain ideas that might helpfully inspire understanding of cooperation and assistance obligations in ESC rights. These include the principles of humanity, neutrality, impartiality and independence that guide humanitarian and disaster-response assistance, with the aim of ensuring that persons in need receive the right aid, at the right time, and delivered in the right way. While these principles are strongly embedded in these bodies of rules, they did not yet find their definite expression in the field of human rights, even less so in development cooperation.[287] As highlighted throughout this book, the focus has been mainly on human rights principles as applied to the recipient of development aid, rather than on the behaviour of donors themselves.

To sum up, there is a great degree of convergence between three sets of rules, in terms of their logic and, in particular, the subsidiary nature of obligations incumbent upon third States. All share common elements; thus the difference is the question of emphasis rather than the content of the norms. The rights that these rules generate for the state in need of assistance are imperfect. The difference between the rules on humanitarian assistance in international humanitarian law and disaster relief, and the rules of international assistance and cooperation in the ESC rights treaties, thus appear narrower than it may seem at first glance. There is, therefore, no tangible reason why the nature of the obligation of assistance and cooperation as envisaged by the ICESCR would be any different.

The Covenant envisages a similar form of 'collective responsibility' for States Parties in attaining the fulfilment of rights secured by it. Significantly, all the bodies of rules discussed here share identical constraints; none are sufficiently precise to address the question of regarding the specific instance the obligations of third states are activated and what the extent of these positive obligations incumbent upon third states is. These constraints evidently derive from the fact that they require a great degree of cohesion within the international community and, as a minimum, institutionalized identification of positive obligations and their enforcement.

3.2 Forms of international assistance and cooperation

Based on the discussions above, it becomes apparent that the Covenant on Economic, Social and Cultural Rights assumes that international cooperation supports governments in the fulfilment of their obligations. The Covenant explicitly requires States Parties to take steps to realize ESC rights individually and through international assistance and cooperation, and its monitoring body, the CESCR,

---

287 The reader may recall the description in Chapter II on the attempts within the UN to push forward the principles of non-selectivity, impartiality and objectivity, and the political context in which these issues were involved.

has stressed that the available resources States Parties must use to the realization of ESC rights can also include those received from international assistance and cooperation:

> The Committee notes that the phrase 'to the maximum of its available resources' was intended by the drafters of the Covenant to refer to both the resources existing within a State and those available from the international community through international cooperation and assistance. Moreover, the essential role of such cooperation in facilitating the full realization of the relevant rights is further underlined by the specific provisions contained in articles 11, 15, 22 and 23. With respect to article 22 the Committee has already drawn attention, in General Comment 2 (1990), to some of the opportunities and responsibilities that exist in relation to international cooperation.[288]

This interpretation does not clarify, however, if States Parties must prioritize the realization of ESC rights when they have these resources at their disposal, regardless of the purpose for which they received such assistance (e.g. whether aid is received for economic growth or liberalization of market economy, etc.). The Limburg Principles clarify this question, confirming that 'the realisation of fundamental freedoms and human rights at the national level should be a *prime purpose* in international assistance and cooperation'.[289]

Article 23 provides a list of possible measures foreseen under Article 2(1) of the ICESCR. According to Article 23 of the ICESCR, the international action for the realization of rights recognized in the Covenant includes 'the conclusion of conventions, the adoption of recommendations, the furnishing of technical assistance, and the holding of regional meetings and technical meetings for the purpose of consultation and study organized in conjunction with the Governments concerned'. For Craven, it is surprising that 'economic assistance', the most 'fundamental form of action', is not foreseen in the provision.[290]

However, it is clear that the language of the provision is indicative only, and therefore other measures are not excluded from the scope of the article. International treaties and agreements related to any of the rights enshrined in the

---

288   CESCR, General Comment No. 3, *op. cit.*, para. 13.
289   See Commentaries to the Limburg Principles 29 and 30 (on Implementation of the International Covenant on Economic, Social and Cultural Rights), which state: 'The idea here is that the realisation of fundamental freedoms and human rights at the national level should be *a prime purpose* in *international assistance and cooperation*' (emphasis added). E.V.O. Dankwa and Cees Flinterman, 'Commentary by the Rapporteurs on the Nature and Scope of States Parties' Obligations', in 9 *Human Rights Quarterly* (1987) 2, pp. 140, 141. See also the *Vienna Declaration and Programme of Action, supra* note 6, para. 4 which states '[t]he promotion and protection of all human rights and fundamental freedoms must be considered as a priority objective of the United Nations in accordance with its purposes and principles, in particular the purpose of international cooperation' (emphasis added).
290   M. Craven, *The International Covenant on Economic, Social and Cultural Rights: A Perspective on Its Development, op. cit.*, p. 147.

covenant may serve as examples of the measures. Examples of conventions regarding provision of assistance have, though, been very scarce in practice.

The case of the Food Assistance Convention has already been given. Another example is World Health Assembly Resolution 58.3 ('Revision of the International Health Regulations'), which is a binding agreement in the framework of activities of the World Health Organization.[291] Accordingly, most development policy frameworks can be considered examples of measures anticipated by the provision. One can add the inventory of 'cooperative' actions that the Human Rights Advisory Committee has identified under the rubric of '*international cooperation in the field of human rights*' discussed earlier.[292]

3.3 Positive measures to create an 'enabling environment'

One of the added values of the concept of the right to development, as high-lighted by its proponents, is that it provides an explicit requirement to create enabling conditions at national and international levels for the realization of human rights. The question, therefore, is whether the international obligation of assistance and cooperation, as provided for by the ICESCR, can extend to measures to be taken 'to actively facilitate a regime that will contribute to the progressive realisation' of ESC rights.[293] The CESCR recognized in a number of general comments 'the existence of structural and other obstacles arising from international factors beyond the control of States', which hinder the enjoyment of ESC rights.[294]

Today, any debate on ESC rights inevitably starts with the ills of economic globalization. Many states have lost policy space in economic, social and political spheres by increasingly ceding their decision-making authority to international actors.[295] Even where governments themselves are responsive, they still may face difficulties in 'maintaining their role as the primary actor in development'.[296] The principal question is whether the two objectives are incompatible. Can a state still be expected to honour its human rights obligations 'while at the same time enabling market forces to take responsibility for many sectors of the economy

---

291 Article 44 of Revision of the International Health Regulations, The Fifty-eighth World Health Assembly, 23 May 2005.
292 See Chapter IV.2.2. Human Rights Council Advisory Committee, 'Study on the Enhance-ment of International Cooperation in the field of human rights, pursuant to Human Rights Council Resolution 13/23', UN doc. A/HRC/19/74, 29 February 2012, paras. 41–44.
293 J. Tobin, *The Right to Health in International Law*, OUP: 2011, p. 345.
294 See e.g. CESCR, General Comment No. 13, The Right to Education, para. 2; General Comment No. 14, The Right to the Highest Attainable Standard of Health, para. 5, and General Comment No. 18, The Right to Work, para. 4.
295 A network of international regulations and commitments of international institutions have limited the powers of states in monetary and fiscal, trade, investment and other important economic areas.
296 K. de Feyter, *World Development Law: Sharing Responsibility for Development*, Intersentia: 2001, p. 68.

that are human rights sensitive, such as the exploitation of natural resources or the provision of services of general interest'?[297]

From a legal point of view, globalization in and of itself does not have any effect on the treaties, and generally 'a state cannot retract its consent to be bound by human rights treaties, simply by arguing that it no longer has the capacity to comply with these obligations due to globalisation'.[298] Developing states voluntarily enter the relationships with the factors that limit their sovereignty and impact their obligations to comply with human rights law treaties. Cognizant of interdependence of national economies, the Summit Outcome 2005 Declaration recognizes:

> *It is for each Government* to evaluate the trade-off between the benefits of accepting international rules and commitments and the constraints posed by the loss of policy space. It is particularly important for developing countries, bearing in mind development goals and objectives, that all countries take into account the need for appropriate balance between national policy space and international disciplines and commitment.[299]

In this context, questions are raised about the capacity of human rights to initiate reforms at the international institutional level, including in the area of economic relations. The source of such an obligation is often found in Article 2(1) of the ICESCR, in addition to the UN Charter obligations on human rights to 'promote respect for and observance of human rights'. Some scholars suggest interpreting the requirement of international assistance and cooperation as a duty to pursue measures through which developing countries are supported in meeting their obligation under the Covenant. It requires 'a positive duty for states to remain actively seized of ways in which the diverse and often competing interests within the international legal system can be reconciled'.[300]

One way to approach the question of the capacity of human rights treaties to instigate changes in the institutional order at the global level has been through the idea that the primary international obligation under human rights is to abstain from inflicting damage on human rights through an existing arrangement, including in the economic sphere. For this duty to be operationalized, certain reforms are required. Such a view is gaining increasing support in the

---

297 W. Benedek, K. de Feyter and F. Marrella, *Economic Globalisation and Human Rights*, CUP: 2007, p. 6.

298 *Ibid.*

299 (emphasis added) Para. 22 (d), which starts by stating:'(d) That the increasing interdependence of national economies in a globalizing world and the emergence of rule-based regimes for international economic relations have meant that the space for national economic policy, that is, the scope for domestic policies, especially in the areas of trade, investment and industrial development, is now often framed by international disciplines, commitments and global market considerations.' UN GA Resolution 60/1, 2005 World Summit Outcome, 24 October 2005.

300 *Ibid.*, p. 347.

doctrine. Theory on this front varies significantly in the level of detail and analysis, but the real hurdle is rather their practical implementation in light of limited practice. These issues will be further discussed in Chapter VI.

Another argument in favour of human rights' capacity to contribute to the global institutional reform is advanced with reference to the principle of coherence discussed in some detail by the ILC in its Fragmentation Study. The basic idea conveyed in the Study is that '[i]n international law there is strong presumption against normative conflict'.[301] From this stems a requirement of harmonization. A considerable body of thought can be identified nowadays on the tension between the human rights regime and diverse, highly specialized areas of international law such as trade, investment, intellectual property, etc.[302] It follows that, contrary to the position that human rights are not capable of addressing structural causes, there are avenues where human rights law contributes to the global institutional reform.[303]

Conclusion

This chapter has aimed at demonstrating the concept of an obligation to cooperate for human rights as distinct from the cooperation for development, yet closely intertwined with it, particularly when it comes to the implementation of the socio-economic rights. The obligation to cooperate for human rights can be traced from the UN Charter through declarations, to specific human rights treaties, whereby international cooperation for ensuring human rights constitutes an essential component of the obligations of states. There is an acceptance at the general level of the existence of such an obligation. However, not all elements

---

301 ILC, Fragmentation of International Law: Difficulties Arising from the Diversification and Expansion of International Law – Report of the Study Group of the International Law Commission, UN doc. A/CN.4/L.682 (13 April 2006), paras. 25, 26.

302 P.M. Dupuy, F. Franconi and E.-U. Petersmann (eds), *Human Rights in International Investment Arbitration*, OUP: 2009; B. Simma, 'Foreign Investment Arbitration: A Place For Human Rights?', 60 *International Comparative Law Quarterly* (July 2011), pp. 573–596. The issue of human rights and trade is particularly well researched, and a select literature includes: S. Joseph, *Blame it on the WTO: A Human Rights Critique*, OUP: 2011; J. Pauwelyn, T. Cottier and E. Burgi, *Human Rights and International Trade*, OUP: 2005; J. Morijn, *Reframing Human Rights and Trade: Potential Limits of a Human Rights Perspective of WTO Law on Cultural and Education Goods and Services*, Intersentia: 2010.

303 In elaborating this issue, Tobin, in the context of duty to cooperate for the right to health, explains that: 'At the same time this onerous requirement that the right to health must be taken into consideration in all matters affecting health is not designed to displace all other legitimate considerations in international relations. States may carry a heavy burden to justify any actions or omissions that will be contrary to an individual's right to health, but this right is not the only or even the paramount consideration relevant in decision making. Importantly, however, the international obligation to co-operate for the purpose of realizing the right to health does operate to recalibrate the balancing process and make visible the right to health in contexts where it may have been overlooked, marginalized, or devalued in the behaviour of states both within and beyond their own jurisdiction.' J. Tobin, *The Right to Health in International Law, op. cit.*, p. 347.

of the obligation to cooperate enjoy the same degree of recognition. The drafting history, negotiations and current debates of the present day all underline the resistance to any implication of a legally binding duty in terms of transfer of resources – the resources that can be essential for ensuring food, water, access to essential healthcare, education and a decent and secure place to live for the prevalent majority of the world.

Finally, it is useful to go back to the theory of law of cooperation to identify the causes of the current situation. It is said that in the absence of central authority in international legal order, only self-interest may serve as a driving force for cooperation. Studies on the 'cooperation' point out that an element of reciprocity needs to be present for cooperation to occur (i.e. if the basis of cooperation is the common end).[304] All parties to the cooperative agreement are to benefit from it. Where there is only one party to benefit, the stimulus for cooperation is lacking. At the international level, there is a positive position towards provision of assistance to developing countries as far as curbing poverty is concerned. In the present-day context, current challenges of globalization have had also an impact on the political undertones of the development aid. Michael Bothe explains: 'poverty and unacceptable inequality stir violent reactions and pose, thus, security problems. Furthermore, the poor which leaves the state of underdevelopment is, in a way, the market of future. Seen in this light, development should be considered as a win–win process.'[305]

The provision on cooperation and assistance is an important starting point for any assessment of human rights legal framework in development. The CESCR has progressively identified some units of obligation to assist and cooperate that seem to transform the normative content of Article 2(1) that originally was interpreted as mainly referring to *cooperation for development*. In line with the genuine direction of the Covenant, the Committee is moving towards defining the obligations in specific terms. It has interpreted the requirement of cooperation in light of the UN Charter and with reference to the notion of 'applicable international law', structuring them together as international obligations flowing from the Covenant. In this chapter, we have discussed only those aspects related to how international action can contribute positively to the attainment of ESC rights. How to make sure that this action, in particular through development cooperation, does not harm socio-economic rights of individuals is the subject of the following chapters.

---

304 Axelrod explains: 'The potential for cooperation arises when each player can help the other. The dilemma arises when giving this cooperation is costly . . . The analysis also shows that the two key requisites for cooperation to thrive are that the cooperation be based on reciprocity, and that the shadow of the future is important enough to make this reciprocity stable.' R. Axelrod, *The Evolution of Cooperation*, Revised Version, Basic Books: 1984, p. 173.
305 M. Bothe, 'Environment, Development, Resources', 318 *Recueil des Cours* (2005), p. 381.

V New legal ideas

Comment on the relationship of the international assistance and cooperation and extraterritorial scope of ESC rights

There have been numerous attempts in academic literature to link 'international assistance and cooperation' under the ICESCR to the notion of the Covenant's extraterritorial application.[1] The Committee on Economic, Social and Cultural Rights has, on occasion, made reference to this notion.[2] The Committee on the Elimination of Discrimination against Women (CEDAW) invoked States Parties' extraterritorial obligations in the context of a housing project.[3] The UN Special

---

1 The amount of literature on the extraterritorial scope of economic, social and cultural rights is impressive. An exemplary list of literature includes: F. Coomans, 'Some Remarks on the Extraterritorial application of the International Covenant on Economic, Social and Cultural Rights' and R Künnemann, 'Extraterritorial application of the International Covenant on Economic, Social and Cultural Rights' in F. Coomans and M. Kamminga (eds), *Extraterritorial Application of Human Rights Treaties*, Intersentia: 2004; S. Skogly, *Beyond National Borders: States's Human Rights Obligations in International Cooperation*, Intersentia: 2006; M. Gibney and S. Skogly, *Universal Human Rights and Extraterritorial Obligations*, University of Pennsylvania Press: 2010; W. Vandenhole, M. Salomon and A. Tostensen (eds), *Casting the Net Wider: Human Rights, Development and New Duty-Bearers*, (Intersentia, 2007); M. Gondek, *The Reach of Human Rights in a Globalising World: Extraterritorial Application of Human Rights Treaties*, Intersentia: 2009; F. Coomans, 'The Extraterritorial Scope of the International Covenant on Economic, Social and Cultural Rights in the Work of the United Nations Committee on Economic, Social and Cultural Rights', 11(1) *Human Rights Law Review* (2011), pp. 1–35; S. Besson, 'The Extraterritoriality of the European Convention on Human Rights: Why Human Rights Depend on Jurisdiction and What Jurisdiction Amounts to', 25 *Leiden Journal of International Law* (2012), pp. 857–884. More recent analyses of the issue include M. Langford, W. Vandenhole, M. Scheinin and W. Van Genugten (eds), *Global Justice, State Dutie : the Extraterritorial Scope of Economic, Social, and Cultural Rights in International Law*, CUP: 2013; G. Giacca, *Economic, Social and Cultural Rights in Armed Conflict, Monograph in International Law Series*, OUP: 2014; W. Vandenhole (ed.), *Challenging Territoriality in Human Rights Law: Building Blocks for a Plural and Diverse Duty-Bearer Regime*, Routledge: 2015; and L. Bartels, 'The EU's Human Rights Obligations in Relation to Policies with Extraterritorial Effects', 25 *European Journal of International Law* (2014), pp. 1071–1091.

2 CESCR, General Comment 19 (on the Right to Social Security), UN doc. E/C.12/GC/19, 4 February 2008, para. 54.

3 CEDAW, Concluding Observations: India, UN doc. CEDAW/C/IND/CO 4–5, 24 July 2014, paras. 14–15. See also Committee on the Rights of the Child, General comment No. 16 (2013) on State obligations regarding the impact of the business sector on children's rights, 17 April 2013.

Rapporteur on the right to food asserted that the undertaking of states to assist and cooperate under socio-economic rights gives rise to extraterritorial obligations.[4] According to the UN Special Rapporteur on the human right to safe drinking water and sanitation, extraterritorial violations may occur, for example, when 'States contribute to human rights violations in the context of development cooperation activities, including by imposing conditions that undermine rights'.[5] More and more development-oriented provisions of the human rights treaties are being dealt with almost exclusively within the paradigm of extraterritorial obligations of states.

This calls for a comment. First and foremost, it raises a question of whether two concepts (obligation of assistance and cooperation on the one hand, and extraterritorial obligations on the other) can be confluent, or are they almost two sides of the same coin? And if they are separate, what is the extent of their mutual reinforcement? Can it be that 'international assistance and cooperation', defined primarily as a means of realizing economic, social and cultural rights, be coextensive with the scope of application of a socio-economic rights treaty? Also, can extraterritorial aspects of ESC rights under the Covenant contribute to a better understanding of the obligation of international assistance and cooperation?

1 Clarification on terminology

The concept of the extraterritorial scope of human rights treaties emerged as a response to (i) situations where states either act directly outside their own territorial boundaries, or (ii) where their domestic actions impact on the rights of individuals living abroad. Different terms have been used in the literature to conceptualize the relationship between a state and the protection of socio-economic rights of an individual(s) in another state: extraterritorial obligations, transnational obligations, transboundary obligations, international obligations, universal obligations, external obligations, inter-state obligations, third state obligations or

4 Report of the Special Rapporteur on the right to food, UN doc. E/CN.4/2005/47, 25 January 2005, paras. 44–46. More recently, Report of the Special Rapporteur on the Right to Food: The Way Forward, UN doc. A/HRC/28/65, 12 January 2015, para. 38ff.
5 Report of the Special Rapporteur on the Human Right to Safe Drinking Water and Sanitation: Common Violations of the Human Rights to Water and Sanitation, UN doc. A/HRC/27/55, 30 June 2014, para. 71. Among the few with more cautious approach on the subject matter see Preliminary Report of the Independent Expert on the Issue of Human Rights Obligations Relating to the Enjoyment of a Safe, Clean, Healthy and Sustainable Environment, UN doc. A/HRC/22/43, 24 December 2012, para. 48, according to which: 'The application of human rights law to transboundary and global environmental harm requires consideration of questions regarding the extraterritorial reach of human rights norms. Those questions are often complex, not least because human rights treaties employ varying language to define the scope of their application. Recent years have seen heightened attention to the extraterritoriality of human rights obligations, but there is still a need for more detailed clarification.'

global obligations.[6] There is, in fact, no common view on how to appropriately formulate the concept in the context of ESC rights.[7]

The notions such as transboundary, transborder or transnational[8] did not acquire a strong following, as they were associated with environmental law and may or may not have a specific geographic connotation.[9] The requirement of international assistance and cooperation, found in Article 2(1) of ICECSR, has also given rise to notions such as global obligations or global responsibility.[10] Although the concept of third state obligations may seem logical in the context of ESC rights, its invocation has been rare among commentators. In a recent publication on the topic, it was suggested that the term transnational obligations is broader and preferable, as it includes both 'extraterritorial human rights obligations as well as *direct* human rights obligations of other actors than States (NSAs)'.[11] Mark Gibney, however, suggests that the most pertinent term in this context is a simple one: human rights obligations.[12]

Perhaps the most commonly used concept is still extraterritorial obligations.[13] This has been the approach of the treaty-based bodies,[14] except from CESCR,

6 For a survey of diverse terms and a full appreciation of important differences between them see M. Gibney, 'On Terminology', in M. Langford, W. Vandenhole, M. Scheinin and W. Van Genugten (eds), *Global Justice, State Duties: the Extraterritorial Scope of Economic, Social, and Cultural Rights in International Law*, CUP: 2013, pp. 32–47.

7 E.g. S. Skogly, *Beyond National Borders: States' Human Rights Obligations in International Cooperation, op. cit.*, pp. 5–6 and W. Vandenhole, 'Third State Obligations under the ICECSR: A Case Study of EU Sugar Policy', 76 *Nordic Journal of International Law* (2007), pp. 71–98.

8 M. Gibney, K. Tomasevski and J. Vedsted-Hansen, 'Transnational State Responsibility for Violations of Human Rights', 12 *Harvard Human Rights Journal* (1999), pp. 267–296; S. Skogly and M. Gibney, 'Transnational Human Rights Obligations', 24 *Human Rights Quarterly* (2002), pp. 781–798.

9 S. Skogly, *Beyond National Borders: States' Human Rights Obligations in International Cooperation, op. cit.*, p. 5.

10 M. Salomon, *Global Responsibility for Human Rights: World Poverty and the Development of International Law*, OUP: 2007.

11 W. Vandenhole (ed.), *Challenging Territoriality in Human Rights Law: Building Blocks for a Plural and Diverse Duty-Bearer Regime*, Routledge: 2015, p. 5. See also M. Gibney and W. Vandenhole (eds), *Litigating Transnational Human Rights Obligations: Alternative Judgments*, Routledge: 2014.

12 One cannot disagree with the argument that: 'the term "human rights" should convey the understanding that all have human rights and that all States have the responsibility to protect those rights-for all people'. M. Gibney, 'On Terminology', in M. Langford, W. Vandenhole, M. Scheinin and W. Van Genugten (eds), *Global Justice, State Duties: the Extraterritorial Scope of Economic, Social, and Cultural Rights in International Law*, CUP: 2013, pp. 32, 47.

13 Here, again, it has been suggested that the use of the term extraterritorial 'is generally understood as having a narrower application, i.e. related to the negative effects of (a State's) policies and activities on the people in another country.' M.E. Salomon, A. Tostensen and W. Vandenhole (eds), *Casting the Net Wider: Human Rights, Development and New Duty-Bearers*, Intersentia: 2007, pp. 3–4.

14 See e.g. the practice of Human Rights Committee (ICCPR), Committee on the Elimination of Discrimination against Women (CEDAW), and Committee on the Rights of the Child (CRC).

which despite its occasional references to the term,[15] has consistently used the 'international obligations' concept without providing any particular explanation. The UN Special Rapporteurs who have taken up this issue frequently have also used the term 'extraterritorial'.[16] In addition, a group of experts who drafted the Maastricht Principles on Extraterritorial Obligations (ETOs) of States in the area of Economic, Social and Cultural Rights opted for the term *extraterritorial*, encompassing both negative and positive obligations (sometimes referred to as global obligations). Indeed, since socio-economic rights are also subject to general principles applied in civil and political rights case law, where the term 'extraterritorial obligation' seems to have been definitively accepted, the term 'extraterritorial' seems more relevant, at least for the time being. In what follows, the basic parameters of the concept of extraterritorial obligations as developed in the area of protection of civil and political rights will be laid down.

2 Extraterritorial application of human rights treaties

Discussions on the human rights consequences of the extraterritorial acts of states have always revolved around civil and political rights, and mainly in relation to the former. The repercussions of external economic and social processes on economic, social and cultural rights are, however, perhaps far more substantial and frequent. Human rights extraterritorial obligations are not yet consistently recognized, even in relation to civil and political rights treaties. Civil and political rights case law has not yet provided all necessary guidance to states, and, instead, courts have dealt with issues with which they have been confronted, on a 'need-to-decide' basis. Today, there is no clear threshold and no substantive rules. As Françoise Hampson points out, the debate is not between general international lawyers and human rights lawyers; rather, it's within and between the latter.[17]

In effect, in international law, states incur responsibility for the conduct of their state agents acting outside their territories.[18] In light of the persistent discussions, Hampson raises a question: 'Is it seriously argued that international law would determine that responsibility exists if there were no substantive basis on which

---

15 CESCR, General Comment No.19, The Right to Social Security, UN doc. E/C.12/GC/19, 4 February 2008.

16 See e.g. B. Frey, Preliminary Report on the Prevention of Human Rights Violations Committed with Small Arms and Light Weapons, UN doc. E/CN.4/Sub.2/2003/29 (2003); Jean Ziegler, Second Submission of the Special Rapporteur on the Right to Food of the United Nations Commission on Human Rights, 2003.

17 F. Hampson, 'The Scope of the Extra-territorial Applicability of International Human Rights Law', in G. Gilbert, F. Hampson and C. Sandoval-Villalba (eds), *The Delivery of Human Rights: Essays in Honour of Professor Sir Nigel Rodley*, Taylor & Francis: 2011, p. 157. A similar point is made by M. Scheinin, 'Just Another Word? Jurisdiction in the Roadmaps of State Responsibility and Human Rights', in M. Langford, W. Vandenhole, M. Scheinin and W. Van Genugten (eds), *Global Justice, State Duties: the Extraterritorial Scope of Economic, Social, and Cultural Rights in International Law*, CUP: 2013, pp. 212–229.

18 International Law Commission, Draft Articles on Responsibility of States for Internationally Wrongful Acts, November 2001, Supplement No. 10 (A/56/10), chp.IV.E.1.

to evaluate the lawfulness of conduct?'[19] One may enquire whether, after all, it is not more a matter of justiciability of human rights than their applicability that is in question.[20] It may be that, indeed, individuals may be less effectively protected from the extraterritorial effects of state conduct under certain human rights treaties than they are under certain regional human rights instruments, which do not require threshold jurisdictional criterion.[21] Martin Scheinin also provides a very useful analysis to demonstrate that 'jurisdiction' is simply an element of the road-map for admissibility determination under human rights treaties.[22] Nonetheless, the extraterritorial scope of civil and political rights has engendered abundant academic work in response to the case law of mainly two bodies, the ECtHR and the Human Rights Committee. Some socio-economic human rights scholars have since joined the debate.

2.1 Defining the scope of obligations under the human rights treaties: Jurisdictional approaches

Any debate on the subject matter starts with the principal enquiry of whether human rights treaties can be applied extraterritorially. The International Court of Justice in its *Wall* opinion,[23] in the case of *DRC v. Uganda*,[24] the UN Human Rights Committee,[25] the Committee on Economic, Social and Cultural Rights in

19 F. Hampson, 'The Scope of the Extra-territorial Applicability of International Human Rights Law', *op. cit.*, p. 182.
20 Compare, for example, the absence of the jurisdictional threshold in the International Covenant on Economic, Social and Cultural Rights (viz. Article 2(1)) and its inclusion in the Optional Protocol to ICESCR (Article 2), whereby the right of individuals to submit communications to the Committee on Economic, Social and Cultural Rights is restricted to those who are 'under the jurisdiction of a State Party'. This in no way limits the scope of international obligations of States Parties to the ICESCR, but does represent an admissibility threshold for the purposes of consideration of individual complaints.
21 V. Moreno-Lax and C. Costello, 'The Extraterritorial Application of the EU Charter of Fundamental Rights: From Territoriality to Facticity, the Effectiveness Model', in S. Peers, T. Hervey, J. Kenner and A.Ward (eds), *The EU Charter of Fundamental Rights: A Commentary*, Hart Publishing: 2014, pp. 1658–1683; L. Bartels, The EU's Human Rights Obligations in Relation to Policies with Extraterritorial Effects, 25 *European Journal of International Law* (2014), pp. 1071–1091.
22 M. Scheinin, 'Just Another Word? Jurisdiction in the Roadmaps of State Responsibility and Human Rights', in M. Langford, W. Vandenhole, M. Scheinin and W. Van Genugten (eds), *Global Justice, State Duties: the Extraterritorial Scope of Economic, Social, and Cultural Rights in International Law*, CUP: 2013, pp. 212–229, p. 222.
23 ICJ, *Legal Consequences of the Construction of a Wall in the Occupied Palestinian Territory*, Advisory Opinion, ICJ Reports 2004, paras. 107–113.
24 ICJ, *Armed Activities on the Territory of the Congo (Democratic Republic of the Congo v. Uganda)*, Judgment of 19 December 2005, ICJ Reports 2005 paras. 219–220.
25 *Delia Saldias de Lopez v. Uruguay*, Comm. No. 52/1979, UN doc. CCPR/C/OP/1, p. 88 (1984); *Lilian Celiberti de Casariego v. Uruguay*, Comm. No. 56/1979, UN doc. CCPR/C/OP/1, p. 92 (1984). See also the HRC's General Comment No. 31, para. 10 of which states: 'States Parties are required by article 2, paragraph 1, to respect and to ensure the Covenant rights to all persons who may be within their territory and to all persons subject

its General Comments[26] and in consideration of country situations[27] all suggest the existence of some degree of extraterritoriality. Similarly, the European[28] and the Inter-American[29] human rights systems have supported the notion of extra-territorial obligations.

The key concept in determining the scope of a state's human rights obligations extraterritorially is jurisdiction.[30] The total cumulus of the case law of the different human rights bodies have led to the development of three criteria to establish whether an individual can be considered as falling within a state's jurisdiction:[31] *de facto* jurisdictional authority or territorial control;[32] control or authority over

---

to their jurisdiction. This means that a State Party must respect and ensure the rights laid down in the Covenant to anyone within the power or effective control of that State Party, even if not situated within the territory of the State Party. As indicated in General Comment 15 adopted at the twenty-seventh session (1986), the enjoyment of Covenant rights is not limited to citizens of States Parties but must also be available to all individuals, regardless of nationality or statelessness, such as asylum seekers, refugees, migrant workers and other persons, who may find themselves in the territory or subject to the jurisdiction of the State Party. This principle also applies to those within the power or effective control of the forces of a State Party acting outside its territory, regardless of the circumstances in which such power or effective control was obtained, such as forces constituting a national contingent of a State Party assigned to an international peace-keeping or peace-enforcement operation.'

26 CESCR, General Comment No.19, The Right to Social Security, UN doc. E/C.12/GC/19, 4 February 2008, para. 54.

27 Committee on Economic, Social and Cultural Rights, 'Concluding Observations of the Committee on Economic, Social and Cultural Rights: Israel', UN doc. E/C.12/1/Add.69, 31 August 2001.

28 ECtHR, *Loizidou v. Turkey*, Preliminary Objections (1995), 310 ECtHR, Series A, paras. 62–64; ECtHR, *Cyprus v. Turkey*, App no. 25781/94, 10 May 2001, para. 77.

29 IAComHR, *Alejandre Jr. and ors v. Republica de Cuba* ('Brothers to the Rescue'), Case 11.589, Report no. 86/99, OEA/Ser.L/V/II.106 Doc. 3 rev., p. 586 (1999), para. 23; *Coard and ors v. United States*, Case 10.951, Report no. 109/99, IACHR, 29 September 1999, para. 37.

30 Thus, for example, according to ICCPR, a State Party incurs obligations vis-à-vis 'all individuals within its territory and subject to its jurisdiction'. Article 2(1), International Covenant on Civil and Political Rights (1966); In a similar vein, the European Convention on Human Rights defines that states owe human rights obligations under the ECHR to 'everyone within their jurisdiction' (Article 1).

31 Sub-Commission on the Promotion and Protection of Human Rights, Working paper on the relationship between human rights law and international humanitarian law by Francoise Hampson and Ibrahim Salama, UN doc. E/CN.4/Sub.2/2005/14, 14 June 2005, para. 82.

32 See ICJ, *Legal Consequences of the Construction of a Wall in the Occupied Palestinian Territory, op. cit.*, paras. 107–112, *DRC v. Uganda* case, *op. cit.*, paras. 216–220; The CESCR's view is that 'the State party's obligations under the Covenant apply to all territories and populations under its effective control': UN doc. E/C.12/1/Add.90, para. 31. The ICJ also endorsed the view of the CESCR; however, both base their consideration of extraterritoriality in a concrete case of occupation, meaning control over a territory. The Committee's treatment of the subject in parallel with references to IHL raises questions as to whether it had considered rights applicable in accordance with the Covenant or as part of IHL. See M. Gondek, *The Reach of Human Rights in a Globalizing World: Extraterritorial Application of Human Rights Treaties, op. cit.*, p. 309.

persons;[33] and the 'cause and effect' criteria. The first approach has been related to cases of military occupation, where 'jurisdiction' is established *prima facie*.[34] Cases involving acts of diplomats and consular agents,[35] as well as cases of detention[36] and unlawful killings,[37] all sharing the common feature of an individual being held in the direct control or authority of state agents, gave rise to the development of the second approach. In the second scenario, what is required is to determine whether a specific act brings the affected person within the 'jurisdiction' of a state.[38]

These two tests may not be easily reconcilable, however, with the types of situations in the development context that we have discussed briefly in the introduction. This is because the common basis for these two tests is the control or physical relationship between the state and the victim. In the case of socioeconomic rights, as well as some other contemporary problems, the 'physical' element may not be present to produce negative effects.[39] In addition, as pointed out, 'because the guaranteeing of ESC rights will often depend on duties to protect and fulfil (or, on positive obligations "not to omit"), the nature of those

33 The European Commission of Human Rights explains this approach as follows: 'authorised agents of a State not only remain under its jurisdiction when abroad, but bring any other person "within the jurisdiction" of that State to the extent they exercise authority over such persons. Insofar as the State's acts or omissions affect such persons, the responsibility of that State is engaged.' *Stocké v. Germany*, Case No. 28/1989/188/248, 19 March 1991. The Human Rights Committee has similarly affirmed that 'it would be unconscionable to so interpret the responsibility under article 2 of the Covenant as to permit a State party to perpetrate violations of the Covenant on the territory of another State, which violations it could not perpetrate on its own territory'. HRC, *López Burgos,* Communication No. 52/1979, p. 12. See also Sub-Commission on the Promotion and Protection of Human Rights, Working paper on the relationship between human rights law and international humanitarian law by Francoise Hampson and Ibrahim Salama, UN doc. E/CN.4/Sub.2/2005/14, 14 June 2005 paras. 86–88. Other relevant case law includes CCPR/C/13/D/52/197, 29 July 1981; IAComHR, *Coard and ors v. United States,* IACHR Report No. 109/99, Case No. 10,951, 29 September 1999, Ann. Rep. IACHR 1999.
34 ECtHR, *Assanidze v. Georgia (GC)*, Application no. 71503/01, ECHR Judgment 8 April 2004, para. 139; ECtHR, *Loizidou v. Turkey*, Application no. 40/1993/435/514, Judgment, 28 November 1996, paras. 52–56.
35 EComHR, *X. v. United Kingdom*, App. No. 7547/76, 15 December 1977. See, however, ECtHR's prounouncement in *Al-Skeini*, limiting the scope of rights owed only to those 'relevant to the situation of that individual'. *Al-Skeini and Others v. The United Kingdom,* Application no. 55721/07, Judgment, 7 July 2011.
36 See e.g. European Commission of Human Rights, *Hess v. UK*, (1975), 2 D&R 72, ECtHR *Ocalan v. Turkey*, App. No. 46221/99, 12 May 2005.
37 ECtHR, *Issa and others v. Turkey*, App. No. 31821/96, 16 November 2004.
38 HRC, *General Comment No. 31, Nature of the General Legal Obligation Imposed on States Parties to the Covenant*, UN doc. CCPR/C/21/Rev.1/Add.13 (2004), para. 10.
39 These include, for example, the right to privacy in digital space, cyber warfare, etc. For the brief summary see the intervention by M. Milanovic, ESIL: *The European Convention on Human Rights and General International Law*, 5 June 2015, www.esil-sedi.eu/node/904. A case in point, e.g., is ECtHR, *Big Brother Watch et al v. UK*, Application no. 58170/13, lodged on 4 September 2013.

duties may make it difficult to identify what specific conduct of the State engenders a "jurisdictional link" between the state and the individual'.[40]

While fact patterns involving these two criteria are not excluded in the development setting, in most cases the 'harm' can be inflicted indirectly, intended or otherwise. Therefore, the third criteria, expressed in the concept of 'control over the infliction of the alleged violation'[41] or the concept of 'cause and effect',[42] can be deemed, perhaps, as a more conceptually appropriate theory of jurisdiction for economic, social and cultural rights. This concept formulates the idea that the state is 'responsible for the (extraterritorial) conduct of [its] agents that adversely affects individuals in another state'.[43] In Hampson's view, '[w]hen a state engages in action in the territory of another state, it is exercising its jurisdiction because the mere fact of the action carries with it a claim of an implied authority to act' and '[w]hether or not the state has international authority for its action in another state, the action itself is an assertion of jurisdiction'.[44]

2.2 Distinguishing jurisdiction in general international law and human rights treaties

Judging by the totality of the human rights case law, it appears jurisdiction has been used as a threshold requirement before identifying whether the responsibility of a state towards an individual can be established. For example, according to the *Banković* case, what was to be established was whether the victim was under the jurisdiction of the state at the time of the conduct in question.[45] In other

40 M. den Heijer and R. Lawson, 'Extraterritorial Human Rights and the Concept of "Jurisdiction"', in M. Langford, W. Vandenhole, M. Scheinin and W. Van Genugten (eds), *Global Justice, State Duties: the Extraterritorial Scope of Economic, Social, and Cultural Rights in International Law*, CUP: 2013, p. 186.
41 Sub-Commission on the Promotion and Protection of Human Rights, Working paper on the relationship between human rights law and international humanitarian law by Francoise Hampson and Ibrahim Salama, UN doc. E/CN.4/Sub.2/2005/14, 14 June 2005, para. 89.
42 C. Cerna, 'Extraterritorial Application of the Human Rights Instruments of the Inter-American System', in F. Coomans and M. Kamminga (eds), *Extraterritorial application of Human Rights Treaties*, Intersentia: 2004, p. 158.
43 W. Vandenhole, 'Third State Obligations under the ICESCR: A Case Study of EU Sugar Policy', *op. cit.*, p. 87. See, however, ECtHR, *Banković and Others v. Belgium and Others* (dec.) [GC], no. 52207/99, ECHR 2001XII, para. 75, rejecting the 'cause-and-effect' notion of jurisdiction.
44 F. Hampson, 'The Scope of the Extra-territorial Applicability of International Human Rights Law', *op. cit.*, p. 168
45 ECtHR, *Banković and Others v. Belgium and Others* (dec.) [GC], no. 52207/99, ECHR 2001XII. C. Greenwood notes: 'Before the question of responsibility is even reached, there is a threshold requirement that the alleged victim must be within the jurisdiction of that state. Moreover, it is the victim, not the agent who commits the alleged violation, who must be within the jurisdiction of the respondent state.' C. Greenwood, Remarks, 'Bombing for Peace: Collateral Damage and Human Rights', 96 *American Society of International Law Proceedings* (2002), p. 100.

terms, for the purposes of establishing jurisdiction, it is not the consequences of the exercise of authority outside national territory that is discussed, but whether the state was entitled to act. In the much commented-on *Banković* case, considered as the statement of the general principle concerning extraterritorial applicability of human rights, the European Court of Human Rights in essence assigned 'jurisdiction' a very restricted meaning, equating it with the notion of territory. The Court found that the Convention could apply outside the territory of a State Party only in 'exceptional circumstances'. The practice of the ECtHR has evoked criticism, not least from one of the judges of the Court.[46]

The way the term 'jurisdiction' had been interpreted in the case law of the human rights bodies spurred a lot of commentary on the actual meaning (or rather its diverse meanings) of the concept in international law,[47] and in human rights law in particular.[48] A consensus opinion on the issue is that jurisdiction serves different functions, under international law on the one hand, and for human rights on the other.[49]

46 According to Judge Bonello, '[a] considerable number of different approaches to extraterritorial jurisdiction have so far been experimented with by the Court on a case-by-case basis, some not completely exempt from internal contradiction'. The Court, in his view, 'could . . . have started the exercise by accepting that this was judicial terra incognita, and could have worked out an organic doctrine of extra-territorial jurisdiction, untrammelled by the irrelevant and indifferent to the obfuscating'. ECtHR, *Case of Al-Skeini and Others v. The United Kingdom*, Judgment 7 July 2011, Concurring Opinion of Judge Bonello, paras. 7 and 29.

47 Most of the discussion on jurisdiction in international law is concerned with the 'State's right of regulation' or right to make legal rules (prescriptive jurisdiction), or the competence of the State to apply laws to individuals or 'to give effect to legal rules' (prerogative or enforcement jurisdiction). As F.A.P. Mann mentions, '[i]t does not matter whether it is exercised by legislative, executive or judicial measures'. F.A.P. Mann, 'The Doctrine of Jurisdiction in International Law', 111 *Recueil des Cours* (1964), p. 13. It is common to make reference to the distinction between diverse forms of jurisdiction in this context and point out that in international law, with regard to criminal matters, the jurisdiction of states is primarily territorial. To this effect, there is a consensus that human rights bodies have made use of this conception of jurisdiction.

48 Jurisdiction in the traditional sense described as 'lawful power to act and hence to its power to decide whether and, if so, how to act, whether by legislative, executive or judicial means'. See B. Oxman, 'Jurisdiction of States', *Max-Planck Encyclopaedia of International Law*, www.mpepil.com.

49 As den Heijer and Lawson point out: 'Although jurisdiction in its function of allocating competences between States appears to have guided the intended delineation of the extent of a State's human rights obligations under the various human rights conventions, it has since become plain that the function of "jurisdiction" in human rights treaties must not be equated with its role in general international law . . . [J]urisdiction under human rights law is not about whether a State is entitled to act, but primarily about delineating as appropriately as possible the pool of persons to which a State ought to secure human rights.' M. den Heijer, R. Lawson, 'Extraterritorial Human Rights and the Concept of "Jurisdiction"', in M. Langford, W. Vandenhole, M. Scheinin and W. Van Genugten (eds), *Global Justice, State Duties: the Extraterritorial Scope of Economic, Social, and Cultural Rights in International Law*, CUP: 2013, p. 163.

To begin with, classical international law doctrine does not probe into the matters of jurisdiction in the context of human rights violations. The basic framework of jurisdiction issues has been set in the well-known *Lotus* case. The PCIJ's approach has been regarded as expansive, i.e. not excluding the possibility of a permissive rule to that effect under international law:

> It does not, however, follow that international law prohibits a State from exercising jurisdiction in its own territory, in respect of any case which relates to acts which have taken place abroad, and in which it cannot rely on some permissive rule of international law. Such a view would only be tenable if international law contained a general prohibition to States to extend the application of their laws and the jurisdiction of their courts to persons, property and acts outside their territory, and if, as an exception to this general prohibition, it allowed States to do so in certain specific cases. But this is certainly not the case under international law as it stands at present. Far from laying down a general prohibition to the effect that States may not extend the application of their laws and the jurisdiction of their courts to persons, property and acts outside their territory, it leaves them in this respect a wide measure of discretion which is only limited in certain cases by prohibitive rules; as regards other cases, every State remains free to adopt the principles which it regards as best and most suitable.[50]

While certain scholars regard *Lotus* as a prevailing approach on the issue in general,[51] certain others view the case as largely anachronistic and confined to the specific context of criminal jurisdiction, and therefore of little use and guidance for the interpretation of human rights.[52] Without regard to the results of the debate on the currency of the *Lotus* standards, the basic framework is that the permissive rule extends to the prescriptive jurisdiction, while enforcement jurisdiction is limited to the territory of the State.[53]

Differing analysis can help to clarify the conceptual confusion in relation to the question of jurisdiction and to shed light on how jurisdictional solutions under human rights law should be (or should have been) appropriately approached. There is by now an agreement in doctrine that for the purposes of human rights, jurisdiction is about delineating the circle of persons to whom a state is obliged to secure human rights. More specifically, the references to and the meaning of territory and jurisdiction in human rights treaties were not designed to deal with the

---

50 PCIJ, *SS Lotus (France v. Turkey)*, PCIJ Reports (1927), Series A, No. 10, p. 19.
51 C. Ryngaert, *Jurisdiction in International Law*, OUP: 2008.
52 H.G. Maier, 'Jurisdictional Rules in Customary International Law', in K.M. Meessen, *Extraterritorial Jurisdiction in Theory and Practice*, Kluwer Law International: 1996, p. 89.
53 To this effect, the PCIJ held that: 'the first and foremost restriction imposed by international law upon a state is that – failing the existence of a permissive rule to the contrary – it may not exercise its power in any form in the territory of another state. In this sense jurisdiction is certainly territorial; it cannot be exercised by a State outside its territory except by virtue of a permissive rule derived from international custom or from a Convention.' PCIJ, *SS Lotus (France v. Turkey)*, PCIJ Reports (1927), Series A, No. 10, pp. 18–19.

issues of accountability for human rights violations, e.g. 'for direct actions taken against individuals outside a state's sovereign territory'. To take the example of the International Covenant on Civil and Political Rights,[54] it is largely agreed that the drafters' reference to territory and jurisdiction in the treaty was meant to simply make sure that the Covenant did *not* generate duties to ensure (positive duties) all of the treaty's provisions to individuals outside their territories (we shall return to this point later).[55]

Quite reasonably, then, the question of accountability for violations of the specific rights as a result of extraterritorial activity is different from the question of jurisdiction as a framework to define the scope of positive duties owed by a state. But irrespective of the theoretical discourse on what is the most appropriate way to interpret the meaning and scope of jurisdiction in human rights treaties, in most scenarios human rights bodies have tried to grapple with the issue of the applicability of human rights norms extraterritorially concerning the 'negative' obligations of a state. As a result, any attempt to frame the current reality through a different category discussed during the drafting would prove inadequate.[56]

Eventually, when confronted with the factual situation of an alleged violation, the practice of the Human Rights Committee has been to suggest interpreting the extraterritorial actions of states as falling within the scrutiny of the Covenant and hence in accordance with the object and purpose of the human rights treaties.[57] Sir Nigel Rodley, applying the rule of interpretation as laid down by the Vienna Convention on the Law of the Treaties, held:

> The ordinary meaning of article 2 was the one given to it by the Committee, and the context included any subsequent practice in the application of the treaty which established the agreement of the States parties regarding its interpretation. It did not include the *travaux préparatoires*, which were a supplementary means of interpretation under article 32 of the Convention. The object and purpose were laid down clearly in the preamble to the Covenant and consisted in protecting humans from the overreaching power of States.[58]

54 Article 2(1), on the nature of the state obligations, stipulates: 'Each State Party to the present Covenant undertakes to respect and to ensure to all individuals within its territory and subject to its jurisdiction the rights recognized in the present Covenant, without distinction of any kind, such as race, colour, sex, language, religion, political or other opinion, national or social origin, property, birth or other status.'
55 See ICJ, *Legal Consequences of the Construction of a Wall in the Occupied Palestinian Territory*, Advisory Opinion, ICJ Reports 2004, para. 109. A thorough analysis can be found in N. Lubell, *Extraterritorial Use of Force against Non-State Actors*, OUP: 2010, pp. 200–201.
56 N. Lubell, *Extraterritorial Use of Force against Non-State Actors*, op cit., p. 202.
57 A. Cassese's observation on the issue is that '[it] is consistent with the object and purpose of human rights obligations: they aim at protecting individuals against arbitrariness, abuse, and violence, regardless of the location where the State conduct occurs.' A. Cassese, *International Law*, OUP: 2005, p. 386.
58 Remarks by N. Rodley, member of the Human Rights Committee, in HRC Consideration of USA Reports, UN doc. CCPR/C/SR.2380, para. 65 in regard to 'Third periodic reports of States parties due in 2003', United States, UN doc. CCPR/C/USA/3, 28 November 2005.

Nowak similarly states that the motive behind the formulation of Article 2(1) of the ICCPR was to limit responsibility of States Parties for the 'legal security of persons who are located on their territory and subject to their sovereign authority'. But '[w]hen States Parties, however, take actions on foreign territory that violate the rights of persons subject to their sovereign authority, it would be contrary to the purpose of the Covenant if they could not be held responsible'.[59]

One author has provided a fairly thorough analysis of all relevant human rights treaties and the meaning attached in these treaties to the notion of jurisdiction. His concluding argument is that 'jurisdiction' has several distinct meanings and, possibly, in the human rights treaties, 'jurisdiction' refers to 'a power a state exercises over a territory, and perhaps over the individuals'.[60]

3 Applicability of ICESCR extraterritorially

The International Covenant on Economic, Social and Cultural Rights belongs to a category of treaties with no provision on their territorial application.[61] Likewise, the Convention on the Elimination of All Forms of Discrimination against Women (CEDAW) and Convention on the Rights of Persons with Disabilities contain no territorial jurisdiction clause. Following the general trend emerging in the jurisprudence of the human rights bodies, authors have started to pay considerable attention to the extraterritorial aspects of the ICESCR.

Whether in light of the years-long process of elaboration of the notion of 'transnational' obligations or in response to the failure to recognize the international dimension of human rights obligations through the concept of right to development, or whether for any other reason, the concept of extraterritoriality has been enthusiastically embraced by the human rights scholarship. The lack of express territorial limitations was seen as an authoritative legal argument to extend the reach of the treaty to virtually all activities of states taking place or having direct or indirect effect on the rights of people outside their territorial borders. The findings of human rights bodies served as a catalyst to move the discussions on the protection of ESC rights into the new plane through a new legal 'idea'.

---

59 M. Nowak, *UN Covenant on Civil and Political Rights: CCPR Commentary*, 2nd edition, Kehl Am Rein: 2005, p. 44.
60 See for a thorough analysis M. Milanovic, 'From Compromise to Principle: Clarifying the Concept of State Jurisdiction in Human Rights Treaties', 8 *Human Rights Law Review* (2008), pp. 411–448; M. Milanovic, *Extraterritorial Application of Human Rights Treaties: Law, Principles, and Policy*, OUP: 2011, p. 54.
61 To remind the reader, Article 2(1) of the ICESCR on the nature of the state obligation states: 'Each State Party to the present Covenant undertakes to take steps, individually and through international assistance and cooperation, especially economic and technical, to the maximum of its available resources, with a view to achieving progressively the full realization of the rights recognized in the present Covenant by all appropriate means, including particularly the adoption of legislative measures.'

3.1 'Jurisdiction' and the ICESCR

As noted earlier, the Covenant does not include the term 'jurisdiction'. Overall, two approaches have been devised to determine the possible extension of application of the Covenant on Economic, Social and Cultural Rights, beyond the territory of a State Party. First, the lack of jurisprudence, or even a general statement by the CESCR on the issue, has seen most authors apply the concept as applied in the jurisprudence on civil and political rights. The second approach is based on the absence of reference to 'territory' and 'jurisdiction' in the Covenant, thus the provision on 'international assistance and cooperation' has been interpreted as implying the extraterritorial applicability of the treaty.[62]

The ICJ's *Advisory Opinion on Legal Consequences of the Construction of a Wall in the Occupied Palestinian Territory*, however, in contrast to human rights scholars, did not consider the existence of the phrase 'international cooperation and assistance' in the treaty as relevant to the question of jurisdiction and instead held that:

> [t]he International Covenant on Economic, Social and Cultural Rights contains no provision on its scope of application. This may be explicable by the fact that this Covenant guarantees rights which are *essentially territorial*.[63]

In this advisory opinion, the Court seems to have set a higher standard of applicability for the ESC rights treaty, compared to the ICCPR.[64] This situation has been reversed to a certain extent. Later, in the contentious case of the *DRC v. Uganda*, the Court, restating its finding of the *Wall* Advisory Opinion on the same measure of extraterritorial applicability of human rights treaties, did not make a reference to the ICCPR but instead employed a broader term of 'international human rights instruments'.[65] In particular, according to the Court, 'international human rights instruments are applicable "in respect of acts done by a State in the exercise of its jurisdiction outside its own territory"'. Thus, the Court resorted to 'a single standard' for all human rights instruments.[66]

Finally, the ICJ may have even further refined its position on the scope of application of human rights treaties. In its decision on Provisional Measures in

---

62 See references in the beginning of this chapter, on the relevant literature.

63 ICJ, *Legal Consequences of the Construction of a Wall in the Occupied Palestinian Territory, op. cit.*, para. 112 (emphasis added).

64 In relation to the extraterritorial applicability of the ICCPR, the ICJ stated in the *Wall* Advisory Opinion that the 'International Covenant on Civil and Political Rights is applicable in respect of acts done by a State in the exercise of its jurisdiction outside its own territory'.

65 ICJ, *Case Concerning Armed Activities on the Territory of the Congo (DRC v. Uganda)*, ICJ 116, Judgment of 19 December 2005, para. 216. It applied this standard to the ICCPR, CRC and the ACHPR. The latter two contain socio-economic rights; however, the Court did not offer separate analysis for them.

66 J. Cerone, 'Jurisdiction and Power: The Intersection of Human Rights Law & the Law of Non-International Armed Conflict in a Transnational Context', *40 Israel Law Review* (2007), pp. 72–128, p. 101.

Application of the International Convention on the Elimination of all Forms of Racial Discrimination (Georgia v. Russian Federation), pointing out the absence of a territorial clause of the treaty, the Court has observed that:

> there is no restriction of a general nature in CERD relating to its territorial application; whereas it further notes that, in particular, neither Article 2 nor Article 5 of CERD, alleged violations of which are invoked by Georgia, contain a specific territorial limitation; and whereas the Court consequently finds that these provisions of CERD generally appear to apply, like other provisions of instruments of that nature, to the actions of a State party when it acts beyond its territory.[67]

The latest pronouncement of the Court leads us to conclude that the Covenant does not *a priori* limit its reach to the national territory. Of evidentiary significance to this effect are also the declarations of the States Parties to the Covenant on Economic, Social and Cultural Rights. When adhering to the ICESCR, Turkey declared that 'it will implement the provisions of this Covenant only to the States with which it has diplomatic relations', and that the ICESCR was ratified exclusively with regard to the national territory 'where the Constitution and the legal and administrative order of the Republic of Turkey are applied'.[68] A number of states objected to Turkey's reservation, stating that it created 'uncertainty as to the States Parties in respect of which Turkey is undertaking the obligations in the Covenant'[69] and that it was 'in the common interest of all states that treaties to which they have chosen to become parties are respected and applied as to their object and purpose by all parties'.[70] While for some the meaning of Turkey's declaration was not clear,[71] according to Greece:

> This reservation is incompatible with the obligation of a State Party to respect and ensure the rights laid down in the Covenant to anyone within the power or effective control of that State Party, even if not situated within the territory of such State Party.[72]

---

67 ICJ, *Application of the International Convention on the Elimination of all Forms of Racial Discrimination (Georgia v. Russian Federation)*, Provisional Measures, Order of 15 October 2008, [2008] I.C.J. Reports 353, paras. 109 and 149 (emphasis added).
68 Turkey: Declaration United Nations Treaty Collection, Chapter IV, Human Rights, http://treaties.un.org/Pages/ViewDetails.aspx?src=TREATY&mtdsg_no=IV-3&chapter=4&lang=en#6.
69 Cyprus: Objection, 26 November 2006, *ibid.*
70 Germany: Objection, 8 November 2004, *ibid.*
71 Sweden: Objection, 15 November 2005, *ibid.* According to Sweden, 'This statement in fact amounts, in the view of the Government of Sweden, to a reservation. The reservation of the Republic of Turkey makes it unclear to what extent the Republic of Turkey considers itself bound by the obligations of the Covenant. In absence of further clarification, therefore, the reservation raises doubt as to the commitment of the Republic of Turkey to the object and purpose of the Covenant.'
72 Greece: Objection, 11 October 2004, *ibid.*

This seems to suggest that some states consider ICESCR obligations, both nega-tive and positive, to be applicable beyond a state's sovereign territory. In light of the above discussion, and consistent with the ICJ's *Wall* Advisory Opinion, later refined in the *DRC v. Uganda* case, one avenue of possible extraterritoriality of the Covenant on Economic, Social and Cultural Rights is *qua* jurisdictional limits.[73]

Contrary to the main argument in the preceding chapter, that international assistance and cooperation is one possible *means of implementation* of states' obligations under ESC rights treaties (as opposed to a self-standing obligation), human rights scholars have adopted an expansive approach to Article 2(1) of the ICESCR. As noted before, the requirement of international assistance and cooperation has been interpreted as a basis for extraterritorial applicability of the Covenant. A standard analysis of extraterritorial obligations with reference to international assistance and cooperation proceeds more or less as follows:

> [The] ICESCR contains explicit references to international cooperation and assistance for the realization of the rights guaranteed therein. It can therefore be said to contain extraterritorial obligations to cooperate internationally for development . . . [which] can be disaggregated into obligations to respect, to protect and fulfill.[74]

The material analysed thus confirms that human rights may be applicable out-side the territory of a state. The question, rather, seems to relate to the circum-stances under which applicability can be envisaged.

3.2 Challenges in applying extraterritoriality principles in the context of development

Notwithstanding the scant assertions of international bodies on the extraterrito-rial applicability of economic, social and cultural rights, it seems that general principles of extraterritorial applicability of the civil and political rights also apply to socio-economic rights.[75] The only problem is that, in situations other than foreign occupation, there is no sufficient clarity as to the extraterritorial scope of the ICESCR. In what follows, it is suggested to review the type of scenarios that may engage 'extraterritorial' applicability of the ICESCR in a development set-ting, with a view to understanding better the suitability of conceptual frameworks developed to deal with the relationship between a state and the protection of socio-economic rights of an individual(s) in another state.

---

73 The limits of the jurisdiction depends on the type of jurisdiction exercised, e.g. for legislative jurisdiction there is no limit in terms of territory, while enforcement jurisdiction cannot be exercised in the territory outside one's own, except for cases of a consent.

74 W. Vandenhole, 'EU and Development: Extraterritorial Obligations under the International Economic, Social and Cultural Rights', *op. cit.*, pp. 85–86.

75 Commentaries to Principle 5, Maastricht Principles on Extraterritorial Obligations of States in the area of Economic, Social and Cultural Rights, and the Commentary by O. De Schut-ter, A. Eide, A. Khalfan, M. Orellana, M.Salomon and I. Seiderman, para. 2.

Potential development-related extraterritorial cases under the ICESCR generally include the following:[76] (i) agricultural practices leading to the export dumping in the developing countries in violation of the right to an adequate standard of living of individuals residing in those countries and (ii) the 'promotion of user fees and cost recovery measures in health projects [in a bilateral or multilateral context], which have had, and continue to have, adverse effects on the right to highest attainable standard of health'[77] (the same practice of increasing user fees can be found in relation to development projects for education,[78] water, sanitation, etc.). In addition, extraterritorial obligations have been found in cases of illegitimate debt accrued as a result of development policies and strategies;[79] technical and financial contributions to government-led land management projects;[80] an extraterritorial obligation has been asserted to fulfil the ESC rights of individuals living in third states;[81] debt repayment and violations of socio-economic rights and so on. Applying a human rights framework, increasingly the NGOs have alleged human rights violations in the context of development cooperation.[82]

76 See generally for six different case studies, FIAN et al., http://www.lancaster.ac.uk/fass/projects/humanrights/documents/FIAN_Oct06_Casestudies.pdf October 2006.
77 W. Vandenhole, 'EU and Development: Extraterritorial Obligations under the International Economic, Social and Cultural Rights', in W. Vandenhole, M. Salomon and A. Tostensen (eds), *Casting the Net Wider: Human Rights, Development and New Duty-Bearers*, Intersentia: 2007, pp. 85–106; W. Vandenhole, 'Third State Obligations Under the ICESCR: A Case Study of EU Sugar Policy', 76 *Nordic Journal of International Law* (2007), pp. 71–98.
78 M. Mustaniemi-Laasko, 'The Right to Education: Instrumental Right Par Excellence', in W. Vandenhole, M. Salomon and A. Tostensen (eds), *Casting the Net Wider: Human Rights, Development and New Duty-Bearers*, Intersentia: 2007, pp. 331–352.
79 F. Coomans and R. Kunnemann (eds), *Cases and Concepts on Extraterritorial Obligations in the Area of Economic, Social and Cultural Rights*, Intersentia: 2012, p. 154ff.
80 Submission to the UN Committee on Economic, Social and Cultural Rights Extraterritorial State Obligations List of Issues in response to the 5th Periodic Report of the Federal Republic of Germany on the implementation of the International Covenant on Economic, Social and Cultural Rights, submitted by Diakonisches Werk der EKD, FIAN Deutschland, Gegenströmung Deutsche Kommission Justitia et Pax, Misereor, Nürnberger Menschenrechtszentrum urgewald, 2011. Eventually, extensive NGO reporting has led the Committee on Economic, Social and Cultural Rights to raise the issue with the State Party. In particular, the Committee expressed its concern that a State Party's development cooperation programme has supported projects that have reportedly resulted in the violation of economic, social and cultural rights, such as in the case of the land-titling project in Cambodia, and reminded the State Party that its development activities should not result in violation of these rights. See CESCR, Concluding Observations: Germany, UN doc. E/C.12/DEU/CO/5, 12 July 2011.
81 See the Zambian Social Cash Transfers Case, in F. Coomans and R. Kunnemann (eds), *Cases and Concepts on Extraterritorial Obligations in the Area of Economic, Social and Cultural Rights*, Intersentia: 2012, p. 180ff.
82 See a series of reports by S. Rockwell and C. Schamas, *A Human Rights Review of the EU and Israel: Relating Commitments to Action, 2003–2004*, Euro-Mediterranean Human Rights Network: 2004; S. Rockwell and C. Schamas, *A Human Rights Review of the EU and Israel: Mainstreaming or Selectively Extinguishing Human Rights, 2004–2005*, Euro-Mediterranean Human Rights Network: 2005; S. Rockwell and C. Schamas, *Third Annual Review on Human Rights in EU–Israel Relations: Accommodating to the 'special' case of Israel 20005–2006*, Euro-Mediterranean Human Rights Network: 2006.

These examples point out at least to two types of scenarios in the development setting that may engage questions related to the extraterritorial operation of the ICESCR. The first relates to protection of individuals from the extraterritorial conduct of a state acting directly outside its territory – promoting, let us say for the sake of simplicity, user fees in the framework of development projects for education. The second scenario would involve a conduct that is not extraterritorial, *per se*, but produces effects outside the territory – put differently, arrangements of a policy or socio-economic nature, taken within the confines of a state, which have an extraterritorial effect on the socio-economic rights of individuals. Again, in simplified terms, a case in point may be a situation akin to the 2015 Greek debt crisis, where economic arrangements and policies adopted by lender states may incur considerable impact on the enjoyment of economic, social and cultural rights of individuals residing in Greece.[83]

More fundamentally, in the development context a wide variety of scenarios will have an inter-state or extraterritorial dimension, as 'development' projects are very often based on cooperative and joint or collective action, involving multiple actors who contribute to the final outcome, and are in some cases harmful. Development is an area of external state activity capable of producing large-scale effects on the situation of the well-being of individuals outside the state's boundaries.[84] It is the essence of development to intervene, to prompt changes. It has even been labelled as an art of large-scale social engineering. However, according to one view, 'domestic economic decisions that have international economic implications, and necessarily global effect upon human conditions, would not bring affected individuals in foreign countries under the jurisdiction of the State in question', suggesting that 'considerations of fairness and expediency require that states would not bear responsibility for indirect or unforeseen consequences of their actions in areas outside their control'.[85] While it is not clear which concerns will need to be taken into consideration – fairness or expediency – the real problem with any practices related to socio-economic fields with human rights implications outside the territory is establishing the necessary link required between the act and the violation.[86]

---

83 For an analysis see FIDH/HLHR, Downgrading Rights: the Cost of Austerity in Greece, 2009, www.etoconsortium.org/nc/en/library/documents/?tx_drblob_pi1%5Bdownload Uid%5D=141.

84 B. Hettne, *Development Theory and the Three Worlds: Towards an International Political Economy of Development*, Longman Scientific & Technical: 1995, p. 38.

85 O. Ben-Naftali and Y. Shany, 'Living in Denial: The Application of Human Rights in the Occupied Territories', 37(17) *Israel Law Review* (2003–04), p. 64.

86 Consider the case of *Zaoi* which appeared before the Court of First Instance of the European Court of Justice concerning development assistance. The applicant claimed the non-contractual liability of the European Union for the death of his wife as a result of a suicide bombing. Particularly, the applicant claimed that the Union was responsible for the death of his wife in a terrorist attack by a Palestinian in Israel. The argument was that the educational system, and a special handbook in particular financed by the EU, incited hatred against Israel, and the Union should be held responsible because of its role as the biggest sponsor of the educational system. The action was based on Article 288 of the EC Treaty. In the case at hand, the Court of First Instance did not recognize any sufficient causal link between the economic support

In addition, complex issues within the development cooperation context would arise in connection with the moment at which violations occur, namely whether they occur at the stage of design or implementation, and how to differentiate between original and consequential violations, or when a violation has not been intended. Difficulties also include establishing a direct link between a *policy* of development cooperation and its effect on ESC rights in the country of the state receiving aid.[87] In the context of development cooperation, there may be challenges in separating the complex causal relationships between conduct and/or omission originating in the international environment from the activities of a particular donor state, as well as separating the donor activities from the activities of the recipient state (or other possible causes).[88] Consider the following example when:

> a vote in Washington to change the wheat price supports for Nebraska can change the price of bread in Calcutta and the price of meat in Kiev. And when major actors take concerted action to produce effects–when, for example, officials from the United States, Japan, and Germany cooperate to manipulate the relative values of the dollar, the yen, and the mark–exports and imports, deficits and taxes, jobs and standards of living, even birthrates and life-expectancies throughout the world far beyond those three countries are affected, for better or worse, as intended or otherwise.[89]

It is often the case that multiple actors are involved in socio-economic processes, making the questions even more complex. What at first sight seems to be an extraterritorial act of a state (donor), is transformed by the state (recipient) into an act or omission of its own. In essence, in development cooperation, decisions are made within cooperative arrangements, with the consent of recipient states; hence actions and decisions of the states (recipient of development cooperation) transform initially extraterritorial conduct into territorial conduct. Such a situation suggests elaboration of sophisticated concepts determining varying degrees of responsibility and means of determining them. At present, broad categories are increasingly used to describe possible sources of harms to human rights of individuals in impoverished parts of the world, such as globalization, global integration of markets, and unequal and unfair economic relations that sustain structural obstacles to many states impeding development. On this basis,

---

of the educational system and the terrorist attack. The Court dismissed the application, as it saw no established causal link between the alleged conduct and the harm claimed. Case T-73/03 *Zaoui and others v. Commission*, 23 April 2003, Order of CFI.

87 Report of the open-ended working group to consider options regarding the elaboration of an optional protocol to the International Covenant on Economic, Social and Cultural Rights on its second session, E/CN.4/2005/52, para. 80.

88 See *infra* section 'The challenge of identifying human rights harm in development process' in Chapter VI.

89 H. Shue, 'Mediating duties', 98(4) *Ethics* (1988), pp. 687–704, p. 694.

it should be conceded that, indeed, the emergences of 'transnational solidarities' challenge the old precepts of jurisdiction.[90]

In the context where global and economic forces are in play, possibilities of attribution to a concrete state or actor may prove precarious. Generally, it is submitted that multilateral contexts are more complex in this regard. Some commentators have tried to address these issues, putting forward different proposals, including the principle of foreseeability,[91] the principle/obligation of due diligence,[92] or even the application of the precautionary principle.[93] Or, to render propositions set out by the Maastricht Principles on the Extraterritorial Obligations of States in the area of Economic, Social and Cultural Rights operative, theoretical analysis is being developed on how to divide responsibility between the national state and other states and actors, as well as between the other actors.[94]

The nature of socio-economic rights themselves adds another layer of complexity to the issue. At the heart of the violation of socio-economic human rights lie systemic or structural causes. Equally, the potential of domestic decisions in the development context (as well as external decisions, such as externally designed economic or social policies) to impact on the socio-economic rights of individuals outside their territories usually goes beyond an individual violation and may result in massive impairment of basic socio-economic rights. In this respect, it seems that there is room to explore these aspects further within the notion of 'grave or systematic violations', as provided for by the Optional Protocol to the ICESCR.[95] All in all, the tests developed for civil and political cases may require

90 As explained: 'By the latter expression [e.g. transnational solidarities] we intend to refer to a set of values and interests, common to each and every state, which are perceived as shared concerns by the international community as a whole. Less theoretically and more pragmatically, the same internationalisation of commercial and financial markets has enormously complicated factual matrices so that the strict application of fairly simple and general rules such as those of the traditional international law of jurisdiction would fall short of doing justice in many cases. Retention of the fairly simplistic formula 'chacun chez soi' seems therefore very inappropriate nowadays.' H.G. Maier, 'Jurisdictional Rules in Customary International Law', *op. cit.*, pp. 84–85.

91 See Principle 9 (Scope of Jurisdiction), Maastricht Principles on Extraterritorial Obligations of States in the Area of Economic, Social and Cultural Rights, October, 2011.

92 M. Salomon, *Global Responsibility for Human Rights: World Poverty and the Development of International Law*, OUP: 2007, pp. 182–183. The Maastricht Principles make use of the term 'obligation to avoid using harm'; see Principle 13 bearing the same title, Maastricht Principles on Extraterritorial Obligations of States in the area of Economic, Social and Cultural Rights.

93 S. Skogly, 'Causality and Extraterritorial Human Rights Obligations', in M. Langford, W. Vandenhole, M. Scheinin, and W. van Genugten (eds), *Global Justice, State Duties: The Extraterritorial Scope of Economic, Social, and Cultural Rights in International Law*, CUP: 2013, pp. 233–258.

94 A. Khalfan and I. Seiderman, 'Extraterritorial Human Rights Obligations: Wider Implications of the Maastricht Principles and the Continuing Accountability Challenge', in W. Vandendole (ed.), *Challenging Territoriality in Human Rights Law: Building Blocks or Plural and Diverse Duty-Bearer Regime*, Routledge: 2015, pp. 15–43.

95 The notion of grave or systematic violations by a State Party of any of the economic, social and cultural rights set forth in the Covenant is included in Article 11 of the Optional Protocol

further refinement and a high degree of sophistication to be able to be accommodate the specificities of violations of the socio-economic rights.

While these issues are starting to become more widely discussed in the human rights analysis, in general international law the question of injurious economic effects is dealt with under the topic of the *effects doctrine* (a variation of objective territorial jurisdiction). According to this doctrine, jurisdiction can be asserted on the basis that the negative (injurious) effect, but not the act or omission itself, occurred in the territory of state.[96] The origin of the effects doctrine is closely associated with the practice of US anti-trust law. Even if the effects doctrine has found some following, it has been very controversial.[97] The main contention was that the effects doctrine would lead to 'unacceptable interferences in the freedom of others to conduct their economic affairs as they choose'.[98] As Simma explains:

> To be sure, economic effects are certainly the result of human action, but it has been argued that there remains a difference in kind between physical constituents of an act realized in a state's territory and the mere economic consequences of the manipulation of market forces . . . It could also be said that such effects are too remote from the initial acts; recognizing them as the 'result' of these initial act could bring almost everything within their ambit. An excessive effects doctrine would indeed bear the risk of creating a sort of jurisdictional 'butterfly effect', since, in the highly interconnected world economy, even inconspicuous and seemingly innocent acts can be traced back as being at the origin of all kinds of negative repercussions.[99]

However, as already alluded to above, it is precisely the interconnectedness of the world economy that serves as a justification to consider the effects doctrine seriously and adapt it to the realities of today's economy. Legal scholars warn that potential problems with the application of the effects doctrine may, however, include the difficulty of identifying which state would have a jurisdiction, not to mention dealing with certain types of international economic

---

to CESCR. In the past, certain forms of systematic violations of socio-economic rights were analysed by Sub-Commission on Prevention of Discrimination and Protection of Minorities. See the Final report on the question of the impunity of perpetrators of human rights violations (economic, social and cultural rights), prepared by Mr El Hadji Guissé, Special Rapporteur, pursuant to Sub-Commission Resolution 1996/24, E/CN.4/Sub.2/1997/8, 27 June 1997.

96 P.A. Malanczuk, *Akehurst's Modern Introduction to International Law*, Routledge: 1997, p. 111. See also K. Raustiala, *Does the Constitution Follow the Flag: The Evolution of Territoriality in American Law*, OUP: 2009.

97 C. Ryngaert, *Jurisdiction in International Law*, OUP: 2008, p. 77ff.

98 R. Higgins, *Problems and Process: International Law and How We Use It*, Clarendon Press: 1994, pp. 74–75.

99 B. Simma and A. Th. Muller, 'Exercise and Limits of Jurisdiction', in J. Crawford and M. Koskenniemi, *The Cambridge Companion to International Law*, CUP: 2012, pp. 134–158, pp. 140–141.

activities.[100] However, 'as long as it is accepted that a state's susceptibility to economic effects brought about by conduct in another state is serious enough to constitute an interest that deserves international legal protection, there is no reason why it should not be recognized as a sufficient nexus for jurisdiction'.[101]

To remedy this gap of accountability for the violations of socio-economic rights in the transborder context, the Maastricht Principles give a broad definition of extraterritorial obligations in the area of economic, social and cultural rights as encompassing: (i) obligations relating to the acts and omissions of a state, within or beyond its territory, that have effects on the enjoyment of human rights outside of that state's territory; and (ii) obligations of a global character that are set out in the UN Charter and human rights instruments to take action, separately and jointly, through international cooperation, in order to realize human rights universally.[102] The problem with the Maastricht Principles, besides the question of their legal status, is that they do not specify the legal source of the extraterritorial obligations they purport to develop.[103]

3.3 The nature of obligations and the question of jurisdiction

In contrast to the foregoing discussion, there is an emerging view, or rather *discovery*, that no jurisdictional threshold should be imposed on the negative state obligations to refrain from doing harm,[104] and even that, by doing so, a state exceeds its authority and violates the sovereignty of the territorial state (including the territorial state's human rights obligations).[105] Roxtrom, Gibney and Einarsen make an important point that jurisdiction relates to 'exclusively Contracting State's positive obligations' and has nothing to do with the negative obligations.[106] They argue that negative obligations under the human rights treaty are owed to everyone everywhere; '[a] universal right could not be guaranteed

---

100 *Ibid.*
101 *Ibid.*
102 The Commentaries to the Principles further clarify that obligations of an extraterritorial nature arise under the first basis (a), because the State has the legal and factual power to regulate the corporation's conduct, and it arises under the second basis (b), due to the obligation a State owes internationally to take separate and joint action. Commentaries to Principle 8, Maastricht Principles on Extraterritorial Obligations of States in the area of Economic, Social and Cultural Rights, and the Commentary by O. De Schutter, A. Eide, A. Khalfan, M. Orellana, M. Salomon and I. Seiderman, www.icj.org/dwn/database/Maas tricht%20ETO%20Principles%20-%20FINAL.pdf.
103 W. Vandenhole, 'Emerging Normative Frameworks on Transnational Human Rights Obligations', EUI Working Papers, RSCAS 2012/17, 2012, p. 4.
104 M. Milanović, *Extraterritorial Application of Human Rights Treaties: Law, Principles, and Policy, op. cit.*, p. 446.
105 N. Lubell, *Extraterritorial Use of Force against Non-State Actors, op. cit.*, p. 210.
106 E. Roxtrom, M. Gibney and T. Einarsen, 'The Nato Bombing Case (Bankovic et al. v. Belgium et al.) and the Limits of the Western Human Rights Protection', 23 *Boston University International Law Journal*, p. 72.

unless the negative duties corresponding to it were universal'.[107] Similarly, Fran-çoise Hampson states that '[i]t would be possible, for example, for states to have the obligation both to respect and to protect a particular right in areas within their control, but only to have an obligation to respect the right where they do not exercise territorial or physical control'.[108]

This line of argument is slowly emerging in terms of analysis. Milanović, for example, is convinced that distinction should be drawn between a state's obligation *to respect* human rights, requiring only obligation of abstention and its obligation *to ensure* human rights, which require the state to take positive measures, including, in certain circumstances, prevention of human rights violations by third parties.[109] For an obligation to respect human rights to exist, states are required to have nothing more than control over the conduct of its own agents.[110] In contrast, positive obligations require a considerable amount of state action and, consequently, control over the area. Control would be required to effectively regulate, or in other words 'to apply the law to the acts of men',[111] to effectively protect the rights of individuals from third parties, and take positive action to implement the rights of individuals by creating institutions, mechanisms of enforcement and so on.[112] Hence, it is proposed to apply the threshold of jurisdiction only to the positive obligations of the state to secure and ensure, while the obligation to respect human rights will not be territorially bound.[113]

The argument is persuasive when seen in light of relevant human rights instruments and their interpretation. Article 2(1) of the Covenant on Civil and Political Rights proclaims that '[e]ach State Party to the present Covenant undertakes to respect and to ensure to all individuals within its territory and subject to its jurisdiction the rights recognized in the present Covenant'. There has been much debate on the conjunctive and disjunctive reading of Article 2(1). On this point, there has been a lot of discussion on the ordinary or plain meaning of the text of the provision. An argument for the conjunctive reading of 'within its territory

---

107 *Ibid.* See also J. Cerone, who suggests that 'the absence of transitive language between "to respect" and "all individuals"' in Article 2 of the ICCPR supports such an interpretation. J. Cerone, 'Jurisdiction and Power: The Intersection of Human Rights Law & the Law of Non-International Armed Conflict in a Transnational Context', *op. cit.*, p. 448.

108 F. Hampson, 'The Scope of the Extra-territorial Applicability of International Human Rights Law', *op. cit.*, p. 165. A similar point is shared by M. Scheinin, 'Just Another Word? Jurisdiction in the Roadmaps of State Responsibility and Human Rights', in M. Langford, W. Vandenhole, M. Scheinin and W. Van Genugten (eds), *Global Justice, State Duties: the Extraterritorial Scope of Economic, Social, and Cultural Rights in International Law*, CUP: 2013, pp. 212–229.

109 M. Milanović, *Extraterritorial Application of Human Rights Treaties: Law, Principles, and Policy, op. cit.*, p. 210.

110 *Ibid.*

111 *Wedding v. Meyler*, 1992 US 573, 584 (1904), cited in F.A.P. Mann, 'The Doctrine of Jurisdiction in International Law', 111 *Recueil des cours* (1964), p. 13.

112 M. Milanović, *Extraterritorial Application of Human Rights Treaties: Law, Principles, and Policy, op. cit.*, p. 210.

113 *Ibid.*, p. 211.

and subject to its jurisdiction' imposing a dual requirement has been provided.[114] The position of the Human Rights Committee itself has been seen to read the text disjunctively.[115] An alternative view is that a conjunctive reading can be only one of the possible ordinary meanings, but not the sole one. In addition, one interpretation suggests that limitation as to jurisdiction (and maybe even when read conjunctively with the 'territory') applies only to the obligation to ensure, whereas the obligation to respect is not subject to any jurisdictional limitations.[116]

In the submission of the US to the Human Rights Committee, the US argued that '[d]uring the negotiating history, the words "within its territory" had been debated and were added by vote, with the clear understanding that such wording would limit the obligations to within a Party's territory'.[117] In effect, reference to territory was introduced by the proposal of the US. At the negotiations of the ICCPR, the US representative, Eleanor Roosevelt, provided the following explanation:

> The purpose of the proposed addition was to make it clear that the draft Covenant would apply only to persons within the territory and subject to the jurisdiction of contracting States. The United States was afraid that without such an addition the draft Covenant might be construed as obliging the contracting States to enact legislation concerning persons who, although outside its territory were technically within its jurisdiction for certain purposes. An illustration would be the occupied territories of Germany, Austria and Japan: persons within those countries were subject to the jurisdiction of the occupying States in certain respects, but were outside the scope of the legislation of those States. Another illustration would be the case of leased territories; some countries leased certain territories from others for limited purposes, and there might be questions of conflicting authority between the lessor nation and the lessee nation.[118]

---

114 See the argument of the US in its 2nd and 3rd periodic report, UN CCPR/C/USA/3, 28 November 2005, p. 109, annex I.
115 See footnote 24.
116 See in particular the line of argument provided by Kunnemann: 'The qualifying clause on territory/jurisdiction in Article 2 ICCPR needs careful reading: Does it pertain to "ensure", where it stands, or both to "respect and ensure"? Do persons for whom the party must ensure the right have to be subject to its jurisdiction, or also those for whom the party has to respect the right. If the second was correct the text should have read "to respect and ensure to all individuals. . ." The fact that it reads instead "to respect and to ensure to all individuals. . ." underlines that the limiting clause refers to "ensure only".' R. Kunnemann, 'Extraterritorial Application of the International Covenant on Economic, Social and Cultural Rights', in F. Coomans and M.T. Kamminga (eds), *Extraterritorial Application of Human Rights Treaties*, Intersentia: 2004, p. 228.
117 HRC, Third periodic reports of States Parties: USA, UN doc. CCPR/C/USA/3, 28 November 2005, p. 109, annex I.
118 Commission on Human Rights, Sixth Session, Summary Records of the Hundred Thirty-Eighth Meeting, UN doc. E/CN.4/SR.138, para. 34.

This passage has been relied upon by the US to interpret a restricted scope of the application of the ICCPR. However, as pointed out elsewhere, it also demonstrates the preoccupation of the negotiators with the prospect of legislating, or a possible norm conflict in the territories to which the US had no title.[119] The preparatory work also shows that negotiators were concerned that 'it was not possible for a State to protect the rights of persons subject to its jurisdiction when they were outside its territory; in such cases, action would be possible only through diplomatic channels'.[120] Another example of the drafting history shows that after an exchange between the US representative and those of the Philippines and Yugoslavia, regarding the possibilities the US would have at its disposal if there was a need to provide US citizens abroad with protection,[121] the representative of Uruguay agreed with the US position and stated that since no state could effectively dispose of an enforcement machinery (judges, police, etc.) in the territory outside its jurisdiction, 'it was evident that States could effectively guarantee human rights only to those persons residing within their territorial jurisdiction. For that reason the Uruguayan delegation would support the United States amendment.'[122] The ICJ in the *Wall* Advisory Opinion also confirms this:

> The *travaux préparatoires* of the Covenant confirm the Committee's interpretation of Article 2 of that instrument. These show that, in adopting the wording chosen, the drafters of the Covenant did not intend to allow States to escape from their obligations when they exercise jurisdiction outside their national territory. They only intended to prevent persons residing abroad from asserting, vis-à-vis their State of origin, rights that do not fall within the competence of that State, but of that of the State of residence.[123]

---

119 M. Milanović, *Extraterritorial Application of Human Rights Treaties: Law, Principles, and Policy, op. cit.*, p. 226.

120 M.J. Bossuyt, *Guide to the 'Travaux Preparatoires' of the International. Covenant on Civil and Political Rights,* Martinus Nijhoff Publishers: 1986, pp. 53–54.

121 In response to the remark of the Philippines whether US citizens denied rights abroad could claim protection of the USA, the US Representative responded: 'if such a case occurred within the territory of a State party to the covenant, the United States Government would insist that the State should honour its obligations under the covenant; if, however, the State in question had not acceded to the covenant, the United States Government would be unable to do more than make representations on behalf of the citizens through the normal diplomatic channels. It would certainly not exercise jurisdiction over a person outside its territory.' UN ESCOR Human Rights Committee, Summary Record of the 194th Meeting, UN doc. E/CN4/SR.194 (1950), para. 16.

122 UN ESCOR Human Rights Committee, Summary Record of the 194th Meeting, UN doc. E/CN4/SR.194 (1950), para. 30.

123 ICJ, *Legal Consequences of the Construction of a Wall in the Occupied Palestinian Territory, op. cit.*, para. 109. See also the comments of J. Cerone, who observed that: 'Thus, with respect to matters within the scope of Palestinian authority, the Court implies that Israel is bound only by negative obligations. This would seem to imply, *a contrario*, that the scope of Israel's obligation in matters within its authority, and beyond the authority of the Palestinians, encompasses positive obligations. This would seem to indicate that as Israel

Here, time and again, if the assertions of the authors of the human rights treaties are read carefully, one can infer that the primary concern was to confine the scope of positive obligations to persons within their borders and that this did not include the question of the responsibility of a state for action taken against individuals outside its sovereign territory. Tomuschat's conclusion was that 'it was the intention of drafters, whose sovereign decision cannot be challenged, to restrict the territorial scope of the Covenant in view of such situations where enforcing the Covenant would be likely to encounter exceptional obstacles. Never was it envisaged, however, to grant States parties unfettered discretionary power to carry out wilful and deliberate attacks against the freedom and personal integrity of their citizens living abroad.'[124]

This distinction between negative and positive obligations and their link to the threshold of jurisdiction is most clearly visible in other examples of the State's treaty-making practice. Article 1(1) of the American Convention on Human Rights, states:

> The States Parties to this Convention undertake *to respect the rights and freedoms recognized herein* and *to ensure to all persons subject to their jurisdiction the free and full exercise of those rights and freedoms*, without any discrimination for reasons of race, colour, sex, language, religion, political or other opinion, national or social origin, economic status, birth, or any other social condition.[125]

It would be fair to infer that the provision attaches the requirement of jurisdiction to 'ensure' rights and freedoms protected by the Convention, whereas the obligation to respect is not linked with the threshold requirement. After all, the *ratio legis* as stipulated in *Issa et al. v. Turkey* is that 'Article 1 of the Convention cannot be interpreted so as to allow a State party to perpetrate violations of the Convention on the territory of another State, which it could not perpetrate on its own territory'.[126]

This line of thinking can also be discerned in the gradual approach adopted in some of the cases of the human rights bodies.[127] Contrary to an 'all or nothing'

---

cedes control, the scope of its obligation is decreased from one encompassing positive and negative obligations to one entailing only negative obligations'. J. Cerone, 'Jurisdiction and Power: The Intersection of Human Rights Law & the Law of Non-International Armed Conflict in a Transnational Context', *op. cit.*, p. 118.

124 C. Tomuschat, individual opinion in *Lopez Burgos v. Uruguay*, No. 52/1979 and *Celibeti v. Uruguay*, No. 56/1979.

125 American Convention on Human Rights, Pact of San José, 22 November 1969 (emphasis added).

126 ECtHR, *Issa and Others v. Turkey*, 16 November 2004, ECHR (2nd sect.) no. 31821/96, 30 March 2005, para. 71.

127 R. Lawson, 'Life after Banković: On the Extraterritorial Application of the European Convention on Human Rights', in R. Lawson, M. Kamminga and F. Coomans (eds), *Extraterritorial Application of Human Rights Treaties*, Intersentia: 2004, p. 120. The European

concept of jurisdiction, as suggested in the *Banković* case,[128] the ECtHR in its subsequent jurisprudence recognized 'varying levels of obligations'. Notable in this respect is the case of *Ilascu*, where the Court acknowledged that 'jurisdiction' can be shared between two or more States Parties.[129] This move can be considered key to understanding situations where 'the *combined* actions of two or more State parties to the Convention have created a situation allegedly in violation of the obligations of each State'.[130]

To return to the main subject of the inquiry, it is to be recalled that the Covenant on Economic, Social and Cultural Rights says nothing about negative obligations. It does not make any distinction between positive and negative. By virtue of Article 2(1), each state 'undertakes to take steps, individually and through international assistance and cooperation . . . with a view to achieving progressively the full realization of the rights recognized in the present Covenant'. The obligation 'to take steps' is inherently of a positive nature. The General Comment on the Nature of State Parties Obligations states:

> The other is the undertaking in article 2 (1) 'to take steps', which in itself, is not qualified or limited by other considerations. The full meaning of the phrase can also be gauged by noting some of the different language versions. In English the undertaking is 'to take steps', in French it is 'to act' ('s'engage à agir') and in Spanish it is 'to adopt measures' ('a adoptar medidas'). Thus while the full realization of the relevant rights may be achieved progressively, steps towards that goal must be taken within a reasonably short time after the Covenant's entry into force for the States concerned. Such steps should be

---

Commission on Human Rights in *W.M. v. Denmark* found that it was evident from the 'constant jurisprudence of the Commission that authorised agents of a State, including diplomatic or consular agents, bring other persons or property within the jurisdiction of that State to the extent that they exercise authority over such persons or property. In so far as they affect such persons or property by the acts or omissions, the responsibility of the State is engaged.' *W.M. v. Denmark*, no. 17392/90, EComHR Decision, 14 October 1992, para. 1.

128 The ECtHR held that 'the wording of Article 1 does not provide any support for the applicants' suggestion that the positive obligation in Article 1 to secure 'the rights and freedoms defined in Section I of this Convention can be divided and tailored in accordance with the particular circumstances of the extra-territorial act in question'. *Banković et al v. Belgium et al*, App. No. 52207/99, ECtHR (2001), para. 75.

129 Recent case-law of the ECtHR can be considered even more generous in its approach. ECtHR, *Case of Chiragov and Others v. Armenia*, Application no. 13216/05, Judgment, 16 June 2015.

130 Some case law of the ECtHR offers a 'relative' concept of jurisdiction. Consider the example of the *Ilascu* case, where the court has identified 'a reduced' scope of jurisdiction, where obligations of Moldova are to be 'tailored to the extent of the jurisdiction effectively exercised'. See for detailed discussion O. De Schutter, 'Human Rights, Globalization and Jurisdiction: Lessons from the European Convention on Human Rights', 6 *Baltic Yearbook of International Law* (2006), pp. 226–228.

deliberate, concrete and targeted as clearly as possible towards meeting the obligations recognized in the Covenant.[131]

Little can be inferred on the issue from the interpretation of the Committee on the nature of States Parties' obligations pertaining to the Covenant which it had adopted in its early years of activity. Rather, the understanding that the socio-economic rights are to be respected coalesced over time through successive interpretation of various rights and the process of identification of the minimum core and justiciable parameters of the ESC rights. In its *Wall* Advisory Opinion, the ICJ also found implicit negative obligations inherent in socio-economic rights by stating that Israel was 'under obligation not to raise any obstacle to the exercise of such rights in those fields where competence has been transferred to Palestinian Authorities'.[132]

In any event, one might even claim that such is the understanding of the CESCR, which has been consistent in its treatment of negative obligations as 'international obligations' rather than extraterritorial ones.[133] The Committee, by using the term 'international obligations', may have intended to underline that negative obligations under the ICESCR are universal. If one proceeds from this reasoning, the extent of the discussion on the extraterritorial applicability of the ICESCR will arise only regarding the meaning and scope of 'international assistance and cooperation'. As discussed earlier, it can be argued that international assistance and cooperation gives an authority for states to act beyond their own territory. This finding leads us back to the concept of international assistance and cooperation as a relevant framework to identify the scope of positive obligations in the external context and what it implies in terms of legal obligations for third states.

Conclusion

What we may conclude is that if the extraterritoriality concept relates solely to the scope of the positive obligations owed outside a state's territory, the term 'international assistance and cooperation' might be considered to determine this scope. The main principles defining the content of international assistance and cooperation, discussed earlier, define international assistance and cooperation as primarily a subsidiary obligation. The exact 'time' when (or the threshold

---

131 CESCR, General Comment No. 3, The Nature of States Parties' Obligations, UN doc. E/1991/23, 14 December 1990, para. 2.
132 ICJ, *Legal Consequences of the Construction of a Wall in the Occupied Palestinian Territory, op. cit.*, para. 112.
133 The Committee, for example, when expressing its position on the on the obligation of other states with regard to sanctions, etc., does not qualify those 'actions' as extraterritorial application of the ICESCR.

needed for) this subsidiary obligation to be activated is not clear with regard to ESC rights.[134]

If, however, one considers extraterritorial aspects from the position of current jurisprudence, the principle to be deduced is that positive obligations are dependent on the degree of control exercised by the State, 'subject to standards of reasonableness'.[135] But the required level of control and corresponding duties arising out of the ICESCR remain unresolved, even less so in relation to the control over the economic situation or effective control over the macro-dimension of socio-economic rights.[136] This chapter also discussed, in some detail, arguments concerning the absence of jurisdictional limits in cases of negative obligation under human rights treaties. The following chapter will discuss this issue in more detail.

134 Similarly, den Heijer and Lawson argue that '[t]hese duties [e.g. international assistance and cooperation] are obviously (and deliberately) formulated in broad and general terms, and their very nature would appear to oppose an interpretation that they should be made dependent upon specific conduct or involvements of a State – other than, perhaps, the resources the State has at its disposal. We would uphold the proposition that those duties should accordingly not be made dependent on the existence of a specific "jurisdictional link" between the State and a particular individual or group of individuals present in a foreign territory.' M. den Heijer and R. Lawson, 'Extraterritorial Human Rights and the Concept of "Jurisdiction"', in M. Langford, W. Vandenhole, M. Scheinin and W. Van Genugten (eds), *Global Justice, State Duties: the Extraterritorial Scope of Economic, Social, and Cultural Rights in International Law*, CUP: 2013, p. 184.

135 On the subject see C. Ryngaert, 'Jurisdiction: Towards a Reasonableness Test', in M. Langford, W. Vandenhole, M. Scheinin and W. Van Genugten (eds), *Global Justice, State Duties: the Extraterritorial Scope of Economic, Social, and Cultural Rights in International Law*, CUP: 2013, pp. 192–212.

136 M. Gondek, *The Reach of Human Rights in a Globalising World: Extraterritorial Application of Human Rights Treaties, op. cit.*, p. 316.

VI Respect for human rights in external activities
Overarching normative principles

Introduction

The resource-related action has been a preferred strategy of international efforts to balance inequality in social and economic terms: aid, preferential treatment, technical assistance, etc. Equally, the meaning of creation of an 'enabling environment' has given way to an interpretation of 'affirmative action' rather than developing an understanding of issues of negligence in development. Since the level of development is singled out as an obstacle to enjoyment of socio-economic rights, the solution to address development challenges (or the lack of) was also seen in providing resources, including through the medium of 'developmental' human rights. Efforts focused on ushering in 'development' rather than on ensuring the way development was promoted or facilitated was not harmful to human rights.

Historically, the social and human impacts of bringing 'development' (both international and national policies and practices) have not always been positive.[1] In practice, however, when the impact of development aid was negative, it was more often addressed by special measures of redress rather than through a change in the economic policies that caused it.[2] This reality compelled legal discourse to

---

1 Rajagopal claims 'it is not the lack of development that caused poverty, inflicted violence, and engaged in destruction of nature and livelihoods; rather it is the very process of bringing development that has caused them in first place'. He further advances his point: 'the mass deportation of 1.5 million people from Phnom Penh by the Khmer Rouge in 1975 is argued to be a crime against humanity, while the mass eviction/deportation of 33 million development refugees from their homes due to development projects such as dams, by the Indian Government, is simply seen as the "social cost" (if at all) of development' in B. Rajagopal, *International Law from Below: Development, Social Movements and Third World Resistance*, CUP: 2003, pp. 21, 195.
2 An example is the transformation of the traditional SAPs towards poverty alleviation. Other examples include the Operational Policies of the WB and the WB instituted High Inspection Panel. In the past, such measures also included compensatory programmes such as the Social Dimensions of Adjustment (SDA Programs that came to close in 1992) which were designed to reduce or 'shield' the poor from the impact of structural adjustments. As Tomasevski pointed out, the term 'safety net' 'has entered development finance rhetoric as the embodiment of such a shield'. K. Tomasevski, 'The Influence of the World Bank and IMF on Economic and Social Rights', 64 *Nordic Journal of International Law* (1995), pp. 385–395, and 391.

focus on ways to compensate for the neglect of human rights within development. Some scholars were even convinced that the work of the human rights community should be entirely geared towards ensuring that development complies with human rights standards, rather than attempting to transform human rights into an 'all-encompassing blueprint' for development.[3]

But how to ensure that economic and/or development policies do not conflict with human rights obligations continues to remain a crucial question.[4] Current debates reveal that increasing attention is being paid by the human rights community to seek adequate responses in this direction. However, analyses are still nascent and far from being systematic. Careful exploration, particularly as to the sources of law involved, is warranted. In the previous chapter, I discussed the emergence of new legal ideas and their possible relevance to this research. The main conclusion was that the concept of extraterritorial obligations is not well established and raises many issues when applied to the context of development.

This chapter discusses and builds on existing legal ideas and arguments elaborated over time, in human rights law specifically and international law generally, to turn the broad thrust of the UN Charter human rights provisions into concrete propositions to guide the behaviour of states. It analyses whether and, if so, to what extent, limits are imposed by international law on respect for human rights in external activities related to development. As in previous chapters, it takes socio-economic rights treaties as a point of departure.

1 Human rights and development cooperation: The factual interplay

An evident first step in discussing the conceptual framework for protection of human rights within development is to describe their factual interaction. The purpose here is to set the framework within which the seeds of the demand of 'what should not be done' in promoting development became visible. That development cooperation activities will implicate the recipient state's obligations under the International Covenant on Economic, Social and Cultural Rights seems unavoidable. As emphasized earlier, even if development puts forward an idealistic and ethical self-perception, it is not, as yet, either perceived or implemented as such in practice. The substantial overlap with the human rights treaty norms makes development policies and activities capable of impacting human rights in diverse ways: positively and negatively, directly and indirectly.[5] The factual interaction is

---

3 K. Tomasevski, *Development Aid and Human Rights Revisited*, 2nd edition, Pinter Publishers: 1993, p. 217.

4 K. Tomasevski, 'Monitoring Human Rights Aspects of Sustainable Development', 8 *American University Journal of International Law and Policy* (1992), p. 88.

5 The factual interaction at the level of policies (multilateral, bilateral) and at the project level covering a wide range of social and human development fields such as delivery of essential services (health, food, etc.) labour, education social security, children, women, etc. *de facto* relate to a range of individual's social and economic as well as civil and political rights.

often presumed to produce situations of ambiguities between human rights logic and development decision-making because, as noted by McInerney-Lankford:[6]

> while there is much substantive congruence, this 'factual overlap' does not automatically align with all the objectives of such operations and those of 'corresponding' human rights treaties. Such activities may not be assumed to reflect or promote the realization of human rights, since few reference or mainstream human rights in their designs and objectives. Moreover, such activities will typically not address any impact on human rights – assessing whether they in fact support human rights or result in human rights harm.[7]

Development is replete with policies and international decision-making that, as the Committee on Economic Social and Cultural Rights long ago stated, 'affect the ability of States to fulfil their treaty obligations'.[8] The question of the impact of international decision-making concerning the balance between growth and distribution, and investment and expenditure, is often invoked as an example.[9] To the extent that they determine national priorities for public spending on social services and the capacity of governments to allocate such resources, questions of compatibility with the human rights normative framework may arise.[10] There is also a correlation between priorities for the allocation of resources at international and national levels.

But unlike other areas such as trade and investment, discussion on legal strategies to ensure a harmonious interface with human rights is lacking in the development field.[11] This is partly because instruments of soft-law or non-legal

---

6 K. Tomasevski, *Development Aid and Human Rights Revisited, op. cit.*, p. 153.

7 S. McInerney-Lankford, 'Human Rights and Development: a Comment on Challenges and Opportunities from a Legal Perspective', 1(1) *Journal of Human Rights Practice* (March 2009), pp. 51–82, p. 53.

8 CESCR, Statement of the United Nations Committee on Economic, Social and Cultural Rights to the Third Ministerial Conference of the World Trade Organization (Seattle, 30 November to 3 December 1999), adopted at its 47th meeting, twenty-first session, held on 26 November 1999, para. 3.

9 As Tomasevski explained, 'Development policies, especially principles of distribution they embody, to a large extent determine the scope for the realization of human rights. The obligations corresponding to economic and social rights, such as principle that human rights should enjoy priority in resource utilization, are seldom translated into development plans.' K. Tomasevski, *Development Aid and Human Rights Revisited, op. cit.*, p. 178.

10 In her mission to Uganda, the then UN Special Rapporteur on the Right to Education (Katarina Tomasevski), observed the conflicting obligations of debt servicing on the one hand, and human rights obligations on the other. According to the Special Rapporteur, '[t]he two types of obligation pull in opposite directions – debt repayment towards diminishing governmental allocations for education and human rights obligations towards increasing such allocations'. Report submitted by Ms Katarina Tomasevski, Special Rapporteur on the right to education, Addendum Mission to Uganda 26 June – 2 July 1999, UN doc. E/CN.4/2000/6 /Add.1, 9 August 1999, para. 35.

11 See Report of the Special Rapporteur on the right to food, Olivier De Schutter, Addendum: Guiding principles on human rights impact assessments of trade and investment agreements, UN doc. A/HRC/19/59/Add.5, 19 December 2011.

approaches to organizing development cooperation activities are applied. These formally have no legal effect, although the practice they generate may contravene human rights law and eventually hinder their protection.[12] The integration of human rights in development theory, policy and practice has always been dependent upon recognition of the existence of a nexus between the two. No significant progress has, however, been achieved since the first time the linkages between economic progress and human rights were identified. In response, debates have increasingly revolved around the question of whether international law addresses the cross-border aspects of human rights violations, in particular socio-economic rights. And, if so, what are the preventive and proactive approaches available to ensure compatibility of policies and practices at the inter-state level with human rights obligations?

2 Proposals on ensuring compliance with human rights: *New, old ideas?*

It would be fair to say that, due in large part to the involvement of civil society at national and international levels, environmental and human rights aspects of development have been raised and exposed. Governments have rarely been concerned with this issue, and so some of the emerging intellectual efforts come from academia and civil society. One way for the human rights community to argue for adherence to human rights norms was to advocate for extraterritorial obligations, which I examined in a separate chapter.[13] Today, another set of academics is showing particular interest in the principles developed in traditional sectors of international law. One view, for example, makes a case for the application of a due diligence standard, as, in the context of international economic interdependence, 'actions and decisions within the global order cannot easily be disaggregated and attributed to a particular state or states for the purposes of state responsibility'.[14] A more refined analysis contends that current international law is based on the independent international responsibility, while what is needed is conceptual tools capable of 'allocating responsibility between a plurality of actors in situations where contributions to harmful outcomes cannot be attributed based on individual causation of each actor'.[15]

Two arguments animate the debate on the significance of due diligence. First, states 'do not often violate ESC rights of individuals living abroad in a *direct*

---

12 At the legal level there is no conflict of norms as long as the relationships between the recipient and donor states are not formalized.
13 See Maastricht Principles on Extraterritorial Obligations (ETOs) of States in the area of Economic, Social and Cultural Rights, in Chapter IV and V.
14 M. Salomon, *Global Responsibility for Human Rights: World Poverty and the Development of International Law*, OUP: 2007, pp. 186–187 (emphasis added).
15 A. Nollkaemper and D. Jacobs, 'Shared Responsibility in International Law: A Conceptual Framework', 32(2) *Michigan Journal of International Law* (2013), pp. 359–438, p. 364.

manner'.[16] Second, in most cases, it is not easy to separate an individual's situation from the general conditions prevalent in his or her country. In light of complex processes typically involved in cross-border socio-economic activities, progressively references are made to the do no harm principles and due diligence standards, as elaborated mainly in the international environmental law. The rules in international environmental law have the logic of prevention at their basis.[17] It is alleged that roughly the same line of process may run through the transboundary economic effects, with devastating consequences on the economic, social and cultural rights of individuals in third countries.[18] The underlying intention of such an analytical approach is sound and it seems to have garnered the support of a number of other scholars.[19]

Let us recall that the approach and terminology used may be newer, but the idea behind proposals to subject development practices to the rule of law is not a revolutionary one.[20] Earlier efforts, such as the NIEO framework and the Charter on Economic Rights and Duties, aimed to structurally transform inequality (albeit confined to international political economy) and also contained elements of prevention, including, among others, the principle of respect for human rights and international obligations as well as the regulation of the activities of transnational corporations.[21] Similarly, the Declaration on Principles of International Law Concerning Friendly Relations and Cooperation among States incorporates fundamental legal limits on state behaviour in pursuance of their

---

16 C. Ryngaert, 'Jurisdiction: Towards Reasonableness Test', in M. Langford W. Vandenhole, M. Scheinin and W. van Genugten (eds), *Global Justice, State Duties: The Extraterritorial Scope of Economic, Social and Cultural Rights in International Law*, CUP: 2013, p. 201.

17 P.-M. Dupuy and C. Hoss, 'Trail Smelter and Terrorism: International Mechanisms to Combat Transboundary Harm', in R. Bratspies and R. Miller (eds), *Transboundary Harm in International Law: Lessons from the Trail Smelter Arbitration*, CUP: 2006, p. 227.

18 For example, Principle 13, setting out the obligation to avoid causing harm, makes reference to the precautionary principle developed in the environmental law in stating that '[u]ncertainty about potential impacts does not constitute justification for said conduct'. In support of their argument, the experts cite the commentaries of the International Law Commission on Article 3 of the Draft Articles on the Prevention of Transboundary Harm from Hazardous Activities (2001), providing that '[t]he State of origin shall take all appropriate measures to prevent significant transboundary harm or at any event to minimize the risk thereof'. Commentary to Maastricht Principles on Extraterritorial Obligations of States in the area of Economic, Social and Cultural Rights by O. De Schutter, A. Eide, A. Khalfan, M. Orellana, M. Salomon and I. Seiderman, www.icj.org/dwn/database/Maastricht%20ETO%20 Principles%20-%20FINAL.pdf, p. 21.

19 S.S. Skogly, 'Causality and Extraterritorial Human Rights Obligations', in M. Langford, W. Vandenhole, M. Scheinin and W. van Genugten (eds), *Global Justice, State Duties: The Extraterritorial Scope of Economic, Social and Cultural Rights in International Law*, CUP: 2013, pp. 233–258.

20 For an in-depth exposition of the topic see P. Alston, *Development and the Rule of Law: Prevention Versus Cure as a Human Rights Strategy*, International Commission of Jurists: 1981.

21 UN GA Resolution 3281 (XXIX), Charter of Economic Rights and Duties of States, UN doc. A/RES/29/3281, 12 December 1974.

development policies externally, among which are the principles of sovereign equality and non-intervention.[22] Of course, the main purpose of the international development law 'project' was to inject the principle of the rule of law into the *process* of development.[23]

The sum total of the instruments of declaratory nature,[24] as well as interpretations given to the socio-economic rights, consistently articulated the creation of conditions conducive for the realization of human rights as an essential component of international measures.[25] If this requirement (i.e. creation of conditions) is to be understood as aiming to eliminate obstacles to socio-economic progress, then, by definition, its content would include rules on ensuring that efforts to support development do not produce negative effects on human rights. This broad-based and generic requirement, however, lacked concreteness in its contents to become operational as a rule.

Therefore, today's legal argumentation in effect attempts to concretize some of the well-known existing principles and rules through the medium of human rights law by applying human rights concepts and framework. Accordingly, states' tripartite obligations to respect, protect and fulfil human rights are interpreted expansively to include acts and omission outside the state's jurisdiction, i.e. affecting individuals residing in third states. Following this rationale, it is argued that states (in our context, donors and creditors) are to respect the human rights of individuals residing in third states.[26] The Montréal Principles on Women's Economic, Social and Cultural Rights,[27] the Quito

22 Declaration on Principles of International Law Concerning Friendly Relations and Cooperation among States in accordance with the Charter of the United Nations, UN GA Resolution 2625, Annex, 25 UN GAOR, Supp. (No. 28), UN doc. A/5217, p. 121 (1970).
23 See ILA Seoul Declaration on the Progressive Development of Principles of Public International Law relating to a New International Economic Order that, among others, proposed the principle of the 'rule of public international law in international economic relations' according to which 'States have a duty to abstain from measures of economic policy, incompatible with their international obligations. The rule of law in international economic relations should be strengthened to this effect.' International Law Association, Report of the Sixty-Second Conference, 62 *International Law Association Reports of Conferences* (1986), p. 449.
24 See Chapters II, III and IV.
25 In particular, Article 3 of the Declaration on the Right to Development; see also Chapter III where in the context of the right to development references were made to the 'enabling factors' that are generally considered as to include (i) the problem of inadequate resources, such as aid, debt, technology transfers, (ii) international trade regime, (iii) asymmetries in global governance, in particular as regards multilateral financial and monetary institutions and (iv) broader issues related to peace, security and disarmament.
26 Earlier and continuous efforts to ensure compliance of development process with human rights standards is advanced in a related but separate subject of the responsibility of international financial institutions. The main arguments in this context have been amply discussed and will not be pursued here.
27 Principle 20 on Due Diligence provides that: 'All states when participating in international financial institutions, trade agreements, or aid and development programs shall apply a due diligence test to assess, foresee, and prevent any adverse consequences of trade agreements, structural adjustment programs, development and humanitarian assistance, and other

Declaration[28] and the Maastricht Principles[29] all follow this logic. It is important to observe that this thinking is not completely contrary to the opinion of some donor states. Practice is crystallizing among certain donors to integrate the 'do no harm' principle in the context of conflict and fragility.[30] While an equally explicit statement of principle applicable to all situations and in all circumstances is still pending, the OECD-DAC's Action-Oriented Policy Paper on Human Rights and Development identifies 'do no harm' as one of its ten principles.[31] Compared to its detailed and comprehensive do no harm policy in conflict situations,[32] the general principle is rather short and lacks the level of detail necessary for their operationalization:

> Donors' actions may affect human rights outcomes in developing countries in positive and negative ways. They can inadvertently reinforce societal divisions, worsen corruption, exacerbate violent conflict, and damage fragile political coalitions if issues of faith, ethnicity and gender are not taken fully into consideration. Donors should promote fundamental human rights, equity and social inclusion, respect human rights principles in their policies and programming, identify potentially harmful practices and develop short, medium and long-term strategies for mitigating the potential for harm.[33]

Likewise, the Accra Agenda for Action supported this position by stating that: 'Developing countries and donors will ensure that their respective development policies and programmes are designed and implemented in ways consistent with their agreed international commitments on gender equality, human

---

economic and social policies on women's economic, social, and cultural rights. Where harm is caused by such agreements or programs, the responsible states and institutions shall implement compensatory measures. This applies at national, regional, and international levels, in public and private spheres of life.' 'Montréal Principles on Women's Economic, Social and Cultural Rights', 26(3) *Human Rights Quarterly*, (2004), pp. 760–778, p. 772.

28 Quito Declaration on the Enforcement and Realisation of Economic, Social, and Cultural Rights in Latin America and the Caribbean, 24 July 1998, paras. 17, 38.

29 Maastricht Principles on Extraterritorial Obligations of States in the area of Economic, Social and Cultural Rights, 17 October 2012.

30 See bilateral donor policy statements on 'do no harm' in conflict situations: SDC, Do No Harm: Tip Sheet, SDC: COPRET, June 2006, German Federal Ministry of Economic Cooperation and Development: Do No Harm Principle, www.bmz.de/en/what_we_do/issues/Peace/development_for_peace/index.html.

31 Organization for Economic Cooperation and Development, Development Assistance Committee, *Action-Oriented Policy Paper on Human Rights and Development* (2007), www.oecd.org/dataoecd/50/7/39350774.pdf.

32 OECD, *Conflict and Fragility, Do No Harm: International Support for State Building*, OECD: 2010.

33 Organization for Economic Cooperation and Development, Development Assistance Committee, Action-Oriented Policy Paper on Human Rights and Development (2007), www.oecd.org/dataoecd/50/7/39350774.pdf, p. 11.

rights, disability and environmental sustainability.'[34] These new terms of donor discourse, however, evolved in a non-binding and voluntary form rather than as a legal obligation. To have lasting importance, the assumption that human rights *tout court* need to be respected in external activities in all circumstances, and at all times, requires firm theoretical foundations. This will ensure that development policies and practices comply with treaty obligations, regardless of the position the actors in the development process, both international and national, take on the nexus between human rights and development and changes in policies.[35]

In this context, one has to observe that scholarship is not always consistent in its use of conceptual constructs but, more crucially, the sources of law to support their argumentation. For example, certain academics seem convinced that cases involving the obligation of states not to violate rights stipulated in the ICESCR in other countries are comparatively straightforward:

> The obligation to respect prohibits a state from directly interfering with the enjoyment of esc rights by persons in other countries. For example, on the basis of the obligation to respect a state should refrain from food embargoes or other coercive measures towards other states. In addition states should refrain from giving trade and producer's subsidies . . . benefiting their own nationals that may be to the detriment of local traders and producers in developing countries. Usually this type of transnational conduct is easy to identify and the negative effects on the esc rights of people in developing countries are often well-documented. It is reasonable to conclude that a foreign state has a rather strong obligation to change its conduct and that it is accountable for such conduct that leads to violations of esc rights of citizens in that other country.[36]

34 Accra Agenda for Action, Third High Level Forum on Aid Effectiveness (2–4 September 2008), para. 13(c). The AAA was agreed at a 2008 Ministerial Conference organized by the Organization for Economic Cooperation and Development, comprising over 100 countries. The Busan Partnership for Effective Development (2011) was much less explicit, stating: 'As we embrace the diversity that underpins our partnership and the catalytic role of development co-operation, we share common principles which – consistent with our agreed international commitments on human rights, decent work, gender equality, environmental sustainability and disability – form the foundation of our co-operation for effective development.' Busan Partnership for Effective Development Co-Operation Fourth High Level Forum on Aid Effectiveness, Busan, Republic of Korea, 29 November – 1 December 2011.

35 This idea has been forcefully articulated by Tomasevski, who stated that the non-compliance with international human rights obligations may not be justified by 'lack of donors' recognition of the linkage between human rights and aid. See K. Tomasevski, *Development and Human Rights Revisited*, 2nd edition, Pinter Publishers: 1993.

36 F. Coomans, 'Some Remarks on the Extraterritorial Application of the International Covenant on Economic, Social and Cultural Rights', in F. Coomans and M. Kamminga (eds), *Extraterritorial Application of Human Rights Treaties*, Intersentia: 2004, pp. 192–193, footnotes omitted.

This position seems to have acquired general support in the literature.[37] However, as rightly noted, '[w]hat seems plain common sense – States are not allowed to do abroad what they are not allowed to do domestically – does not necessarily make legal sense'.[38] First, legal logic sometimes overlooks the fact that the case law of human rights bodies on respect of human rights in the territory of third states is often hinged upon the question of jurisdiction.[39] Second, arguments developed on the basis of the general comments of the Committee on Economic, Social and Cultural Rights, UN General Assembly resolutions on human rights, and unilateral coercive measures, as well as reports of the human rights special procedures, may be convincing; however, strictly speaking these sources are not legally binding.[40] This has not escaped the attention of international financial institutions. Commenting on the interpretations of the Committee as to the meaning and scope of obligations of international cooperation, the legal counsel of the International Monetary Fund made a thinly veiled reference to the legal status of the normative pronouncements of human rights bodies.[41]

Equally, little substantiation is provided on the question of the activities of the states as members of international organizations, which requires states to take positive measures to ensure conformity with their treaty obligations. In this context, one should recall the recently endorsed UN Guiding Principles on Business and Human Rights, which state:

> At present States are not generally required under international human rights law to regulate the extraterritorial activities of businesses domiciled in their territory and/or jurisdiction. Nor are they generally prohibited from doing so, provided there is a recognized jurisdictional basis. Within

---

37 See the references in the Chapter V on Extraterritorial Obligations related to the ESC rights, but particularly: S. Skogly, *Beyond National Borders: States' Human Rights Obligations in International Cooperation*, Intersentia: 2006; W. Vandenhole, 'Third State Obligations Under the ICESCR: A Case Study of EU Sugar Policy', 76 *Nordic Journal of International Law* (2007), pp. 73–100.

38 W. Vandenhole, 'The Limits of Human Rights Law in Human Development', in E. Claes, W. Devroe and B. Keirsbilck (eds), *Facing the Limits of the Law*, Springer: 2009, pp. 355–374, p. 362.

39 The previous chapter's analysis concluded that the jurisprudence of the human rights, judicial and quasi-judicial, is indicative of a general statement of principle that envisages the application of human rights treaties extraterritorially in very exceptional circumstances, such as territorial control or physical control.

40 F. Coomans, 'Some Remarks on the Extraterritorial Application of the International Covenant on Economic, Social and Cultural Rights', in F. Coomans and M. Kamminga (eds), *Extraterritorial Application of Human Rights Treaties*, Intersentia: 2004, pp. 192–193, fottnote 26, referring to the Commission on Human Rights Resolution 2002/22 on Human rights and unilateral coercive measures.

41 The Legal Counsel stated that: 'It is of course for States parties to ascertain the extent of their obligations of international cooperation.' F. Gianviti, Economic, Social and Cultural Human Rights and the International Monetary Fund, Working Paper, E/C.12/2001/WP.5, 7 May 2001, para. 26.

these parameters some human rights treaty bodies recommend that home States take steps to prevent abuse abroad by business enterprises within their jurisdiction.[42]

Thus, reference to the term 'present' seems to indicate the possibility of future developments, where regulation of extraterritorial activities of companies is the obligation of the home state as well. In the same vein, Olivier De Shutter affirms that '[t]he contemporary, mainstream view is that there exists no general obligation imposed on States, under international human rights, to exercise extraterritorial jurisdiction (understood here as a combination of adjudicative and prescriptive jurisdiction) in order to contribute to the protection and promotion of internationally recognized human rights outside their national territory'.[43] He also reminds us that if there is a positive obligation of states to protect the rights of individuals from acts of non-state actors, such obligations have only been affirmed in situations falling under a state's jurisdiction. Consequently, 'in the current state of development of international law, a clear obligation for States to control private actors operating outside their national territory, in order to ensure that these actors will not violate the human rights of others, has not crystallized yet'.[44]

In recognition of these challenges, general principles of international law and legal mechanisms developed in special international law are relied upon in an attempt to flesh out prohibitive and preventive aspects of cross-border socio-economic activities. For example, the commentaries on the Maastricht Principles on the ETOs of States in the area of Economic, Social and Cultural Rights often apply the principles and rules developed in environmental law to the case of socio-economic rights, including the precautionary principle, issues of foreseeability and causality as developed in the Draft Principles on the Allocation of Loss in the Case of Transboundary Harm, etc.

It is, of course, entirely possible to apply the rules by analogy, given the 'area-related' development of legal rules in international law, but this will depend on whether one adheres to the conception of international law as a 'coherent and just legal order' and/or whether conditions for analogous application are met.[45] For example, analogous application is justified where a gap exists, which means the issue in question must not be regulated by any rule or principle of international law.[46] From this standpoint, the question remains whether there is indeed

42 Commentary to Principle 2, Guiding Principles on Business and Human Rights: Implementing the United Nations 'Protect, Respect and Remedy' Framework, UN doc. A/HRC/17/31, 21 March 2011, p. 7. See also J. Crawford, *Legal Opinion on Third Party Obligations with respect to Israeli Settlements in the Occupied Palestinian Territories*, TUC: 2012.

43 O. De Schutter, *International Human Rights Law: Cases, Materials, Commentary*, CUP: 2010, p. 162.

44 *Ibid.*, p. 162.

45 S. Voneky, 'Analogy in International Law', *Max Planck Encyclopaedia of International Law*, www.mpepil.com.

46 *Ibid.*

no rule or principle of international law that could regulate the cross-border aspects of socio-economic rights violations. Should guidance not therefore be looked for in the general legal principles and rules found therein? Is there any special rule applicable in relation to human rights?

3 International law and cross-border aspects of socio-economic rights

3.1 General obligation to avoid causing harm and exercise due diligence

It would be ambitious to attempt here anything like a complete analysis of a concept such as due diligence. The following is thus merely a comment on some aspects of the concept of due diligence that may be relevant to the discussion on ensuring compliance with human rights norms.

The starting point is that states are to avoid causing harm. The famous *Trail Smelter* Arbitral Decision held that states were not allowed 'to use or permit the use of [their] territory in such a manner as to cause injury by fumes in or to the territory of another or the properties of persons therein, when the case is of serious consequence and the injury is established by clear and convincing evidence'.[47] In effect, the principle enshrined in the *Trail Smelter* case and reaffirmed in the *Nuclear Weapons* Advisory Opinion[48] as well as the Rio Declaration, is believed to have attained the status of customary law in the field of environmental protection.[49] In the *Corfu Channel* case, the International Court of Justice stated that '[i]t is true, as international practice shows, that a State on whose territory or in whose waters an act contrary to international law has occurred, may be called upon to give an explanation'[50] and that 'certain general and well-recognized principles' include the principle that 'every State's obligation not to allow knowingly its territory to be used for acts contrary to the rights of other States'.[51]

---

47 *Trail Smelter Arbitration, United States v. Canada,* UN Reports of International Arbitral Awards (UNRIAA), 16 April 1938 and 11 March 1941, Vol. III, pp. 1905–1982 or American Journal of International Law, Vol. 33 (1939), p.182 and Vol. 35 (1941), p. 684.

48 In the *Nuclear Weapons* Advisory Opinion, the International Court of Justice reaffirmed the general obligation of states 'to ensure that activities within their jurisdiction and control respect the environment of other States or of areas beyond national control'. ICJ, *Legality of the Threat or Use of Nuclear Weapons,* Advisory Opinion, ICJ Reports 1996, p. 226, para. 29.

49 O. Schachter, 'The Emergence of International Environmental Law', 44 *Journal of International Affairs* (1991), p. 462, stating that: 'On its own terms, [the "do no harm" principle] has not become State practice: States generally do not "ensure that the activities within their jurisdiction do not cause damage" to the environments of others.'

50 *Corfu Channel (U.K. v. Albania.),* Merits, 1949 ICJ Reports 4, Judgment of 9 April 1949, p. 18.

51 *Ibid.,* p. 22.

As Professor Dupuy observes, this principle is a direct consequence of the basic premise of international law, namely sovereign equality and reciprocity: 'Ceci est particulièrement vrai s'agissant des conséquences des activités qu'un Etat déterminé peut entreprendre à l'intérieure de sa propre zone de compétence. Il devra veiller à s'assurer que des dommages ou préjudices divers ne seront pas entrainés sur le territoire des autres Etats par ses propres activités ou celles qu'il autorise.'[52]

The *Trail Smelter* and *Corfu Channel* cases thus offer 'an appropriate starting point for consideration of the general international law on transboundary harm, as it was from this arbitration that a central principle of international law [i.e. due diligence] was introduced'.[53] While it is clearly the case that development of the obligation of due diligence is at the core of the development of international law on transboundary harm, it is also true that the content and nature of the obligation of due diligence may change according to the subject matter under consideration.[54] The obligation of prevention or the due diligence obligation is thus a principle of law of general application. The primary obligation of states to prevent transboundary socio-economic harm therefore can be said to derive from the principle of *sic utere tuo ut non laedas*.[55] But even if this is so, the grounds for a claim of due diligence in relation to the cross-border aspects of socio-economic activities are more murky. First, there is little to no state practice from which general standards of what due diligence would require in the prevention of socio-economic harm can be extracted. Second, references in General Assembly Declarations, including encouragement to all international donors and development banks to 'seek to ensure that their own policies and programmes will advance the attainment of agreed development goals', are too modest.[56] Relevant documents speak of 'enhancing coherence and consistency' and improving good governance at 'all levels' in the reform of international financial and trade systems.[57]

---

52 P.-M. Dupuy, *Droit International Public*, 5e edition, Dalloz: 2000, p. 99. See also Max Huber, according to whom, 'The development of the national organisation of States during the last few centuries and, as a corollary, the development of international law have established this principle of the exclusive competence of the State in regard to its own territory in such a way as to make it the point of departure in settling most questions that concern international relations.' *Island of Palmas (Neth./U.S.)*, 2 R.I.A.A. 829, 838 (Perm. Ct. Arb. 1928) (Huber, sole arb.).
53 P.-M. Dupuy and Cristina Hoss, 'Trail Smelter and Terrorism: International Mechanisms to Combat Transboundary Harm', *op. cit.*, p. 226. These pronouncements were based on *Alabama Arbitration* of 1872, in J.B. Moore, International Arbitrations, vol. 1, Gov't Printing Press, USA, p. 653.
54 *Ibid.*, p. 226.
55 E.g. the maxim 'so use your own as not to injure another's property'.
56 Commitment 2(h) Copenhagen Declaration of World Summit for Social Development, UN doc. A/CONF.166/9, 6–12 March 1995. As noted in previous chapters, upcoming Sustainable Development Goals (to be adopted September 2015) give some cause for hope. Current zero draft stipulates that '[t]he new Agenda recognizes the need to build peaceful, just and inclusive societies, based on respect for human rights (including the right to development), the rule of law and effective and accountable institutions. These are fundamental requirements for the achievement of sustainable development.' (para. 28).
57 Monterrey Consensus of the International Conference on Financing for Development March 2002; UN GA Resolution 60/1, 2005 World Summit Outcome, 24 October 2005.

The strongest and most recent improvements include a general pronouncement such as '[w]e commit to respecting all human rights'.[58] It would be too early, however, to say that the concept of due diligence in the transboundary socio-economic context is consolidated.

The question of the adverse effects of economic activities was raised in the framework of the ILC's work on international liability for injurious consequences arising out of acts not prohibited by international law.[59] The Special Rapporteur of the Commission, M.C.W. Pinto, commenting on the scope of topic, stated:

> The techniques of the present topic – that is, the promotion of painstaking individual adjustment of competing interests in particular subject areas to reconcile liberty of action with freedom from adverse transboundary effects – might well be more productive of solutions in the economic area than undue reliance upon rules curtailing freedom of action.[60]

However, the extension of the scope of the ILC's draft articles to the adverse effects of activity in the economic sphere was set aside and not pursued. This was due to, first, that there was 'no possibility of proceeding inductively from the evidence of State practice in the field of the physical uses of territory to the formulation of rules or guidelines in the economic field', and, second, there was an understanding that 'such a step might retard the emergence of general support for development of the topic as such'.[61]

Thus far, there is neither a primary treaty obligation nor state practice to that effect. It is even doubtful if an obligation upon states exists to ensure that economic activities within their jurisdiction and control do not negatively impact on other states. The position that one state should not hinder the development of another and eliminate obstacles to development seems to be a widely accepted formulation.[62] Such a principle is considered an international minimum standard. However, the content of this obligation to not hinder (i.e. what should *not* be done to hinder

---

58 Outcome document of the Third International Conference on Financing for Development: Addis Ababa Action Agenda, UN doc. A/CONF.227/L.1, 15 July 2015, para. 1.

59 The Chairman of the Commission, Reuter, announced that 'the draft could be limited to transboundary problems pertaining to the physical environment and that questions involving the most delicate problems that might arise in the economic sector could be set aside'. Official Records of the General Assembly, Thirty-seventh Session, Sixth Committee, 37th meeting, para. 12.

60 Fourth report on international liability for injurious consequences arising out of acts not prohibited by international law, by Robert Q. Quentin-Baxter, Special Rapporteur, UN doc. A/CN.4/373 and Corr. 1 & 2, para. 15.

61 M.C.W. Pinto, 'Reflections on International Liability for Injurious Consequences Arising out of Acts not Prohibited by International Law', 16 *Netherlands Yearbook of International Law* (1985), pp. 17–48, p. 45.

62 The Vienna Declaration and Programme of Action Adopted by the World Conference on Human Rights in Vienna on 25 June 1993, para. 10; see also Declarations of Cairo World Population and Development Summit, 1994; the Copenhagen World Summit for Social Development, 1995; the Beijing Fourth World Conference on Women, 1995; and Millennium Declaration 2000.

development) is unclear. To date, there is no basic criteria to make it possible to determine whether a state has acted diligently or not in its social and economic activities with cross-border effects. A developing state would not be able to hold a group of developed states responsible for a particular socio-economic activity or even a development approach, for example, if it considers that their policies hinder its own development path, unless there is a breach of a specific treaty obligation.[63]

This being said, there are some initiatives underway to elaborate basic elements of the obligation of prevention in certain sectors of economic activity.[64] In the context of development cooperation specifically, some policy arrangements are visible. Indeed, over the last few years, bilateral donors and major development institutions have put more and more emphasis on the idea of policy coherence for development. While on the surface, the rationale at the basis of policy coherence revolves around the idea of 'the most efficient possible use of . . . [development aid] resources', the concept of policy coherence in development draws its basis from a number of normative principles.[65]

The European Consensus for Development, which sets out the European vision for development, defines 'promoting policy coherence' as one of its main objectives.[66] To promote policy coherence, the EU takes 'account of the objectives of development cooperation in all policies that it implements which are likely to affect developing countries, and that these policies support development objectives'.[67] These areas include, among others, trade, agriculture, fisheries, social

---

63 U. Khaliq, *Ethical Dimensions of the Foreign Policy of the European Union: A Legal Appraisal*, CUP: 2008, p. 63.

64 See UNCTAD, Draft Principles on Promoting Responsible Sovereign Lending and Borrowing, April 2011, http://unctad.org/en/docs/gdsddf2011misc1_en.pdf, and also a related study UNCTAD/M. Goldmann, A Comparative Survey Written for the United Nations Conference on Trade and Development: Responsible Sovereign Lending and Borrowing: the View from Domestic Jurisdictions, February 2012.

65 According to Philipp Dann, the normative bases for deriving the principle of coherence in development are diverse. These include the principles of cost-effectiveness (also closely identified with concepts of result orientation and concentration), the principle of alignment and the principle of coordination and management of development aid. P. Dann, *The Law of Development Cooperation: A Comparative Analysis of the World Bank, the EU and Germany*, CUP: 2012, pp. 285–295. See also Chapter II. According to another view, the preoccupation of the OECD-DAC donors with policy coherence is a form of a response to the growing diversification of donors, viz. non-traditional donor states that are not part of the OECD framework.

66 Policy coherence can be defined as a 'concept that expresses the ambition to make sure that all policy areas that affect developing countries contribute positively to the objectives of development cooperation'. N. Keijzer, 'The Future of Development Cooperation: from Aid to Policy Coherence for Development?', European Centre for Development Policy Management (ECDPM), April 2012, p. 2.

67 Joint statement by the Council and the representatives of the governments of the Member States meeting within the Council, the European Parliament and the Commission on European Union Development Policy: 'The European Consensus', 2006/C 46/01, 24 February 2006, para. 35.

dimension of globalization, employment and decent work, migration, research and innovation, information society, transport and energy.[68] Similarly, the OECD is taking steps towards designing a broad framework to enhance policy coherence for development (PCD).[69]

The more enticing question is whether a 'policy coherence for development' or 'whole of government' (e.g. coherence of policies within government) approach, as promulgated by development cooperation actors, can be coextensive with the '*do no harm*' standard. If one describes the concept of PCD 'as efforts to minimize contradictions and to build synergies between policies *other than development cooperation* that have an impact on developing countries', this may indeed be the case.[70] However, it seems that the concept of policy coherence for development is more than just 'minimizing the adverse impact that public policies can have in developing countries', and also includes positive efforts to integrate 'development concerns' across all fields.[71] In the same spirit, the Addis Ababa Action Agenda stipules: 'We commit to *pursuing policy coherence* and an enabling environment for sustainable development at all levels and by all actors and to reinvigorating the global partnership for sustainable development.'[72] From this perspective, since human rights is an integral part of the notion of sustainable development, policy coherence for development and the obligation to respect international human rights are interrelated.[73]

Whether there is an obligation of prevention or a duty of a state towards the socio-economic rights of the people outside of its territory who suffer the consequences of its socio-economic actions will be examined further below, after consideration of the obligation to respect human rights under international law.

---

68 For example, in paragraph 36, the Consensus document specifies measures to be taken in the area of agriculture: 'Within the framework of the reformed Common Agriculture Policy (CAP), the EU will substantially reduce the level of trade distortion related to its support measures to the agricultural sector, and facilitate developing countries' agricultural development. In line with development needs, the EU supports the objectives of asymmetry and flexibility for the implementation of the EPAs.' *Ibid.*

69 OECD Strategy on Development, Meeting of the OECD Council at Ministerial Level Paris, 23–24 May 2012, p. 5, www.oecd.org/pcd/. See also OECD, *Better Policies for Development: Recommendations for Policy Coherence,* OECD, 2011.

70 T.F. McInerney, *Strategic Treaty Management: Practice and Implications,* CUP: 2015, pp. 164–165.

71 OECD, Policy Framework for Policy Coherence for Development, Working Paper no. 1, 2012, p. 3.

72 Outcome document of the Third International Conference on Financing for Development: Addis Ababa Action Agenda, UN doc. A/CONF.227/L.1, 15 July 2015, para. 9.

73 For a discussion see S. McInerney-Lankford, 'Human Rights and Development: Regime Interaction and the Fragmentation of International Law', in H. Cissé , S. Muller, C. Thomas and C. Wang (eds), *Legal Innovation and Empowerment for Development, the World Bank Legal Review,* Vol. 4, World Bank: 2013, pp. 123–159.

3.2 General obligation to respect human rights

There is no *expressis verbis* provision in international human rights treaties requiring states to not violate the human rights of individuals residing in other states or to be respectful of human rights when conducting their external activities, including in the area of development cooperation. The common preambular paragraph of the International Covenant on Civil and Political Rights and the International Covenant on Economic, Social and Cultural Rights notes that:

> in accordance with the Universal Declaration of Human Rights, the ideal of free human beings enjoying civil and political freedom and freedom from fear and want can only be achieved if conditions are created whereby everyone may enjoy his civil and political rights, as well as his economic, social and cultural rights.[74]

This preambular paragraph appears as the closest reference to the issue of promotion and protection of human rights at the international level. Perhaps the only relevant provision is the requirement of 'international assistance and cooperation' for the implementation for socio-economic rights in the ICESCR, CRC, and CRPD. The primary obligation derives from the UN Charter provisions to promote respect for all human rights. It is posited here that an obligation to respect fundamental human rights is to be found in general international law. This conclusion emerges from a number of cases decided by the International Court of Justice.

3.2.1 Jurisprudence of the International Court of Justice

Examination and analysis of the Court's views on human rights has been the subject of comprehensive academic treatment.[75] Most of the cases to be examined

74 Paragraph 4 of the Preamble, ICCPR.
75 The most recent extensive writing includes: B. Simma, 'Human Rights before the International Court of Justice: Community Interest Coming to Life?', in H.P. Hestermeyer, D. Konig, N. Matz-Luck, V. Roben, A. Seiber-Fohr, P.-T. Stoll and S. Voneky (eds), *Coexistence, Cooperation and Solidarity: Liber Amirocum Rudiger Wolfrum*, Martinus Nijhoff Publishers: 2012 Vol. I, p. 577; S. Sivakumaran, 'The International Court of Justice and Human Rights', in S. Joseph and A. McBeth (eds), *Research Handbook on International Human Rights Law*, Edward Elgar Publishing: 2010, p. 299. G. Zyberi, *The Humanitarian Face of the International Court of Justice: its Contribution to Interpreting and Developing International Human Rights and Humanitarian Law Rules and Principles* (with a bibliography covering the literature up to and including 2007), Intersentia: 2008; R. Higgins, 'The International Court of Justice and Human Rights', 20(4) *Leiden Journal of International Law* (2007), pp. 745–51; J. Grimheden, 'The International Court of Justice – Monitoring Human Rights' in G Alfredsson and others (eds), *International Human Rights Monitoring Mechanisms. Essays in Honour of Jakob Th Moeller*, 2nd revised edition, Martinus Nijhoff Publishers: 2009, pp. 249–262. For earlier treatment of the subject see E. Schwelb, 'The International Court of Justice and the Human Rights Clauses of the Charter', 66 *American Journal of International Law* (1972), pp. 337–351; N.S. Rodley, 'Human Rights and Humanitarian Intervention: The Case Law of the World

here have been adjudicated in the period which is known as the phase of modest engagement of the Court with human rights issues, compared to its recent jurisprudence, where the ICJ has been seized with cases where issues of international human rights law made up the substantive questions put before it.[76] What follows is a *tour d'horizon* of the ICJ's application of human rights in cases before the court that look into the question of an obligation to respect human rights as an obligation under general international law.[77] The Court's views are particularly pertinent as they develop human rights related questions from an inter-state perspective.

The first enunciation of the fundamental principles of international human rights law comes from one of the earliest cases before the Court: the *Corfu Channel* case. The case is notable for a range of important legal issues it dealt with, but the focus here will be on the obligation of coastal states to notify the existence of sea mines, referring to this obligation as being based 'on certain general and well-recognized principles, namely: elementary considerations of humanity, even more exacting in peace than in war'.[78] The concept was further qualified as an 'intransgressible principle of international customary law'[79] and later in the *Wall* Opinion, the Court viewed this rule together with many humanitarian law rules as 'essentially of an *erga omnes* character'.[80] This distinction between what it called bilateral obligations and obligations *erga omnes*, i.e. 'towards the international community as a whole', was drawn in the famous *obiter dictum* of the *Barcelona Traction* case, which, from the onset, dealt with the diplomatic protection of shareholders. According to the Court these *erga omnes* obligations were:

> By their very nature . . . the concern of all States. In view of the importance of the rights involved, all States can be held to have a legal interest in their protection; they are obligations *erga omnes*.

Court', 38 *International Comparative Law Quarterly* (1989), pp. 321–333; S.M. Schwebel, 'Human Rights in the World Court', in R.S Pathak (ed.), *International Law in Transition: Essays in Memory of Judge Nagendra Singh*, Martinus Nijhoff Publishers: 1992, pp. 267–290; S.M. Schwebel, *The Treatment of Human Rights and of Aliens in the International Court of Justice*, in V. Lowe and M. Fitzmaurice (eds), *Fifty Years of the International Court of Justice: Essays in Honour of Sir Robert Jennings*, CUP: 1996, pp. 327–350.

76 B. Simma, 'Human Rights before the International Court of Justice: Community Interest Coming to Life?' *op. cit.*, p. 577, dividing the evolution of the Court's human rights engagement into two phases, the first where the ICJ displayed a self-restraint towards the issue, and the second, when the Court more readily embraced human rights questions.

77 Human rights issues have already appeared before the predecessor of the Court, the Permanent Court of International Justice. On the question of the contribution of the PCIJ to human rights see R. Goy, 'La Cour Permanente de Justice Internationale et Les Droits De L'Homme', in G. Cohen-Jonathan (ed.), *Liber Amicorum Marc-André Eissen*, Bruylant: 1995, pp. 199–232.

78 ICJ, *Corfu Channel Case, (UK v. Albania)*, (Merits), Judgment of 9 April 1949, ICJ Reports 1949, p. 22.

79 ICJ, *Legality of the Threat or Use of Nuclear Weapons*, Advisory Opinion, 8 July 1996, ICJ Reports 1996 (I), p. 257, para. 79.

80 ICJ, *Legal Consequences of the Construction of a Wall in the Occupied Palestinian Territory*, Advisory Opinion, ICJ Reports 2004, para. 157.

Such obligations derive, for example, in contemporary international law, from the outlawing of acts of aggression, and of genocide, as *also from the principles and rules concerning the basic rights of the human person*, including protection from slavery and racial discrimination.[81]

The Court has thus suggested that *erga omnes* obligations may derive *inter alia* from the principles and rules concerning the basic rights of the human person, and listed the prohibition of slavery and racial discrimination as examples. While the issue is picked up again in more detail below, it will suffice here to mention that the expression used by the Court, i.e. the 'basic rights of the human person', further complicates the subject, as it raises the question as to which rights can be qualified as 'basic'. In the passage above, the list of examples related to what can be regarded as basic rights, although non-exhaustive, is confined to three: the prohibition of genocide, protection from slavery and racial discrimination. It is suggested that by choosing the wording, 'basic rights of the human person', the Court intended to make it clear that not all human rights rules and principles have an *erga omnes* character.[82] This conclusion is further supported by the Court's treatment of the issue of 'denial of justice'. In addressing the claim of Belgium in this regard, the Court held that:

> With regard to more particularly to human rights, to which reference has already been made in paragraph 34 of this Judgment [e.g. specifying obligations *erga omnes*[83]], it should be noted that these also include protection against denial of justice. However, on the universal level, the instruments which embody human rights do not confer on States the capacity to protect the victims of infringements of such rights irrespective of their nationality.[84]

The Court's assessment was evidently based on prevailing realities at the time of the decision, where there was as yet no mechanism for individual complaint

---

81 ICJ, *Barcelona Traction, Light and Power Company, Limited,* ICJ 1970, paras. 33–34 (emphasis added).

82 P.H. Kooijmans, 'In the Shadow land Between Civil War and Civil Strife: Some Reflections on the Standard-setting Process', in A.J.M. Delissen and G.J. Tanja (eds), *Humanitarian Law of Armed Conflict Challenges Ahead. Essays in Honour of Frits Kalshoven*, Martinus Nijhoff Publishers: 1991, p. 235; M. Ragazzi, *The Concept of International Obligations Erga Omnes*, OUP: 2000, p. 140.

83 Paragraph 34 of the ICJ Judgment stated: 'Such obligations derive, for example, in contemporary international law, from the outlawing of acts of aggression, and of genocide, as also from the principles and rules concerning the basic rights of the human person, including protection from slavery and racial discrimination. One of the corresponding rights of protection have entered into the body of general international law.' ICJ, *Reservations to the Convention on the Prevention and Punishment of the Crime of Genocide, Advisory Opinion,* ICJ Reports 1951, p. 23; others are conferred by 'international instruments of a universal or quasi-universal character': ICJ, *Barcelona Traction, Light and Power Company, Limited,* ICJ Reports 1970, paras. 32, 34 .

84 *Barcelona Traction, ibid.,* para. 91.

under universal human rights treaties.[85] On balance, the *Barcelona Traction* case can be regarded as a monument to the international legal order, transforming the very texture of the protection of human rights at the international level, identifying instances in which every state has a legal interest to protect.

A year later, the ICJ decided the *Namibia* case in response to a General Assembly request for an advisory opinion on *South West Africa*, in which the Court delivered its much criticized decision in 1966. The Advisory Opinion of 1971 confirmed the position of the UN Security Council on the illegality of the continued presence of South Africa in Namibia. In this context, the ICJ invoked the pledge of UN Member States under the UN Charter to promote respect and observance for human rights and found that:

> Under the Charter of the United Nations, the former Mandatory had pledged itself to observe and respect, in a territory having an international status, human rights and fundamental freedoms for all without distinction as to race. To establish instead, and to enforce, distinctions, exclusions, restrictions and limitations exclusively based on grounds of race, colour, descent or national or ethnic origin which constitute a denial of fundamental human rights is a flagrant violation of the purposes and principles of the Charter.[86]

Schwelb captured well the significance of the Court's pronouncement: '[w]hen the Court speaks of "conformity with the international obligations assumed . . . under the Charter", or talks of "a violation of the purposes and principles of the Charter", or mentions the pledge to observe and respect human rights and fundamental freedoms for all and much more so when it finds that certain actions "constitute a denial of fundamental human rights" and classifies them as "a flagrant violation of the purposes and principles of the Charter", it leaves no room for doubt that, in its view, the Charter does impose on the Members of the United Nations legal obligations in the human rights field.'[87]

---

85 There is also a proposition that the Court refers to the notion of denial of justice as being part of international law, and that there could be a distinction between the principles and rules concerning the basic rights of the human person that gave rise to obligations towards the international community and protection against denial of justice. N. Rodley, 'Human Rights and Humanitarian Intervention: the Case Law of the World Court', 38 *International and Comparative Law Quarterly* (1989), p. 331.

86 ICJ, *Legal Consequences for States of the Continued Presence of South Africa in Namibia (South West Africa) notwithstanding Security Council Resolution 276 (1970)*, Adrisory Opinion, ICJ Reports 1971, para. 131. As Schwelb notes: 'The purpose of the Organization consisting in promoting and encouraging respect for human rights and for fundamental freedoms for all is *set* forth in Article 1 (3). When the Court finds that South Africa's policy constitutes a flagrant violation of the purposes and principles of the Charter, it clearly does not intend to convey the idea that only Article 1 (3) has been violated. This follows from the fact that the Court refers to the pledge of Member States which is contained in Chapter IX (Article 56) of the Charter. What is meant is a violation of the relevant provisions of the Charter, *i.e.*, its human rights clauses, as a whole.' E. Schwelb, 'The International Court of Justice and the Human Rights Clauses of the Charter', 66 *American Journal of International Law* (1972), p. 349.

87 *Ibid.*, p. 348.

Nigel Rodley draws a similarly important conclusion in that the pronounce-ment of the Court signifies that '[t]he Charter provisions are therefore not just hortatory and programmatic', but a legally binding obligation.[88] It is also sig-nificant that the Court not only refers to the human rights provisions set out in the purposes and principles of the UN Charter, but to the entire corpus of human rights provisions in the Charter. This conclusion can be derived from the reference to the 'pledge' of the member States contained in Article 56 of the Charter.[89]

Another case of relevance to our discussion is the *Tehran Hostages* case. In *Tehran Hostages*, the Court established a violation of human rights, as found in the UN Charter and Universal Declaration of Human Rights, in the context of applicable rules of general international law.[90] In the view of the Court, 'the Universal Declaration of Human Rights is a document of sufficient legal status to justify its invocation by the Court in the context of a State's obligations under general international law'.[91] The use of the wording of 'fundamental principles' of the UDHR yet begs a question whether the Court is actually making a distinc-tion between 'fundamental' and 'other' principles, and what would constitute the content of these 'fundamental' principles – a question raised above. While it leaves a possibility for a restrictive reading, and in the context of the case the prohibition of torture could be said to constitute such a fundamental principle, it is also possible that the Court was 'simply stating that the Declaration as a whole propounds fundamental principles recognized by general international law'.[92] But even if the expression used by the Court is read restrictively, it clearly does

---

88 N. Rodley, 'Human Rights and Humanitarian Intervention: the Case Law of the World Court', *op. cit.*, p. 324.

89 This point summarizes the conclusion arrived at by Schwelb. In his view, 'what is meant is a violation of relevant provisions of the Charter, i.e. its human rights clauses as a whole'. E. Schwelb, 'The International Court of Justice and the Human Rights Clauses of the Char-ter', *op. cit.*, p. 349.

90 In paragraph 90 the Court stated: 'On the basis of the foregoing detailed examination of the merits of the case, the Court finds that Iran, by committing successive and continuing breaches of the obligations laid upon it by the Vienna Conventions of 1961 and 1963 on Diplomatic and Consular Relations, the Treaty of Amity, Economic Relations, and Consular Rights of 1955, and the applicable rules of general international law, has incurred respon-sibility towards the United States.' As Rodley (*op. cit.*, p. 325) notes, the formulation of 'applicable rules of international law' is 'itself interesting', as the pleadings of the US were based on the Treaty of Amity between the USA and Iran, where obligation to provide 'the most constant protection and security' and 'human and reasonable treatment' were pro-vided. And in paragraph 91, the Court held that 'Wrongfully to deprive human beings of their freedom and to subject them to physical constraint in conditions of hardship is in itself manifestly incompatible with the principles of the Charter of the United Nations, as well as with the fundamental principles enunciated in the Universal Declaration of Human Rights.' ICJ, *United States Diplomatic and Consular Staff in Tehran*, Judgment, ICJ Reports 1980, p. 3.

91 N. Rodley, 'Human Rights and Humanitarian Intervention: the Case Law of the World Court', *op. cit.*, p. 326.

92 *Ibid.*

not foreclose any further legal developments of what may constitute a 'fundamental' principle.

The *Nicaragua* case is also acknowledged to have found that human rights
are part of general international law. According to Rodley, to reach such a conclusion, the judgement in *Nicaragua* should be placed in a proper context. He
offers the following reading of the case: 'if one reads what the Court says about
human rights in the light of its central argument (i.e. they cannot be invoked to
justify armed intervention), one finds that the Court tends to confirm its recognition that human rights principles are part of general international law.'[93] The
Court, in examining the commitment of Nicaragua to the Organization of American States in relation to its domestic political system (democracy and free elections), as well as respect for human rights, had concluded that these matters fall
within the domestic jurisdiction and recalled that every state has a fundamental
right to choose and implement its own political, economic and social systems.[94]
It further took a view that while there was 'a possibility of a State binding itself
by agreement in relation to a question of domestic policy, such as that relating
to the holding of free elections on its territory', Nicaragua did not do so, given
that its commitments were not legal undertakings.[95] The Court then stated that:

> Nicaragua is accused by the 1985 finding of the United States Congress of
> violating human rights. This particular point requires to be studied indepen-
> dently of the question of the existence of a 'legal commitment' by Nicaragua
> towards the Organization of American States to respect these rights; the
> absence of such a commitment would not mean that Nicaragua could with
> impunity violate human rights.[96]

Again, Rodley's interpretation is useful here in that what the Court is trying
to say in this passage is that the human rights violations of Nicaragua could be
examined under a source other than the specific undertakings of Nicaragua under
the OAS, i.e. under customary law.[97] The absence of a formal legal commitment

---

93 *Ibid.*, p. 328.
94 ICJ, *Military and Paramilitary Activities in und against Nicaragua (Nicaragua v. United
    States of America)*, Judgment, ICJ Reports 1986, para. 258.
95 *Ibid.*, paras. 259, 260 and 261.
96 *Ibid.*, para. 267.
97 N. Rodley, 'Human Rights and Humanitarian Intervention: the Case Law of the World
    Court', *op. cit.*, p. 328. Rodley's reading of the case is: 'Nicaragua allegedly pledged itself
    to the Organisation of American States legally to respect human rights together with other
    values. In fact the pledge should be seen as political rather than legal, but this is no obstacle
    to the Organisation acting: this is because Nicaragua is party to a number of human rights
    treaties including the Pact of San Jose. As such it is subject to implementation measures
    that do not constrain other States. These measures had yielded results (in the form of two
    reports) that would have permitted the Organisation to act, if they had found serious human
    rights violations and wished to act on the basis of them. So the United States has nothing to
    complain about in terms of the opportunities for the Organisation to deal with the human
    rights situation in Nicaragua.' *Ibid.*, p. 329.

thus does not preclude the possibility of international responsibility when human rights violations occur. The question before the Court, he continues, was not about the existence of such an obligation to respect fundamental human rights, but its implementation and the limited question before it, namely whether they gave a basis for the US military action, which they certainly did not, as the Court specified.

The aforementioned cases evidence the fact that although human rights issues played a rather ancillary role to the context of the cases in question, they do contain important formative elements for the way human rights constituted themselves in the international legal order. The important conclusion to be derived from the present analysis of the selected jurisprudence of the International Court of Justice is that UN Charter human rights provisions are of a binding character; 'the principles and rules of international law concerning the basic rights of the human person' create obligations *erga omnes*, and these principles and rules can be found in the UN Charter and the Universal Declaration of Human Rights.[98] The ICJ 'has unambiguously accepted that the obligation to respect fundamental human rights is an obligation under general international law'.[99]

3.2.2 The doctrine on the obligation to respect human rights

The conclusion formulated on the basis of the ICJ's case law in the preceding section can be supported further by the position of the Institut de Droit International (IDI), expressed in its Resolution on the Protection of Human Rights and the Principle of Non-intervention in Internal Affairs of States adopted at its session in Santiago de Compostela in 1989. In its resolution, the Institut suggested that the very obligation of states to ensure the protection of human rights is an obligation *erga omnes*.[100] Article 1 of the resolution puts forward the following:

> Human rights are a direct expression of the dignity of the human person. The obligation of States *to ensure their observance* derives from the recognition of this dignity as proclaimed in the Charter of the United Nations and in the Universal Declaration of Human Rights.
>
> This international obligation, as expressed by the International Court of Justice, is *erga omnes*; it is incumbent upon every State in relation to the international community as a whole, and every State has a legal interest in the protection of human rights. The obligation further implies a duty of

---

98 *Ibid,*. p. 326.

99 B. Simma and P. Alston, 'The Sources of Human Rights Law: Custom, Jus Cogens, and General Principles', 12 *Australian Year Book of International Law* (1988–1989), p. 105.

100 In 2015, at its 67th session, the International Law Commission decided to include the topic of jus cogens. See UN doc. A/69/10. Session de Saint-Jacques-de-Compostelle 1989, La protection des droits de l'homme et le principe de non-intervention dans les affaires intérieures des Etats, www.idi-iil.org/idiF/resolutionsF/1989_comp_03_fr.PDF.

solidarity among all States to ensure as rapidly as possible the effective protection of human rights throughout the world.[101]

As such, this resolution clearly suggests that the general obligation to ensure respect for human rights as proclaimed in the UN Charter and the UDHR is itself an *erga omnes* obligation. The reference to the UN Charter and UDHR was read by Yoram Dinstein as all rights recognized in the Universal Declaration,[102] an interpretation not readily accepted by some authors.[103] Indeed, the Resolution of the IDI does not define the term 'human rights', while the reference to the UDHR seems to suggest a broad thrust of the term.[104] The text of the resolution suggests a degree of hierarchy only at the level of legal consequences.[105] Article 2(3) specifies that:

> Violations justifying recourse to the measures referred to above shall be viewed in the light of their gravity and of all the relevant circumstances. Measures designed to ensure the collective protection of human rights are particularly justified when taken in response to especially grave violations of these rights, notably large-scale or systematic violations, as well as those infringing rights that cannot be derogated from in any circumstances.

Article 2(3) suggests a distinction should be drawn between derogable and non-derogable rights, in that in the case of the former, the actions by third states

---

101 Emphasis added. The English version of Article 1 creates ambiguity when stating that the obligation of states to ensure human rights 'as expressed by the International Court of Justice, is *erga omnes*.' It can be read as referring to the term *erga omnes*, as used by the Court in its dictum in *Barcelona Traction*, and the list of *erga omnes* would be limited to those examples provided for in the famous passage. However, the French text is explicit, in that it refers to the terminology as used by the Court, rather than to the Court's qualification of *erga omnes*. The original text of the resolution of the IDI, in French, reads as follows:

> Les droits de l'homme sont l'expression directe de la dignité de la personne humaine. L'obligation pour les Etats d'en assurer le respect découle de la reconnaissance même de cette dignité que proclament déjà la Charte des Nations Unies et la Déclaration universelle des droits de l'homme.
>
> Cette obligation internationale est, selon une formule utilisée par la Cour internationale de Justice, une obligation *erga omnes*; elle incombe à tout Etat vis-à-vis de la communauté internationale dans son ensemble, et tout Etat a un intérêt juridique à la protection des droits de l'homme. Cette obligation implique au surplus un devoir de solidarité entre tous les Etats en vue d'assurer le plus rapidement possible une protection universelle et efficace des droits de l'homme.

102 Y. Dinstein, 'The Erga Omnes Applicability of Human Rights', 30 *Archiv des Völkerrechts* (1992), p. 17.

103 M. Ragazzi, *The Concept of International Obligations Erga Omnes*, OUP: 2000, p. 144.

104 This is evidenced by the discussion during the drafting where the initial reference to 'fundamental' human rights was later rejected.

105 T. Koji, 'Emerging Hierarchy in International Human Rights and Beyond: From the Perspective of Non-Derogable Rights', 12(5) *European Journal of International Law* (2001), pp. 917–941, p. 936.

should be in response to 'especially grave violations' or 'large-scale or systematic violations' of these rights, while for the latter, such a threshold does not seem to be required. The former category of rights, i.e. derogable rights, should thus go beyond an isolated incident of the violation and, on the condition of consistency and grossness, can give rise to obligations *erga omnes*. This degree of hierarchy is also evident in the subsequent Article 4(b) of the resolution of the IDI, which states that 'la mesure sera proportionnée à la gravité de la violation'.

It seems safe to conclude that the IDI has supported the theory that the general obligation to respect human rights is in itself an obligation *erga omnes*. Fitzmaurice, in a special report submitted to the Institut de Droit International (much earlier before the resolution was adopted), referred to the principle of a general duty – 'common law' duty – to respect human rights, which according to him, not only formed part of international customary law but had pre-existed in much the same way as the rules embedded in the Nuremberg Charter.[106] Thus, for the purposes of this chapter, a central point is that there is a general principle to respect and to avoid causing harm to human rights. This principle can be said to have a life of its own, independently from the question of rights giving rise to obligations towards the international community, as well as their scope and the legal consequences stemming therefrom.[107]

---

106 Sir G. Fitzmaurice, 'Special Report: The Future of Public International Law and of the International Legal System in the Circumstances of Today', Institut de Droit International, *Livre du Centenaire 1873–1973. Evolution et perspectives du droit international,* Basel: 1973, p. 323. Burghenthal is also convinced of the idea that 'the protection of human rights knows no international boundaries, and that the international community has an obligation to ensure that governments guarantee and protect human rights wherever they may be violated has captured the imagination of mankind'. T. Buergenthal, 'International Human Rights in an Historical Perspective', in J. Symonides (ed.), *Human Rights: Concepts and Standards,* Ashgate, UNESCO Publishing: 2000, p. 4.

107 Article 38 of the VCLT states: 'Nothing in articles 34 to 37 precludes a rule set forth in a treaty from becoming binding upon a third State as a customary rule of international law, recognized as such.' 'That provision of the 1969 and the 1986 Vienna Conventions is clear in conceding that for a norm to bind a third State as a customary rule of international law it ought to be recognized as such (i.e., the source of the binding character of such norm being custom, not the treaty itself). It thus appears that, independently of the rules of the law of treaties concerning the effects of treaties on third States, Article 38 of the two Vienna Conventions was meant to be purely a reservation in support of the *legitimacy* of the process whereby principles contained in treaties may become binding on non-parties through being recognized as customary rules. Article 38 of the two Vienna Conventions thus retains its importance not only with regard to States but also in relation to international organizations: these latter, even though not normally participating as parties in codification conventions, which play a significant role in the evolution of international custom, have nevertheless to apply the rules enshrined in such conventions. Article 38, although – as already indicated – not affecting the process of formulation itself of customary law, "does not prejudge" in one way or another the possibility that the effects of that process might extend – besides States – to international organizations. This is significant, for the present purposes, as some international organizations, in the discharge of their functions, operate in the field of the safeguard of human rights.' A.A. Cancado-Trindade, 'Co-existence and Co-ordination of Mechanisms of International Protection of Human Rights (at Global and Regional Levels)', 202 *Recueil des Cours* (1987), p. 84.

Whether this *communis opinio* stands the test of some of the development actors, such as the IFIs, is far from clear. The basic contention advanced unofficially by the legal adviser of the IMF, Francois Gianvitti, in an occasion organized by the Committee on Economic, Social and Cultural Rights, was that the rights set out in the Covenant have to be part of general or customary international law to have a direct effect on the Fund.[108] The suggestion that socio-economic rights formed part of general or customary international law was not accepted by the IMF, despite an insistence on this point by human rights bodies.

3.2.3 Discovering the content of human rights in the obligation to respect

Attempting to identify the contours of a customary character of a right not only is a daunting task but, as Theodor Meron has warned, requires an 'overconfident' observer.[109] Such an inquiry, in its range and ambition, cannot be feasibly accommodated here. The purpose is rather to synthesize the relevant theoretical constructions and arguments as regards the customary status of socio-economic rights. At the onset, it needs to be reiterated that there is perhaps no issue more examined and less understood than the subject of customary human rights law. When it comes to socio-economic rights, they are hardly ever analysed by the scholarship in the context of the discussions on the content of customary human rights law. The basic provisions of the UN Charter generating obligations to respect human rights are certainly not confined to a few 'classic' civil and political human rights.[110]

The UDHR has often been used as a shortcut for evidence of the customary status of virtually all individual human rights. But this assertion is not commonly held. It is not clear the extent to which the UDHR has come to be regarded as an authoritative interpretation of Charter-based provisions or as binding as a matter of customary law. The assertion that states are bound by 'each and every provision' of the Declaration as a matter of customary law may indeed be regarded as an 'overstatement'.[111]

As far as socio-economic rights are concerned, in a study of 20 years ago examining the content of customary law evidenced in the Declaration, Hurst Hannum reached the following conclusion:

> *Articles 22 through 27* [of the UDHR] deal primarily with economic, social, and cultural rights, including social security, the right to work, the right to

---

108 F. Gianvitti, Economic, Social and Cultural Human Rights and the International Monetary Fund, Working Paper, UN doc. E/C.12/2001/WP.5, 7 May 2001, paras. 19–21.

109 T. Meron, *Human Rights and Humanitarian Norms as Customary Law*, Clarendon Press: 1989, pp. 46, 95.

110 As Henkin agrees: 'But "human rights" in the Charter may well have included more. By 1945, virtually every State was a welfare State, and the Charter declared that the peoples of the United Nations were determined "to promote social progress and better standards of life in larger freedom".' L. Henkin, 'International law: politics, values and functions: general course on public international law', 216 *Recueil des Cours* (1989), p. 234.

111 M. Kamminga, *Inter-State Accountability for Violations of Human Rights*, University of Pennsylvania Press: 1992, p. 133.

rest and leisure, the right to an adequate standard of living, the right to education, and the right to participate in cultural life. Despite the fact that the
United States, in particular, has often denied the status of "rights" to these
norms, they may enjoy wider international support than some of the civil
and political rights traditionally emphasized in U.S. jurisprudence. However, they are rarely referred by either commentators or courts in discussions
of the content of customary international human rights law. The following
rights would seem to enjoy sufficiently widespread support as to be at least
potential candidates for rights recognized under customary international
law: the right to free choice of employment; the right to form and join trade
unions; and the right to free primary education, subject to a state's available
resources. Many rights included within these articles are closely related to
other rights, such as the right to life and the prohibition against arbitrary
discrimination.[112]

As can be seen, Hannum's list of ESC rights and their components as candidates
for customary status, with the exception of the right to free primary education,
require negative obligations and have civil and political right-related origins. The
Committee on Economic, Social and Cultural Rights has adopted a broader view
on this issue, observing that: 'even in a situation of armed conflict, fundamental
human rights must be respected and that basic economic, social and cultural
rights, as part of the minimum standards of human rights, are guaranteed under
customary international law and are also prescribed by international humanitarian
law'.[113] The characterization of the minimum core of the socio-economic rights
as customary international law has not, however, been supported by thorough
legal analysis.[114] Generally, the literature tends to display caution with regard to
attaching a character of customary law to socio-economic rights.

The topic accommodates differing views among scholarship.[115] For some
scholars, socio-economic rights are not firmly established under the category
of customary international law.[116] On the other side of the spectrum, certain
authors have tried to shed light on the extent socio-economic rights have attained

---

112 H. Hannum, 'The Status of the Universal Declaration of Human Rights in National and
International Law', 25 *Georgia Journal of International and Comparative Law* (1995–
1996), pp. 348–349.

113 CESCR, Concluding Observations: Israel, UN doc. E/C.12/1/Add.90, 26 June 2003,
para. 31.

114 See, however, A. Cassimatis, *Human Rights Related Trade Measures Under International
Law: the Legality of Trade Measures Imposed in Response to Violations of Human Rights Obligations under General International Law*, Martinus Nijhoff Publishers: 2007, pp. 72–86.

115 T. Meron, *Human Rights and Humanitarian Norms as Customary Law*, Clarendon Press:
1989; O. Schachter, 'International Law in Theory and Practice: General Course in Public
International Law, 178 *Recueil des cours* (1982), p. 337.

116 T. Meron, 'On a Hierarchy of International Human Rights', 80(1) *American Journal of
International Law* (1986), p. 80; P.-M. Dupuy, *Droit International Public*, 5th edition,
Dalloz: 2000, p. 213.

(or are likely to attain) the status of customary international law. Oscar Schachter holds the view that a strong case can be made with respect to the right to subsistence, or 'at least' the right to food.[117] There is, in fact, wide support for the proposition that at least some aspects of the right to food are part of customary law.[118] This support may also stem from the fact that the text of Article 11 of the Covenant itself stipulates that 'the States Parties to the present Covenant [recognize] the fundamental right of everyone to be free from hunger'. Philip Alston's analysis of the legal status of the Millennium Development Goals suggests that those minimum sets of goals adopted on the basis of agreement and consistently endorsed by virtually all states in development fora may have crystallized into customary human rights law.[119]

At the same time, there have been debates as to whether constructing the status of human rights generally in terms of customary law is appropriate. In their prominent analysis, Alston and Simma proposed a view that human rights law does not stand the traditional test of custom formation; most of the human rights standards will hardly meet the requirement of actual state practice.[120] The socio-economic rights in particular may be unable to substantiate the presence of the main prerequisites of customary law. Instead, they draw attention to the third source mentioned in the Article 38 of the Statute of International Court of Justice, namely 'the general principles of law recognized by civilised nations'. Adopting a broad definition of 'general principles',[121] this source of law 'seems to conform more closely than the concept of custom to the situation where a norm invested with strong inherent authority is widely accepted even though widely violated'.[122] Alston and Simma, referring to the jurisprudence of the International Court of Justice, some of which was referred to in the previous section, point out that the Court, while accepting that the obligation to respect human rights is an obligation under general international law, never expressly spoke of custom.

This brings us back to an examination of whether the concept of the 'basic' or 'fundamental' human rights that the Court referred to incorporates socio-economic dimensions. As the Draft Articles on State Responsibility for Wrongful

---

117 O. Schachter, 'International Law in Theory and Practice: General Course in Public International Law, 178 *Recueil des cours* (1982), p. 337.

118 S. Narula, 'The Right to Food: Holding Global Actors Accountable Under International Law', *Working Paper Number 7*, Center for Human Rights and Global Justice, 2006.

119 P. Alston, 'Ships Passing in the Night: The Current State of the Human Rights and Development Debate seen through the Lens of the Millennium Development Goals', 27(3) *Human Rights Quarterly* (2005), pp. 755–829.

120 B. Simma and P. Alston, 'The Sources of Human Rights Law: Custom, Jus Cogens, and General Principles', *op. cit.*, p. 82.

121 Simma and Alston suggest that the notion 'general principles' should not be restricted to mean solely to legal principles developed in *foro domestica*. The authors explain: 'For the drafters of the Statute the decisive point was that such principles were not to be derived from mere speculation; they had rather to be made objective through some sort of general acceptance or recognition by States.' *Ibid.*, p. 102.

122 *Ibid.*

Acts makes clear, the notion is fluid and may evolve in the future.[123] The quali-
fication of what is 'basic' inevitably touches upon the question of hierarchy of
human rights, the logic of which demonstrates the presence of many problems.
First of all, the question of hierarchy generally in international law is subject to
dispute.[124] Second, examination of the subject necessarily requires an inquiry into
related concepts of *jus cogens, erga omnes*, and non-derogable and core rights, all
of which not only are subject to academic controversy but are also marked by
the lack of consensus on their identity.[125] There are, in fact, many complex posi-
tions within these categories and in relation to the hierarchy. What is clear, as a
minimum, is that the question of hierarchy in international law and human rights
law are in a dialectical relationship: 'hierarchy affects human rights' and 'human
rights give birth to hierarchy in general'.[126]

At any rate, as Professor Dupuy notes, '[i]l est évident qu'une hiérarchisation
des droits et libertés à garantir s'expose à la contestation', as it inevitably leads
one to fall into the trap of value judgement and arbitrariness.[127] Creating a hierarchy in human rights according to their fundamental character is hardly reconcilable with the theory of indivisibility and interdependence of human rights.[128]
But leaving the indivisibility discourse and its internal theoretical inconsistencies
aside,[129] it is the analysis of treaty texts that causes us to consider that states did

123 According to the Commentary on the ILC draft: 'Nor is it the function of the articles
to provide a list of those obligations which under existing international law are owed to
the international community as a whole. This would go well beyond the task of codifying
the secondary rules of State responsibility, and in any event, such a list would be only of
limited value, as the scope of the concept will necessarily evolve over time.' Commentary
on Article 48, Draft articles on Responsibility of States for Internationally Wrongful Acts,
with commentaries, contained in International Law Commission, Report on the work of
its fifty-third session (23 April – 1 June and 2 July – 10 August 2001), GAOR Fifty-Sixth
Session, Supplement No. 10, UN doc. A/56/10, p. 127.
124 J.H.H. Weiler and A. L. Paulus, 'The Structure of Change in International Law or Is There
a Hierarchy of Norms in International Law?', 8 *European Journal of International Law*
(1997), pp. 545–565.
125 I. Brownlie, *Principles of Public International Law*, 7th edition, OUP: 2008, pp. 562–563
126 T. Koji, 'Emerging Hierarchy in International Human Rights and Beyond: From the Perspective of Non-Derogable Rights, *op. cit.*, p. 939.
127 P.-M. Dupuy, *Droit International Public*, *op. cit.*, p. 213; Meron also is of view that 'the
characterisation of some rights as fundamental results largely from our own subjective perceptions of their importance'. T. Meron, 'On a Hierarchy of International Human Rights',
op. cit., p. 8.
128 T. van Boven, 'Distinguishing Criteria of Human Rights', in K. Vasak (ed.), *The International
Dimensions of Human Rights*, UNCESCO: 1982, p. 43. The preambles of the Covenants on
Economic, Social and Cultural Rights and Civil and Political Rights refer to each other, and,
following the Tehran Conference on Human Rights of 1968, indivisibility of human rights
have been reaffirmed and is an incontrovertible component of the human rights discourse.
129 Not only does it not take into consideration the hierarchy debate in general international
law, but it also does not correspond to the certain human rights theories, such as the idea
of 'minimum core of socio-economic rights'. It is understandable that, as Koji says, 'most
human rights scholars tend to use theories as a means of promoting human rights and indeed
pay little attention to theoretical consistency.' T. Koji, 'Emerging Hierarchy in International
Human Rights and Beyond: From the Perspective of Non-Derogable Rights', *op. cit.*, p. 925.

not give all human rights the same status.[130] Strictly from a consensualist conception of international law, 'some rights are obviously more important than other human rights'.[131]

Although there is no set of agreed criteria for differentiating between the higher rights and ordinary rights, one of the widely accepted methods used is the concept of non-derogable rights.[132] On this basis, the list of non-derogable rights provided by Article 4(2) of the ICCPR, and Article 12 (2) of the ECHR, or Article 27 of ACHR and even that of Common Article 3 of the Geneva Conventions of the 1949, evidences the absence of explicit references to any of the socio-economic rights. A list common to all treaties includes the right to life, the prohibition of slavery, prohibition of torture or of cruel, inhuman or degrading treatment or punishment and prohibition of retroactive penal measures.

Obviously, certain of the enumerated rights in the list, particularly the right to life[133] and prohibition of torture, contain economic and social rights elements.[134] International criminal law is pointed out as a relevant field in search of criteria to deduce the fundamental character of certain human rights and thus locating them in the framework of the imperative norms of international law.[135] Put in these terms, legal corollaries of socio-economic rights can be found amply in the content of crimes under the Rome Statute and hence may evidence their fundamental nature for the protection of basic rights of human person.[136]

At the same time, authors like Steven S. Marks support the idea of the selection of rights common to several human rights treaties to serve as a common list of rights applicable equally in exceptional circumstances such as underdevelopment,

130 P.-M. Dupuy, *Droit International Public, op. cit.*, p. 213.
131 T. Meron, 'On a Hierarchy of International Human Rights', *op. cit.*, p. 4.
132 For a critique of the concept of 'emergency' as a legacy of colonialism in human rights discourse see B. Rajagopal, *International Law from Below: Development, Social Movements and Third World Resistance, op. cit.*, pp. 176–177.
133 General Comment on Article 6 (Right to Life, General Comment No. 6, adopted 30 April 1982, Hum. Rts. Comm., 16th Sess., reprinted in Compilation of General Comments and General Recommendations Adopted by Human Rights Treaty Bodies, p. 127, UN doc. HRI/GEN/1/Rev.6 (2003). See also protection of the right to health through the prism of the right to housing in HRC, Concluding Observations: Canada, UN doc. CCPR/C/79/Add.105, 7 April 1999, para. 12; and HRC, Concluding Observations: Canada, UN doc. CCPR/C/CAN/CO/5, 20 April 2006.
134 For an excellent overview, see U. Khaliq and R. Churchill, 'The Protection of Economic and Social Rights: A Particular Challenge?', in H. Keller and G. Ulfstein (eds), *UN Human Rights Treaty Bodies: Law and Legitimacy*, CUP: 2012, pp. 199–260.
135 P.-M. Dupuy, *Droit International Public, op. cit.*, p. 217. On the possible relevance of the gravity of violations of human rights see Geneva Academy of International Humanitarian Law and Human Rights, *What Amounts to 'a Serious Violation of International Human Rights Law'? An Analysis of Practice and Expert Opinion for the Purpose of the 2013 Arms Trade Treaty*, Academy Briefing No. 6, August 2014.
136 For example, very cursorily one can name by way of example elements within crimes against humanity stipulated in Article 7(2)(b), as well as socio-economic rights elements in war crimes: Article 8(2)(b)(iii), (iv), (ix), (xxiv), (xxv) and Article 8(2)(e)(ii),(iv),(xii), Rome Statute of the International Criminal Court.

natural disasters and armed conflict.[137] According to Tomasevski, in any event, the categories of 'fundamental' human rights are not helpful or particularly relevant to the context of development.[138] This view therefore proposes the 'relevance' criterion to be developed and applied. In other words, a situation-specific method of defining 'clusters' of the rights most affected in a specific context would be helpful.

Last but not least, it is worth mentioning that parallel to these is a separate theory based on the basic needs approach. This approach, regarded by some as important, is premised on the idea that the realization of human rights is dependent upon fulfilment of basic subsistence needs.[139]Obviously, this approach may be subject to criticism for 'committing the naturalistic fallacy of deducing norm from fact, but determination of basic human needs should be recognized as a result of the philosophical consideration that no human right can be realized without the fulfilment of such basic needs'.[140] This theory is in line with the position of the Committee on Economic, Social Cultural Rights on minimum core rights. As Eibe Riedel further clarifies:

> In relation to ESC-rights generally, one is not talking about a grand, extravagant bouquet of every conceivable social blessing, but of no more than minimum subsistence levels, necessary for survival – the minimum for existence. Every person is entitled to the core esc-rights, indispensable for leading a life in dignity. Such basic social rights in no way differ from other freedom rights.[141]

The subsistence or certain elements of the right to adequate standard of living are clearly making gains at least in the *opinio juris* of states, albeit advanced under labels distant from rights terminology.[142] In any event, what is lacking is the consistent application of these basic 'rights' in practice.[143]

---

137 See S.P. Marks, 'Principles and Norms of Human Rights Applicable in Emergency Situations: Underdevelopment, Catastrophes and Armed Conflicts', in K. Vasak (ed.), *The International Dimensions of Human Rights*, UNESCO: 1982, Vol. I, pp. 175–215.
138 K. Tomasevski, 'Monitoring Human Rights Aspects of Sustainable Development', *op. cit.*, p. 96.
139 D. Shelton, 'Are There Differentiations among Human Rights? *Jus Cogens*, Core Human Rights, Obligations *Erga Omnes* and Non-Derogability', in Venice Commission, *The Status of International Treaties on Human Rights*, Council of Europe Publishing: 2006, p. 177 et seq.
140 T. Koji, 'Emerging Hierarchy in International Human Rights and Beyond: From the Perspective of Non-Derogable Rights', *op. cit.*, p. 926.
141 E. Riedel, 'International Covenant on Economic, Social and Cultural Rights (1966)', *Max Planck Encyclopaedia of International Law*, www.mpepil.com, para. 53.
142 The basic needs concept advanced under diverse labels (poverty reduction, improvement of standards of living, well-being of population) has consolidated over the past decade as one of the main, if not the central, goals of development.
143 IACtHR, The Realisation of Economic, Social and Cultural Rights in the Region, Annual Report of the Inter-American Commission on Human Rights, 1993, OEA/Ser.L/V.II.85, Doc. 9, rev., 11 February 1994, pp. 519–534.

3.2.4 *An example of a fundamental human right: Obligation not to deprive a people of its own means of subsistence*

Given the fragmentary and inconclusive material available in relation to the socio-economic content of 'basic' or 'fundamental' human rights, it is perhaps useful to adhere to the examples of fundamental rights found in the Draft Articles on Responsibility of States for Internationally Wrongful Acts. Article 50 of the Draft Articles sets out the obligations not affected by countermeasures, among which are the obligations for the protection of fundamental human rights in paragraph 1(b).[144] In the commentaries on the relevant provision, the Draft Articles enumerate the jurisprudence and doctrine on the limits to countermeasures.[145] They also mention certain human rights provisions not subject to derogation, as identified by human rights treaties. In addition to these, interestingly, reference is made to the effect of economic sanctions as dealt with by the Committee on Economic, Social and Cultural Rights. The commentary further summons up analogies that 'can be drawn from other elements of general international law' and in this context recalls the unconditional prohibition of starvation as a method of warfare,[146] as well as the final sentence of paragraph 2 of Common Article 1 to the International Covenants: 'In no case may a people be deprived of its own means of subsistence.'[147] Before examining the work of the ILC, a few comments of general nature are in order in relation to this elusive provision.

The formula appears in the context of Article 1(2) in the 1966 Covenants, along with the norm stipulating the sovereignty of people over natural wealth and resources.[148] Very little information is available on the meaning and implication of the sub-norm in the preparatory work to the international covenants. Nor has doctrine attempted to provide any systematic clarification, often treating the provision very marginally against the background of a broader question of self-determination.[149]

---

144 Article 50(1)(b) on Obligations not affected by countermeasures of the ILC Draft Articles on State Responsibility, paragraph 1 reads: 'Countermeasures shall not affect: . . . b) obligations for the protection of fundamental human rights.'

145 In particular, the *Portuguese Colonies case (Naulilaa incident)*, UNRIAA, Vol. II (Sales No. 1949.V.1), p. 1011, pp. 1025–1026 (1928) and the Institut de Droit International Resolution of 1934, *Régime des représailles en temps de paix*, Session de Paris.

146 Article 54(1), Protocol Additional to the Geneva Conventions of 12 August 1949, and relating to the Protection of Victims of International Armed Conflicts (Protocol I).

147 International Law Commission, Report on the work of its fifty-third session (23 April – 1 June and 2 July – 10 August 2001), GAOR Fifty-Sixth Session, Supplement No. 10, UN doc. A/56/10, p. 132.

148 The full text of Common Article 1(2) of the 1966 International Covenants on human rights reads as follows:

> All peoples may, for their own ends, freely dispose of their natural wealth and resources without prejudice to any obligations arising out of international economic cooperation, based upon the principle of mutual benefit, and international law. In no case may a people be deprived of its own means of subsistence.

149 So far the only exception is B. Saul, D. Kinley and J. Mowbray, *The International Covenant on Economic, Social and Cultural Rights: Commentary, Cases, and Materials*, OUP: 2014, pp. 116–121.

Intermittently, however, it was invoked in contexts as diverse as genocide, occupation, and indigenous peoples' rights,[150] though without a detailed analysis of its legal implications in those settings. Interestingly, the provision is not referred to in the 1962 General Assembly Resolution on Permanent Sovereignty over Natural Resources or the 1970 Declaration of Principles of International Law Concerning Friendly Relations and Cooperation among States or even the Declaration on the Right to Development. Attempts have been made to treat the provision as the basis for subsistence rights; in particular, in the context of the right to food.[151] The Committee on Economic, Social and Cultural Rights has taken a similar stance, invoking the sub-provision in the context of the right to water.[152]

According to Cassese, the sub-norm may 'be read to nullify even arrangements "freely made" by the people "for their own ends" if these arrangements deprive the people of its means of subsistence. It presumably nullifies the obligation to pay any compensation required under international law where such compensation

150 Article 20, the Declaration on the Rights of Indigenous Peoples, 13 September 2007. See also the application of the provision in the practice of the Human Rights Committee. E.g. the Human Rights Committee in its consideration of the report of Canada noted that 'as the State party acknowledged, the situation of the aboriginal peoples remains "the most pressing human rights issue facing Canadians". In this connection, the Committee is particularly concerned that the State party has not yet implemented the recommendations of the Royal Commission on Aboriginal Peoples (RCAP). With reference to the conclusion by RCAP that without a greater share of lands and resources institutions of aboriginal self-government will fail, the Committee emphasizes that the right to self-determination requires, *inter alia*, that all peoples must be able to freely dispose of their natural wealth and resources and that they may not be deprived of their own means of subsistence (art 1, para. 2). The Committee recommends that decisive and urgent action be taken towards the full implementation of the RCAP recommendations on land and resource allocation. The Committee also recommends that the practice of extinguishing inherent aboriginal rights be abandoned as incompatible with Article 1 of the Covenant.' HRC, Concluding Observations: Canada, UN doc. CCPR/C/79/Add.105 (1999), para. 8. In its Concluding Observations on Sweden: 'The Committee is concerned at the limited extent to which the Sami Parliament can have a significant role in the decision-making process on issues affecting the traditional lands and economic activities of the indigenous Sami people, such as projects in the fields of hydroelectricity, mining and forestry, as well as the privatization of land (arts. 1, 25 and 27 of the Covenant). The State party should take steps to involve the Sami by giving them greater influence in decision-making affecting their natural environment and their means of subsistence.' UN doc. CCPR/CO/74/SWE (2002), para. 15.
151 See e.g. FAO, *The Right to Adequate Food in Emergencies*, UN: 2002, p. 23, where the provision has been included in the 'normative content of right to food', i.e. 'Deprivation of food and of means of subsistence. Article 1(2) of the ICCPR and of the ICESCR states that "in no case may a people be deprived of its own means of subsistence".'
152 General Comment No. 15 on the Right to Water (Articles 11 and 12 of the Covenant), states: 'Taking note of the duty in article 1, paragraph 2, of the Covenant, which provides that a people may not "be deprived of its means of subsistence", States parties should ensure that there is adequate access to water for subsistence farming and for securing the livelihoods of indigenous peoples.' UN doc. E/C.12/2002/11, para. 7.

would deprive the people of its means of subsistence.'[153] However, this explanation provides little information on the potential importance of the provision with respect to the substantive rights guaranteed by the Covenant.[154] In the drafting history, the original wording of the sub-norm appeared as follows:

> In no case may a people be deprived of its own means of subsistence on the grounds of any rights that may be claimed by other States.[155]

Generally, there was considerable controversy regarding the provision. The Saudi Arabian delegate clarified that the means of subsistence intended:

> to prevent a weak or penniless government from seriously compromising a country's future by granting concessions in the economic sphere – a frequent occurrence in the nineteenth century. The second sentence of paragraph 2 was intended to serve as a warning to all who might consider resorting to such unfair procedures.[156]

In the view of Alston, examples of the cases given in the period of drafting suggest that it would be appropriate for the supervisory mechanism 'to concern itself in the future with cases where this provision is alleged to have been violated by virtue of the deprivation of a people of its subsistence food production', yet, as he warned, 'in view of the complexity of issue, its essentially economic and social nature, the difficulty of demonstrating causality, and the Committee's generally cautious approach, it is unlikely that the Committee will take such issues in the foreseeable future'.[157] Alston's assessment holds, to a large extent, valid even today. Nonetheless, the CESCR had taken some small but significant steps in applying the sub-norm in the context of the right to self-determination, finding some concrete violations that fall within its scope:

> The Committee urges the State party to respect the right to self-determination as recognized in article 1, paragraph 2, of the Covenant, which provides that 'in no case may a people be deprived of its own means of subsistence'. Closure restricts the movement of people and goods, cutting off access to external markets and to income derived from employment and livelihood.

---

153 A. Cassese, 'The Self-determination of Peoples', in L. Henkin (ed.), *The International Bill of Rights: the Covenant on Civil and Political Rights*, Columbia University Press: 1981, pp. 92–106.

154 P. Alston, 'International Law and the Human Rights to Food', in P. Alston and K. Tomasevski (eds), *The Right to Food: Towards a System for Supervising States' Compliance with the Right to Food*, Martinus Nijhoff Publishers: 1984, p. 24.

155 Commission on Human Rights, Report of the 8th Session, 1952, 14 ESCOR (1952) Supplement no. 4 (E/CN.4/669), para. 91, adopted by 10 votes to 6, with 2 abstentions. *Ibid.*, para. 70.

156 Saudi Arabia, UN doc. A/C.3/SR.672, 25 November 1955, para. 36.

157 P. Alston, 'International Law and the Human Rights to Food', *op. cit.*, p. 24.

The Committee also calls upon the Government to give full effect to its obligations under the Covenant and, as a matter of the highest priority, to undertake to ensure safe passage at checkpoints for Palestinian medical staff and people seeking treatment, the unhampered flow of essential foodstuffs and supplies, the safe conduct of students and teachers to and from schools, and the reunification of families separated by closures.[158]

The provision has received some attention in the work of the International Law Commission in the context of state responsibility. In the framework of the provision providing for the obligation of states to make reparations under the Draft Articles on State Responsibility, the text of draft Article 42 was originally far more extensive and included in paragraph 3 the following sentence:

In no case shall reparation result in depriving the population of a State of its own means of subsistence.

The purpose of this requirement was obviously to define the limits of reparations.[159] Different views were expressed as to whether the provision should be retained with respect to reparation. The provision proved to be controversial, with some members expressing a view that the provision was of 'critical importance for developing countries',[160] while, on the other hand, many States objected to the provision, 'as it would be abused by States to avoid their legal obligations and erode principle of full reparation'.[161]

Although in the final text the provision in question was not retained, discussions at the International Law Commission provide useful insights on the meaning of the provision.[162] The sub-norm that appears in both Covenants on human rights was said to have 'its validity in international law',[163] and as contained in the Covenants, reflected a 'legal principle of general application'.[164] The problem was particularly placed 'in the category of massive and systematic human rights violations'.[165]

---

158 CESCR, Concluding Observations: Israel, UN doc. E/1999/22, para. 265.
159 J. Crawford, A. Pellet, S. Olleson and K. Parlett (eds), *The Law of International Responsibility: A Commentary*, OUP: 2010, p. 565ff.
160 Yearbook of International Law Commission 2000, Vol. 1, UN doc. A/CN.4/SER.A/2000, p. 21, para. 23.
161 Yearbook of International Law Commission 2000, Vol. 1, UN doc. A/CN.4/SER.A/2000, p. 23, para. 43.
162 The wording of the paragraph 3 of Article 42 has been heavily criticized by many governments, except Germany. See Yearbook of International Law Commission 2000, Vol. 1, p. 5, para. 17.
163 *Ibid.*, para. 100.
164 International Law Commission, Report of the International Law Commission on the work of its forty-eighth session, 6 May – 26 July 1996, Official Records of the General Assembly, Fifty-first session, Supplement No. 10, UN doc. A/51/10, p. 66.
165 Yearbook of International Law Commission 2000, Vol. 1, UN doc. A/CN.4/SER.A/2000, p. 191, para. 23. See also the Prohibition of starvation of the civilian population as a method of warfare, Article 54(1) of the Additional Protocol of 1977 to the Geneva Conventions of 12 August 1949, Rome Statute of the International Criminal Court, Article 8(2)(b)(xxv).

Concerns expressed at the ILC were soon afterwards raised in the Eritrea–Ethiopia Claims Commission. The Commission stated that the size of the parties' claims 'raised potentially serious questions involving the intersection of the law of State responsibility with fundamental human rights norms'.[166] Acknowledging first that both Eritrea and Ethiopia are parties to the ICCPR and ICESCR, the Commission went on to highlight that even if the issue as it appeared before the International Law Commission (i.e. in the context of reparations) was not retained, '[*t*]*hat does not alter the fundamental human rights law rule of common Article I(2), which unquestionably applies to the Parties*'.[167] The Commission further stated that:

> Awards of compensation of the magnitude sought by each Party would impose crippling burdens upon the economies and populations of the other, notwithstanding the obligations both have accepted under the Covenants. Ethiopia urged the Commission not to be concerned with the impact of very large adverse awards on the affected country's population, because the obligation to pay would fall on the government, not the people. The Commission does not agree. Huge awards of compensation by their nature would require large diversions of national resources from the paying country – and its citizens needing health care, education and other public services – to the recipient country. In this regard, the prevailing practice of States in the years since the Treaty of Versailles has been to give very significant weight to the needs of the affected population in determining amounts sought as post-war reparations.[168]

Having regarded the sub-norm contained in Article 1(2) of the Covenants as the relevant rule of international law, the Commission stated that it could not disregard the fact that a 'large damage award' could result in the 'serious injury to its population if such damages to be paid'. Hence, it considered 'whether it was necessary to limit its compensation awards in some manner to ensure that the ultimate financial burden imposed on a Party would not be so excessive, given its economic condition and its capacity to pay, as to compromise its ability to meet its people's basic needs'.[169] Towards the end, however, the Commission concluded that 'it need not decide the question of possible capping of the award in light of the Parties' obligations under human rights law'.[170]

166 Eritrea Ethiopia Claims Commission, *Eritrea's Damages Claims between The State of Eritrea and The Federal Democratic Republic of Ethiopia*, The Hague, 17 August 2009, para. 19.
167 Eritrea Ethiopia Claims Commission, *Eritrea's Damages Claims between The State of Eritrea and The Federal Democratic Republic of Ethiopia*, The Hague, 17 August 2009, para. 19 (emphasis added).
168 *Ibid.*, para. 21.
169 *Ibid.*, para. 22.
170 Eritrea Ethiopia Claims Commission, *Eritrea's Damages Claims between The State of Eritrea and The Federal Democratic Republic of Ethiopia*, The Hague, 17 August 2009, para. 23.

The importance of the ILC's and Eritrea–Ethiopia Claims Commission's contribution to the topic is that they took the sub-norm, 'in no case may a people be deprived of its own means of subsistence', outside the context of self-determination and treated the principle as a self-standing norm of international law of general application. A conclusion one can reach as a result of this cursory review is that this principle of general international law is relevant not only to the cases of reparations and countermeasures, but by definition applies to development agreements and policies involving both states and non-state actors. This is evidenced by the approach taken in the Draft Articles where the provision was placed in the context of the protection of fundamental human rights.

It is interesting that the principle has not been invoked in the recent human rights analysis of the Greek debt crisis or economic sanctions.[171] As noted, however, even though Article 1(2) recognizes that economic self-determination of peoples is without prejudice to any obligations arising out of international economic cooperation, these international economic obligations are subject to the prohibition of depriving a people of its own means of subsistence – a non-derogable core of the provision.[172] Indeed, where international economic obligations compromise the ability of a state to meet its people's basic needs or a blockade brings a 'severe human dignity crisis resulting from the deteriorated public services, widespread poverty, food insecurity, . . . unemployment and . . . aid dependence',[173] a violation of Article 1(2) is still possible.

Writing as far back as in 1984, Alston already referred to this provision as a 'sub-norm' with great potential.[174] Could this norm potentially apply to a range of policies, both at national and international levels, as a safeguard or as a norm that includes the obligation to respect a range of rights enshrined in the International Covenants? A strong case can be made for an affirmative answer. The norm performs both the function of the obligation to avoid damaging

171 OHCHR, Greek crisis: Human rights should not stop at doors of international institutions, says UN expert, Press Statement by the United Nations Independent Expert on foreign debt and human rights, Juan Pablo Bohoslavsky, 2 June 2015, www.ohchr.org/EN/News Events/Pages/DisplayNews.aspx?NewsID=16032&. See also Legal Brief Prepared for the Special Committee of the Hellenic Parliament on the Audit of the Greek Debt (Debt Truth Committee), Economic Policy Conditionality, Socio-Economic Rights and International Legal Responsibility: The Case of Greece 2010–2015, 15 June 2015 by Olivier De Schutter and Margot E. Salomon.

172 B. Saul, D. Kinley and J. Mowbray, *The International Covenant on Economic, Social and Cultural Rights: Commentary, Cases, and Materials*, OUP: 2014, pp. 116–121.

173 Report of the international fact-finding mission to investigate violations of international law, including international humanitarian and human rights law, resulting from the Israeli attacks on the flotilla of ships carrying humanitarian assistance, UN doc. A/HRC/15/21, 27 September 2010, para. 40.

174 He notes: 'this sub-norm would seem to be of major significance for the right to food in the area when the proliferation of cash crops for export appears to be a major threat to the adequate production of subsistence foods for the masses in a growing number of countries'. P. Alston, 'International Law and the Human Rights to Food', *op. cit.*, p. 24.

core socio-economic rights and defines, albeit in vague and general terms, the scope of the rights protected. Its synthetic but categorical provision stands as self-explanatory.

3.3 Non-intervention and unilateral coercive measures of economic character

As far as the negative effects of economic and social policies on third states are concerned, general principles of international law, such as those expressed in the UN Charter and 1970 Friendly Relations and Cooperation Declaration,[175] set out the basic framework through the principle of the prohibition of intervention. This Declaration states: 'No State may use or encourage the use of economic, political or any other type of measures to coerce another State in order to obtain from the subordination of the exercise of its sovereign rights and to secure from it advantages of any kind.' In Resolution 3016 (XXVII), the General Assembly was more concrete in terms of what measures could fall within the intervention in economic fields, declaring that '*actions, measures or legislative regulations* by States aimed at coercing, directly or indirectly, other States engaged in the change of their internal structure' would be in violation of not only the UN Charter and the 1970 Declaration but also the 2nd International Development Strategy.[176] The Charter of Economic Rights and Duties of States, although frail in its legal weight, provided a more forceful articulation of the principle.[177] The

---

175 UN GA Resolution 2625, UN GAOR, 25th Session, 1883d Plen. mtg., Suppl. No. 28, 24 October 1970, p. 121, which is regarded as reflecting customary international law. The principles contained in the Declaration were reconfirmed in the Millennium Declaration, UN GA Resolution 55/2 of 8 September 2000 and in the UN GA Resolution 60/1, *2005 World Summit Outcome*, and GAOR 60th Session Supp 49 vol. 1, 24 October 2005. See also Peaceful and Neighbourly Relations among States, UN doc. A/1236 (XII), 14 December 1957; Declaration on the Inadmissibility of Intervention in the Domestic Affairs of States and the Protection of their Independence and Sovereignty, UN doc. A/2131 (XX), 21 December 1965; Status of the Implementation of the Declaration on the Inadmissibility of Intervention in the Domestic Affairs of States and the Protection of their Independence and Security, UN doc. A/Res/2225 (XXI), 19 December 1966; Charter of Economic Rights and Duties of States, UN doc. A/Res/3281(XXIX), 12 December 1974; Declaration on the Establishment of the New International Economic Order, UN doc. A/Res/3201 (S-VI), 1 May 1974; Non-interference in the Internal Affairs of States, UN doc. A/Res/31/91, 14 December 1976; Noninterference in the Internal Affairs of States, UN docs. A/Res/32/153, 19 December 1977; A/Res/33/74, 15 December 1978; A/Res/34/101, 14 December 1979; A/Res/35/159, 12 December 1980; Declaration on the Inadmissibility of Intervention and Interference in the Internal Affairs of States, UN doc. A/Res/36/103, 9 December 1981.
176 UN GA Resolution 3016 (XXVII) on Permanent Sovereignty over Natural Resources of Developing Countries, 18 December 1972 (emphasis added).
177 It stated, *inter alia*, that '[a]ll States have the duty to conduct their mutual economic relations in a manner which takes into account the interest of other countries. In particular all States should avoid prejudicing the interests of developing countries.' A/Res/3281(XXIX), 1 May 1974.

1981 Declaration on the Inadmissibility of Intervention and Interference in the Internal Affairs of States referred to the duty of states to prevent the use of transnational corporations under its jurisdiction and control as instruments of political pressure or coercion against other states. Thus, the prohibition of economic coercion is one possible application of the principle of non-intervention, with bilateral programmes possibly falling within its scope.[178]

The General Assembly, the Commission on Human Rights, the Human Rights Council, as well as international conferences of the 1990s, produced a number of resolutions on the question of human rights and unilateral coercive measures.[179] The Vienna Declaration and Programme of Action on Human Rights declared that:

> The World Conference on Human Rights calls upon States to refrain from any unilateral measure not in accordance with international law and the Charter of the United Nations that creates obstacles to trade relations among States and impedes the full realization of the human rights set forth

178 B.E. Carter acknowledges that '[c]ategorization is not easy because, in part, States – as well as individuals, corporations, or other entities within these States – engage daily in a wide variety of international economic activity . . . [t]hese activities, however, can be grouped roughly into five major categories, as uses of or limits on: (a) bilateral government programmes, such as foreign assistance and aircraft landing rights; (b) exports from the sender State; (c) imports from the target country; (d) private financial transactions, such as on bank deposits and loans for trade or investment; and (e) the activities of international financial institutions ("IFIs"), such as the World Bank'. B.E. Carter, 'Economic Coercion', *Max Planck Encyclopaedia of International Law*, www.mpepil.com.

179 See for example for the latest one, UN GA Resolution Unilateral economic measures as a means of political and economic coercion against developing countries, A/RES/66/186, 6 February 2012; UN GA Resolution Human rights and unilateral coercive measures, A/RES/66/156, 20 March 2012; HRC, Human rights and unilateral coercive measures, A/HRC/RES/19/32, 19 April 2012. The tradition of these resolutions is long-standing and go back to the instruments specifically targeted on non-intervention: Economic Measures as a Means of Political and Economic Coercion against Developing Countries, UN docs. A/Res/39/210 (1984), A/Res/40/185 (1985), A/Res/41/165 (1986), A/Res/42/173 (1987), A/Res/44/215 (1989), A/Res/46/210 (1991), A/Res/48/168, (1993); Unilateral Economic Measures as a Means of Political and Economic Coercion against Developing Countries, UN docs. A/Res/52/181 (1997), A/Res/54/200 (1999), A/Res/56/179 (2001), A/Res/58/198 (2003), A/Res/60/185 (2005), A/Res/62/183 (2007); Respect for the Principles of National Sovereignty and Non-interference in the Internal Affairs of States in Electoral Processes, UN docs. A/RES/44/147 (1989), A/RES/45/151 (1990), A/RES/46/130 (1991), A/RES/47/130 (1992), A/RES/48/124 (1993), A/RES/50/172 (1995), A/RES/52/119 (1997), A/RES/54/168 (1999); Respect for the Principles of National Sovereignty and Non-interference in the Internal Affairs of States in Electoral Processes as an Important Element for the Promotion and Protection of Human Rights, UN doc. A/Res/56/154, 13 February 2002. On embargos on Cuba, see e.g. UN doc. A/RES/62/3, 30 October 2007, which was adopted by 184 votes to 4 (Israel, Marshall Islands, Palau, United States), with 1 abstention (Federated States of Micronesia) and three states absent (Albania, El Salvador, Iraq). For the debate see A/62/PV.38. The UN SC has affirmed the importance of non-interference in internal affairs: Resolution 1790 (2007).

in the Universal Declaration of Human Rights and international human rights instruments, in particular the rights of everyone to a standard of living adequate for their health and well-being, including food and medical care, housing and the necessary social services. The World Conference on Human Rights affirms that food should not be used as a tool for political pressure.[180]

Despite these enunciations in, strictly speaking, non-binding declarations (except for the 1970 Declaration), the prohibition of non-intervention has been rather narrowly construed in the jurisprudence as well as in the day-to-day practice of states.[181] The fact that economic sanctions are not prohibited and are imposed by states is a significant factor in an assessment of the issue. The ICJ, in response to the claims of Nicaragua that the United States had violated the principle of non-intervention through withdrawal of economic aid, reduction of quotas, and a trade embargo, held in the *Nicaragua* case that:

> While admitting in principle that some of these actions were not unlawful in themselves, counsel for Nicaragua argued that these measures of economic constraint add up to a systematic violation of the principle of non-intervention. At this point . . . the Court has merely to say that it is unable to regard such action on the economic plane as is here complained of as a breach of the customary-law principle of non-intervention.[182]

The conduct of the US that Nicaragua complained about, even if not qualified as a breach by the Court, is the most frequent and among 'the most effective methods of pressure', with potentially severe consequences[183] for states depending significantly on aid.[184] While a reading of the texts suggests that economic measures are not excluded from the scope of the non-intervention norm, the central element of the definition is the 'requirement of coercion'. Therefore, the actual problem is in constructing an argument 'that a state's sovereign will can be overborne through imposition of economic measures'.[185] In light of this, it could be that the Court in *Nicaragua* did not find that the actions amounted to a violation of the non-intervention prohibition, in view of the concrete circumstances of the case, while a different legal evaluation may be developed with regard to a different set of facts.

---

180 The Vienna Declaration and Programme of Action of the World Conference on Human Rights (1993), para. 31.
181 There is, however, a perception that in the Latin American region the issue has a normative character. This is due to the fact that Article 20 of the OAS Charter states: 'No State may use or encourage the use of coercive measures of an economic or political character in order to force the sovereign will of another State and obtain from it advantages of any kind.'
182 ICJ, *Military and Paramilitary Activities in und against Nicaragua (Nicaragua v. United States of America)*, Judgment, 27 June 1986, pp. 244–245.
183 M. Janejad and M. Wood, 'The Principle of Non-intervention', 22 *Leiden Journal of International Law* (2009), pp. 345–381, p. 370.
184 *Ibid.*, p. 371.
185 *Ibid.*, pp. 370–371.

The second component of the economic coercion concept is an intention to 'change some policies or practices or even its governmental structure' of the target state.[186] In relation to this criterion it is suggested to look at the practice of the IMF and the WB. Their decisions go very far towards changing the policy of states at many levels in dramatic ways. However, rarely are the actions of the IFIs regarded as intervention.[187] Nonetheless, a pertinent question remains as to whether recent applications of the policy adjustments in states facing severe economic crises may fall within the ambit of 'subordination of will' and thus amount to economic coercion.

The prohibition of non-intervention is too imprecise a notion to provide an answer as to whether the use of development aid to induce changes in the internal regulatory framework of the states, in disregard of their human rights obligations, violates the norm. Overall, in the context of the UN resolutions, referred to above, on unilateral coercive measures, one recurrent issue has been the imposition of an economic, commercial and financial embargo on Cuba by the US. Even though many states were opposed to the extraterritorial effects of such measures, they did not condemn the embargo as such. The EU, for example, while condemning the extraterritorial effects of the US actions, was of the view that the 'trade policy of the United States towards Cuba is fundamentally a bilateral issue'.[188]

The debate on the issue historically took place between developed and developing states, the former limiting the general prohibition of Article 2(4) of the UN Charter only to the use of military force, while the latter clearly saw economic coercion within the ambit of the norm. The second interpretation is problematic, as the proposal to include prohibition against economic coercion had been rejected in the drafting of the Charter.[189] Since the issue has been highly debated over the decades, the UN SG concluded that 'there is no clear consensus in international law as to when coercive measures are improper, despite relevant treaties, declarations, and resolutions adopted in international organizations which try to develop norms limiting the use of such measures'.[190] Perhaps the conditions imposed on the developing countries in exchange for development aid are the most difficult aspect of the economic coercion concept. As Detlev Chr. Dicke remarks, '[a]s long as the developing countries

---

186 A.F. Lowenfeld, *International Economic Law*, OUP: 2002, p. 698.
187 For a recent case study see Legal Brief Prepared for the Special Committee of the Hellenic Parliament on the Audit of the Greek Debt (Debt Truth Committee), Economic Policy Conditionality, Socio-Economic Rights and International Legal Responsibility: The Case of Greece 2010–2015, 15 June 2015 by Olivier De Schutter and Margot E. Salomon.
188 Necessity of ending the economic, commercial and financial embargo imposed by the United States of America against Cuba, UN GA 62nd session, 38th plenary meeting, 30 October 2007, p. 19.
189 UNCIO, *Documents of the United Nations Conference on International Organization*, Vol. 6, United Nations Information Organizations: 1945, p. 334.
190 UN GA, Economic Measures as a Means of Political and Economic Coercion against Developing Countries: Note by the Secretary–General, UN doc. A/48/535, 25 October 1993, Agenda Item 91(a), 1.

prefer – quite understandably – to receive aid rather than complaining publicly against ominous conditions, it will remain very difficult to achieve any progress in this field'.[191]

Assessment of the legality of economic measures can be said to be quintessentially context-specific, depending on the nature of the measures, applicable conventional and customary international law, and an assessment of circumstances precluding wrongfulness of such measures. It will not be irrelevant to suggest that in view of the controversies over the issue, some states have transferred the debate into the realm of human rights discourse.[192] A recent study of the Office of the High Commissioner on Human Rights, pursuant to Resolution 15/24 of the Human Rights Council, conducted a synthesis of issues on the topic of impact of unilateral coercive measures on the enjoyment of human rights, stating that 'it follows that unilateral coercive measures regardless of their legality under particular body of international law, may negatively impact human rights in various ways'.[193]

4 The practice of the CESCR on cross-border aspects of economic, social and cultural rights

4.1 Due diligence in human rights generally

The obligations of prevention in the field of human rights were elaborated in a more detailed manner by the practice of the UN Human Rights Committee[194] and

191 D. C. Dicke, 'The Concept of Economic Coercion: a Wrong in Itself', in P. J.I.M. de Waart, Dr P. Peters and E.M.G. Denters (eds), *International Law and Development*, Martinus Nijhoff Publishers: 1988, pp. 187–191, p. 190. Erik M.G. Denters: 'The relevance of public international law is also difficult to recognize when studying aspects of IMF conditionality. Available literature shows that conditionality is considered to belong mainly to the realm of economic and political sciences and most international lawyers have failed to identify conditionality as a legal concept. This attitude of aloofness may be one of the reasons why, apart from IMF instruments, there are no well defined principles of international law available that must be respected by the IMF in its relationship with States requesting access to the Fund's resources.' Erik M. G. Denters, 'IMF Conditionality: Economic, Social and Cultural Rights, and the Evolving Principle of Solidarity', in P. J.I.M. de Waart, Dr P. Peters and E.M.G. Denters (eds), *International Law and Development*, Martinus Nijhoff Publishers: 1988, pp. 235–243, p. 235.
192 See Annual Report of the Secretary General on human rights and unilateral coercive measures, UN doc. A/66/272, 5 August 2011.
193 Thematic Study of the Office of the United Nations High Commissioner for Human Rights on the impact of unilateral coercive measures on the enjoyment of human rights, including recommendations on actions aimed at ending such measures, UN doc. A/HRC/19/33, 11 January 2012, para. 4.
194 HRC, General Comment No. 31, para. 8: 'However the positive obligations on States Parties to ensure Covenant rights will only be fully discharged if individuals are protected by the State, not just against violations of Covenant rights by its agents, but also against acts committed by private persons or entities that would impair the enjoyment of Covenant rights in so far as they are amenable to application between private persons or entities. There

the CESCR in their General Comments.[195] Similarly, the European,[196] African[197] and Inter-American[198] human rights systems have contributed to the understanding of the obligation of due diligence in protection of human rights. The obligation of due diligence was extensively elaborated within the scope of the right to life, but also in relation to the prohibition of torture and inhuman and degrading treatment,[199] the rights to liberty and security of person,[200] the right to respect for private and family life, and the right to safe environment,[201] protection of children,[202]

---

may be circumstances in which a failure to ensure Covenant rights as required by article 2 would give rise to violations by States Parties of those rights, as a result of States Parties' permitting or failing to take appropriate measures or to exercise due diligence to prevent, punish, investigate or redress the harm caused by such acts by private persons or entities.' See also HRC, General Comment No. 6 on the Right to Life, 30 April 1982, paras. 3–4.

195 See the discussion in the following section.
196 Among others, the case law of the ECtHR includes *Osman v. UK*, Judgment of 28 October 1998, Reports 1998-VIII, paras. 115, 116; *Mahmut Kaya v. Turkey*, Judgment of 28 March 2000, Reports 2000-III, para. 101; *Kilic v. Turkey*, Judgment of 28 March 2000, Reports 2000-III, para. 76; *Paul and Audrey Edwards v. UK*, Judgment of 14 March 2002, Reports 2002-II, para. 56; *Keenan v. UK*, Judgment of 3 April 2001, Reports 2001-III, paras. 89–93; *Tais v. France*, Judgment of 1 June 2006, paras. 96, 98; *Mastromatteo v. Italy*, Judgment of 25 September 2002, Reports 2002-VIII, paras. 74–77; *McCann et al. v. UK*, Judgment of 27 September 1995, Series A No. 324, para. 212; *Ergi v. Turkey*, Judgment of 28 July 1998, Reports 1998-IV, paras. 79–81, 86; *Isayeva et al. v. Russia*, Judgment of 24 February 2005, No. 57950/00, paras. 170–171;
197 ACHPR, *Zimbabwe Human Rights NGO Forum v. Zimbabwe* (No. 245/2002), Fortieth Session, 15–29 November 2006, Twenty-First Activity Report of the African Commission on Human and Peoples' Rights, EX.CL/322 (X), p. 54, paras. 143, 146, 147.
198 IACtHR, *Neira Alegria et al. v. Peru*, Judgment of 19 January 1995, Series C. No. 20, paras. 65–76; *Velásquez-Rodriguez v. Honduras*, Judgment of 29 July 1988, Series C. No. 4, paras. 166, 172, 174, 175; *Godínez Cruz v. Honduras*, Judgment of 20 January 1989, Series C. No. 5, paras. 175–186; *The 19 Tradesmen v. Colombia*, Judgment of 5 July 2004, Series C. No. 109, paras. 152–156.
199 Examples of jurisprudence include: ECtHR, *Z et al. v. UK*, Judgment of 10 May 2001, Reports 2001-V, para. 73; *Mahmut Kaya v. Turkey*, Judgment 28 March 2000, Reports 2000-III, para. 115; *Ilascu et al. v. Moldova and Russia*, Judgment of 8 July 2004, Reports 2004-VII, paras. 313, 331; From the case law of IACtHR, examples include: IACtHR, *Velásquez Rodríguez v. Honduras*, Judgment of 29 July 1988, Series C. No. 4, para. 187; *Godínez Cruz v. Honduras*, Judgment of 20 January 1989, Series C. No. 5, para. 197; *Tibi v. Ecuador*, Judgment of 7 September 2004, Series C. No. 114, paras. 142–162; *The 'Juvenile Reeducation Institute' v. Paraguay*, Judgment of 2 September 2004, Series C. No. 112, para. 151 et seq.
200 ECtHR, *Kurt v. Turkey*, Judgment of 25 May 1998, *Reports* 1998-III; *Anguelova v. Bulgaria*, Judgment of 13 June 2002, Reports, 2002-IV; *Orhan c. Turquie*, Judgment of 18 June 2002, www.echr.coe.int/echr; *Kurt v. Turkey*, Judgment of 25 May 1998, Reports 1998-III, para. 124; HRC, *Delgado Páez v. Colombia* (195/1985), Communication of 12 July 1990, Report 1990, pp. 49, para. 5.5.
201 ECtHR, *Powell and Rayner v. UK*, Judgment of 21 February 1990, Series A. No. 172; *López Ostra v. Spain*, Judgment 19 December 1994, Series A. No. 303-C; *Hatton et al. v. UK*, Judgment of 2 October 2001, www.echr.coe.int/echr, para. 97.
202 HRC, *Mónaco de Gallicchio v. Argentina* (400/1990), Communication of 3 April 1995, Report 1995, pp. 10 et seq, para. 10.5; *Thomas v. Jamaica* (800/1998), Communication of 8 April 1999, Report 1999, pp. 287 et seq., para. 6.6.

freedom of expression and assembly,[203] etc. The practice of the Inter-American Court (IACtHR) is particularly interesting, as it has adopted a broad approach in defining the content of the due diligence obligations in relation to the right to life to encompass the creation of decent conditions of life in the case of *Street Children*.[204] For example, in the case of *Street Children*, with reference to Article 4 of the American Convention, the IACtHR held that:

> In essence, the fundamental right to life includes not only the right of every human being not to be deprived of his life arbitrarily, but also the right that he will not be prevented from having *access to the conditions that guarantee a dignified existence*. States have the obligation to guarantee the creation of the conditions required in order that violations of this basic right do not occur and, in particular, the duty to prevent its agents from violating it. [emphasis added]

In this case, the Court, with reference to Article 19 on the rights of the child, found a violation in particular when states 'do not prevent them [e.g. children] from living in misery, thus depriving them of the minimum conditions for a dignified life and preventing them from the "full and harmonious development of their personality", even though every child has the right to harbour a project of life that should be tended and encouraged by the public authorities so that it may develop this project for its personal benefit and that of the society to which it belongs'.[205] Similarly, in the case of the *Yakye Axa Indigenous Community*, the Court confirmed that the right to life comprises 'not only the right of every human being not to be arbitrarily deprived of his life, but also the right that conditions that impede or obstruct access to a decent existence', and that the state has an obligation of 'generating minimum living conditions that are compatible with the dignity of the human person and of not creating conditions that hinder or impede it'.[206] The Court went on to conclude that the right to life has been abridged 'for not taking measures regarding the conditions that affected their possibility of having a decent life'.[207]

These cases of course included circumstances concerning the behaviour of states within their respective borders. The idea of obligations to adopt measures

203 ECtHR, *Özgür Gündem v. Turkey*, Judgment 16 March 2000, Reports 2000-III, para. 43; ECtHR, *Plattform 'Ärzte für das Leben' v. Austria*, Judgment 21 June 1988, Series A. No. 139, para. 32.

204 IACtHR, *Case of the 'Street Children' (Villagrán-Morales et al.) v. Guatemala*, Judgment of 19 November 1999, Series C. No. 63, para. 144.

205 *Ibid.*, para. 191.

206 IACtHR, *The Yakye Axa Indigenous Community v. Paraguay*, Judgment of 17 June 2005, Series C. No. 125, paras. 161–162.

207 *Ibid.*, para. 176. In the practice of the ECHR, certain cases can be identified where the protection of the right to life implied prevention of dangers to health of a person. These include *L.C.B. v. UK*, Judgment of 9 June 1998, Reports 1998-III, para. 36; *Velikova v. Bulgaria*, Judgment of 18 May 2000, Reports 2000-VI; *Anguelova v. Bulgaria*, Judgment of 13 June 2002, Reports 2002-IV.

to prevent violations of human rights in a cross-border context has been recently confirmed by the ICJ in the *Genocide* case[208] as well as in the case of the *DRC v. Uganda*.[209] The first case is remarkable, as the Court for the first time discussed in detail the duty to prevent human rights violations taking place abroad.[210]

While the court in this case cautioned that its decision applied only to the Genocide Convention,[211] the merit of the pronouncement is that the Court drew a distinction between the duty to prevent and the duty of repression of the crime by stating that the former obligation is 'both normative and compelling' and 'has its own scope', i.e. is a primary obligation.[212] Even though the case concerned

208 ICJ, *Application of the Convention on the Prevention and Punishment of the Crime of Genocide (Bosnia and Herzegovina v. Serbia and Montenegro)*, Judgment, ICJ Reports 2007, para. 430.

209 ICJ, *Armed Activities on the Territory of the Congo (Congo v. Uganda)*, ICJ Judgment, 19 December 2005, paras. 209–211.

210 The Court's assessment of the issues was the following: 'In this area the notion of "due diligence", which calls for an assessment *in concreto*, is of critical importance. Various parameters operate when assessing whether a State has duly discharged the obligation concerned. The first, which varies greatly from one State to another, is clearly the capacity to influence effectively the action of persons likely to commit, or already committing, genocide. This capacity itself depends, among other things, on the geographical distance of the State concerned from the scene of the events, and on the strength of the political links, as well as links of all other kinds, between the authorities of that State and the main actors in the events. The State's capacity to influence must also be assessed by legal criteria, since it is clear that every State may only act within the limits permitted by international law; seen thus, a State's capacity to influence may vary depending on its particular legal position vis-à-vis the situations and persons facing the danger, or the reality, of genocide. On the other hand, it is irrelevant whether the State whose responsibility is in issue claims, or even proves, that even if it had employed all means reasonably at its disposal, they would not have sufficed to prevent the commission of genocide. As well as being generally difficult to prove, this is irrelevant to the breach of the obligation of conduct in question, the more so since the possibility remains that the combined efforts of several States, each complying with its obligation to prevent, might have achieved the result – averting the commission of genocide – which the efforts of only one State were insufficient to produce.' ICJ, *Application of the Convention on the Prevention and Punishment of the Crime of Genocide (Bosnia and Herzegovina v. Serbia and Montenegro)*, Judgment, ICJ Reports 2007, para. 430. See e.g. the discussions in C. Ryngaert, 'Jurisdiction: Towards Reasonableness Test', in M. Langford W. Vandenhole, M. Scheinin and W. van Genugten (eds), *Global Justice, State Duties: The Extraterritorial Scope of Economic, Social and Cultural Rights in International Law*, CUP: 2013, p. 203.

211 It held that it 'does not . . . purport to establish a general jurisprudence applicable to all cases where a treaty instrument, or other binding legal norm, includes an obligation for States to prevent certain acts. Still less does the decision of the Court purport to find whether, apart from the texts applicable to specific fields, there is a general obligation on States to prevent the commission by other persons or entities of acts contrary to certain norms of general international law.' It stressed that it will instead 'confine itself to determining the specific scope of the duty to prevent in the Genocide Convention, and to the extent that such a determination is necessary to the decision to be given on the dispute before it'. *Application of the Convention on the Prevention and Punishment of the Crime of Genocide (Bosnia and Herzegovina v. Serbia and Montenegro), op. cit.*, para. 429.

212 The full paragraph reads as follows: 'The obligation on each contracting State to prevent genocide is both normative and compelling. It is not merged in the duty to punish, nor

an obligation in the context of genocide, many commentators are of the view that the Court has provided a useful test of general application as, first, the case in point relates to a human rights violation and, second, the context in which due diligence has been applied is extraterritorial. As is generally the case with due diligence obligations, its application is context-specific and requires different measures in different circumstances. While in the words of the Court, 'various parameters' operate in this regard, the Court gave examples of these parameters, including the 'capacity of the State to influence'. As the Court highlighted, this capacity to influence varies; it therefore provided elements such as geographical distance of the state concerned from the scene of the events and on the strength of links of all other kinds. In this context, the Court further notes that 'a State's capacity to influence may vary depending on its particular legal position vis-à-vis the situations and persons facing the danger, or the reality, of genocide'.[213]

4.2 The practice of the Committee on Economic, Social and Cultural Rights

The text of the International Covenant on Economic, Social and Cultural Rights does not incorporate the general obligation to ensure all rights enshrined in the Covenant, as is the case with the International Covenant on Civil and Political Rights. In contrast, the Convention on the Rights of the Child as well as the Convention on the Rights of Persons with Disabilities, which encompass both civil and political rights, and economic, social and cultural rights, require States Parties to 'ensure' the rights enshrined therein.[214] Notwithstanding the quality of 'progressive realization' being attached to socio-economic rights generally, the CESCR has iterated in its interpretations of various rights the obligation of prevention and protection, including the principle of *sic utere laedas*.

The Committee was the main vehicle to try to transcribe the broadly formulated provisions of the Covenant. It has provided some clarifications on the content of norms relevant to the development process, fleshing out elements of negative obligations, as well as identifying positive obligations to protect human rights. In the previous chapter on international assistance and cooperation for

---

can it be regarded as simply a component of that duty. It has its own scope, which extends beyond the particular case envisaged in Article VIII, namely reference to the competent organs of the United Nations, for them to take such action as they deem appropriate. Even if and when these organs have been called upon, this does not mean that the States parties to the Convention are relieved of the obligation to take such action as they can to prevent genocide from occurring, while respecting the United Nations Charter and any decisions that may have been taken by its competent organs.' *Ibid.*, para. 427.

213 ICJ, *Application of the Convention on the Prevention and Punishment of the Crime of Genocide (Bosnia and Herzegovina v. Serbia and Montenegro)*, Judgment, ICJ Reports 2007, para. 430.

214 Article 1 of the Convention on the Rights of Persons with Disabilities stipulates: 'The purpose of the present Convention is to promote, protect and ensure the full and equal enjoyment of all human rights and fundamental freedoms by all persons with disabilities, and to promote respect for their inherent dignity.'

human rights, it was pointed out that the obligation of assistance and cooperation, as envisaged by Article 2(1) of the Covenant, can hardly be regarded as a
self-standing and independent obligation. However, the approach taken by the
Committee on Economic, Social and Cultural Rights as well as a number of commentators has been different on the issue.

While initially the Committee described the nature of obligations under
international assistance and cooperation in terms of positive actions, later it
expanded its scope and content to include the obligation to prevent harm
and to exercise due diligence.[215] As concluded previously in this writing, in so
doing, the Committee seems to construe a complex argument on the basis of a
number of legal sources. At first, the Committee adopted the approach of the
ILC, focusing on the obligations of conduct and result,[216] but later it adopted
the tripartite typology of obligations to respect, protect and fulfil.[217] The contours of the obligations prescribed by the Committee are not so precise. Some
indication can be found through analysis of a number of its general comments
on the Covenant.

The obligation to respect, as meaning the duty to abstain from depriving someone from a right he or she already enjoys, was raised with regard to the work of
the UN specialized agencies. According to the Committee, 'international agencies' are to avoid any involvement in projects which are in contravention with
human rights standards.[218] In relation to development cooperation activities, the
Committee has advised UN agencies 'to do their utmost to ensure that their
activities are fully consistent' with the enjoyment of human rights.[219] Obligations
prescribed here by the Committee are clearly obligations of prevention:

> Every effort should be made, at each phase of a development project, to
> ensure that the rights contained in the Covenants are duly taken into account.
> This would apply, for example, in the initial assessment of the priority needs

---

215 CESCR, General Comment No. 3, The Nature of States Parties' Obligations, UN doc.
E/1991/23, 14 December 1990, para. 14, cited in full in Chapter IV.

216 *Ibid.*, para. 1, which reads: 'Article 2 is of particular importance to a full understanding of
the Covenant and must be seen as having a dynamic relationship with all of the other provisions of the Covenant. It describes the nature of the general legal obligations undertaken
by States parties to the Covenant. Those obligations include both what may be termed
(following the work of the International Law Commission) obligations of conduct and
obligations of result.'

217 CESCR, General Comment No. 12, The Right to Adequate Food, UN doc. E/CN.12/
1999/5, 12 May 1999.

218 Comment No. 2, para. 6 stipulates *inter alia*: 'In negative terms this means that the international agencies should scrupulously avoid involvement in projects which, for example,
involve the use of forced labour in contravention of international standards, or promote
or reinforce discrimination against individuals or groups contrary to the provisions of the
Covenant, or involve large scale evictions or displacement of persons without the provision
of all appropriate protection and compensation.' CESCR, General Comment No. 2, International Technical Assistance Measures, UN doc. E/1990/23, 2 February 1990, para. 6.

219 *Ibid.*

of a particular country, in the identification of particular projects, in project design, in the implementation of the project, and in its final evaluation.[220]

Concrete content of due diligence standards in this respect are not yet elaborated. The Committee has developed the obligation to respect in relation to the right to housing,[221] including in the context of international technical assistance measures, the right to food,[222] the right to health[223] and the right to water. In particular in relation to rights to food, health, and water, it has explicitly referred, with varying degrees of language, to the obligation to 'respect' in 'other countries'. In addition to this, resolutions of the United Nations General Assembly on the right to food indicate that the right to adequate food requires 'the adoption of appropriate environmental and social policies, at both the national and international levels, oriented to the eradication of poverty and the fulfilment of human rights for all', and provide that 'all States should make all efforts to ensure that their international policies of a political and economic nature, including international trade agreements, do not have a negative impact on the right to food in other countries'.[224] In relation to the right to health, states are 'to prevent third parties from violating the right in other countries, if they are able to influence these third parties by way of legal or political means'.[225] In the context of the right to water:

> [t]o comply with their international obligations in relation to right to water, States parties *have to respect* the enjoyment of the right in other countries . . .

---

220 *Ibid.*, para. 8.
221 On the Right to Adequate Housing, the Committee among others referred to '[i]nternational financial institutions promoting measures of structural adjustment should ensure that such measures do not compromise the enjoyment of the right to adequate housing. States parties should, when contemplating international financial cooperation, seek to indicate areas relevant to the right to adequate housing where external financing would have the most effect'. CESCR, General Comment No. 4, The Right to Adequate Housing, contained in document UN doc. E/1992/23, 13 December 1991, para. 19.
222 The CESCR, on the Right to Food, stated: 'In implementing commitment [to take joint and separate action within international assistance and cooperation], *States parties should take steps to respect* the enjoyment of the right to food in other countries, to protect that right, to facilitate access to food and to provide the necessary aid when required.' CESCR, General Comment No. 12, The Right to Adequate Food, UN doc. E/CN.12/1999/5, 12 May 1999, para. 36.
223 The Committee referred to: 'States parties *have to respect* the enjoyment of the right to health in other countries, and to prevent third parties from violating the right in other countries, if they are able to influence these third parties by way of legal or political means, in accordance with the Charter of the United Nations and applicable international law.' CESCR, General Comment No. 14, The Right to the Highest Attainable Standard of Health, UN doc. E/C.12/2000/4, 11 August 2000, para. 39.
224 For example, UN GA Resolution 64/159 on the Right to Food (adopted without a vote), UN doc. A/RES/64/159, 10 March 2010, paras. 20 and 32.
225 CESCR, General Comment No. 14, The right to the highest attainable standard of health, UN doc. E/C.12/2000/4, 11 August 2000, para. 39.

> Any activities undertaken within the State party's jurisdiction should not deprive another country of the ability to realize the right to water for persons in its jurisdiction.[226]

This paragraph is more elaborate than other comments, as it also defines that '[i]nternational cooperation requires States Parties to refrain from actions that interfere, directly or indirectly, with the enjoyment of the right to water in other countries'.[227] Additionally, the CESCR, with respect to the right to water, stressed that 'water should never be used as an instrument of political and economic pressure'.[228] Apart from general formulas of the duty to respect, the Committee gave examples of instances of how States should perform their obligation of prevention. For instance, 'States parties should, in international agreements whenever relevant, ensure that the right to adequate food is given due attention and consider the development of further international legal instruments to that end.'[229] Even if the Committee chose to employ the cautious language with references such as 'obligation' to give 'due attention and consider', what it essentially did is to reiterate here the principle *lex prior derogat legi posteriori*. It is helpful to recall that the European Commission of Human Rights in 1958 already reiterated this general rule by stating that:

> it is clear that, if a State contracts treaty obligations and subsequently concludes another international agreement which disables it from performing its obligations under the first treaty, it will be answerable for any resulting breach of its obligations under the earlier treaty.[230]

A more forceful enunciation has been formulated by Judge Weeramantry in his Separate Opinion, in the *Gabčíkovo-Nagymaros Case*: 'Treaties that affect human rights cannot be applied in such a manner as to constitute denial of human rights human rights as understood at the time of their application.'[231] Equally, 'the same inter-temporal rule is also applicable as regards international human rights customary rules'.[232] At this point, it is to be recalled that the former World

226 CESCR, General Comment No. 15, The Right to Water, UN doc. E/C.12/2002/11, 20 January 2003, para. 31 (emphasis added).
227 *Ibid.*
228 *Ibid.*, para. 32.
229 CESCR, General Comment No. 12, The Right to Adequate Food, UN doc. E/CN.12/1999/5, 12 May 1999 and CESCR, General Comment No. 14, The Right to the Highest Attainable Standard of Health, UN doc. E/C.12/2000/4, 11 August 2000, para. 39.
230 ECommHR, Decision no 235/56 of 10 June 1958, Yearbook 2, 256, p. 300.
231 ICJ, *Gabčíkovo-Nagymaros Project (Hungary–Slovakia)*, Judgment, ICJ Reports 1997, Separate Opinion of Judge Weeramantry, p. 7.
232 P.-M. Dupuy, 'Unification Rather than Fragmentation of International Law? The case of International Investment Law and Human Rights Law', in P.-M. Dupuy, F. Francioni and E.-U. Petersmann (eds), *Human Rights in International Investment Arbitration*, OUP: 2009, p. 54

Bank General Counsel, Ibrahim Shihata, when discussing obligations of states under the UN Charter, opined that obligations of Member States under the UN Charter prevail over their other treaty obligations, including those under the Bank's Articles of Agreement, by virtue of an explicit provision reflected in Article 103 of the UN Charter.[233]

The Committee also addressed obligations of states acting in the capacity of members of international organizations such as the IMF and WB, encouraging a State Party 'to do all it can to ensure that the policies and decisions of those organizations are in conformity with the obligations of States parties to the Covenant, in particular the obligations contained in articles 2 (1), 11, 15, 22 and 23 concerning international assistance and cooperation'.[234] The 'do no harm' obligation has been raised in the context of sanctions. The standards developed by the Committee in relation to sanctions are relevant to development cooperation, as aid also falls within the ambit of economic sanctions.[235] The obligation to protect 'at least the core content of the economic, social and cultural rights' of individuals in the targeted state according to the Committee derives from the UN Charter obligations. The Committee further makes the following comment:

> When the affected State is also a State party, it is doubly incumbent upon other States to respect and take account of the relevant obligations. To the extent that sanctions are imposed on States which are not parties to the Covenant, the same principles would in any event apply given the status of the economic, social and cultural rights of vulnerable groups as part of general international law, as evidenced, for example, by the near-universal ratification of the Convention on the Rights of the Child and the status of the Universal Declaration of Human Rights.

---

233 I.F.I. Shihata, *The World Bank Legal Papers*, Martinus Nijhoff Publishers: 2000, p. 266.
234 See e.g. Concluding Observations: Italy, UN doc. E/2001/22, para. 126, where the CESCR encouraged the Government of Italy 'as a member of international organizations, in particular IMF and the World Bank, to do all it can to ensure that the policies and decisions of those organizations are in conformity with the obligations of States parties to the Covenant, in particular the obligations contained in article 2, paragraph 1, concerning international assistance and cooperation'. In Concluding Observations Belgium, UN doc. E/2001/22, para. 493, the Committee reproduced the recommendation it had made in relation to Italy, while with respect to Japan, it opted for the word 'urge' instead of 'encourage', and in addition to the obligations contained in Article 2(1), it referred to Articles 11, 15, 22 and 23. Government Concluding Observations Japan, UN doc. E/C.12/1/Add.67, para. 37; see also Concluding Observations: Germany, UN doc. E7 C.12/1/Add.68, para. 31.
235 The CESCR's view is that economic sanctions have a dramatic impact upon rights recognized by the ICESCR: 'Thus, for example, they often cause significant disruption in the distribution of food, pharmaceuticals and sanitation supplies, jeopardize the quality of food and the availability of clean drinking water, severely interfere with the functioning of basic health and education systems, and undermine the right to work.' CESCR, General Comment No. 8, Economic Sanctions and Economic, Social and Cultural Rights, UN doc. E/C.12/1997/8, 12 December 1997, para. 3.

As De Schutter has pointed out, the reference to '*doubly*' incumbent upon other states, would 'seem to betray a certain hesitation among the members of the Committee about whether the obligations of the States adopting sanctions have their source in the international undertakings of those States, or instead in the rights recognized to the population of the targeted State. The reality, however, is that it can be both, and both at the same time.'[236]

With respect to the state or group of states responsible for imposition, maintenance or implementation of the sanctions, the Committee made three conclusions that 'follow logically from the recognition of economic, social and cultural human rights'.[237] One is that ESC rights 'must be taken fully into account when designing an appropriate sanctions regime'. The CESCR did not prescribe any particular measure; however, it listed some possible actions.[238] The second is the monitoring of the situation of ESC rights, as '[w]hen an external party takes upon itself even partial responsibility for the situation within a country (whether under Chapter VII of the Charter or otherwise), it also unavoidably assumes a responsibility to do all within its power to protect the economic, social and cultural rights of the affected population'.[239]

In relation to development cooperation, the Committee stated that socio-economic rights include core obligations derived from 'minimum essential levels' of the rights to food, education and health, which it considered 'non-derogable' and which it found to give rise to international responsibilities:

> Thus, according to the Committee, the core obligations of economic, social and cultural rights have a crucial role to play in national and international developmental policies, including anti-poverty strategies. When grouped together, the core obligations establish an international minimum threshold that all developmental policies should be designed to respect. In accordance with General Comment No. 14, it is particularly incumbent on all those who can assist, to help developing countries respect this international minimum threshold. If a national or international anti-poverty strategy does not reflect this minimum threshold, it is inconsistent with the legally binding obligations of the State party.[240]

---

236 O. De Schutter, *International Human Rights Law: Cases, Materials, Commentary, op. cit.*, p. 166.
237 CESCR, General Comment No. 8, Economic Sanctions and Economic, Social and Cultural Rights, UN doc. E/C.12/1997/8, 12 December 1997, paras. 10–14. It concluded that these rights should be fully taken into account when designing a sanction regime, putting in place an effective monitoring and response to any disproportionate suffering experienced by the vulnerable groups in the targeted group through international assistance and cooperation.
238 *Ibid.*, para. 17.
239 *Ibid.*, para. 18.
240 CESCR, Poverty and the International Covenant on Economic, Social and Cultural Rights: Statement of the Committee to the Third United Nations Conference on the Least Developed Countries (25th session; E/2002/22-E/C.12/2001/17, annex VII), paras. 16–17.

On many occasions, in its dialogue on state reporting, the Committee had enquired 'as to whether the State party, as a member of international financial organizations, in particular the International Monetary Fund and the World Bank, does all it can to ensure that the policies and decisions of those organizations are in conformity with the obligations of States parties to the Covenant'.[241] With respect to the right to work, more elaborate clarifications were provided:

> States parties that are members of international financial institutions, in particular the International Monetary Fund, the World Bank and regional development banks, should pay greater attention to the protection of the right to work in influencing the lending policies, credit agreements, structural adjustment programmes and international measures of these institutions. The strategies, programmes and policies adopted by States parties under structural adjustment programmes should not interfere with their core obligations in relation to the right to work and impact negatively on the right to work of women, young persons and the disadvantaged and marginalized individuals and groups.[242]

Within the framework of 'international obligations' of States Parties, obligations of due diligence were also referred to in General Comment No. 14 on the right to health. This Comment stipulates that states have to take measures 'to prevent third parties from violating the right in other countries, if they are able to influence these third parties by way of legal or political means, in accordance with the Charter of the United Nations and applicable international law'.[243] States must prevent their own citizens and companies from violating the right to water of individuals and communities in other countries.[244]

The obligation of prevention also encompasses the bilateral and multilateral negotiations settings as indicated above in the framework of protection of the right to work.[245] Due attention should be given to the right to water in

---

241 See the list of issues to be taken up in connection with the consideration of the third periodic report of the Netherlands UN doc. E/C.12/NLD/Q/3, para. 4. The CESCR raised one, both or all three issues above in relation to Italy, Austria, Finland, Netherlands, Belgium, France, Sweden, UK, Australia, Switzerland, New Zealand and Spain reports. Replies to the Committee's questions include Italy (HR/CESCR/NONE/2004/3), Finland (E/C.12/FIN/Q/5/Add.1), Netherlands (E/C.12/NLD/Q/3/Add.1), Belgium (E/C.12/BEL/Q/3/Add.1), Sweden (E/C.12/SWE/Q/5/Add.1), UK (E/C.12/GBR/Q/5/Add.1), Australia (E/C.12/AUS/Q/4/Add.1), Switzerland (E/C.12/CHE/Q/2–3/Add.1), New Zealand (E/C.12/NZL/Q/3/Add.1), Spain (E/C.12/ESP/Q/5/Add.1).
242 CESCR, General Comment No. 18, The Right to Work, UN doc. E/C.12/GC/18, 6 February 2006, para. 30.
243 CESCR, General Comment No. 14, The Right to the Highest Attainable Standard of Health, UN doc. E/C.12/2000/4, 11 August 2000, para. 39.
244 CESCR, General Comment No. 15, The Right to Water, UN doc. E/C.12/2002/11, 20 January 2003, para. 33.
245 General Comment 18 on the Right to Work, para. 30, which stipulates: 'To comply with their international obligations in relation to article 6 [right to work], States parties should endeavour to promote the right to work in other countries as well as in bilateral and multilateral negotiations.'

international agreements and in relation to the conclusion and implementation of other international and regional agreements. When entering into these international obligations, States Parties should take steps to ensure that these instruments do not adversely impact upon the right to water.[246] In its preceding statements, the CESCR required or encouraged states to 'ensure' or to 'do all [they] can', as well as to influence third parties 'by way of legal or political means', 'if they are able to'. This clearly confirms the obligation of best efforts.

The above review demonstrates that the Committee has integrated and emphasized the component of prevention at the very centre of the realization of socio-economic rights in an international context. It had used the obligation of cooperation and assistance as a principle guiding its interpretation and systematization of law. It can be asserted that the principle of due diligence is steadily emerging as a relevant legal tool in the realm of activities of states, with a potential negative impact on human rights. The credit for adapting the well-established principle of international law as earlier noted goes mainly to the Committee and to the academic commentary,[247] but as Professor Dupuy and Cristina Hoss point out, 'the very nature of the general due diligence obligation is to offer the necessary flexibility to respond to most of the potential conflicts between the states'.[248]

Despite the progress achieved, the scope and content of an obligation to prevent harm on ESC rights in the cross-border context is still very abstract. The Committee so far has provided examples of settings where the obligation to avoid causing harm to ESC rights should be exercised. What has not been sufficiently developed are the means or content of due diligence obligations. Relevant parameters include only broad requirements 'to do the utmost' or 'to do all it can', 'give due attention' or 'consider development of legal instruments' to ensure compliance at least with a minimum threshold of socio-economic rights. Although states have often been advised to conduct human rights impact assessments in the area of trade and investment,[249] only the Committee

---

246   See also the General Comment No. 15 on the Right to Water, para. 35, where the CESCR also stated that '[a]greements concerning trade liberalization should not curtail or inhibit a country's capacity to ensure the full realization of the right to water'.

247   S. Skogly, *Beyond National Borders: Beyond National Borders: States' Human Rights Obligations in International Cooperation, op. cit.*

248   P.-M. Dupuy and C. Hoss, 'Trail Smelter and Terrorism: International Mechanisms to Combat Transboundary Harm', in R. Bratspies and R. Miller (eds), *Transboundary Harm in International Law: Lessons from the Trail Smelter Arbitration*, CUP: 2006, p. 206.

249   Committee on Economic, Social and Cultural Rights, Concluding observations: Ecuador, UN doc. E/C.12/1/Add.100, para. 56; Committee on the Rights of the Child, Concluding observations: El Salvador, UN doc. CRC/C/15/Add.232, para. 48; Committee on the Elimination of Discrimination against Women, Concluding observations: Colombia, UN doc. CEDAW/C/COL/CO/6, para. 29; Concluding observation: the Philippines, UN doc. CEDAW/C/PHI/CO/6, para. 26; and Concluding observations: Guatemala, UN doc. CEDAW/C/GUA/CO/6, para. 32; Report of the Special Rapporteur on the right to food, O. De Schutter on his mission to the World Trade Organization, UN doc. A/HRC/10/5/Add.2, 4 February 2009, paras. 37–38.

on the Rights of the Child has provided an explicit statement of the general requirement of impact assessments including in the design of the development policies.[250]

Sector-specific guidelines on human rights impact assessments of trade and investment agreements, as well as business and human rights, provide some elements that could contribute to the consolidation of an effective device to map out risks, given there is little overall on the issue and its relationship with states obligations under the Covenant.[251] To date, there has been no systematic discussion of the human rights impact assessments in the development process – a subject that seems to be warranted for an obligation of prevention to become operative.[252] Human rights indicators framework, developed only recently, lays the groundwork for further elaboration of impact assessments.[253]

5 The practical application of the obligation 'do no harm'

Having ascertained that, as a minimum, development policies and practices are to avoid causing damage to the socio-economic rights of individuals and that international law provides a firm basis for this, the next issue to address is to map out challenges to the operationalization of this basic requirement. It is often assumed by doctrine that the obligation of abstention or the duty to respect human rights is quite straightforward – i.e. unproblematic. It is also said that prohibitive norms (what states should not do) are easier to identify and comply with. The discussion that follows aims to demonstrate that these basic premises need further qualification when applied to the development context. It sets out insufficiencies both in human rights on the one hand and development on the other, the tackling of which constitutes a prerequisite for devising an operational '*do no harm*' framework for the development context.

---

250 CRC, General Comment 05 (2003), General Measures of Implementation for the Convention on the Rights of the Child, CRC/GC/2003/5, para. 45.
251 Guiding principles on human rights impact assessments of trade and investment agreements, Report of the Special Rapporteur on the right to food, Olivier De Schutter, UN doc. A/HRC/19/59/Add.5, 11 December 2011; Guiding Principles on Business and Human Rights: Implementing the United Nations 'Protect, Respect and Remedy' Framework, UN doc. A/HRC/17/31, 21 March 2011.
252 In 1979, the UN Secretary General proposed, *inter alia*, to consider requiring a '"human rights impact statement" . . . to be undertaken prior to the commencement of specific development projects or in connexion with the preparation of an overall development plan or programme'. The International Dimensions of the Right to Development as a Human Right in relation with other Human Rights based on International Cooperation, including the Right to Peace, taking into account the Requirements of the New International Economic Order and the Fundamental Human Needs, Report of the Secretary-General, UN doc. E/CN.4/1334 (1979), para. 314.
253 OHCHR, *Human Rights Indicators: A Guide to Measurement and Implementation*, UN: 2012.

5.1 The challenge of identifying human rights harm in the development process

The starting point is that operationalization of the broad-based requirement of the 'do no harm' principle needs to take into account the complex relationships and processes development entails. First and foremost, a clear understanding of the ways development generates risks needs to be established. Certainly, determination of the extent to which development policy and activity interferes with or causes harm to human rights would depend on the particular facts, as well as to considerations of causation. But demonstration of a foundation in fact of human rights concerns over development interventions is something that human rights analysis will often struggle with.

To begin with, due to the complexity of the development architecture,[254] there is no established perception of how to calibrate and manage the human rights risks it generates. In fact, human rights analysis is sparse beyond the project-based model of development. The locus of human rights risks may include development cooperation at macro (international) and meso (national) levels.[255] Macro-level development planning is not easy to understand, as its scope can potentially be very expansive.[256] It is a well-known fact that at this level, development planning is an internationalized process 'to such an extent that national sovereignty (economic or developmental) no longer constitutes an operative concept for most developing countries'.[257]

What characterizes development cooperation is the great distance between the original providers of funds and the designers of policy, and the final situation at the level of people affected by such policies and measures. Between the donors and individuals of developing countries, a great many organizations work in the field of development.[258] These many organizations include aid organizations (public,

254 As Degnbol-Martinussen and Engberg-Pedersen state, 'the dialogue between donor and recipient changed from being mostly a technical dialogue about capital, technology and organization, to an all-encompassing political dialogue about the structure of society and management of society's development processes'. J. Degnbol-Martinussen and P. Engberg-Pedersen, *Aid: Understanding International Development Cooperation*, 2nd edition, Zed-Books: 2005, p. 41.

255 For example, one of the outcomes of the aid effectiveness discourse is that policy-oriented development cooperation has become a 'norm', which meant the majority of development cooperation activities aim at reform and restructuring of different sectors in the recipient state. C. Tan, 'Evolving Aid Modalities and their Impact on the Delivery of Essential Services in Low-Income Countries', *Law, Social Justice and Global Development*, 5 October 2005, p. 4

256 The MDGs and particularly the Monterrey Consensus recognize trade, investment and debt, among others, as 'vital components' of national and international development efforts.

257 K. Tomasevski, 'Monitoring Human Rights Aspects of Sustainable Development', *op. cit.*, p. 87.

258 See the discussion of 'Actors in Aid Interaction' in J. Degnbol-Martinussen and P. Engberg-Pedersen, *Aid: Understanding International Development Cooperation, op. cit.*, pp. 174–199.

private) in the donor countries that manage funds; private enterprises and organizations; multilateral organizations; international NGOs; administrations in the recipient countries that integrate aid into national planning, budgeting, implementation and accounting;[259] ministries and organizations in central and local administrations receiving and using aid; project implementation units; local organizations in developing countries receiving aid and/or participating in the implementation of projects; etc. All these actors can be implicated in one process (for example, reforming the justice sector, or combating malnutrition). Where the origins of harm are dispersed among many development actors, trying to single out a causal nexus and attributing responsibility to an individual development actor can be complicated.

Furthermore, in between the failings of development and the harmful effects felt at an individual and/or collective level, there are layers of complexity related to the economic, fiscal, monetary processes and forms, and extraterritorial effects of the domestic socio-economic policies and activities. The composite, multilayered character of causality involved across the development cooperation setting and the difficulty of attributing the genesis of negative impact to any individual donor/actor is a challenge to standard techniques and analysis of attribution of responsibility for human rights abuses. It is possible that the multidimensional nature of the problem may not fit neatly within the traditional human rights framework of obligations to respect and protect suggested by current doctrine and can pose challenges to their operationalization at the system-wide context.

Furthermore, human rights implications of development policies are not well understood beyond the observable discord at the aggregate level. For example, the omission in the MDG Goal 2 (on universal primary access to education) of the requirement that education should be free and compulsory in accordance with the human rights provision on the right to education clearly is only one identifiable example of inconsistency.[260] Whether there are other sources of contradiction between development and human rights below the surface of visible is less clear. There is currently little to no assessment of certain highly specialized areas of development and on the capacity of development processes to produce human rights impacts. In our assessment, the extent to which, for example, development financing techniques may contain uncharted problems for human rights is not well researched, at least not systematically.[261]

---

259 As mentioned elsewhere, the difficulty of the development context is that the development policies and activities are typically endorsed by the governments, which further complicate the matter for the purposes of the attribution of responsibility.

260 While it is the right of every child to receive free and compulsory education according to the international human rights treaties, the development strategies have converted this right into a long-term development goal for which no accountability mechanism is prescribed.

261 Apart from relatively well-researched terrains as PRSP and the World Bank's Poverty Reduction Strategy Credits (PRSCs), little analysis is available on the financial instruments of development/donors such as Sector-wide Approaches (SWAPs), Community Driven Development (CDD) and Output-based Aid. For an overview of financing instruments for development see C. Tan, 'Evolving Aid Modalities and their Impact on the Delivery of Essential Services in Low-Income Countries', *Law, Social Justice and Global Development*, 5 October 2005.

As an example, the Community Driven Development initiative, which enjoys high popularity among donors, channels decision-making and funds for development directly to community groups, bypassing central authorities.[262] On the face of it, the financing technique can be qualified as a progressive instrument directly empowering 'poor men and women'. Critics, however, question the initiative on several counts: lack of state control may undermine the central government's capacity to plan development programmes, national budget, weakens coordination and in the absence of national control of basic service delivery, weakens the prospects of universal coverage.[263] Similar critique is advanced towards other financing instruments:[264] '[p]lacing service delivery outside the remit of national and local governments do [*sic*] not guarantee adequate regulation as to consistency of services, quality and universal access'.[265] Put in these terms, development cooperation can be a distinctive area as regards causality and modes of interaction with human rights. Integration of human rights concerns into the design of the broad-based conceptual framework of development policies to prevent potential risks is therefore only one of the first necessary steps.

The aforementioned example on financing techniques is just an illustration that the basic requirement to 'do no harm' or to 'respect' can be broad. Operationalization of the 'do no harm' rule will require extensive knowledge of the relationship between development and human rights and it is not clear whether the concept is capable of integrating the true scale of the development paradigm. Particularly, given that the socio-economic rights implications have been the least visible aspect of the development and human rights convergence debate, there may be many more issues to investigate to provide practical details for operationalization of the duty to 'respect'. To date, human rights analysis has mainly focused on project-based models of causality, i.e. on the areas where the most direct and immediate impact of development activities can be seen, e.g. in large-scale international development projects, including

262 The World Bank defines CDD as 'an approach that gives control over planning decisions and investment resources to community groups and local governments'. See Community Driven Development, www.worldbank.org/.
263 See C. Tan, 'Evolving Aid Modalities and their Impact on the Delivery of Essential Services in Low-Income Countries', *op. cit.*, pp. 9–11.
264 On the Output-Based Aid, Celine Tan has written: 'Output-based aid has more or less the same effect on the delivery of essential services. While the financing of the services may be contingent upon service delivery and/or performance outcomes, OBA projects can also have sustainability challenges as services are contracted out to private service providers. This has implications for government regulation of essential services provision similarly to those of the CDD approaches. As OBA requires contractors to put up a substantial initial outlay, bidders for OBA contracts are restricted to companies or large not-for-profit organisations with means to raise the capital. . . . Many private firms charge "user fees" for their services and the priority for resource allocation is determined by the companies, usually on the basis of profit, rather than on issues of social justice or poverty reduction.' *Ibid.*, p. 10.
265 *Ibid.*

construction of big dams that resulted in adverse consequences to the livelihoods of communities.[266]

As for the systemic or structural dynamics, no specific methodology has been developed as yet. The complex ways that development interacts at the macro level with finance and economy are less well understood, partly because these areas in themselves are extremely complex subjects. The origin of the human rights harm therefore can be spread across the development system. In development cooperation, it is not simply the donor–recipient continuum but a complex process involving diverse actors and activities engaged in a particular segment at the different stages of a bigger process. Discharging the respect-bound obligations by development institutions will require due diligence as a 'comprehensive, proactive attempt to uncover human rights risks, actual and potential, over the entire life cycle of a project or business activity, with the aim of avoiding and mitigating those risks'.[267] Without understanding the risks that development may produce, and, particularly, unless development policies and activities are not comprehensively mapped against human rights standards, it will be difficult to delineate any operative content to the obligations of the respect and protect framework.

Added to this, demonstration of human rights harm has always been made contingent upon empirical evidence, as often 'allegations of . . . a negative impact are not accepted by aid agencies because there is no statistical proof for it'.[268] Evidence of contradiction between the logic of development and human rights as a general matter is limited to the availability of empirical data, subject of course to methodological limitations.[269] To this adds the continuing challenge of measuring

---

266 As a result of the Narmada Project in India and the World Bank commissioned Morse report, this issue has been understood as a concern not only for the state where the project is initiated but also for the international community as well. According to Skogly, '[t]here is no doubt that in certain extraterritorial situations acts or omissions that lead to human rights violations may be easier to identify than others. For instance, if a State that agrees to provide assistance for educational facilities in another State does this on the condition that education will be available to boys only, this would clearly be an act that creates discrimination in the access to education, a violation of Article 13 of the International Covenant on Economic, Social and Cultural Rights. Likewise, if a State that supports educational facilities in another State fails to consider the actual access of both genders to a school (for instance by not ensuring that there are separate lavatories for boys and girls on the premises), and thus creating a *de facto* situation of discrimination, this may be an omission that directly results in violation of the right to education for either boys or girls.' S. Skogly, 'Causality and Extraterritorial Human Rights Obligations', in M. Langford, W. Vandenhole, M. Scheinin, and W. van Genugten, *Global Justice, State Duties: The Extraterritorial Scope of Economic, Social, and Cultural Rights in International Law*, CUP: 2013, pp. 233–258, p. 234.

267 Business and human rights: Towards operationalizing the 'protect, respect and remedy' framework, Report of the Special Representative of the Secretary-General on the issue of human rights and transnational corporations and other business enterprises, J. Ruggie, A/HRC/11/13, 22 April 2009, para. 71.

268 K. Tomasevski, *Development Aid and Human Rights Revisited, op. cit.*, p. 176.

269 Mac Darrow excellently summarizes the role and limits of empirical evidence in the context of the activities international financial institutions which largely apply to development cooperation in general. M. Darrow, *Between Light and Shadow, The World Bank, The International Monetary Fund and International Human Rights Law*, Hart Publishing: 2003, p. 54.

development itself, as characterized by inconsistent empirical evidence.[270] From a human rights perspective, there have been useful attempts to develop conceptual models of human rights influence 'in order to illustrate the kinds of presumptive effects [of development] on human rights' that can serve as the basis for appraisal of human rights impacts of the development interventions.[271] Be that as it may, Mac Darrow makes an important point in relation to the significance of empiricism in matters related to human rights:

> to limit the expression of values such as human rights purely to quantitative and instrumental analysis, is to risk ignoring their essential character and importance. Irrespective of whether education, food, or free speech helps or hinders growth, project performance or prevailing development ideals on the empirical evidence, one of the basic premises . . . is that questions of fundamental 'human right' as a matter of principle cannot simply be laid upon the table and bargained away on the same basis as any other factor in development.[272]

Similarly, to date, the human rights community has carried the burden of proving that development had harmful effects.[273] The suggestion is that this process should be reversed, as is the case in environmental protection. Hence, 'the burden of proving that a development intervention will not harm human rights is on those responsible for its design and implementation'.[274]

To conclude, the important point to make here is that for the 'do no harm' principle to be operational, comprehensive analysis of development activities against human rights obligations should be carried forward. Such an in-depth analysis will, however, require clarity as to the normative scope of the human rights involved.

270 To give one example, the UNDP Human Development Report 2010's retrospective assessment of key trends over the past 40 years found that there was no significant correlation between economic growth and improvements in health and education, particularly in low and medium income countries. UNDP, *Human Development Report 2010–20th Anniversary Edition. The Real Wealth of Nations: Pathways to Human Development*, HDR 2010, pp. 4, 45 et seq.

271 See M. Darrow, *Between Light and Shadow, The World Bank, The International Monetary Fund and International Human Rights Law, op. cit.*, pp. 62–63, discussing S. de Vylder's study 'Development Strategies, Macro-economic Policies and the Rights of the Child', Discussion paper for Radda Barnen, Stockholm (1996).

272 *Ibid.*, p. 56. See also on the limits of indicators in P. Dann, *The Law of Development Cooperation: A Comparative Analysis of the World Bank, the EU and Germany*, CUP: 2013, p. 147f.

273 K. Tomasevski, *Development Aid and Human Rights Revisited, op. cit.*, p. 155.

274 *Ibid.*, p. 215; see the Committee's concluding observations on Switzerland where it recommended that 'the State party undertake an impact assessment to determine the possible consequences of its foreign trade policies and agreement on the enjoyment by the population of the State party's partner countries, of their economic, social and cultural rights'. CESCR, Concluding observations: Switzerland, UN doc. E/C.12/CHE/CO/2–3, 26 November 2010, para. 24.

5.2 Uncertainties and challenges of ESC rights

It is proposed that two factors have mitigated the way human rights were complied with in the process of development and have had an impact on their integration into the corpus of development practice. The first relates back to the traditional conception of human rights as civil and political rights, which did not immediately relate to development understood mainly in economic growth terms.[275] The longstanding non-recognition and misconception of the legal quality of socio-economic rights contributed to the construction of the place of human rights in the development paradigm.[276] Legal theory has long proved that the line of divide between the two sets of rights is permeable and that the dichotomy between negative (civil and political rights) and positive (ESC rights) can no longer be sustained. Important intellectual work is being secured to transform old certainties about the resource-based nature of these rights towards identifying the entire spectrum of obligations, from obligation of abstention to obligation of due diligence.[277]

The reality is that the concept of ESC rights is still contested and they 'are still not taken seriously as fundamental human rights'.[278] Donor approaches underline the divisibility of human rights. Human rights have been (and continue to be) visualized as mainly civil and political rights in the practice of donors. Correlation between the historiography of socio-economic rights and their integration into development practice is rarely discussed and acknowledged as a relevant aspect of the human rights and development convergence discourse, except for the CESCR.[279] One reason could be '[w]ho gets to speak for human rights, and

---

275 The treaty guaranteeing ESC rights speaks of 'progressive realisation to the maximum available resources', while its civil and political counterpart requires that the rights it encompasses be respected and ensured.

276 Certain authors attach a restrictive reading of the obligations flowing from the ICESCR. See for example M. Bossuyt, 'La distinction entre les droits civils et politiques et les droits économiques, sociaux et culturels', Vol. VIII (4) *Revue des droits de l'homme* (1975), pp. 783–820; E.W. Vierdag, 'The Legal Nature of the Rights Granted by the International Covenant on Economic, Social and Cultural Rights', 9 *Netherlands Yearbook of International Law* (1978), p. 69 et seq.

277 See in particular R. Pisillo Mazzeschi, 'Responsabilité de l'état pour violation des obligations positives relatives aux droits de l'homme', 333 *Recueil des Cours* (2008).

278 O. De Schutter (ed.), *Economic, Social and Cultural Rights as Human Rights*, Human Rights Law Series, Edward Elgar Publishing: 2013; M. Dowell-Jones, *Contextualising the International Covenant on Economic, Social and Cultural Rights: Assessing the Economic Deficit*, Martinus Nijhoff Publishers: 2004, p. 1.

279 The Committee on Economic, Social and Cultural Rights's view is that there is a connection between the neglect of these rights 'in the social development context' with the political and ideological controversies, which tended to portray ESC rights 'as being solely the concern of either the Communist countries or a handful of developing countries'. CESCR, Statement to the World Summit for Social Development and the International Covenant on Economic, Social and Cultural Rights, tenth session, E/1995/22-E/C.12/1994/20 and Corr. 1, annex V, para. 7. Exceptions include K. Tomasevski's works, in particular K. Tomasevski, *Development Aid and Human Rights Revisited, op. cit.*; B. Rajagopal, *International Law from Below: Development, Social Movements and Third World Resistance, op. cit.*

consequently what gets spoken about as human rights'[280] But crucially, as Louis Henkin observed, the lack of a monitoring mechanism for ESC rights has given an impression that:

> economic-social rights are not rights, or that the international law on economic-social rights is not perceived as entailing legally binding obligations. One may suggest instead that the Covenant assumes that compliance is not the important concern: States wish to comply and will do so if they have the necessary resources. Therefore the international preoccupation has been not with compliance but with enhancing resources, with economic development of States so as to enable them to comply.[281]

The second factor, identifying the relevance of human rights, presupposes clarity of substantive human rights provisions. For human rights to live up to their intended role in the current critique amid resistance to development practices, clear-cut definitions of what they imply for a development context are needed. In general terms, states and donors, as well as development institutions, be they at the national or international level, need to know the exact content of human rights implications of their activities and what steps to take to be in compliance with the treaty. The level of precision in the definition of obligations is an important factor in preventing human rights violations, particularly at the stage when development cooperation players design their activities. However, as Professor Dupuy points out, the difficulty with ESC rights is that they 'may be the object of different interpretations, as their exact meaning and bearing are not necessarily always stripped of all ambiguity'.[282]

Disagreements persist not only at the level of the content but also on the question of *what* means are necessary to give the socio-economic rights a real meaning.[283] Compared to the period when socio-economic rights provisions were formulated, they have seen momentous developments in terms of interpretation of their normative content,[284] which evolved in the general comments

---

280 Rajagopal, *ibid.*, p. 188.
281 L. Henkin, 'International Law: Politics, Values and Functions', 216 *Recueil des cours* (1989), p. 270.
282 P.-M. Dupuy, 'Unification Rather than Fragmentation of International Law? The case of International Investment Law and Human Rights Law', *op. cit.*, pp. 54–55.
283 For a comprehensive assessment of the difficulties raised by the ambiguity of the ESC rights in the context of investment dispute settlements see P.-M. Dupuy, 'Unification Rather than Fragmentation of International Law? The case of International Investment Law and Human Rights Law', *ibid.*, pp. 54–55 and P. Thielbörger, 'The Human Right to Water Versus Investor Rights: Double-Dilemma or Pseudo-Conflict?', in P.-M. Dupuy and E.-U. Petersmann (eds), *ibid.*, pp. 488–510.
284 The Committee's efforts equilibrated to a certain extent the imbalance between civil and political and socio-economic rights in terms of their normative substance. The Committee posited that 'there is no Covenant right which could not, in the great majority of systems, be considered to possess at least some significant justiciable dimensions'. CESCR, General

of the treaty bodies, dialogue with states, and concluding observations, and in the work of Special Rapporteurs.[285] The only problem, already mentioned, is that these interpretations are materially disconnected from the text of the treaty itself, and even if there are no objections by governments to its progressive interpretations, they remain 'undoubtedly a form of soft-law'.[286] It is hoped that the operationalization of the Optional Protocol to the ICESCR may provide a further opportunity for normative development.[287] With the exception of a visible minority,[288] there is a broadly shared view that '[o]nly case law is able to explain

---

Comment No. 9: The domestic application of the Covenant, E/C.12/1998/243 December 1998, para. 10. For a nuanced analysis of the question of justiciability particularly in light of the 'progressive realisation' of ESC rights, see R. Pisillo Mazzeschi, 'Responsabilité de l'état pour violation des obligations positives relatives aux droits de l'homme', *op. cit.*, p. 455.

285 See e.g. Jean Ziegler, *Second Submission of the Special Rapporteur on the Right to Food of the United Nations Commission on Human Rights*, 2003; Report of the Special Rapporteur on the right of everyone to the enjoyment of the highest attainable standard of physical and mental health: Mission to Uganda, Paul Hunt, UN doc. A/HRC/4/28/Add.3, 21 March 2007.

286 U. Khaliq and R. Churchill, 'The Protection of Economic and Social Rights: A Particular Challenge?', in H. Keller and G. Ulfstein (eds), *UN Human Rights Treaty Bodies: Law and Legitimacy*, CUP: 2012, p. 206.

287 This aspect is also not without controversy. Three strands of critique (even theories) can be distinguished. First, certain authors maintain that without understanding the underlying macroeconomic context of rights, the 'consideration of individual complaints under specific provisions of the Covenant may further alienate the Covenant/Committee from economic discourse by atomising the Covenant into its legal individual components' (M. Dowell Jones, *Contextualising the International Covenant on Economic, Social and Cultural Rights: Assessing the Economic Deficit, op. cit.*, pp. 169–172). Second, related to the first, is the critique of the difficulty to tackle the structural problems inherent in non-realisation of ESC rights through the optic of individual claims (see e.g. K. Tomasevski, 'The Influence of the World Bank and IMF on Economic and Social Rights', *op. cit.*, pp. 385–395, p. 395.). Third, there is a more cautious approach towards the justiciable aspects of the ESC rights. For instance, Mazzeschi suggests that justiciability should be read within the context of a 'progressive realisation' of ESC rights: 'Cela signifie que ces droits, sauf quelques cas particuliers, ne sont pas immédiatement et entièrement justiciable devant les juges internes, mais produisent seulement *quelques effets justiciables* jusqu'au moment où ils seront, avec le temps, réalisés entièrement. Autrement dit, sauf quelques exceptions, les obligations prévues par l'ICESCR n'ont pas de caractère immédiat, ne sont pas *self-executing* et ne sont donc même pas immédiatement justiciable devant les juges internes ; or contraire elles produisent *certaines obligations particulières* pour les Etats, leur violation n'a lieu que dans certains cas particuliers . . . et elle ne pourra donc être invoquée par les sujets privés devant les juges internes seulement que dans certains cas et avec modalités particulières' (R. Pisillo Mazzeschi, 'Responsabilité de l'état pour violation des obligations positives relatives aux droits de l'homme', *op. cit.*, p. 455.).

288 There is a small circle of authors who question the suitability of case-by-case approach to the systemic issues the ESC rights pose. In relation to the clarification of the normative content of the Covenant through the medium of a complaints mechanism, M. Dowell-Jones argued that 'the adoption of such a protocol [Optional protocol to the ICESCR] would be extremely premature given the ongoing conceptual uncertainty surrounding many of the Covenant's provisions, including its key obligation – article 2(1) ICESCR, as well as the

the vague formulations typical for human rights norms by outlining through concrete examples the exact obligations contained in a human rights norm'.[289]

The second caveat is a criticism at a deeper level with respect to the human rights theory itself. The basic question raised is whether the human rights concept provides a shield from economic abuse of power or even if it recognizes development-produced forms of violations.[290] Rajagopal, for example, questions the capacity of human rights to embrace the category of economic violence and states that '[i]t is unfortunately true that violence committed in the name of development remains 'invisible' to the human rights discourse'.[291] According to him, 'economic violence – that is, violence caused by the market – is treated as out of bounds of human rights law, even as it attempts to assert itself as the sole liberatory discourse in the Third World'.[292] He asks, in particular, 'why is the violence of development, which has claimed and has continued to claim millions of "victims", never as visible as some other types of violence?'[293]

It is not possible within the confines of this section to address all the points Rajagopal raises on the relationship between human rights (and law) and violence in general, but the reason this critique has been brought up is his call for disciplinary introspection regarding the selective recognition of some forms of violence to the exclusion of others. It is true that classic human rights scholarship did not deal profoundly with these questions. Yet, it would be unfair to assert that human rights analysis has been blind to these issues, as well as to the concept of economic abuse of power, generally. Although there is no discernible solid assessment of different issues at stake, a separate, slender, but critical, literature has developed over time on the neglect of the indissoluble links of the socio-economic human rights covenant with the macroeconomic context and alleged disregard of this basic element by the human rights community.[294]

---

evident lack of macroeconomic expertise among the Committee. Too many fundamental issues concerning the scope and practical implications of the Covenant remain unclear, indeed many have hardly been discussed at all.' M. Dowell-Jones, *Contextualising the International Covenant on Economic, Social and Cultural Rights: Assessing the Economic Deficit*, *op. cit.*, p. 185.

289 U. Kriebaum, 'Privatizing Human Rights: The Interface between International Investment Protection and Human Rights', in A. Reinisch and U. Kriebaum (eds), *The Law of International Relations – Liber Amicorum Haspeter Neuhold*, Eleven International Publishing: 2007, pp. 165–189.

290 The term 'abuse of economic power', to the knowledge of authors, has been invoked mainly in the works of K. Tomasevski, *Development Aid and Human Rights Revisited, op. cit.*, and B. Rajagopal, *International Law from Below: Development, Social Movements and Third World Resistance, op. cit.*, who uses a slightly different terminology (e.g. economic violence) to convey the same concept.

291 Rajagopal, *ibid.*, p. 195.

292 *Ibid.*, p. 196.

293 *Ibid.*, p. 202.

294 Generally for a critique relevant to development context see K. Tomasevski, 'The Influence of the World Bank and IMF on Economic and Social Rights', 64 *Nordic Journal of International Law* (1995), pp. 385–395, who also argues that 'The focus on poverty requires another change in the human rights discourse a move away from the emphasis on legislative

This criticism revolves around disquiet over attempts to use the medium of international human rights law and legal methodology to improve socio-economic conditions without due consideration of economic conditionality of the implementation of ESC rights (e.g. to the 'maximum available resources' the text of the treaty says[295]). The criticism is made towards the economic deficit in the quality and consistency of the Committee's treatment of the economic dimension of the ESC rights. The predominantly juro-centric focus of human rights analysis and the capacity of the Committee are identified as an immediate reason for the disregard of the economic dimension.[296]

The inevitable consequence of such neglect, it is argued, produces pronouncements of a high level of generality and of little practical use to States Parties. The internal criticism underlines a need for departure from a primary focus on legal measures and instead posits the ESC rights within the reality of a constant change of economics. Hence, 'the import of Covenant guarantees must be subject to continual reassessment in light of the *ebb and flow* of the fluid relationship of State and individual within the parameters of evolving economic conditions and needs'.[297] Since economic conditions are mutating, the structure of ESC rights undergoes transformation in view of the socio-economic conditions. Therefore, 'it is imperative that the Covenant is conceptualized dynamically in light of evolving possibilities and needs, rather than statically as a linear progression of implementation according to the level of development of any particular economy'.[298] The economic deficit in the analysis of ESC rights in itself is a major finding, but the foregoing proposals seem to attempt to reconcile them with a currently operating configuration of the state and the market. Additionally, the macro- and micro-economic approaches proposed rely on economic theory and analysis, which are beset with complexity, and about which there is a considerable divergence of views.

---

measures as the key method for implementing human rights obligations and more attention to economic policies and measures. Human Rights rely on legislative measures, while poverty eradication necessitates changed development finance policies', p. 393. For a systematic view, see M. Dowell-Jones, *Contextualising the International Covenant on Economic, Social and Cultural Rights: Assessing the Economic Deficit, op. cit.*

295 Article 2(1), ICESCR.

296 The Committee has been described as not in a position to interpret the substantive provisions, as 'this group comprised predominantly of lawyers is not endowed with the type of expertise and operational capability necessary to assess complex macroeconomic and fiscal policy information in order to determine whether a State party is pursuing appropriate policies and has taken proper steps to implement the Covenant given its particular socio-economic profile'. M. Dowell-Jones, *Contextualising the International Covenant on Economic, Social and Cultural Rights: Assessing the Economic Deficit, op. cit.*, p. 43. Similarly, M. Craven viewed that the Committee was not 'able to assist States in developing social programmes or restructuring their economic relations; it lacked the technical, administrative or financial means to do so . . . Individual members might have some knowledge, but the general level of expertise was low.' CESCR, Summary record of the 22nd meeting, UN doc. E/C.12/1995/SR.22, 18 May 1995, para. 30.

297 *Ibid.*, pp. 7–8 (emphasis added).

298 *Ibid.*, p. 8.

By way of conclusion, and as a general comment to both of the aforesaid opinions, what may be true is that there is much disagreement among economists about what economic theory is adequate, and whether known alternatives to the received model of market and state can produce different results.[299] The legal difficulties stemming from socio-economic rights are inherent to it by virtue of their belonging to the province of law and economics. To this effect, the contours of the economic dimensions of ESC rights are far from being clear as yet, and the mysterious nature of the macroeconomic realm renders all speculations on ESC rights proximate. This conclusion may sound like a well-known platitude, narrowing down the problem to the point where no solutions may be envisaged. But it rightly points out that the economic contingency of human rights is less well understood in the theory and practice of human rights, and more systematic research is required to develop methods of integrating economic analysis.[300]

Finally, to assess whether any clarifications on the nature and scope of ESC rights relevant to the development context exist, it is useful to inquire into the current practice of the CESCR's dialogue with states, particularly those that engage in development cooperation. The starting point is the treaty reporting guidelines. The earlier version of these guidelines was preoccupied with the use of development cooperation to promote the implementation of rights.[301] The new Guidelines require states to report under Article 2 of the ICESCR on 'the impact of international economic and technical assistance and cooperation, whether received or provided by the State party, on the full realization of each of the Covenant rights in the State party or, as the case may be, in other countries, especially developing countries'.[302]

299 P. Krugman, How Did Economists Get It So Wrong?, *The New York Times*, 9 September 2009, www.nytimes.com/2009/09/06/magazine/06Economic-t.html?_r=2&pagewanted=1&em; see also for the critique of the received models in the field: The State of Economics: The Other-Worldly Philosophers, and Financial Economics: Efficiency and Beyond, *The Economist*, 16 July 2009, www.economist.com/node/14030288 and www.economist.com/node/14030296, respectively.

300 M. Dowell-Jones, *Contextualising the International Covenant on Economic, Social and Cultural Rights: Assessing the Economic Deficit*, Martinus Nijhoff Publishers: 2004, p. 10.

301 In particular, whether 'any effort is made to ensure' that development cooperation is used on a priority basis, to promote the realisation of economic, social and cultural rights. Revised General Guidelines Regarding the Form and Contents of Reports to Be Submitted by States Parties under Articles 16 and 17 of the International Covenant on Economic, Social and Cultural Rights, UN doc. E/C.12/1991/1, 17 June 1991, Part A, para. 3.

302 Guidelines on Treaty-Specific Documents to Be Submitted By States Parties under Articles 16 And 17 of the International Covenant on Economic, Social And Cultural Rights, E/C.12/2008/224 March 2009, adopted by the Committee on Economic, Social and Cultural Rights at its 49th meeting (forty-first session) on 18 November 2008, taking into consideration the guidelines on a common core document and treaty-specific documents, as contained in the harmonized guidelines (HRI/GEN/2/Rev.5), p. 9. The Harmonized Guidelines, in relation to the ICESCR on Article 2, paragraph 7, require information whether if the 'State participates in development cooperation, . . . any effort [is] made to ensure that it is used, on a priority basis, to promote the realization of economic, social and cultural rights?'

In addition, states are required to indicate the following in their reports: 'mechanisms in place to ensure that a State party's obligations under the Covenant are fully taken into account in its actions as a member of international organizations and international financial institutions, as well as when negotiating and ratifying international agreements, in order to ensure that economic, social and cultural rights, particularly of the most disadvantaged and marginalized groups, are not undermined'.[303] These two indicia complement the general requirement of the harmonized Guidelines[304] and are comparatively more elaborate than information required under other human rights treaties.[305] The new guidelines evidence a progression from a mere indication of the volume, towards a more qualitative assessment.

Nonetheless, this does not address the fact that generally there has been no sustained supervision of either the development cooperation's contribution to the realization of the ESC rights, or its impact. It is not clear what states are to report on the impact of aid provided on full realization of each of the Covenant rights and what level of detail is required. And when states do provide valuable material, no meaningful follow-up is undertaken to clarify non-resource-related parameters of development cooperation: whether development programmes did 'all they can' to avoid causing harm and what measures were taken to that effect.

An example is in order to demonstrate this. The review of select state reports shows that only one State Party, Belgium, provided a detailed account about its development cooperation policy, outlining sectors contributing to the realization of ESC rights.[306] The commendable approach of Belgium was to provide sufficiently detailed information reflecting on the state of development cooperation contribution under each right protected by the Covenant.[307] The report traced

---

303 *Ibid.*, para. 3(c).
304 Harmonized guidelines generally require the states to provide information, in the case of recipient states, on the extent of development cooperation or other assistance which supports human rights promotion, including budgetary allocations, and for states providers, the extent of development cooperation provided supporting the promotion of human rights in those countries. Compilation of Guidelines on the Form and Content of Reports to be Submitted by States Parties to the International Human Rights Treaties, HRI/GEN/2/Rev.5, 29 May 2008, para. 43(i) under the title Development cooperation and assistance.
305 Along similar lines, the specific requirements exist for the Convention on the Right of the Child requiring information mainly on human and financial resources allocated 'in particular within bilateral assistance programmes'. Compilation of Guidelines on the Form and Content of Reports to Be Submitted By States Parties to the International Human Rights Treaties, HRI/GEN/2/Rev.5, 29 May 2008, para. 43(i) under the title Development cooperation and assistance. Annex on CRC, para. 12. According to paragraph 12(b), States receiving aid are also to inform about the total resources received and the percentage allocated to programmes for children.
306 CESCR, Belgium: Third periodic reports submitted by States parties under Articles 16 and 17 of the Covenant, E/C.12/BEL/3, 21 September 2006.
307 *Ibid.* The State report included a separate section on development cooperation under Articles 2, 6, 7, 8, 9, 10, 11, 12, 13 and 14 of the Covenant on Economic, Social and Cultural Rights.

the state's contribution in as diverse settings as multilateral cooperation, outlining all the activities it supported, directly or indirectly, and linking them to specific normative provisions. The country's own assessment of its development legislation was that 'although the act does not explicitly refer to the Covenant, some . . . sectoral and cross-cutting priorities certainly have a direct or indirect impact on economic, social and cultural rights'.[308] Instead, the Committee, in its list of issues, raised the question of measures the reporting state intended to take to reach the objective of 0.7% of GDP for ODA. In addition, as if the Committee considered the information on development cooperation insufficient, it asked to 'report on ways the development cooperation policies of the State party contribute to the realization of economic, social and cultural rights in developing countries'.[309]

The report of Belgium is a clear example where the Committee missed an opportunity to go into a more detailed examination of the realization of socioeconomic rights in the context of development cooperation, and investigate further the types of impact it can produce given the breadth of information at hand and the transparency demonstrated by the reporting state. Similarly, the concluding observations it reached were extremely limited in content and utility and cannot qualify as an encouraging message for the reporting state to pursue a more complex and critical analysis of its development activities.[310]

The review of the treaty-reporting process reveals that the Committee systematically raises almost exclusively the issue of the quantitative contribution of a State Party to development.[311] On a regular basis, although less consistently, the CESCR questioned the extent to which the State Party seeks to promote economic, social and cultural rights.[312] The Committee rarely underlined the important dimension

308 *Ibid.*, para. 6.
309 List of Issues raised in relation to Third periodic report submitted by Belgium, UN doc. E/C.12/BEL/Q/3, 10 April 2007, para. 2.
310 The relevant paragraph of the Concluding observation states: 'The Committee, while noting with satisfaction that the State party already devotes 0.5 per cent of its gross domestic product (GDP) to official development assistance (ODA), recommends that the State party increase its official development assistance to 0.7 per cent of its GDP, as recommended by the United Nations, and continue to strengthen its activities in the area of international cooperation.' Concluding Observations: Belgium, UN doc. E/C.12/BEL/CO/3, 4 January 2008, para. 27.
311 In total, ten country reports covering the period of sessions from 2007–2012 have been examined: Germany: UN doc. E/C.12/DEU/5, 27 June 2010; New Zealand: UN doc. E/C.12/NZL/3, 17 January 2011; Spain: UN doc. E/C.12/ESP/5, 31 January 2011; Switzerland: UN doc. E/C.12/CHE/2–3, 17 July 2009; UK: UN doc. E/C.12/GBR/5, 31 January 2008; Australia: UN doc. HRI/CORE/AUS/2007, 22 July 2008; Sweden: UN doc. E/C.12/SWE/5, 6 September 2006; France: UN doc. E/C.12/FRA/3, 15 March 2007; Belgium: UN doc. E/C.12/BEL/3, 21 September 2006; Finland: UN doc. E/C.12/FIN/5, 8 February 2006.
312 New Zealand: List of Issues, UN doc. E/C.12/NZL/Q/3, 14 June 2011; Spain: List of Issues, UN doc. E/C.12/ESP/Q/5, 2 September 2011; UK: Dialogue, Session Report, para. 26 question by N. Schrijver: UN doc. E/C.12/2009/SR.14, 20 May 2009; Sweden: List of Issues, UN doc. E/C.12/SWE/Q/5, 13 December 2007; France: List of Issues, UN doc. E/C.12/FRA/Q/3, 26 December 2007, and see also the Session Report on dialogue with France: UN doc. E/C.12/2008/SR.3, 7 May 2008; Belgium: List of Issues, UN doc. E/C.12/BEL/Q/3, 10 April 2007.

of the requirement to 'respect' the rights protected by the Covenant in the process of delivering development cooperation, even if it believes states have a duty to do so. Only on one occasion did the Committee express concern that a development cooperation programme 'reportedly' resulted in the violation of economic, social and cultural rights.[313] The case concerned a donor State Party's support to a land-titling project in the framework of cooperation for development in Cambodia. The CESCR previously commented on the case of access to lands in the framework of the Cambodian treaty reporting under the ICESCR.[314] Although in the dialogue with the Donor State the CESCR raised the question of the availability of a project-impact assessment, in its concluding observations the Committee recommended that the development cooperation policies 'do not result' in a violation of ESC rights, but rather contribute to their realization.[315]

The CESCR has not yet developed focused questions to allow for a meaningful assessment. A question naturally arises as to whether systematic reference to the volume of ODA in the Committee's monitoring of state compliance with the Covenant did not strengthen a largely resource-based perception of the development dimension of the treaty – a perception that might have crystallized and consolidated over time into a main definition at the expense of other important non-monetary and non-economic dimensions of compliance.

Conclusion

This chapter has considered whether there are rules under international law that require the respect of human rights in the transborder context. While the basic idea may seem indisputable, the human rights scholarship has preferred to use alternative conceptions, even sideways as it were, arguing for the extraterritorial scope of the Covenant on Economic, Social and Cultural Rights or applying by analogy the legal principles devised for the protection of environment in order to argue for the existence of such an obligation. These approaches are not necessarily inaccurate. However, it appears that international law firmly embeds the notion that the obligation to do no harm to human rights is a minimum standard. The jurisprudence of the International Court of Justice has considered this minimum standard as a general principle of international law. The baseline norm conveys the idea that states are to desist from damaging human rights of individuals in third states, and this applies to all human rights.[316]

---

313 CESCR, Concluding Observations: Germany, UN doc. E/C.12/DEU/CO/5, 12 July 2011, para. 11.
314 CESCR, Concluding Observations: Cambodia, UN doc. E/C.12/KHM/CO/1, 12 June 2009, paras. 15, 16.
315 CESCR, Concluding Observations: Germany, *op. cit.*
316 Principle 13 of the Maastricht Principles states: 'States must desist from acts and omissions that create a real risk of nullifying or impairing the enjoyment of economic, social and cultural rights extraterritorially. The responsibility of States is engaged where such nullification or impairment is a foreseeable result of their conduct. Uncertainty about potential impacts does not constitute justification for such conduct.' Maastricht Principles on Extraterritorial Obligations of States in the area of Economic, Social and Cultural Rights.

It would be misleading, however, not to point out a further caveat concerning socio-economic rights, which from the outset were identified as the rights most implicated in the development process. In some respect, cross-border aspects of socio-economic rights are only an emerging idea. The Committee on Economic, Social and Cultural Rights has clarified different parameters involved; however, there remains much ambiguity related, although not exclusively, to the content of the rights to a larger degree contingent on an economic framework. Nonetheless, this aspect is not decisive for putting into practice a minimum accepted standard of avoiding causing harm. This implies transformation of the very texture of the policies and practice of development actors towards embracing the legal dimension of human rights.

VII General conclusion

The introduction to this research proposed that criteria for linking human rights and development policies and practices should be sought within the international human rights law framework.

My analysis began by characterizing and contextualizing human rights in development discourse. It attempted to chart the trajectory of human rights over past decades in development policies. The survey of development policy and practice may usefully inform us as to whether current development arrangements leave any space for the legal integration of human rights. It is difficult in this process to dissociate the topic from the complex narrative of development itself, and particularly its relationship with the law in general. The body of principles and rules, identified as international development law, has played a modest role in advancing the development of poor states. More and more voices are joining the call to revisit the fundamental questions underlying the development paradigm and applicable legal principles. This is so because at the global level there is little to suggest any substantial improvement in human well-being. The progress that has been achieved contrasts starkly with persistent, systemic poverty. Needless to say, the recent global financial crisis and accompanying recession have reduced significantly the expected results from the 'Millennium Development Goals' and strategies.

Despite harsh criticism of it from some quarters, at least in the near future the development paradigm will not be abandoned. Even critics agree that it is very unlikely that radical alternatives should be pursued. The main challenge is, rather, to refocus current policies and practices on 'human development'. There is a great deal of work for the legal discipline in particular. Lawyers are called upon to reconstruct international development law 'away from ideological polemics of the past, to make it autonomous and to educate about the array of rules . . . [and] give unity and new visibility to a branch of law that has been left completely untended'.[1] International human rights law is a key ingredient in the reconstruction of the body of law concerned with the problems of development, not least because human rights are one of the main components of the many definitions of

---

1 E. Jouannet, *The Liberal-Welfarist Law of Nations: A History of International Law*, CUP: 2012, p. 299.

development, but also because there is at least a minimal consensus across all disciplines that the ultimate objective of development is to improve the human condition. There is therefore a genuine momentum to identify and define as precisely as possible the legal norms related to the human rights and development interface. It is a complex endeavour to assess whether human rights law can serve as a framework to structure the relationship of states and regulate their behaviour in the economic sphere, and whether it can serve as an instrument of change for reform in financing, debt servicing and institutional structures engaged in these issues.

A step in the direction of answering this problem is to visualize human rights law broadly, as a concept concerned with civil and political rights as much as with economic and social rights. For the most part, it has always been the development praxis that determined the scope for human rights in the process of development. Although development discourse in its early days saw the challenges of development in global economic structures and attempted to find solutions at the inter-state level, human rights concepts were used to advance this structural transformation at the global level, systematized under the well-known concept of the right to development. Later on, development discourse focused on the internal structures of a state as a challenge and obstacle to development, while human rights were engaged in helping to define the relationship of the developing state with its own citizens. The reality is that human rights are important in both environments: global and domestic. The challenges of development have to be met at many levels. Equality, respect for human rights, and the rule of law between states are as important as they are within a state. Assessment of the impact of development policies and practices of donors on the lives of individuals is as important as the human rights performance of developing countries.

These initial reflections assisted in setting the context and the choice of this study, which is concerned only with the narrow question of the normative framework of human rights, as related to the externally designed and planned development strategies and cooperation. The starting point for the discussion on the normative framework is the concept of the right to development. Despite some scepticism that always persisted with regard to the normative precision of the right to development, it has served, to paraphrase Georges Abi-Saab, as a unifying conceptual framework. It pulled together many different parameters of the human rights and development relationship, linking closely the national and international dimensions of obligations in relation to development of a human person. While some progress is visible regarding the individual dimension of the right to development, the inter-state dimension of the right remains highly contentious. The question is, then, if the right to development derives its normative force from existing sources under international law, namely the UN Charter and the International Covenant on Economic, Social and Cultural rights, should we not define the right to development as an interpretation of these sources? There is little discussion of whether the obligations to cooperate and assist, as envisaged in both the UN Charter and the ICESCR, are not sufficient in themselves to provide a legal framework for understanding the relationship between human rights and the development process.

The UN Charter and the ICESCR create legally binding obligations on states to cooperate for human rights, including through cooperation for development. In particular, socio-economic human rights treaties normatively absorb 'cooperation for development', qualifying it as an important means for achieving human rights, and provide additional elements as to its purpose and scope. By phrasing the *problématique* more broadly, we also find that international law in general as yet does not provide answers to some of the important questions raised in the context of international cooperation and assistance. Even in cases of severe distress, be it armed conflict, disaster situations or extreme poverty, if there is a right to assert or to receive assistance (for states, on behalf of individuals), it has to be directed towards the international community, and not towards any individual state.

This finding does not, however, detract from the general validity of the concept of international assistance and cooperation, given that the 'rules' on assistance are only one element of the entire structure. Finally, the normative concerns of human rights not only are related to the question of resources and how development policies and practices can positively influence human well-being. The notion also may require states to refrain from conduct that may harm the human rights of individuals residing abroad. This argument is further supported by reference to general principles of law. International law in explicit terms requires states to respect, as a minimum, fundamental human rights, an obligation which is binding upon all participants in the development process in all circumstances and at all times.

Perhaps we do not need sophisticated but contentious legal arguments based on the notion of the territorial application of human rights to advance this basic concept. The problem is that the exercise of due diligence or obligation of prevention which is inherent in the notion of avoiding causing harm has not as yet found its way into development policies and practices. What is further needed is to clarify the requirement to respect human rights through comprehensive analysis of the diverse ways development policies and practices generate risks for human rights, along with the concrete normative content of the human rights concerned. What is the contribution of international law to the question of the human rights and development interface? In order to find an answer, it is necessary to return to the original design of the UN Charter. Let us recall, in ending, that the preamble to the UN Charter determined that in order:

> to reaffirm faith in fundamental human rights, in the dignity and worth of the human person, in the equal rights of men and women and of nations large and small, and . . .
>
> to promote social progress and better standards of life in larger freedom,

we must '*employ* international machinery for the promotion of the economic and social advancement of all peoples'.[2]

---

2 Preambular paragraphs 2, 4 and 8, UN Charter (emphasis added).

Table of cases

III ICTY

IV Arbitration

V European Court of Justice

VI European Commission of Human Rights

VII European Court of Human Rights

VIII Inter-American Commission of Human Rights

IX Inter-American Court of Human Rights

X African Commission of Human and Peoples Rights

XI Claims Commissions

XII Human Rights Committee

Table of legal instruments and documents

I Universal Treaties

II Regional Treaties

III Declarations

IV National Legislation, Policies and Guidelines

Austria

Belgium

Canada

Denmark

Finland

United Kingdom

United States of America

V Other Instruments

UNITED NATIONS DOCUMENTS

I General Assembly Resolutions

II ECOSOC Documents

III International Law Commission

IV Other Documents

V Human Rights Bodies

Human Rights Committee

a) General Comments

b) State Reports

c) Concluding Observations

Committee on Economic, Social and Cultural Rights

c) State Reports

d) Concluding Observations

Committee on the Rights of the Child

Committee on the Elimination of Discrimination against Women

a) Concluding Observations

Charter-based Bodies

Bibliography

Abi-Saab, G., 'Cours général de droit international public', 207 *Recueil des Cours* (1987).

Abi-Saab, G., 'Le droit au développement', 44 *Annuaire suisse de droit international* (1988), pp. 9–24.

Abi-Saab, G., 'Wither the International Community', 9(2) *European Journal of International Law* (1998), pp. 248–265.

Abi-Saab, G., 'The Legal Formulation of the Right to Development', in R.-J. Dupuy (ed.), *The Right to Development at the International Level*, The Hague Academy of International Law: 1980, pp. 159–175.

Ago, R., 'Opening Statement', in R.-J. Dupuy (ed.), *The Right to Development at the International Level*, The Hague Academy of International Law: 1980, pp. 3–4.

Akpinarli, N., *The Fragility of the 'Failed State' Paradigm: A Different International Law Perception of the Absence of Effective Government*, Brill: 2010.

Alston, P. (ed.), *Peoples' Rights*, Oxford University Press: 2005.

Alston, P., *Development and the Rule of Law: Prevention versus Cure as a Human Rights Strategy*, International Commission of Jurists: 1981.

Alston, P., 'Human Rights and the New International Development Strategy', 10(3) *Bulletin of Peace Proposals* (1979), pp. 281–290.

Alston, P., 'Making Space for New Human Rights: The Case of the Right to Development', 1 *Harvard Human Rights Yearbook* (1988), pp. 3–40.

Alston, P., 'Revitalising United Nations Work on Human Rights and Development', 18 *Melbourne University Law Review* (1991), pp. 216–257.

Alston, P., 'Ships Passing in the Night: The Current State of the Human Rights and Development Debate Seen Through the Lens of the Millennium Development Goals', 27(3) *Human Rights Quarterly* (2005), pp. 755–829.

Alston, P., 'Shortcomings of a Garfield the Cat Approach to the Right to Development', 15 *California Western International Law Journal* (1985), pp. 510–518.

Alston, P., 'The United Nations' Specialized Agencies and Implementation of the International Covenant on Economic, Social and Cultural Rights', 18 *Columbia Journal of Transnational Law* (1979–1980), pp. 79–118.

Alston, P., and G. Quinn, 'The Nature and Scope of States Parties' Obligations under the International Covenant on Economic, Social and Cultural Rights', *9 Human Rights Quarterly* (1987) pp. 156–229.

Alston, P., and K. Tomasevski, *The Right to Food: Towards a System for Supervising States' Compliance with the Right to Food*, Martinus Nijhoff Publishers: 1984.

Anand, R., *Confrontation or Cooperation? International Law and Developing Countries*, Dordrecht, Martinus Nijhoff Publishers: 1987.

Arangio-Ruiz, G., *The UN Declaration on Friendly Relations and the System of the Sources of International Law*, Sijthoff & Noordhoff: 1979.

Axelrod, R. *The Evolution of Cooperation*, Revised Version, New York: 1984.

Bartels, L., 'The EU's Human Rights Obligations in Relation to Policies with Extraterritorial Effects', 25 *European Journal of International Law*, (2014), pp. 1071–1091.

Baxi, U., 'Normative Content of a Treaty as Opposed to the Declaration on the Right to Development: Marginal Observations', in S.P. Marks (ed.), *Implementing the Right to Development: the Role of International Law*, Friedrich Ebert Stiftung: 2008, pp. 47–52.

Bedjaoui, M., 'Some Unorthodox Reflections on "the Right to Development"', in Snyder F. and P. Slinn (eds), *International Law of Development: Comparative Perspectives*, Abingdon: 1987, pp. 87–116.

Bedjaoui, M., 'L'humanité en quête de paix et de développement', Cours général de droit international public (2004), Vol. II, 325 Recueil des Cours (2006).

Benedek, W., K. de Feyter and F. Marrella, *Economic Globalization and Human Rights*, Cambridge University Press: 2007.

Ben-Naftali, O., and Y. Shany, 'Living in Denial: The Application of Human Rights in the Occupied Territories', 37 *Israel Law Review* (2003–04), pp. 17–118.

Besson, S., 'The Extraterritoriality of the European Convention on Human Rights: Why Human Rights Depend on Jurisdiction and What Jurisdiction Amounts to', 25 *Leiden Journal of International Law* (2012), pp. 857–884.

Bissio, R., Application of the criteria for periodic evaluation of global development partnerships – as defined in Millennium Development Goal 8 – from the right to development perspective: the Paris Declaration on Aid Effectiveness, Paper presented for Eighth session Working Group on the Right to Development High Level Task Force on the implementation of the right to development, UN doc. A/HRC/8/WG.2/TF/CRP.7, 31 December 2007.

Bissio, R., 'The Paris Declaration on Aid Effectiveness', in OHCHR, *Realizing the Right to Development Essays in Commemoration of 25 Years of the United Nations Declaration on the Right to Development*, UN: 2013, pp. 233–247.

Bobbio, N., *The Age of Rights*, Polity Press: 2005, reprint.

Boisson de Chazournes, L., and L. Condorelli, 'Common Article 1 of the Geneva Conventions revisited: Protecting Collective interests', 887 *The International Review of the Red Cross* 2000, pp. 67–87.

Boisson de Chazournes, L., and L. Condorelli, 'Quelles perspectives pour la responsabilité de protéger?' in A. Auer , A. Flückiger, and M. Hottelier (eds), *Les droits de l'homme et la constitution: études en l'honneur du Professeur Giorgio Malinverni*, Genève, Schulthess, 2007, pp. 329–337.

Bossuyt, M., 'La distinction entre les droits civils et politiques et les droits économiques, sociaux et culturels', VIII(4) *Revue des droits de l'homme* (1975), pp. 783–820.

Bossuyt, M.J., *Guide to the 'Travaux Préparatoires' of the International Covenant on Civil and Political Rights*, Martinus Nijhoff Publishers: 1986.

Bothe, M., 'Environment, Development, Resources', 318 Recueil des Cours (2005).

Bouony, L., Article 56, in J.-P. Cot and A. Pellet (eds), *La Charte des Nations Unies: commentaire article par article*, 3rd edition, Economica & Bruylant: 2005, pp. 1480–1508.

Brownlie, I., 'The Rights of Peoples in Modern International Law', in J. Crawford (ed.), *The Rights of Peoples*, Clarendon Press: 1988, pp. 1–16.

Brownlie, I., *Human Right in Development*, Commonwealth Secretariat Human Rights Unit Occasional Paper: 1989.

Brownlie, I., *Principles of Public International Law*, 7th edition, Oxford University Press: 2008.

Buergenthal, T., 'International Human Rights in an Historical Perspective', in J. Symonides (ed.), *Human Rights: Concepts and Standards*, Ashgate, UNESCO Publishing: 2000, pp. 3–25.

Campanelli, D., 'Principle of Solidarity', *Max Planck Encyclopaedia of International Law*, www.mpepil.com.

Cancado Trinidade, A.A., 'Legal Dimensions of the Right to Development as a Human Right: Some Conceptual Aspects', *Global Consultation on the Realization of the Right to Development as a Human Right*, Geneva, 8–12 January 1990, HR/RD/1990/CONF.36.

Cancado-Trindade, A.A. 'Co-existence and co-ordination of mechanisms of international protection of Human Rights (at global and regional levels)', 202 Recueil des Cours (1987).

Carter, B.E., 'Economic Coercion', *Max Planck Encyclopaedia of International Law*, www.mpepil.com.

Carty, A., 'The Third World Claim to Economic Self-Determination: Economic Rights of Peoples: Theoretical Aspects', in S.R. Chowdhury, E.M.G. Denters and P. J.I.M. de Waart (eds), *The Right to Development in International Law*, Martinus Nifhoff Publishers: 1992, pp. 43–60.

Cassese, A., 'The Self-determination of Peoples', in L. Henkin (ed.), *The International Bill of Rights: the Covenant on Civil and Political Rights*, Columbia University Press: 1981, pp. 92–106.

Cassese, A., *International Law in a Divided World*, Clarendon Press: 1986.

Cassimatis, A., *Human Rights Related Trade Measures Under International Law: the Legality of Trade Measures Imposed in Response to Violations of Human Rights Obligations under General International Law*, Martinus Nijhoff Publishers: 2007.

Cerna, C., 'Extraterritorial Application of the Human Rights Instruments of the Inter-American System', in F. Coomans and M. Kamminga (eds), *Extraterritorial application of Human Rights Treaties*, Intersentia: 2004, pp. 141–175.

Cerone, J., 'Jurisdiction and Power: The Intersection of Human Rights Law & the Law of Non-International Armed Conflict in a Transnational Context', 40 *Israel Law Review* (2007), pp. 72–128.

Chun, L., 'Human Rights and Democracy: The Case for Decoupling', in 5(3) *International Journal of Human Rights* (2001), pp. 19–44.

Coomans F., and M.T. Kamminga, *Extraterritorial Application of Human Rights Treaties*, Intersentia: 2004.

Coomans, F., 'Some Remarks on the Extraterritorial application of the International Covenant on Economic, Social and Cultural Rights' in F. Coomans and M. Kamminga (eds), *Extraterritorial Application of Human Rights Treaties*, Intersentia: 2004, pp. 183–201.

Coomans, F., 'The Extraterritorial Scope of the International Covenant on Economic, Social and Cultural Rights in the Work of the United Nations Committee on Economic, Social and Cultural Rights', 11(1) *Human Rights Law Review* (2011), pp. 1–35.

Coomans, F., and R. Kunnemann (eds), *Cases and Concepts on Extraterritorial Obligations in the Area of Economic, Social and Cultural Rights*, Intersentia: 2012.

Craven, M., *The International Covenant on Economic, Social and Cultural Rights: A Perspective on Its Development*, Oxford University Press: 1995.

Crawford, J., (ed.), *The Rights of Peoples*, Clarendon Press: Oxford, 1988.

Crawford, J., et al. (eds), *The Law of International Responsibility: A Commentary*, Oxford University Press: 2010.

Crawford, J., and M. Koskenniemi, *The Cambridge Companion to International Law*, Cambridge University Press: 2012.

Dankwa, E.V.O., and C. Flinterman, 'Commentary by the Rapporteurs on the Nature and Scope of States Parties' Obligations', 9(2) *Human Rights Quarterly* (1987), pp. 136–146.

Dann, P., 'Accountability in Development Aid Law: the World Bank, UNDP and Emerging Structures of Transnational Oversight', 44 *Archiv des Völkerrechts* (2006), pp. 381–404.

Dann, P., *The Law of Development Cooperation: A Comparative Analysis of the World Bank, the EU and Germany*, Cambridge University Press: 2013.

Dann, P., and L. Vierck, 'Paris Declaration on Aid Effectiveness (2005)/Accra Agenda for Action (2008)', *Max Planck Encyclopaedia of International Law*, www.mpepil.com.

Darrow, M., *Between Light and Shadow: the World Bank, the IMF and International Human Rights Law*, Hart Publishing: 2003.

Darrow, M., 'The Millennium Development Goals: Milestones or Millstones? Human Rights Priorities for the Post-2015 Development Agenda', 15(1) *Yale Human Rights and Development Journal* (2012), pp. 55–127.

Darrow, M., and A. Tomas, 'Power, Capture, and Conflict: A Call for Human Rights Accountability in Development Cooperation', 27(2) *Human Rights Quarterly* (2005), pp. 471–538.

de Feyter, K., *World Development Law: Sharing Responsibility for Development*, Intersentia: 2001.

de Feyter, K., *Human Rights: Social Justice in the Age of Market, Global Issues in a Changing World*, Zedbooks: 2005.

de Mesquita, J.B., *International Covenant on Economic, Social and Cultural Rights: Obligations of International Assistance and Cooperation*, Human Rights Centre, University of Essex: 2002.

De Schutter, O., 'Human Rights, Globalization and Jurisdiction: Lessons from the European Convention on Human Rights', 6 *Baltic Yearbook of International Law* (2006), pp. 183–245.

De Schutter, O., *International Human Rights Law: Cases, Materials, Commentary*, Cambridge University Press: 2010.

De Schutter, O., (ed.), *Economic, Social and Cultural Rights as Human Rights*, Human Rights Law Series, Edward Elgar Publishing: 2013.

de Waart, P., 'State Rights and Human Rights as Two Sides of One Principle of International Law: the Right to Development', in P. de Waart, P. Peters and E. Denters (eds), *International Law and Development*, Dordrecht: 1988.

Degnbol-Martinussen, J., and P. Engberg-Pedersen, *Aid: Understanding International Development Cooperation*, Zed Books: 2005.

Delbruck, J., 'The International Obligation to Co-operate-An Empty Shell or A Hard Law Principle of International Law? – A Critical Look at A Much Debated Paradigm of Modern International Law', in H.P. Hestermeyer et al. (eds), *Coexistence, Cooperation and Solidarity: Liber Amicorum Rudiger Wolfrum*, Vol. 1, Brill/Nijhoff: 2011, pp. 3–16.

Delbruck, J., (ed.), *International Law of Cooperation and State Sovereignty: Proceedings of an International Symposium of the Kiel Walther-Shucking-Institute of International Law, May 23–26, 2001*, Dunker and Humbold: 2001.

den Heijer, M., and R. Lawson, 'Extraterritorial Human Rights and the Concept of "Jurisdiction"', in M. Langford, W. Vandenhole, M. Scheinin and W. Van Genugten (eds), *Global Justice, State Duties : the Extraterritorial Scope of Economic, Social, and Cultural Rights in International Law*, Cambridge University Press: 2013, pp. 153–191.

Denters, E.M.G., 'IMF Conditionality: Economic, Social and Cultural Rights, and the Evolving Principle of Solidarity', in P. J.I.M. de Waart, P. Peters and E.M.G. Denters (eds), *International Law and Development*, Martinus Nijhoff Publishers: 1988, pp. 235–243.

Detrick, S., *Commentary on the United Nations Convention on the Rights of the Child*, Kluwer International: 1999.

Dinstein, Y., 'Collective Human Rights of Peoples and Minorities', 25 (1) *International and Comparative Law Quarterly* (1976), pp. 102–120.

Dinstein, Y., 'The Erga Omnes Applicability of Human Rights', 30 *Archiv des Völkerrechts* (1992), pp. 16–37.

Donnelly, J., 'In Search of the Unicorn: The Jurisprudence and Politics of the Right to Development', 15 *California Western International Law Journal* (1985), pp. 473–509.

Donnelly, J., *Universal Human Rights in Theory and Practice*, Cornell University Press: 2003.

Dos Santos, T., 'The Structure of Dependence', 60 *The American Economic Review* 2, Papers and Proceedings of the Eighty-second Annual Meeting of the American Economic Association (May 1970), pp. 231–236.

Dos Santos, T., 'The Crisis of Development Theory and the Problem of Dependence in Latin America', in H. Bernstein (ed.), *Underdevelopment and Development: The Third World Today*, Harmondsworth 1973, pp. 57–80.

Dowell Jones, M., *Contextualising the International Covenant on Economic, Social and Cultural Rights: Assessing the Economic Deficit*, Martinus Nijhoff Publishers: 2004.

Dupuy, P.-M., 'International Law: Torn between Coexistence, Cooperation and Globalization: General Conclusions', 9 *European Journal of International Law* (1998), pp. 278–286.

Dupuy, P.-M., *Droit International Public*, 5th edition, Dalloz: 2000.

Dupuy, P.-M., 'L'unité de l'ordre juridique international: cours général de droit international public', 297 Recueil des Cours (2002).

Dupuy, P.-M., and C. Hoss, 'Trail Smelter and Terrorism: International Mechanisms to Combat Transboundary Harm', in R. Bratspies and R. Miller, *Transboundary Harm in International Law: Lessons from the Trail Smelter Arbitration*, Cambridge University Press: 2006, pp. 225–239.

Dupuy, P.-M., E.-U. Petersmann and F. Francioni, *Human Rights in International Investment Law and Arbitration*, Oxford University Press: 2009.

Dupuy, R.-J., 'Communauté internationale et disparités de développement: cours général de droit international public', 165 Recueil des Cours (1979).

Eide, A., C. Krause and A. Rosas (eds), *Economic, Social and Cultural Rights. A Textbook*, Dordrecht: 1995.

Endicott, M., 'The Definition of Investment in ICSID Arbitration: Development Lessons for the WTO?', in M.W. Gehring and M.-C. Cordonier Segger (eds),

Sustainable Development in World Trade Law, Kluwer Law International: 2005, pp. 379–410.

Escobar, A., *Encountering Development: The Making and Unmaking of the Third World*, Princeton University Press: 1995.

Escobar, A., 'Power and Visibility: Development and the Invention and Management of the Third World', 3(4) *Cultural Anthropology* (1988), pp. 428–443.

Fine, B., 'Economics and ethics: Amartya Sen as point of departure', 1(1) *The New School Economic Review* (2004), pp. 151–62.

Fisler Damrosch., L., 'Obligation of Cooperation in the International Protection of Human Rights', in J. Delbruck (ed.), *International Law of Cooperation and State Sovereignty: Proceedings of an International Symposium of the Kiel Walther-Shucking-Institute of International Law, May 23–26, 2001*, Dunker and Humbold: 2001, pp. 15–45.

Fitzmaurice, G., 'Special Report: The Future of Public International Law and of the International Legal System in the Circumstances of Today', Institut de Droit International, *Livre du Centenaire 1873–1973. Evolution et perspectives du droit international*, Basel: 1973.

Fleck, D., 'International Accountability for Violations of the *Ius in Bello*: The Impact of the ICRC Study on Customary International Humanitarian Law', 11(2) *Journal of Conflict & Security Law* (2006), pp. 179–199.

Flory, M., 'Adapting International Law to the Development of the Third World', 26 *Journal of African Law* (1982), pp. 12–20.

Flory, M., 'La 4e Décennie pour le Développement', 36 *Annuaire française de droit international* (1990), pp. 606–613.

Franck, T.M., 'The Emerging Right to Democratic Governance', 86 *American Journal of International Law* (1992), pp. 46–91.

Frankovits, A., 'Introduction: A Rights-Based Approach to Development and the Right to Development', 3 *Human Rights and Development Yearbook* (2002), pp. 3–14.

French, D., '"From Seoul With Love" – The Continuing Relevance Of The 1986 Seoul ILA Declaration on Progressive Development of Principles of Public International Law Relating to a New International Economic Order', 55 *Netherlands International Law Review* (2008), pp. 3–32.

Friedmann, W., *The Changing Structure of International Law*, Columbia University Press: 1964.

Fukuda-Parr, S., and A.E. Yamin, 'The power of numbers: A critical review of MDG targets for human development and human rights', 56(1) *Development* (2013), pp. 58–65.

Fukuda-Parr, S., A.E. Yamin, and J. Greenstein, 'The Power of Numbers: A Critical Review of Millennium Development Goal Targets for Human Development and Human Rights', 15(2–3) *Journal of Human Development and Capabilities* (2014), pp. 105–117.

Garcia-Bolivar, O.E., Economic Development at the Core of the International Investment Law Regime, Paper presented at the International Investment Treaty Law and Arbitration Conference, Sydney, Australia, 19–20 February 2010.

Garcia-Bolivar, O.E., *Defining an ICSID Investment: Why Economic Development Should be the Core Element*, International Institute for Sustainable Development, 13 April 2012, www.iisd.org.

Ghai, Y., 'Human Rights and Governance: The Asia Debate', 15 *Australia Yearbook of International Law* (1994), pp. 1–34.

Giacca, G., *Economic, Social and Cultural Rights in Armed Conflict, Monograph in International Law Series*, Oxford University Press: 2014.

Gianviti, F., Substantive Issues Arising in the Implementation of ICESCR: Working Paper, UN doc. E/C.12/2001/WP.5, 7 May 2001.

Gibney, M., 'On Terminology', in M. Langford, W. Vandenhole, M. Scheinin and W. Van Genugten (eds), *Global Justice, State Duties : the Extraterritorial Scope of Economic, Social, and Cultural Rights in International Law*, Cambridge University Press: 2013, pp. 32–47.

Gibney, M., and S. Skogly (eds), *Universal Human Rights and Extraterritorial Obligations*, University of Pennsylvania Press: 2010.

Gibney, M., and W. Vandenhole (eds), *Litigating Transnational Human Rights Obligations: Alternative Judgments*, Routledge: 2014.

Gibney, M., K. Tomasevski and J. Vedsted-Hansen, 'Transnational State Responsibility for Violations of Human Rights', 12 *Harvard International Law Journal* (1999), pp. 267–295.

Gondek, M., *The Reach of Human Rights in a Globalising World: Extraterritorial Application of Human Rights Treaties*, Intersentia: 2009.

Gore, C., 'The New Development Cooperation Landscape: Actors, Approaches, Architecture', 25 *Journal of International Development* (2013), pp. 769–786.

Goy, R., 'La Cour Permanente de Justice Internationale et Les Droits De L'Homme', in G. Cohen-Jonathan (ed.), *Liber Amicorum Marc-André Eissen*, Bruylant: 1995, pp. 199–232.

Greenwood, C., Remarks, 'Bombing for Peace: Collateral Damage and Human Rights', 96 *American Society of International Law Proceedings* (2002), pp. 100–194.

Grimheden, J., 'The International Court of Justice – Monitoring Human Rights', in G. Alfredsson et al. (eds), *International Human Rights Monitoring Mechanisms. Essays in Honour of Jakob Th Moeller*, 2nd revised edition, Martinus Nijhoff Publishers: 2009, pp. 249–262.

Guder, L., *The Administration of Debt Relief by the International Financial Institutions A Legal Reconstruction of the HIPC Initiative*, Springer: 2009.

Hamida, W.B., 'Two Nebulous ICSID Features: The Notion of Investment and the Scope of Annulment Control: *Ad Hoc* Committee's Decision in *Patrick Michell v. Democratic Republic of Congo*', 24(3) *Journal of International Arbitration* (2007), pp. 287–306.

Hampson, F., 'The Scope of the Extra-territorial Applicability of International Human Rights Law', in G. Gilbert, F. Hampson and C. Sandoval-Villalba (eds), *The Delivery of Human Rights: Essays in Honour of Professor Sir Nigel Rodley*, Taylor & Francis: 2011, pp. 157–183.

Hannum, H., 'The Status of the Universal Declaration of Human Rights in National and International Law', 25 *Georgia Journal of International and Comparative Law* (1995–1996), pp. 287–398.

Henkaerts, J-M., and L. Doswald-Beck, *Customary Rules of International Humanitarian Law*, ICRC Study (Vols. I and II), Cambridge University Press: 2005.

Henkin, L., 'International Human Rights as "Rights"', 1 *Cardozo Law Review* (1979), pp. 425–447.

Henkin, L., 'International Law: Politics, Values and Functions', 216 Recueil des Cours (1989).

Hettne, B., *Development Theory and the Three Worlds: Towards an International Political Economy of Development*, Longman Scientific & Technical: 1995.

Hickey, S., and D. Mitli (eds), *Human Rights-Based Approaches to Development*, Kumarian Press: 2009.

Higgins, R. *Problems and Process: International Law and How We Use It*, Clarendon Press: 1994.

Higgins, R., 'The International Court of Justice and Human Rights,' 20(4) *Leiden Journal of International Law* (2007), pp. 745–751.

Hirsch, M., 'Developing Countries', *Max Planck Encyclopaedia of Public International Law*, www.mpepil.com.

Ibhawoh, B., 'The Right to Development: The Politics and Polemics of Power and Resistance', 33(1) *Human Rights Quarterly* (2011), pp. 76–104.

ILA, New Delhi Declaration of Principles of International Law Relating to Sustainable Development, 2 April 2002, 70th International Law Association Conference, New Delhi, India (2002).

ILA, 'Report of Seventieth Conference', 70 *International Law Association Reports of Conferences* (2002).

ILA, 'Report of the Seventy-First Conference', 71 *International Law Association Conference Report* (2004).

ILA, 'Report of the Sixty-First Conference', 61 *International Law Association Reports of Conferences* (1984).

ILA, 'Report of the Sixty-Second Conference', 62 *International Law Association Reports of Conferences* (1986).

ILA, 'Report of the Sixty-Seventh Conference', 67 *International Law Association Reports of Conferences* (1996).

ILA, 'Report of the Sixty-Sixth Conference', 66 I*nternational Law Association Reports of Conferences* (1994).

Institut de Droit International, Resolution of 2003 on Humanitarian Assistance, Bruge Session.

Institut de Droit International, Session de Saint-Jacques-de-Compostelle 1989, La protection des droits de l'homme et le principe de non-intervention dans les affaires intérieures des Etats.

Jacoby, E.H., 'Dilemma of the World Bank: Comment to the Annual Report 1972', 4(3) *Development and Change*, pp. 95–100.

Janejad, M., and M. Wood, 'The Principle of Non-intervention', 22 *Leiden Journal of International Law* (2009), pp. 345–381.

Joannet, E., 'How to Depart from the Existing Dire Conditions of Development', in A. Cassese (ed.), *Realizing Utopia: The Future of International Law*, Oxford University Press: 2012, pp. 392–418.

Jolly, R., 'Adjustment with a Human Face: A UNICEF Record and Perspective on 1980s', 19(12) *World Development* (1991), pp. 1807–1821.

Joseph, S., *Blame it on the WTO: A Human Rights Critique*, Oxford University Press: 2011.

Jouannet, E., 'What Is the Use of International Law? International Law as A 21st Century Guardian Of Welfare', 28 *Michigan Journal of International Law* (2006–2007), pp. 815–862.

Jouannet, E., *The Liberal-Welfarist Law of Nations: A History of International Law*, Cambridge University Press: 2012.

Kamminga, M.T., *Inter-state Accountability for Violations of Human Rights*, University of Pennsylvania Press: 1992.

Karimova, T., and G. Golay, 'Principle 5: Poverty Eradication', in J.E. Viñuales (ed.), *The Rio Declaration on Environment and Development: A Commentary*, OUP: 2015, pp. 181–207.

Keijzer, N., The Future of Development Cooperation: from Aid to Policy Coherence for Development?, European Centre for Development Policy Management (ECDPM), April 2012.

Kenig-Witkowska, M.M., 'The UN Declaration on the Right to Development in Light of Its Travaux Preparatoires', in P. J.I.M. de Waart, P. Peters and E. Denters (eds), *International Law and Development*, Martinus Nijhoff Publishers: 1988, pp. 382–388.

Khalfan, A., and I. Seiderman, 'Extraterritorial Human Rights Obligations: Wider Implications of the Maastricht Principles and the Continuing Accountability Challenge', in W. Vandendole (ed.), *Challenging Territoriality in Human Rights Law: Building Blocks or Plural and Diverse Duty-Bearer Regime*, Routledge: 2015, pp. 15–43.

Khaliq, U., and R. Churchill, 'The Protection of Economic and Social Rights: A Particular Challenge?' in H. Keller and G. Ulfstein (eds), *UN Human Rights Treaty Bodies: Law and Legitimacy*, Cambridge University Press: 2012, pp. 199–260.

Khaliq, U., *Ethical Dimensions of the Foreign Policy of the European Union: A Legal Appraisal*, Cambridge University Press: 2008.

Koji, T., 'Emerging Hierarchy in International Human Rights and Beyond: From the Perspective of Non-Derogable Rights', 12(5) *European Journal of International Law* (2001), pp. 917–941.

Kooijmans, P.H., 'In the Shadow land Between Civil War and Civil Strife: Some Reflections on the Standard-setting Process', in A.J.M. Delissen and G.J. Tanja (eds), *Humanitarian Law of Armed Conflict Challenges Ahead. Essays in Honour of Frits Kalshoven*, Martinus Nijhoff Publishers: 1991, pp. 225–247.

Kriebaum, U., 'Privatizing Human Rights: The Interface between International Investment Protection and Human Rights', in A. Reinisch and U. Kriebaum (eds), *The Law of International Relations – Liber Amicorum Haspeter Neuhold*, Eleven International Publishing: 2007, pp. 165–189.

Künnemann, R., 'Extraterritorial Application of the International Covenant on Economic, Social and Cultural Rights', in F. Coomans and M.T. Kamminga (eds), *Extraterritorial Application of Human Rights Treaties*, Intersentia: 2004, pp. 201–232.

Langford, M., W. Vandenhole, M. Scheinin and W.Van Genugten (eds), *Global Justice, State Duties: the Extraterritorial Scope of Economic, Social, and Cultural Rights in International Law*, Cambridge University Press: 2013.

Lauterpacht, H., *International Law and Human Rights*, Stevens & Sons: 1950.

Lawson, R., 'Life after Bankovic: On the Extraterritorial Application of the European Convention on Human Rights' in R. Lawson, M. Kamminga and F. Coomans (eds), *Extraterritorial Application of Human Rights Treaties*, Intersentia: 2004, pp. 83–124.

Lowenfeld, A.F., *International Economic Law*, Oxford University Press: 2002.

Lubell, N., *Extraterritorial Use of Force against Non-State Actors*, Oxford University Press: 2010.

Macrae, J., *Aiding Recovery? The Crisis of Aid in Chronic Political Emergencies*, London: 2001.

Mahiou, A., 'International Law of Development', *Max Planck Encyclopedia of Public International Law*, www.mpepil.com.

Maier, H.G., 'Jurisdictional Rules in Customary International Law', in K.M. Meessen (ed.), *Extraterritorial Jurisdiction in Theory and Practice*, Kluwer Law International: 1996, pp. 64–101.

Malanczuk, P.A., *Akehurst's Modern Introduction to International Law*, Routledge: 1997.

Mann, F.A.P., 'The Doctrine of Jurisdiction in International Law', 111 Recueil des Cours (1964).

Marks, S., 'Human rights and Development', in S. Joseph and A. McBeth (eds), *Research Handbook On International Human Rights Law*, Edward Elgar Publishing: 2010, pp. 167–196.

Marks, S., 'Obligations to Implement the Right to Development: Philosophical, Political and Legal Rationales', in B.A. Andreassen and S.P. Marks (eds), *Development as a Human Right: Legal, Political and Economic Dimensions*, Intersentia: 2010.

Marks, S., and A. Clapham, *International Human Rights Lexicon*, Oxford University Press: 2005.

Marks, S., 'Prospects for Human Rights in the Post-2015 Development Agenda', in J. Kozma, A. Muller-Funk and M. Nowak (eds), *Vienna+20: Advancing the Protection of Human Rights Achievements, Challenges and Perspectives 20 Years After the World Conference*, Ludwig Boltzmann Institute of Human Rights, Studies Series, Vol. 31, Neuer Wissenschaftlicher Verlag: 2014, pp. 291–306.

Marks, S., B. Rudolf, K. De Feyter and N. Schrijver, 'The Role of International Law' in OHCHR, *Realizing the Right to Development Essays in Commemoration of 25 Years of the United Nations Declaration on the Right to Development*, UN: 2013, pp. 445–468.

Marks, S.P., 'Principles and Norms of Human Rights Applicable in Emergency Situations: Underdevelopment, Catastrophes and Armed Conflicts', in K. Vasak (ed.), *The International Dimensions of Human Rights*, Vol. I, UNESCO: 1982, pp. 175–215.

Martin, M., 'Assessing the HIPC Initiative: The Key Policy Debates', in J.J. Teunissen and A.Akkerman (eds), *HIPC Debt Relief: Myths and Reality*, The Hague: Forum on Debt and Development: 2004, pp. 11–47.

Mawdsley, E., 'Human Rights and South-South Development Cooperation: Reflections on the "Rising Powers" as International Development Actors', 36(3) *Human Rights Quarterly* (2014), pp. 630–652.

M'Baye, K., 'Le droit au développement comme un droit de l'homme', 5 *Revue des droits de l'homme* (1972), pp. 503–534.

McInerney, T.F., *Strategic Treaty Management: Practice and Implications*, Cambridge University Press: 2015.

McInerney-Lankford, S., 'Human Rights and Development: Some Institutional Perspectives', 25(3) *Netherlands Quarterly of Human Rights* (2007), pp. 459–509.

McInerney-Lankford, S., 'Human Rights and Development: a Comment on Challenges and Opportunities from a Legal Perspective', 1(1) *Journal of Human Rights Practice* (2009), pp. 51–82.

McInerney-Lankford, S., 'International Financial Institutions and Human Rights: Select Perspectives on Legal Obligations', in D.D. Bradlow and D.B. Hunter (eds), *International Financial Institutions and International Law*, Kluwer Law International: 2010, pp. 239–285.

McInerney-Lankford, S., 'Human Rights and Development: Regime Interaction and the Fragmentation of International Law', in H. Cissé, S. Muller, C. Thomas and C. Wang (eds), *Legal Innovation and Empowerment for Development, the World Bank Legal Review*, Vol. 4, 2013, pp. 123–159.

McInerney-Lankford, S., and H.-O. Sano, *Human Rights Indicators in Development: An Introduction*, World Bank: 2010.

McLachlan, C., 'The Principle of Systemic Integration and Article 31(3)(c) of the Vienna Convention', 54 *International Comparative Law Quarterly* (2005), pp. 279–320.

McWhinney, E., 'The Concept of Cooperation', in M. Bedjaoui (ed.), *International Law: Achievements and Perspectives*, Martinus Nijhoff Publishers: 1991, pp. 424–436.

Mégret, F., 'International Human Rights Law Theory', in A. Orakhelashvili (ed.), *Research Handbook on the Theory and History of International Law*, Research Handbooks in International Law Series, Edward Elgar: 2011, pp. 199–231.

Meron, T., *Human Rights and Humanitarian Norms as Customary Law*, Clarendon Press: 1989.

Milanovic, M., 'From Compromise to Principle: Clarifying the Concept of State Jurisdiction in Human Rights Treaties', 8 *Human Rights Law Review* (2008), pp. 411–448;

Milanovic, M., *Extraterritorial Application of Human Rights Treaties: Law, Principles, and Policy*, Oxford University Press: 2011.

Monshipouri, M., and C.E. Welch, 'The Search for International Human Rights and Justice: Coming to Terms with the New Global Realities', 23(2) *Human Rights Quarterly* (2001), pp. 370–401.

Moreno-Lax V., and C. Costello, 'The Extraterritorial Application of the EU Charter of Fundamental Rights: From Territoriality to Facticity, the Effectiveness Model', in S. Peers, T. Hervey, J. Kenner and A.Ward (eds), *The EU Charter of Fundamental Rights: A Commentary*, Hart Publishing: 2014, pp. 1658–1683.

Morijn, J., *Reframing Human Rights and Trade: Potential Limits of a Human Rights Perspective of WTO Law on Cultural and Education Goods and Services*, Intersentia: 2010.

Mustaniemi-Laasko, M., 'The Right to Education: Instrumental Right Par Excellence', in W. Vandenhole, M. Salomon and A. Tostensen (eds), *Casting the Net Wider: Human Rights, Development and New Duty-Bearers*, Intersentia: 2007, pp. 331–352.

Narula, S., 'The Right to Food: Holding Global Actors Accountable Under International Law', 44 *Columbia Journal of Transnational Law* (2006), pp. 691–800.

Nelson, P., 'Human Rights, The Millennium Development Goals, and the Future of Development Cooperation', 25(12) *World Development* (2007), pp. 2041–2055.

Neumayer, E. 'Do Human Rights Matter in Bilateral Aid Allocation? A Quantitative Analysis of 21 Donor Countries', 84(3) *Social Science Quarterly* (2003), pp. 650–666.

Nollkaemper, A., and D. Jacobs, 'Shared Responsibility in International Law: A Conceptual Framework', 32(2) *Michigan Journal of International Law* (2013), pp. 359–438.

Nowak, M., *UN Covenant on Civil and Political Rights: CCPR Commentary*, Kehl Am Rein: 1993.

Orford, A., 'Globalization and the Right to Development', in P. Alston (ed.), *Peoples' Rights*, Oxford University Press: 2005, pp. 127–185.

Osmani, S. 'Some Thoughts on the Right to Development', in Franciscans International, *The Right to Development: Reflections on the Right to Development – Reflections on the First Four Reports of the Independent Expert on the Right to Development*, Geneva: 2003, pp. 34–45.

Oxman, B., 'Jurisdiction of States', *Max-Planck Encyclopaedia of International Law*, www.mpepil.com.

Palacio, A., 'The Way Forward: Human Rights and the World Bank', in S. Puri (ed.) *Development Outreach*, World Bank Institute: 2006, pp. 35–36.

Pauwelyn, J., T. Cottier and E. Burgi, *Human Rights and International Trade*, Oxford University Press: 2005.

Pellet, A., 'The Functions of the Right to Development: A Right to Self-Realisation', 3 *Third World Legal Studies* (1984), pp. 129–139.

Pictet, J.S., *The Geneva Conventions of 12 August 1949*, Commentary, Fourth Geneva Convention Relative to the Treatment of Civilian Persons in Time of War ICRC: 1958.

Pinelli, C., 'Conditionality', *Max Planck Encyclopaedia of International Law*, www.mpepil.com.

Pinto, M.C.W., 'Reflections on International Liability for Injurious Consequences Arising out of Acts not Prohibited by International Law', 16 *Netherlands Yearbook of International Law* (1985), pp. 17–48.

Piron, L.H., 'The Right to Development: A Review of the Current State of the Debate', ODI: April 2002.

Pisillo Mazzeschi, R., 'Responsabilité de l'état pour violation des obligations positives relatives aux droits de l'homme', 333 Recueil des Cours (2008).

Pogge, T., 'The First United Nations Development Goal: A Cause for Celebration', 5(3) *Journal of Human Development and Capabilities* (2004), pp. 337–397.

Ragazzi, M., *The Concept of International Obligations Erga Omnes*, Oxford University Press: 2000.

Rajagopal, B., 'Counter-hegemonic International Law: rethinking human rights and development as a Third World strategy', 27(5) *Third World Quarterly* (2006), pp. 767–783.

Rajagopal, B., *International Law from Below: Development, Social Movements and Third World Resistance*, Cambridge University Press: 2003.

Raustiala, K., *Does the Constituion Follow the Flag: The Evolution of Territoriality in American Law*, Oxford University Press: 2009.

Rich, R., 'The Right to Development as an Emerging Human Right', 23 *Virginia Journal of Internaitonal Law* (1982–1983), pp. 287–328.

Rich, R., 'The Right to Development: A Right of Peoples?', in J. Crawford (ed.), *The Rights of Peoples*, Clarendon Press: 1988, pp. 39–54.

Riedel, E. 'International Covenant on Economic, Social and Cultural Rights (1966)', *Max Planck Encyclopaedia of International Law*, www.mpepil.com.

Riedel, E. 'Article 55 (c)', in B. Simma et al. (eds), *The Charter of the United Nations. A Commentary*, 2nd edition, Oxford University Press: 2012, pp. 918–941.

Riedel, E., 'New Bearings in Social Rights? The Communications Procedure Under the ICESCR', in U. Fastenrath et al., *From Bilateralism to Community Interest: Essays in Honour of Bruno Simma*, Oxford University Press: 2011, pp. 575–589.

Rishmawi, M., *A Commentary on the United Nations Convention on the Rights of the Child, Article 4 – The Nature of States Parties' Obligations*, Martinus Nijhoff Publishers: 2006.

Rist, G., *The History of the Development: from Western Origins to Global Faith*, London: Zedbooks: 2002.

Rodley, N.S., *Human Rights and Humanitarian Intervention: The Case Law of the World Court*, 38 *International Comparative Law Quarterly* (1989), pp. 321–333.

Rostow, W.W., *The Stages of Economic Growth: A Non-Communist Manifesto,* Cambridge University Press: 1960.

Roxtrom, E., M. Gibney and T. Einarsen, 'The Nato Bombing Case (Bankovic et al. v. Belgium et al.) and the Limits of the Western Human Rights Protection', 23 *Boston University International Law Journal*, pp. 55–136.

Rudolf, B., 'The Relation of the Right to Development to Existing Substantive Treaty Regimes', in S. Marks (ed.), *Implementing the Right to Development: the Role of International Law*, Friedrich Ebert Stiftung: 2008, pp. 105–116.

Ryngaert, C., *Jurisdiction in International Law*, Oxford University Press: 2008.

Ryngaert, C., 'Jurisdiction: Towards a Reasonableness Test', in M. Langford, W. Vandenhole, M. Scheinin and W. Van Genugten (eds), *Global Justice, State Duties: the Extraterritorial Scope of Economic, Social, and Cultural Rights in International Law*, Cambridge University Press: 2013, pp. 192–212.

Saith, A., 'From Universal Values to Millennium Development Goals: Lost in Translation', 37(6) *Development and Change* (2006), pp. 1167–1199.

Salomon, M., 'Legal Cosmopolitanism and the Normative Contribution of the Right to Development', in S.P. Marks (ed.), *Implementing the Right to Development: the Role of International Law*, Friedrich Ebert Stiftung: 2008, pp. 17–26.

Salomon, M., *Global Responsibility for Human Rights: World Poverty and the Development of International Law*, Oxford University Press: 2007.

Sandvik-Nylund, M., *Caught in Conflicts: Civilian Victims, Humanitarian Assistance and International Law*, 2nd revised edition, Abo Akademi University, Institute for Human Rights: 2003 – VIII.

Sano, H.-O., 'Does Human Rights-Based Development Make a Difference?', in M.E. Salomon, A. Tostensen and W. Vandenhole (eds), *Casting the Net Wider: Human Rights, Development and New Duty-Bearers*, Intersentia: 2007, pp. 63–81.

Sano, H.-O., 'The Drivers of Human Rights Change in Development', in P. Gready and W. Vandenhole (eds), *Human Rights and Development in the New Millennium: Towards a Theory of Change*, Routledge: 2014, pp. 29–49.

Santos, A., 'The World Bank's Uses of the "Rule of Law" Promise in Economic Development', in D. Trubek and A. Santos (eds), *The New Law and Economic Development*, Cambridge University Press: 2006, pp. 253–300.

Sassoli, M., 'The Role of Human Rights and International Humanitarian Law in New Types of Armed Conflicts', in Orna Ben-Naftali (ed.), *International Humanitarian Law and International Human Rights Law*, OUP: 2011, pp. 34–94.

Saul, B., D. Kinley and J. Mowbray, *The International Covenant on Economic, Social and Cultural Rights: Commentary, Cases, and Materials*, Oxford University Press: 2014.

Schachter, O., 'Implementing the Right to Development: Programme of Action', in S.R. Chowdhury, E.M.G. Denters and P. J.I.M. de Waart (eds), *The Right to Development in International Law*, Martinus Nifhoff Publishers: 1992, pp. 27–30.

Schachter, O., 'International Law in Theory and Practice: general course in public international law', 178 Recueil des Cours (1982).

Schachter, O., 'The Emergence of International Environmental Law', 44 *Journal of International Affairs* (1991), pp. 457–492.

Schachter, O., 'The Evolving International Law of Development', 15(1) *Columbia Journal of Transnational Law* (1976), pp. 1–16.

Scheinin, M., 'Just Another Word? Jurisdiction in the Roadmaps of State Responsibility and Human Rights', in M. Langford, W. Vandenhole, M. Scheinin and W. Van Genugten (eds), *Global Justice, State Duties: the Extraterritorial Scope of Economic, Social, and Cultural Rights in International Law*, Cambridge University Press: 2013, pp. 212–229.

Schreuer C., et. al., *The ICSID Convention: A Commentary*, 2nd edition, Cambridge Univeristy Press: 2009.

Schrijver, N., 'A Missionary Burden or Enlightened Self-Interest? International Law in Dutch Foreign Policy', 57 *Netherlands International Law Review* 2010.

Schrijver, N., 'Agenda for Development', *Max Planck Encyclopaedia of International Law*, www.mpepil.com.

Schrijver, N., 'The Evolution of Sustainable Development in International Law: Inception, Meaning and Status', 329 Recueil de Cours (2007).

Schrijver, N., *Development without Destruction: the UN and Global Resource Management*, IUP: 2010.

Schwebel, S.M., 'Human Rights in the World Court', in R.S Pathak (ed.), *International Law in Transition: Essays in Memory of Judge Nagendra Singh*, Martinus Nijhoff Publishers: 1992, pp. 267–290.

Schwebel, S.M., 'The Treatment of Human Rights and of Aliens in the International Court of Justice', in V. Lowe and M. Fitzmaurice (eds), *Fifty Years of the International Court of Justice: Essays in Honour of Sir Robert Jennings*, Cambridge University Press:1996, pp. 327–350.

Schwelb, E., The International Court of Justice and the Human Rights Clauses of the Charter, 66 *American Journal of International Law* (1972), pp. 337–351.

Sen, A., *Development as a Freedom*, Oxford University Press: 1999.

Sengupta, A., 'Preface', in S.P. Marks (ed.), *Implementing the Right to Development: the Role of International Law*, Friedrich Ebert Stiftung: 2008, pp. 8–10.

Sengupta, A., 'The Human Right to Development', in B.A. Andreassen and S.P. Marks (eds), *Development as a Human Right: Legal, Political and Economic Dimensions*, Intersentia: 2010, p. 13–44.

Sepúlveda Carmona, M., 'Obligations of "international assistance and cooperation" in an Optional Protocol to the International Covenant on Economic, Social and Cultural Rights', 24(2) *Netherlands Quarterly of Human Rights* (2006), pp. 271–305.

Shelton, D., 'Are There Differentiations among Human Rights? *Jus Cogens*, Core Human Rights, Obligations *Erga Omnes* and Non-Derogability', in Venice Commission, *The Status of International Treaties on Human Rights*, Council of Europe Publishing: 2006.

Shihata, I.F.I., *The World Bank Legal Papers*, Martinus Nijhoff Publishers: 2000.

Shihata, I.F.I., 'Exclusion of Political Considerations in the Bank's Articles – Its Meaning and Scope in the Context of the Institution's Evolution', in I.F.I. Shihata, F. Tschofen and A.R. Parra (eds) *The World Bank in a Changing World: Selected Essays*, Martinus Nijhoff Publishers: 1991.

Shihata, I.F.I., 'Political Activity Prohibited', in I.F.I. Shihata, *The World Bank Legal Paper*, Martinus Nijhoff Publishers: 2000, pp. 219–244.

Shue, H., 'Mediating duties', 98(4) *Ethics* (1988), pp. 687–704.

Shue, H., *Basic Rights: Subsistence, Affluence, and U.S. Foreign Policy*, 2nd edition, Princeton University Press: 1996.

Shwelb, E., 'The Law of Treaties and Human Rights', in W.M. Reisman and B.H. Weston (eds), *Towards the World Order and Human Dignity: Essays in Honour of Myres S. McDougal*, Free Press: 1976, pp. 262–290.

Simma, B., 'From Bilateralism to Community Interest in International Law', 250 Recueil de Cours (1994).

Simma, B., 'Human Rights and State Responsibility', in A. Reinisch and U. Kriebaum (eds), *The Law of International Relations – Liber Amicorum Hanspeter Neuhold*, Eleven International Publishing: 2007, pp. 359–381.

Simma, B., 'Human Rights before the International Court of Justice: Community Interest Coming to Life?' in H.P. Hestermeyer, D. Konig, N. Matz-Luck, V. Roben, A. Seiber-Fohr, P.-T. Stoll and S. Voneky (eds), *Coexistence, Cooperation and Solidarity: Liber Amirocum Rudiger Wolfrum*, Vol. I, Brill/Nijhoff: 2011, pp. 577–603.

Simma, B., 'Foreign Investment Arbitration: A Place For Human Rights?', 60 *International Comparative Law Quarterly* (July 2011), pp. 573–596.

Simma, B., 'Mainstreaming Human Rights: The Contribution of the International Court of Justice', 3(1) *Journal of International Dispute Settlement* (2012), pp. 7–29.

Simma, B., and Alston, P., 'The Sources of Human Rights Law: Custom, Jus Cogens, and General Principles', 12 *Australian Year Book of International Law* (1988–1989), pp. 82–108.

Simma, B., and A. Th. Muller, 'Exercise and Limits of Jurisdiction', in J. Crawford and M. Koskenniemi, *The Cambridge Companion to International Law*, Cambridge University Press: 2012, pp. 134–158.

Sivakumaran, S., 'The International Court of Justice and Human Rights' in S. Joseph and A. McBeth (eds), *Research Handbook on International Human Rights Law*, Edward Elgar Publishing: 2010, pp. 299–325.

Skogly, S., *The Human Rights Obligations of the World Bank and the International Monetary Fund*, Cavendish Press: 2001.

Skogly, S.I., *Beyond National Borders: States' Human Rights Obligations in International Cooperation*, Intersentia: 2006.

Skogly, S., 'Causality and Extraterritorial Human Rights Obligations', in M. Langford, W. Vandenhole, M. Scheinin, and W. van Genugten, *Global Justice, State Duties: The Extraterritorial Scope of Economic, Social, and Cultural Rights in International Law*, CUP: 2013, pp. 233–258.

Skogly, S., and M. Gibney, 'Transnational Human Rights Obligations', 24 *Human Rights Quarterly* (2002), pp. 781–798.

Snyder, F., 'Law and Development in the Light of Dependency Theory', 14 *Law and Society Review* (1980), pp. 723–804.

Stiglitz, J., More Instruments and Broader Goals: Moving Toward the Post-Washington Consensus, The 1998 WIDER Annual Lecture (Helsinki, Finland), 7 January 1998.

Stokke, O., *UN and Development: From Aid to Cooperation*, IUP Press: 2009.

Stoll, P.T., 'Article 55 (a) and (b)', in B. Simma, D.-E. Khan, G. Nolte and A. Paulus (eds), *The Charter of the United Nations A Commentary*, 3rd edition, Oxford University Press: 2013.

Sumner, A., and R. Mallett, *The Future of Foreign Aid Development Cooperation and the New Geography of Global Poverty*, Palgrave Macmillan: 2012.

Tams, C., *Enforcing Obligations Erga Omnes in International Law*, Cambridge University Press: 2005.

Tan, C., 'Evolving Aid Modalities and their Impact on the Delivery of Essential Services in Low-Income Countries', *Law, Social Justice and Global Development*, 5 October 2005, www.go.warwick.ac.uk/elj/lgd/2005_1/tan.

Tan, C., 'The New Disciplinary Framework: Conditionality, New Aid Architecture and Global Economic Governance', chapter for J. Faundez and C. Tan (eds), *International Law, Economic Globalization and Developing Countries*, accessed SSRN, pp. 1–22.

Tobin, J., *The Right to Health in International Law*, Oxford University Press: 2011.

Tomasevski, K., 'The Influence of the World Bank and IMF on Economic and Social Rights', 64 *Nordic Journal of International Law* (1995), pp. 385–395.

Tomasevski, K., *Development Aid and Human Rights*, St Martin's Press: 1989.

Tomasevski, K., 'Monitoring Human Rights Aspects of Sustainable Development', 8 *American University Journal of Law and Policy* (1992), pp. 77–102.

Tomasevski, K., *Development Aid and Human Rights Revisited*, 2nd edition, Pinter Publishers: 1993.

Tomasevski, K., *Responding to Human Rights Violations: 1946–1999*, Martinus Nijhoff Publishers: 2000.

Tomasevski, K., 'Human Rights Obligations: Making Education Available, Accessible, Acceptable and Adaptable', in *Right to Education Primer No. 3*, SIDA: 2001.

Tourme-Jouannet, E., *What is a Fair International Society? International Law Between Development and Recognition*, Hart Publishing: 2013.

Uvin, P., 'From the Right to Development to the Rights-based Approach: How "Human Rights" Entered Development', 17(4–5) *Development in Practice* (2007), pp. 597–606.

van Boven, T., 'Distinguishing Criteria of Human Rights', in K. Vasak (ed.), *The International Dimensions of Human Rights*, UNCESCO: 1982, p. 43–60.

van Boven, T., 'Is There an Emerging Right to Good Governance'?', 3 *Netherlands Quarterly on Human Rights* (1995), pp. 304–310.

Vandenhole, W., 'The Human Right to Development as a Paradox', 36(3) *Verfassung und Recht in Übersee. Law and Politics in Africa, Asia and Latin America* (2003), pp. 377–404.

Vandenhole, W., 'EU and Development: Extraterritorial Obligations under the International Economic, Social and Cultural Rights', in W. Vandenhole, M. Salomon and A. Tostensen (eds), *Casting the Net Wider: Human Rights, Development and New Duty-Bearers*, Intersentia: 2007, pp. 85–106.

Vandenhole, W., 'Third State Obligations under the ICESCR: A Case Study of EU Sugar Policy', 76 *Nordic Journal of International Law* (2007), pp. 71–98.

Vandenhole, W., 'Economic, Social and Cultural Rights in the CRC: Is There a Legal Obligation to Cooperate Internationally for Development?', 17 *International Journal of Children's Rights* (2009), pp. 23–63.

Vandenhole, W., 'The Limits of Human Rights Law in Human Development', in E. Claes, W. Devroe and B. Keirsbilck (eds), *Facing the Limits of the Law*, Springer: 2009, pp. 355–374.

Vandenhole, W., Emerging Normative Frameworks on Transnational Human Rights Obligations, EUI Working Papers, RSCAS 2012/17, 2012, pp. 1–24.

Vandenhole, W., (ed.), *Challenging Territoriality in Human Rights Law: Building Blocks for a Plural and Diverse Duty-Bearer Regime*, Routledge: 2015.

Vandenhole, W., M. Salomon and A. Tostensen (eds), *Casting the Net Wider: Human Rights, Development and New Duty-Bearers*, Intersentia: 2007.

Vierdag, E.W.,'The Legal Nature of the Rights Granted by the International Covenant on Economic, Social and Cultural Rights', 9 *Netherlands Yearbook of International Law* (1978), pp. 69–105.

Viñuales , J.E. (ed.), *The Rio Declaration on Environment and Development: A Commentary*, Oxford University Press: 2015.

Virally, M., 'La 2e décennie des Nations Unies pour le développement – Essai d'interprétation para-juridique', 16 *Annuaire français de droit international* (1970), pp. 9–33.

Virally, M., 'Vers un droit international du développement', 11 *Annuaire français de droit international* (1965), pp. 3–12.

Voneky, S., 'Analogy in International Law', *Max Planck Encyclopaedia of International Law*, www.mpepil.com.

Watson, J.S., 'The Limited Utility of International Law in the Protection of Human Rights', 74 *Proceedings of the ASIL* (1980), pp. 1–6.

Weiler, J.H.H., and A.L. Paulus, 'The Structure of Change in International Law or Is There a Hierarchy of Norms in International Law?', 8 *European Journal of International Law* (1997), pp. 545–565.

Dijkstra, G., The New Aid Paradigm – A Case for Policy Incoherence, Background Paper for World Economic and Social Survey, 2010.

Wolfensohn, J.D., 'Some Reflections on Human Rights and Development', in P. Alston and M. Robinson (eds), *Human Rights and Development: Towards Mutual Reinforcement*, Oxford University Press: 2005, pp. 19–24.

Wolfrum, R., 'International Law of Cooperation', *Max Planck Encyclopaedia of International Law*, www.mpepil.com.

Wolfrum, R., 'International Law of Cooperation', Encyclopedia of Public International Law Vol. II, Elsevier, 1995, pp. 1242–1247.

Wolfrum, R. 'Article 1', in B. Simma et al. (eds), T*he Charter of the United Nations. A Commentary*, 2nd edition, Oxford University Press: 2012, pp. 39–47.

Wolfrum, R. 'Article 55', in B. Simma et al. (eds), *The Charter of the United Nations. A Commentary*, 2nd edition, Oxford University Press: 2012, pp. 897–917.

Wolfrum, R. 'Article 56', in B. Simma et al. (eds), *The Charter of the United Nations. A Commentary*, 2nd edition, Oxford University Press: 2012, pp. 941–944.

Zamora, S., 'Economic Relations and Development', in O. Schachter and C. Joyner (eds), *United Nations Legal Order*, Vol. 1, Cambridge: 1995, pp. 503–576.

Zyberi, G., *The Humanitarian Face of the International Court of Justice: its Contribution to Interpreting and Developing International Human Rights and Humanitarian Law Rules and Principles*, Intersentia: 2008.

UN reports

A New Global Partnership: Eradicate Poverty and Transform Economies Through Sustainable Development: The Report of the High-Level Panel of Eminent Persons on the Post-2015 Development Agenda, 30 May 2013.

Annex II, Summary of the discussions held regarding the issue of international cooperation to be considered by the Ad Hoc Committee, UN doc. A/AC.265/2004/WG/1.

Compilation of Guidelines on the Form and Content of Reports to be Submitted by States Parties to the International Human Rights Treaties, HRI/GEN/2/Rev.5, 29 May 2008.

Consolidation of findings of the High-level Task Force on the Implementation of the Right to Development, UN doc. A/HRC/15/WG.2/TF/2/Add.1, 25 March 2010.

Country study: Review of Progress and Obstacles in the Promotion, Implementation, Operationalization and Enjoyment of the Right to Development — Country studies on the right to development – Argentina, Chile and Brazil, UN doc. E/CN.4/2004/WG.18/3, 23 January 2004.

Daily summary of discussion at the sixth session 1 August 2005, vol. 7, No. 1 of 1 August 2005.

E/C.12/2008/2, 24 March 2009, adopted by the Committee on Economic, Social and Cultural Rights at its 49th meeting (forty-first session) on 18 November 2008, taking into consideration the guidelines on a common core document and treaty-specific documents, as contained in the harmonized guidelines, HRI/GEN/2/Rev.5.

FAO, Human Rights Principles: PANTHER, www.fao.org/righttofood/about-right-to-food/human-right-principles-panther/ru/.

FAO, The Right to Adequate Food in Emergencies, Rome: 2002.

Fifth report: Fifth report of the independent expert on the right to development, Mr Arjun Sengupta, submitted in accordance with Commission resolution 2002/69 – Frameworks for development cooperation and the right to development, UN doc. E/CN.4/2002 /WG.18/6, 16 September 2002.

Final report on the question of the impunity of perpetrators of human rights violations (economic, social and cultural rights), prepared by Mr El Hadji Guissé, Special Rapporteur, pursuant to Sub-Commission resolution 1996/24, UN doc. E/CN.4/Sub.2/1997/8, 27 June 1997.

First report: Study on the current state of progress in the implementation of the right to development submitted by Mr Arjun K. Sengupta, independent expert, pursuant to Commission resolution 1998/72 and General Assembly resolution 53/155, UN doc. E/CN.4/1999/WG.18/2, 27 July 1999.

Fourth report: Fourth report of the independent expert on the right to development, Mr Arjun Sengupta, submitted in accordance with Commission resolution 2001/9, UN doc. E/CN.4/2002/WG.18/2, 2 March 2002.

Green, M., and S. Randolph., Consultant report – Right to development criteria and corresponding operational sub-criteria, Bringing Theory into Practice: Operational Criteria for Assessing Implementation of the International Right to Development, UN doc. A/HRC/15/WG.2/TF/CRP.5, 14 January 2010.

Guidelines on Treaty-Specific Documents to Be Submitted By States Parties under Articles 16 And 17 Of The International Covenant On Economic, Social And Cultural Rights.

ILO, Minutes of the 115th Session of the Governing Body (Sixth sitting, Fourth report) 50 (1951).

ILO, Resolution concerning the recurrent discussion on social protection (social security), adopted by the ILC at its 100th session, June 2011.

ILO, Social Protection Floor for a Fair and Inclusive Globalization Report of the Advisory Group chaired by Michelle Bachelet, ILO: 2011.

ILO, Social Protection Floors for Social Justice and a Fair Globalization, Report IV, document for the ILC 2012, 101st session, 28 February 2012.

Inter-sessional open-ended working group on a draft optional protocol to the Convention on the Rights of the Child on involvement of children in armed conflicts

Comments on the Report of the Working Group, UN doc. E/CN.4/2000/WG.13/2/Add.1.

Joint statement of the Chairpersons of the United Nations human rights treaty bodies, presented at the High-level Plenary Meeting of the General Assembly on the Millennium Development Goals, New York, 20–22 September 2010.

OHCHR, Claiming the MDGs: A Human Rights Approach, UN: 2008.

OHCHR, Frequently Asked Questions on a Human Rights-Based Approach to Development Cooperation, UN: 2006.

OHCHR, Human Rights and Poverty Reduction: A Conceptual Framework, UN: 2004.

OHCHR, Thematic Study of the Office of the United Nations High Commissioner for Human Rights on the impact of unilateral coercive measures on the enjoyment of human rights, including recommendations on actions aimed at ending such measures, UN doc. A/HRC/19/33, 11 January 2012.

Preliminary Report of the Independent Expert on the Issue of Human Rights Obligations Relating to the Enjoyment of a Safe, Clean, Healthy and Sustainable Environment, UN doc. A/HRC/22/43, 24 December 2012.

Preliminary study of the independent expert on the right to development, Mr Arjun Sengupta, on the impact of international economic and financial issues on the enjoyment of human rights, submitted in accordance with Commission resolutions 2001/9 and 2002/69, UN doc. E/CN.4/2003/WG.18/2, 27 January 2003.

Rapporteur on The right to Food, O. De Schutter on his mission to the World Trade Organization, UN doc. A/HRC/10/5/Add.2, 4 February 2009.

Report of Secretary-General, Trends and Progress in International Development Cooperation, UN doc. E/2010/93, 10 June 2010.

Report of the Open-ended Working Group to Consider Options Regarding the Elaboration of an Optional Protocol to the International Covenant on Economic, Social and Cultural Rights on its Second Session, UN doc. E/CN.4/2005/52.

Report of the Open-ended Working Group to Consider Options Regarding the Elaboration of an Optional Protocol to the International Covenant on Economic, Social and Cultural Rights on its Third Session, 2006, UN doc. E/CN.4/2006/47.

Report of the Open Working Group of the General Assembly on Sustainable Development Goals, UN doc. A/68/970, 12 August 2014.

Report of the Secretary-General, Progressive Development of the Principles and Norms of International Law Relating to the New International Economic Order, UN doc. A/39/504/Add.1, 23 October 1984.

Report of the Secretary-General K. Annan, In Larger Freedom: Towards Development, Security and Human Rights for All, UN doc. A/59/2005, 21 March 2005.

Report of the Secretary-General, Accelerating progress towards the Millennium Development Goals: options for sustained and inclusive growth and issues for advancing the United Nations development agenda beyond 2015, UN doc. A/66/126, 11 July 2011.

Report of the Secretary-General, Agenda for Development, UN doc. A/48/935, 6 May 1994.

Report of the Secretary-General, Human Rights and Unilateral Coercive Measures, UN doc. A/66/272, 5 August 2011.

Report of the Secretary-General, Keeping the Promise; A Forward-Looking Review to Promote an Agreed Action Agenda to Achieve the Millennium Development Goals by 2015, February 2010.

Report of the Secretary-General, Road map towards the implementation of the United Nations Millennium Declaration, UN doc. A/56/326, 6 September 2001.

Report of the Secretary-General, Strengthening of the United Nations: an Agenda for Further Change, UN doc. A/57/387, 9 September 2002.

Report of the Secretary-General, The International Dimensions of the Right to Development as a Human Right in Relation with Other Human Rights Based on International Cooperation, Including the Right to Peace, Taking into Account the Requirements of the New International Economic Order and the Fundamental Human Needs, UN doc. E/CN.4/1334, 2 January 1979.

Report of the Secretary-General, We the peoples: the role of the United Nations in the twenty-first century, UN doc. A/54/2000, 27 March 2000.

Report of the Special Rapporteur B. Frey, Preliminary Report on the Prevention of Human Rights Violations Committed with Small Arms and Light Weapons, UN. doc. E/CN.4/Sub.2/2003/29, 25 June 2003.

Report of the Special Rapporteur Mr Danilo Türk, The Realization of Economic, Social and Cultural Rights, E/CN.4/Sub.2/1992/16, 3 July 1992.

Report of the Special Rapporteur on the promotion and protection of human rights and fundamental freedoms while countering terrorism, Martin Scheinin, UN doc. A/HRC/6/17, 21 November 2007.

Report of the Special Rapporteur on the right of everyone to the enjoyment of the highest attainable standard of physical and mental health: Mission to Uganda, Paul Hunt, UN doc. A/HRC/4/28/Add.3, 21 March 2007.

Report of the Special Rapporteur on the Right to Adequate Food, A. Eide, UN Commission on Human Rights, The Right to Adequate Food as a Human Right, UN doc. E/CN.4/Sub.2/1987/23, 7 July 1987.

Report of the Special Rapporteur on the Right to Food of the United Nations Commission on Human Rights, Jean Ziegler, Second Submission, March 2003.

Report of the Special Rapporteur on the right to food, Olivier De Schutter, UN doc. A/HRC/19/59/Add.5, 11 December 2011.

Report of the Special Rapporteur on the right to food, Olivier De Schutter, Addendum: Guiding principles on human rights impact assessments of trade and investment agreements, UN doc. A/HRC/19/59/Add.5, 19 December 2011.

Report of the Special Rapporteur on the Right to Food: The Way Forward, UN doc. A/HRC/28/65, 12 January 2015.

Report of the Special Representative of the Secretary-General on the issue of human rights and transnational corporations and other business enterprises, J. Ruggie, Business and human rights: Towards operationalizing the 'protect, respect and remedy' framework, UN doc. A/HRC/11/13, 22 April 2009.

Report of the working group on a draft optional protocol to the Convention on the Rights of the Child on involvement of children in armed conflicts on its sixth session, UN doc. E/CN.4/2000/74.

Report submitted by Ms. Katarina Tomasevski, Special Rapporteur on the right to education, Addendum Mission to Uganda 26 June–2 July 1999, UN doc. E/CN.4/2000/6 /Add.1, 9 August 1999.

Revised General Guidelines Regarding the Form and Contents of Reports to Be Submitted by States Parties Under Articles 16 and 17 of the International Covenant on Economic, Social and Cultural Rights, UN doc. E/C.12/1991/1, 17 June 1991, Part A.

Robinson, M., United Nations High Commissioner for Human Rights, Development and Rights: the Undeniable Nexus, UN General Assembly Special Session on the

Implementation of the Outcome of the World Summit for Social Development, Geneva, 26 June 2000.

Second report: Report of the independent expert on the right to development, Note by the Secretary-General, UN doc. A/55/306, 17 August 2000.

Secretary-General's Report, Renewing the United Nations: a Programme for Reform, UN doc. A/51/950, 14 July 1997.

Sixth report: Review of progress and obstacles in the promotion, implementation, operationalization, and enjoyment of the right to development Consideration of the sixth report of the independent expert on the right to development – Implementing the right to development in the current global context, UN doc. E/CN.4/2004/WG.18/2, 17 February 2004.

Special Rapporteur on the Human Right to Safe Drinking Water and Sanitation: Common Violations of the Human Rights to Water and Sanitation, UN doc. A/HRC/27/55, 30 June 2014.

Synthesis Report of the Secretary-General on the Post-2015 Sustainable Development Agenda, The Road to Dignity by 2030: Ending Poverty, Transforming All Lives and Protecting the Planet, UN doc. A/69/700, 4 December 2014.

Third report: Third report of the independent expert on the right to development, Mr Arjun Sengupta, submitted in accordance with Commission resolution 2000/5, UN doc. E/ CN.4/2001/WG.18/2, 2 January 2001.

UN Commission on Human Rights, Report of the Eighth Session (14 April to 14 June 1952), ECOSOC Official Records Fourteenth Session, Suppl. No. 4, Annex I.

UN Commission on Human Rights, Report on the Thirty-Third Session, 62 UN ESCOR Supp. (No. 6), UN doc. E/5927 (1978).

UN Commission on Human Rights, Sixth Session, Summary Records of the Hundred Thirty-Eights Meeting, UN doc. E/CN.4/SR.138.

UN Commission on Human Rights, Study on the current state of progress in the implementation of the right to development, by Mr Arjun K. Sengupta, independent expert, UN doc. E/CN.4/1999/WG.18/2, 27 July 1999.

UN DEA, The United Nations Development Agenda: Development for All: Goals, Commitments and Strategies agreed at the United Nations World Conferences and Summits since 1990, United Nations, Economic and Social Affairs: 2007.

UN Human Rights Council Advisory Committee, Report on Enhancement of International Cooperation in the Field of Human Rights, prepared by E. Decaux and updated by L. Boisson de Chazournes, present Rapporteur, A/HRC/AC/8/3, 12 December 2011.

UN Human Rights Council, R. Malhotra, Implementing the Right to Development — A Review of the Task Force Criteria and Some Options, UN doc. A/HRC/12/WG.2/TF/CRP.6, 31 March 2009.

UN Human Rights Council, Working Group on the Right to Development, Report on Expert Consultation, The criteria and operational sub-criteria for the implementation of the right to development, UN doc. A/HRC/15/WG/2/TF/CRP/4, 18 January 2010.

UN Sub-Commission on the Promotion and Protection of Human Rights, Concept Document on the Right to Development, Working Paper submitted by Florizelle O'Connor, UN doc. E/CN.4/Sub.2/2005/23, 24 June 2005.

UN Sub-Commission on the Promotion and Protection of Human Rights, Working paper on the relationship between human rights law and international humanitarian law by Francoise Hampson and Ibrahim Salama, UN doc. E/CN.4/Sub.2/2005/14, 14 June 2005.

UN, An opening Declaration, Transforming our World by 203 New Agenda for Global Action, Zero Draft, June 2015.

UN, Global Compact, Corporate Sustainability and the United Nations Post-2015 Development Agenda Perspectives from UN Global Compact Participants on Global Priorities and How to Engage Business Towards Sustainable Development Goals, Report to the UN Secretary-General, 17 June 2013.

UN, Measures for the Economic Development of Underdeveloped Countries: Report by a Group of Experts appointed by the Secretary-General of the United Nations, NY: United Nations, DEA, May 1951.

UN, Protection of Persons in the Event of Disasters, Memorandum prepared by the Secretariat, Doc. A/CN.4/590, 11 December 2007.

UN, Summary of the Report hosted by the President of the General Assembly on advancing the United Nations development agenda beyond 2015, 4 November 2011.

UN, The Human Rights Based Approach to Development Cooperation: Towards a Common Understanding Among UN Agencies (the 'Stamford Statement'), 2003.

UN, The Millennium Development Goals Report 2010, New York: 2010.

UN, The Millennium Development Goals Report 2015, New York: 2015.

UNCIO Documents of the United Nations Conference on International Organization, Vol. 6, United Nations Information Organizations, New York: 1945.

UNCTAD, Development Implications of International Investment Agreements, IIA Monitor No. 2 (2007), UN 2007.

UNCTAD, Draft Principles on Promoting Responsible Sovereign Lending and Borrowing, April 2011.

UNCTAD, Economic Development in Africa Report 2010, South-South Cooperation: Africa and the New Forms of Development Partnership, UN, Geneva: 2010.

UNCTAD, Follow-up to the Millennium Summit and Preparations for High-level Plenary Meeting of the General Assembly on the Millennium Development Goals: New Development Paths. Reconnecting the Millennium Development Goals to the Development Agenda: an UNCTAD Perspective, Geneva, June 2010.

UNCTAD, The Least Developed Countries Report 2010: Towards a New International Development Architecture for LDCs, New York and Geneva: 2010.

UNCTAD, The Least Developed Countries Report 2014: Growth with Structural Transformation: A Post-2015 Agenda, Geneva: 2014.

UNCTAD/M. Goldmann, A Comparative Survey Written for the United Nations Conference on Trade and Development: Responsible Sovereign Lending and Borrowing: the View from Domestic Jurisdictions, February 2012.

UNDG, Human Rights Mainstreaming Mechanism: Operational Plan 2011–2013, November 2011, https://undg.org/wp-content/uploads/2015/04/UNDG-HRM-Operational-Plan-Nov-20-2011.pdf.

UNDP, Human Development Report 1990: Concept and Measurement of Human Development, New York, Oxford University Press: 1990.

UNDP, Human Development Report 2010–20th Anniversary Edition. The Real Wealth of Nations: Pathways to Human Development, HDR 2010.

UNDP, Staff Opinion, The Paris Declaration and National Ownership: From de Jure to de Facto, October 2007, No.1.

UNESCO, 'Le droit à l'assistance humanitaire: actes du Colloque international organisé par l'Unesco', UNESCO, SHS-95/CONF.805/3.

UNESCO, The Human Rights Based Approach and the United Nations System, Desk Study Prepared by A. Frankovits, UNESCO: 2006.

Index

For Product Safety Concerns and Information please contact our EU
representative GPSR@taylorandfrancis.com
Taylor & Francis Verlag GmbH, Kaufingerstraße 24, 80331 München, Germany

www.ingramcontent.com/pod-product-compliance
Ingram Content Group UK Ltd.
Pitfield, Milton Keynes, MK11 3LW, UK
UKHW052031210425
457613UK00032BA/1002